y of Congress Cataloging in Publication Data
ntry under title:

956.94
I85

in the Begin era.

Book had its origins in a conference that was held at
ltimore Hebrew College on April 8, 1979"—Pref.
ibliography: p.
cludes index.
ontents: Likud 1977-81/by Effraim Torgovnik—Likud
ver/by David Pollock—Changing domestic policy,
81/by Ira Sharkansky and Alex Radian—[etc.]
. Israel—Politics and government—Congresses.
in, Menachem, 1913-   —Congresses. I. Freedman,
t Owen.
25.P3A177   1982   956.94'054   82-13329
  0-03-059376-X

Published in 1982 by Praeger Publishers
CBS Educational and Professional Publishing
a Division of CBS Inc.

©1982 by Praeger Publishers

23456789 052 987654321

Printed in the United States of America

ISRAEL
IN THE
BEGIN
ERA

edited by
Robert O. Freedman

PRA

PRAEGER SPECIAL STUDIES • PRAEGE

To my wife Sharon whose companionship makes life worthwhile.

Contents

v

Preface

This book had its origins in a conference that was held at the Baltimore Hebrew College on April 8, 1979. At that time, almost two years into the first term of the Likud government, it had become clear that Menachem Begin had made a major impact on the Israeli political scene. First and foremost, of course, was the peace treaty signed with Egypt on March 26, 1979—the first such peace treaty Israel had ever signed with an Arab neighbor. Perhaps equally important, however, was the impact Begin had made in the area of Israeli domestic politics. Indeed, Begin had moved Likud from its perennial position as an opposition party before the 1977 elections to become the governing party, and he was to lead the Likud to a reelection victory in June 1981. In the process, Likud consolidated its position as one of Israel's two major parties, thereby creating a major change in the political dynamics of Israeli politics, since before 1977 it had always been the Labor Alignment that dominated the Israeli political scene.

Given the changes in Israel that were already apparent by October 1978 when the conference was first planned, it was felt by the conference's organizers that an academic meeting devoted to the domestic and foreign policy trends in the first part of Begin's Likud government would be a useful initial step in the preparation of a book that would analyze the first full parliamentary term of the Begin government. This volume is the outgrowth of that effort. With contributors from both Israel and the United States who approach the Begin era from a number of different disciplines and different points of view, it is felt that *Israel in the Begin Era* is a balanced treatment of the thrust of Israeli politics from the elections of May 1977, which brought Prime Minister Begin's Likud party to power, to its reelection in June 1981.

As this book was going to press, the Israeli army invaded Lebanon to eliminate the PLO artillery, which had become an increasing danger to Israel's northern region. While the outcome of the Israeli operation in Lebanon was still in doubt at press time, it is felt that this book will provide useful background for understanding the Israeli move, for Prime Minister Begin's decision to send Israeli forces into Lebanon, and for the possible domestic repercussions of that operation.

The conference, and this book which resulted from it, was made possible by generous grants from the Zionist Academic Council and the Maryland Chapter of the American Jewish Congress, along with support from the Baltimore Jewish Community Relations Council and the Peggy Meyerhoff Pearlstone School of Graduate Studies of the Baltimore Hebrew College. The support of all of these institutions is deeply appreciated. In addition, the Israeli Embassy was helpful in providing data for the book; and the Baltimore Hebrew College Library staff and its director, Dr. Jesse Mashbaum, provided a number of supporting research services. Finally, special thanks are due to my supersecretary, Mrs. Elise Baron, who typed the manuscript while also helping to manage the graduate program of the Baltimore Hebrew College.

Robert O. Freedman
Baltimore, June 1982

Introduction

The election victory scored by the Begin-led Likud party in the 1981 Israeli elections returned Prime Minister Begin to power for a second consecutive term. By 1981 he had clearly made his mark, most directly because of the peace treaty Israel had signed with Egypt, as he was the first Israeli leader to achieve such a success. In addition, by leading his Likud party to its election victory after being virtually written off in the public opinion polls six months prior to the elections, Begin clearly put his stamp on the Israeli political scene. What, in fact, was Israel like during Begin's first term? What were the changes he enacted and what was the nature of Israeli politics during his period of rule? These are some of the questions that are dealt with in this book, which focuses on the politics of Israel during the Begin era. Since so much has already been written about Israel's foreign policy during the 1977–81 period, some of it by participant observers such as Foreign Minister Moshe Dayan and Defense Minister Ezer Weizmann,[1] the primary emphasis of this book is on Israeli domestic politics and, in particular, on the political dynamics that were operative within Israel's most important political parties. Thus two chapters have been devoted to the Likud, one on its consolidation of power in the 1977–81 period and the other on its internal political dynamics and its relations with its coalition partners. Another chapter is devoted to Israel's religious parties, which were the Likud's most important coalition partners in the 1977–81 period, following the disintegration of the Democratic Movement for Change. A fourth chapter deals with the Labor party and how it reacted to being in the opposition for the first time in Israel's history. The Israeli Arabs, while not (yet) formed into a political party, are clearly a growing force on the Israeli scene and are dealt with in another chapter of the book. A sixth chapter analyzes the Begin government's efforts to bring about change in Israel's socioeconomic system.

While the primary focus of the book is on Israel's domestic politics, two chapters are devoted to its foreign policies. One, written from the perspective of

1

superpower competition in the Middle East, analyzes the impact of the Egyptian-Israeli peace agreement and Israeli West Bank settlement policy on regional politics. The other discusses the ambiguous nature of "autonomy" and analyzes the difficulties confronting any attempt to create genuine autonomy for the Palestinian Arabs of the West Bank and Gaza.

The rise of the Likud to power, and the consolidation of the party's political power once in office, are the central themes discussed by Efraim Torgovnik in the first chapter of this volume. After discussing the reasons for Likud's success in the 1977 elections, he discusses some of the internal difficulties the party had in exercising its power, difficulties that stemmed both from inexperience and the contradictory socioeconomic policies espoused by the two major Likud factions, Herut and the Liberals. Torgovnik shows that by the beginning of 1981, Herut's basically populist approach had won out over the free market capitalism of the Liberals, a development that greatly enhanced Likud's reelection hopes since much of its electoral support came from lower socioeconomic groups. Torgovnik also shows how Sadat's visit enhanced Begin's legitimacy as Israel's prime minister, and how, over the course of the 1977–81 period, Likud became more unified as Herut asserted greater dominance over the other Likud factions. These developments were due in no small part to Begin himself, and Torgovnik attributes the consolidation of the Likud during the 1977–81 period and its second consecutive election victory to Begin alone. Indeed, Torgovnik goes so far as to call the Likud "Begin-dependent."

The central role of Begin is also a major topic discussed by David Pollock in his analysis of the Likud party and its coalition partners. In addition to discussing the roles of such prominent, but politically rather impotent Israelis as Moshe Dayan, Ezer Weizmann, and Yigal Hurvitz, who were to leave the government in protest against Begin's policies, Pollock analyzes the Democratic Movement for Change (DMC), which was to join the government in October 1977 and the Tehiya party, which was to be formed from opponents of Begin's Camp David policy who defected from Likud. After recounting the gradual disintegration of the DMC, Pollock concludes that while the party was rather ineffectual, it was, at least, able to somewhat delay the establishment of Jewish settlements on the West Bank. If the DMC was to disintegrate during the 1977–81 period, the Liberal faction of Likud, the second largest faction in the party after Herut, was to be rent by internal strife, primarily between Yitzhak Moda'i and Simcha Ehrlich. While the two struggled, the Liberals lost positions of influence within the government, including the Finance Ministry. Nevertheless, despite protests from some members of Herut, Begin, mindful of his political alliance with Liberal leader Simcha Ehrlich, awarded the Liberals the same proportion of seats on the Likud party list in 1981 as they had received in 1977—thereby assuring Likud of the Liberals' loyalty. While factional infighting was particularly pronounced in the Liberal faction of Likud, it was also present in the Herut faction, albeit in a more subdued way. In the course of his analysis, Pollock examines the various factions in Herut, along with the strengths of the potential successors to Begin, although he cautions against predicting the emergence of any successor to Begin so long as the Israeli leader is healthy—so great had his power and influence within the party become by the end of 1981.

One of the challenges facing any opposition party when it achieves power—particularly one that had been in the opposition as long as the Likud—is to effect policy changes that will distinguish it from previous governments. Yet there are numerous obstacles to effecting such changes, even for such a powerful political figure as Menachem Begin. Indeed, as Ira Sharkansky and Alex Radian indicate in their analysis of the Begin government's efforts to change long-established Israeli domestic policies, the prime minister encountered a number of difficulties. Thus, he was unable to nationalize health care, sell many government corporations, or get a national pension law enacted despite pledges to do so. The two authors, while noting that the Israeli government's preoccupation, if not obsession, with security and foreign policy issues necessarily limited the amount of time and energy its top figures could devote to domestic issues, also point out other important obstacles to domestic policy change, which included an inherited bureaucracy and powerful institutions still controlled by Labor, such as the Histadrut. In addition, they note that even in spheres where policy changes were enacted, such as the establishment of the Project Renewal program and the extension of free tuition to all four years of high school, such programs had already been under discussion by previous Labor governments, so there is some question about how innovative the Begin government really was.

Finally, the authors show that in the economic sphere, where most of the domestic policy changes have taken place, the Begin government has come full circle. After first trying out a series of free market reforms and cutting subsidies, it was to return to a major subsidy system quite similar to the one that had been operative under Labor. Indeed, one of the factors that aided the Likud's reelection campaign was the subsidy system introduced by Yoram Aridor, Begin's third finance minister.

As the Likud party was consolidating its power, Labor was suffering from the effects of its election defeat. After analyzing the reasons for Labor's loss in the 1977 elections, Myron Aronoff contends that the party's top leaders never fully understood the factors that led to the party's election failure. Consequently, they failed to undertake the fundamental changes, including the creation of a genuinely democratized nomination system for the party's Knesset list, which would have enabled the party to regain the confidence of the public and invigorate the party's rank and file. Other problems that plagued Labor included severe infighting between former Prime Minister Yitzhak Rabin and Labor party leader Shimon Peres, and conflict between major groups and factions within the party. After discussing the changing alignments within the Labor party in the 1977–81 period, Aronoff goes on to trace its role as an opposition to the Likud-led government coalition. He also discusses the serious mistakes made by Labor in the 1981 election campaign, mistakes that enabled the Likud party to return to power.

If the Labor party was unable to solve its most serious problems during the 1977–81 period, initially the two religious parties appeared to be far better off. After a brief analysis of the role of religion in Israel, and the emergence of a civil religion to the country, Daniel Elazar analyzes political developments within the National Religious Party (NRP) and Agudat Israel during Begin's first term in office. He indicates that while the NRP emerged with great optimism from the 1977 elections, and hoped to take a very active role in the government, internecine quarrels between NRP doves and hawks and the breakaway of the North African Sephardi faction (TAMI) headed by Aharon Abuhatzeira soon led to near political disaster for the NRP, which lost half of its parliamentary seats in the 1981 elections.

By contrast, Agudat Israel made many political gains during Begin's first term, as it negotiated successfully for increased funding for its institutions and a greater degree of general religious observance by the state. Elazar, who carefully distinguishes between Israel's small number of religious fanatics, and the vast majority of Israel's Orthodox religious community, sees a further strengthening of Agudat Israel in the future. He also foresees an increasingly dim political future for Israel's Labor Alignment unless it can develop a more positive attitude toward Israel's religious communities, which have become increasingly sympathetic to the Likud party, in general, and to Prime Minister Begin, in particular.

If Begin's policies have been attractive to large numbers within Israel's Orthodox Jewish community, they have been far less satisfying to Israel's Arab minority, as Ian Lustick points out in his analysis of the Israeli Arabs in the Begin era. After indicating that many of Begin's policies toward the Israeli Arab community are carryovers from previous Labor governments, he also points out that the Begin government's rhetoric has been considerably harsher, as a number of members of the Likud government have viewed the Arabs as "aliens" or "enemies" within the midst of Israel. Not unnaturally, Israeli Arabs have reacted to government rhetoric, to its actions, such as land confiscation from Negev Bedouin, and to continued perceived discrimination in housing and economic development by becoming increasingly radicalized and Palestinianized, although the Begin government has cracked down on any manifestation of pro-PLO activity. Meanwhile, various Israeli Arab organizations have arisen to challenge Rakah, the Israeli Communist party, which over the last several decades had emerged both as a spokesman for Israel's Arabs and the recipient of an increasing proportion of their votes in Israeli national elections. Interestingly enough, however, despite appeals for votes and calls for an election boycott by the PLO by Rakah, there was a sharp increase in the Israeli Arab vote for the Labor Alignment in the 1981 elections. While, as Lustick points out, this may have been a move by the Israeli Arabs to try to oust a hostile Begin government and bring the somewhat more sympathetic Labor party back to power, it should also be noted that the Labor party, if it indeed proves sympathetic to Israeli Arab concerns, may also garner a larger degree of Arab support in future elections as the increasingly educated and sophisticated Arab electorate realizes that Rakah cannot really help it. In any case, Lustick argues, unless the Likud-dominated coalition government changes its policies in the near future, more confrontation between the Israeli government and the Israeli Arab community is likely to occur.

In turning to the international aspects of the Begin era, perhaps the most important achievement of the Begin government was to achieve a peace treaty with Egypt, its most important Arab neighbor. As mentioned above, participant observers such as Moshe Dayan and Ezer Weizmann have written extensively about the peace process from an Israeli perspective. Consequently, the often tortuous peace process is discussed in this volume from the perspective of the two superpowers by Robert O. Freedman. Freedman contends that while the United States, under Jimmy Carter, was initially seeking to foster a general Arab-Israeli peace settlement, when this proved impossible, Washington moved to support a separate Egyptian-Israeli peace agreement, while at the same time continuing to seek to expand the peace to take in Jordan, the Palestinian Arabs (including the PLO), and as many other Arab states as possible—a policy that was to bring it into increasing conflict with Israel. For its part, the Soviet Union, after initially being invited by the United States to participate in a general settlement of the Arab-Israeli conflict, tried first to prevent the Egyptian-Israeli peace agreement from being signed and later sought to reinforce Egyptian President Sadat's isolation in the Arab world, which resulted from the treaty. Moscow followed this strategy in an effort to achieve an "anti-imperialist" unity in the Arab world, which could be used to weaken the Western position in the region. Unfortunately for Moscow, the anti-Sadat unity in the Arab world was not long in dissipating, in part because of the Soviet Union's invasion of Afghanistan and in part because of the outbreak of the Iran-Iraq war, both of which split the centrist Arabs (Saudi Arabia, Kuwait, Jordan, the UAE, and Morocco) from the radicals (Syria, South Yemen, Algeria, the PLO, and Libya). Moscow, however, sought to take advantage of a number of Begin's actions during this period, such as the building of settlements on the West Bank, the expulsion of Arab officials from Hebron, the formal annexation of East Jerusalem, the confrontation with Syria over its missiles in Lebanon, the bombing of the Iraqi nuclear reactor, and the bombing of PLO offices in Beirut to both divert Arab attention from its own invasion of Afghanistan and to reestablish the long-sought "anti-imperialist" Arab unity; but the Soviet Union was to achieve only limited success in its efforts. Freedman concludes, however, that so long as there is a competition for influence in the Middle East between the United States and the Soviet Union, Moscow, which supports Israel's existence, will seek to exploit Israeli actions on the West Bank and elsewhere in the region, to undermine the U.S. position in the Middle East while strengthening its own.

Perhaps the most controversial issue to arise following the Camp David agreements was the nature of the "autonomy" promised to the Arabs of the West Bank and Gaza. Writing from the perspective of a specialist in international law, Robert Friedlander asserts that the concept of autonomy has little meaning and that most attempts to provide autonomy have had negligible results. Friedlander also discusses the increasingly negative relationship between the United Nations General Assembly (thought by some to be a quasi-legislative body in international law) and the state of Israel, and he contends that the U.N. General Assembly resolutions supporting the PLO have been counterproductive, hardening the position of the Israeli government not only against that organization but also against the prospect of any genuine autonomy for the Palestinians. Friedlander concludes that the prospects for autonomy for the Palestinians are dim in part because of the inclinations of the Begin government, in part because of the ambiguity of the term, and in part because of the hostility toward Israel of both the PLO and the bulk of the Arab world.

In sum, perhaps the most striking conclusion that can be drawn from this collection of essays about Israel during the first term of the Likud government under Prime Minister Menachem Begin is the major personal role that Begin has achieved in directing government policy. Indeed, time after time, whether in government coalition politics, domestic policy debates, or foreign policy decisions, it was Begin's will that prevailed. At the same time, Begin was the cement that held both the factionalized Likud party and the government together. It is clear that Israeli politics in the 1977–81 period would have been very different if Menachem Begin was not his country's prime minister, and it would also appear that Israeli politics may change considerably when he departs from the political scene.

NOTE

1.   See Moshe Dayan, *Breakthrough: A Personal Account of the Egyptian-Israeli Peace Negotiations* (New York: Alfred A. Knopf, 1981) and Ezer Weizmann, *The Battle for Peace* (New York: Bantam Books, 1981).

1   Likud 1977-81:
The Consolidation of Power

Efraim Torgovnik

INTRODUCTION

Politics is unkind to political parties that lose their bid for power and are relegated to the opposition. There they have only their principles, contested goals, and rhetoric to keep them warm. To the winning, newly elected parties, without prior experience in government, politics is also cruel. They soon find that principles and goals adhered to for years and popularized in electoral politics are not easily operationalized and implemented. The preelection dreams of wielding power and affecting change are confronted by the realities of the socio-economic-political system. The public's appetite for costly social benefits and subsidies does not diminish with the election of an opposition party to the government. Budgetary changes are difficult to achieve, old ways are institutionalized and supported by an entrenched bureaucracy and interest groups, and general structures are set against the newcomer.

Environmental constraints on new governments are present in different political systems, even in systems with a tradition of changes of the party at the helm. This was noted by Martin Lipset and more recently in the memoirs and diaries of Richard Crossman.[1] The Israeli situation is different. The Likud was a party "born for opposition." In May 1977 the party won enough seats in the Israeli Knesset (parliament) to head a coalition government. It was 29 years since the establishment of the state, and the Likud had had no real prior experience in government.[2] Furthermore, in the political institutions the Jewish community evolved in Palestine in the mid-1920s, there was hardly any participation by the various wings that preceeded the modern Likud.

From a theoretical perspective, the lack of experience and the systemic constraints on newly elected governments do not preclude their potential ability to decide, act, and cope with prevalent situations and constraints. However, in order to succeed in government and effect change, a newly elected party would require: (1) a solid parliamentary base, (2) an ideologically close coalition, (3) leadership and legitimacy, (4) a tradition of party discipline, and (5) an ability to influence key decision centers, for example, through appointment. Success of newly elected parties may be considered in light of the following proposition: Crisis situations are likely to enhance the capacity of newly elected parties to cope with the challenges of governing and they may even succeed in evolving new policies.[3] In a system where foreign policy plays a key role in government, and the international environment induces domestic policy changes, there is opportunity for the emergence of leadership.

This chapter deals with an ongoing situation: the Begin era and, more specifically, with the Likud party in power. Research on ongoing events is rather hazardous because the very situations and issues researched are in a state of flux. The domain of research is in danger of being defined by ephemeral events. The problems faced by the newly elected government may permeate and become the problems of the research. Due recognition is given to this situation, and therefore the categories selected as a framework of analysis of the Likud in power are made clear and include:

1. *Structural setting:* In a proportional representation system such as Israel's there is a tendency toward the proliferation of political bodies. In electoral politics groups tend to congregate in political alignments. In these, each political subunit is assured a measure of recognition, influence, and a share of power. This is achieved mainly by institutionalizing each group's right to party decision centers. These are the key structural features of the Labor Alignment and the Likud.[4] A major problem emerges with parties having such a structure. When they are in government, they must make decisions, formulate policy, and, especially, mobilize support, but from a political base that is fractionalized. The issue involves the relationship between party and government. When the fractionalized party structure also reflects a measure of ideological (and other) divergences, a government will face numerous constraints on its freedom to decide.

2. *Preparedness to rule:* Parties that have spent a long period in opposition may advocate positions different from what they would have advocated had the party perceived itself as a potential ruling body. Duverger and others[5] categorize parties as doctrinaire when they advance positions at the extreme ends of a left to right continuum. Doctrinaire parties often do not think of themselves as serious competitors for power. They seek members, adherents, and exposure. The question we pose is, to what extent was the Likud ready structurally, ideologically, and experientially to assume power after being in the opposition since the establishment of the state and having had only minor experience in government? Were the Likud's platform and goals useful in guiding a Likud government?

3. *Attitudinal and behavioral factors:* These two categories provide a critical base for the analysis of decision making. To what extent is there a convergence between the Likud's goals and proposed programs compared with what was actually decided and done?

4. *Capacity to decide:* Has the Likud shown a capacity to translate normative utterances to decisions on governmental policy and to effect a change of policies of the former Labor government? The discussion deals with two policy areas: security and peace and socioeconomic policy. Success in these domains is likely to contribute to the legitimization of the newly elected party and contribute to its reelection.

THE LIKUD'S RISE TO POWER

The Likud party was formally established in July 1973. It is a federation of former parties and political groups: Herut, Liberals, La'am, Free Center, a group headed by Ariel Sharon, and the Movement for a Greater Israel. The Likud's rise to power is significant because it provides an understanding of the social milieu that established the Likud as the ruling party. The party structure that emerged bears on its policy making capacity. The discussion here will consist of two parts: (1) the formation of the Likud in 1973 and (2) the Likud's actual rise to power.

Background

The key figure in the formation of the Likud ("unity" in Hebrew) is former general Ariel Sharon. His role then should be related to his ability to wield power in the subsequent Likud governments, where he serves as chief advocate of an aggressive settlements policy on the West Bank. In 1973, Sharon lurked in the background of the new political body—the Likud. He entered the Liberal party, which was then aligned with Begin's Herut under the name Gahal. Emulating the Labor Alignment, he proposed to the two Gahal parties the establishment of a large party consisting of the center-right groups, which would become the alternative to Labor. He proposed to include in this Likud, the splinter political group of the Free Center, which had previously broken away from the Herut party, and whose leader, Shmuel Tamir, remained at odds with Menachem Begin and was considered politically untouchable. Due to his inexperience in politics, however, Sharon quickly alienated the party's apparatus, but this served to strengthen his popular public image.

The importance of the Unity party was clear. It would change the old image of Gahal as a permanent opposition. A large political body with popular personalities would be likely to challenge the ruling but weakening Ma'arach Labor Alignment. Sharon's ability to initiate the new Likud was related to his status in the army. In the 1973 war he emerged as a war hero. He led the troops that turned the tide—crossed the Suez Canal, invaded Egypt, and stopped only 60 miles from Cairo. The political implications of Sharon's war record did not fail to immediately become apparent. As in war, he had become the alternative to failing generals, so in politics he and the Likud would become, in the minds of many, the alternative to the confused Ma'arach. With Sharon's ascent, it became conclusively clear that the army was the training ground for political leaders.[6] Similarly, prior to 1977, Ezer Weizmann of Herut was not taken seriously by the political pros. However, he helped the Herut gain respectability. After failing to compete for leadership against no less than Begin himself, the latter proceeded to mock Weizmann publicly, referring to him as a "cute naughty boy," which resulted in Weizmann's withdrawal from party activity. Sharon's initiative brought Weizmann back. The two were able to patch up old feuds and join forces in a center-right coalition. It should be noted that the ideological base of these ex-generals is vague, at best. Their interest is mainly in policy, notably in the domain of security and territories. Therefore, they became open prey to a market hungry for popular figures.

In this discussion it is important to note that by 1973 the Likud had gained sufficient legitimacy to be considered open for popular ex-military leaders to join. Previously this was uncommon. In a broader sense this pursuit of ex-generals has implications for the Israeli political system. It points to the inability of the political parties to replenish and raise a new generation of leaders from within.[7]

The years following 1973 appeared hard for Labor. It was a closed party, hamstrung by domineering factions and leaders like Golda Meir. Newcomers assessed correctly that they had little chance for advancement in Labor. Its public image was also tarnished by the dynamic recruitment of leaders in the Likud, compared with Labor, which appeared closed and static. Newcomers to politics assessed correctly the high chances for personal mobility in the Likud. The Likud also held a coherent hawkish position. Furthermore, after 1973 it became progressively clear that Labor was perceived by the public as unable to manage the economy.[8] It was during this period that many key leaders of the Labor party defected to form a new party, the Democratic Movement for Change.[9] One of the most significant signs of weakness in a political party is its inability to keep adherents, and to attract personalities and retain them. While Labor was showing these signs of weakness, the Likud and the Democratic Movement for Change showed a great ability to attract popular personalities.

The 1973 "war elections" were a major success for the Likud, which gained 13 parliamentary seats. In May 1977 their day arrived. The Democratic Movement for Change drew support for its 15 seats in the Knesset mainly from disillusioned Labor voters. This disillusionment was a result of the 1973 war and its aftermath, which left many in Israel with doubts about Labor's ability to rule. These doubts were augmented by a series of corruption cases in Labor's ranks and the then Premier Rabin's involvement in a criminal court case. Moreover, Israel had undergone demographic changes resulting in increased support of young voters for the hawkish Likud. These factors formed the background for the success of the center-right block as an alternative to Labor and caused the erosion of the psychological dominance of Labor. Outsiders to politics such as Arik Sharon and Ezer Weizmann were able to join forces in a center-right coalition to confront the 29-year-old dominant Labor Alignment, and the "outsiders" helped secure the Likud victory.

THE ACTUAL FORMATION OF THE LIKUD

Sharon, it was reported, conducted what amounted to classroom discussions with old pros from Herut and the Liberals in order to overcome their opposition and fears for their snug power positions in the fractionalized structure.[10] The very negotiations exposed anonymous factional leaders who preferred to give in to Sharon, relying, correctly, on their persisting organizational strength in order to retain their positions. The Labor faction in the Liberals, for example, secured its seats under the new arrangements.[11] The proposal for a center-right alignment to stand against the Labor Alignment became the exciting news of the day. It was difficult to oppose. Weizmann found in Sharon's proposal an opportunity to return to politics gracefully. He conditioned his return on having Gahal accept additional groups under its umbrella.[12] Begin, it is alleged, at first opposed the new Likud. It threatened Herut and signified a change in his closely controlled, relatively small political organization. Personal aspects were also present. Under the new conditions Begin would be required to accept Shmuel Tamir of the Free Center, who had previously split with Herut. Begin's opposition to an alliance with people such as Tamir should be understood in a broader perspective beyond the personal feud between these two persons. Tamir signified a potential ideological flexibility or pragmatism that might be introduced into the doctrinaire structure that Begin fostered and that gave shelter to what appeared to be an outdated conception of a greater Israel. Furthermore, during the years 1968-73 Tamir became one of the most impressive and effective voices in Israeli politics, while Begin joined the National Unity Government following the Six-Day War and became rather ineffective as an opposition force. In any case, Tamir did not join the Likud during the critical elections of 1977. He sought his fortune with the Democratic Movement for Change. Nonetheless, after heading a secession within that movement, he and his faction joined the Likud government and he became Minister of Justice. In 1981 he asked to join the Likud party and was flatly rejected. The Tamir case suggests that the Likud had difficulties in viewing itself as a large party ready to face the inner conflicts inevitably accompanying such a structure.

THE LIKUD VICTORY OF 1977

The Likud was officially formed following a decision of Gahal's executive committee on July 22, 1973. Begin and the Herut gave their support, foreseeing the prospects of political gain during the forthcoming election.[13]

In order for the Likud to win, a number of factors would have to be present, such as (1) weakening the dominance of Labor and (2) establishing sufficient legitimacy for voters to break with a tradition of more than a quarter of a century of party identification. These changes came about around 1977. The Democratic Movement for Change enabled many voters to break with Labor, while the Likud vote was hardly affected. Second, Labor dominance was shattered due to the political, attitudinal, and demographic changes that took place among Israel's voters, notably (1) a lack of identification with Labor among young voters who also did not identify with past achievements identified with Labor; (2) an emerging differentiation, which, in its most generalized terms, can be stated as follows: the Labor vote came mainly from the middle and upper classes, and this vote in 1977 was split between two parties; (3) the Likud became progressively identified as the party of the masses[14] (see Table 1.1).

TABLE 1.1
**Likud Electoral Gains with a Variety of Age Groups
Compared with Labor during Four Elections (percent)**

Age Group	Labor Alignment				Likud			
	1969	1973	1977	1981	1969	1973	1977	1981
Under 24	40	39	20	21	36	44	51	47
25–39	54	37	25	32	30	44	34	37
40–49	61	48	38	30	25	35	29	45
Over 50	62	54	53	40	21	23	23	30

Source: Special thanks are due to Professor Asher Arian for making survey data available. The 1981 data is based on a survey conducted during May-June 1981.

The progressive electoral gains of Likud (and previously Gahal) can be seen in Table 1.2.

One of the paradoxes of the 1977 election is that the Likud, considered a center-right party, gained among the lower socioeconomic groups, while Labor lost its "natural constituency" and became progressively identified with what some referred to as the "establishment."[15] The shift to the Likud may be summarized as follows:

TABLE 1.2
Electoral Gains of Likud (Knesset seats)

Year	Gains
1965*	26 (as Gahal)
1969	26 (as Gahal)
1973	39
1977	43
1981	48

*In 1965, the Gahal party included the Liberals and Herut.

1. The Likud's major component, Herut, always had a populist base, which supported its hawkish positions. Public opinion in general shifted in this direction, and in 1977 a deteriorating economic situation encouraged the lower strata to seek their fortunes outside Labor.[16]

2. Begin's leadership style appealed to these people for both his hawkish stand and his sensitivity to Jewish symbols.

3. The Likud, implicitly, through its hawkish policies and promises for economic reform and betterment, appealed directly to the poorer sector of the voters, who are mostly Jews of distinct ethnic origins.

4. Among the young voters the Likud made significant inroads—a process that has been continuing for some time. In 1973, 31.6 percent of the age group of 18–34 voted Likud, compared with 22.7 percent for Labor. In 1977 the proportions were 53.8 percent Likud and 26.1 percent Labor. The gains among the young might be tentatively explained on the basis of: (a) their position on security and peace, which is largely influenced by their lives under conditions of war, (b) their cynical attitude toward the then ruling Labor Alignment and their lack of identification with old symbols associated with that party, and lastly (c) their proclivity to change.

5. Not the least important factor in the Likud's rise to power was Begin's stature as a leader. Yitzhak Rabin, who became prime minister following the 1973 war, was not a candidate in 1977. Shimon Peres was appointed at the very last minute. It appeared suddenly that Begin remained the only historic figure on the scene. He belonged to the generation of the founding fathers, if not by his age then by being their bitter political opponent. He became an asset to his party, to the dismay of Labor, which had figured that his old image of being to the right of mainstream politics would work against him. The May 1977 election may be described as one of voter

assertiveness. It showed, what was not even conceived of for nearly three decades, that a dominant party can be toppled. No future elections in Israel are likely to be the same, as indeed the 1981 election results show. Party identification as a key factor in choice has to be reconsidered, as well as the role of the party apparatus and public relations, especially the role of TV and personalities.

COMPONENTS OF THE LIKUD AND POLICY

The literature suggests that a party consisting of institutionalized subunits is likely to be constrained in its capacity to reach a consensus on aims and methods of domestic and foreign policy.[17] The capacity of a government to rule is contingent on its leader's ability to secure consensus or support from his political party. These dimensions of party and government refer to a situation where the various factions of the party are ideologically differentiated groups, whose leaders often compete with the established leadership. With a minor exception, this is not the case in the Likud. True, the various groups—Herut, Liberals, La'am, and Greater Israel—are institutionalized parts within the Likud and receive an agreed upon share of power, and their leaders seek key governmental positions. However, the small attitudinal and ideological divergence among them is not reflected in actual behavioral situations. (The conflict that emerged over the Camp David peace agreement, however, was an exception. Its opponents in the Greater Israel group and the Herut included seven Knesset members). In 1977, however, the various groups were able to write their platform and agree on it. A high level of agreement was expected at first among the Likud's subgroups who were all bent on winning the election. The agreement, however, did not negate the capacity of groups and key Likud personalities to affect policies. Their effectiveness might be measured in a number of ways: first, in terms of their ability to have a role in policy; second, in the ability of a group or individuals to mobilize resources; third, in terms of access to leaders and a strong bargaining position within the party. The strength of these dimensions would also depend on the size and character of the government coalition and on the extent to which each group or individual was needed within that coalition.

Arik Sharon provides an example of policy effectiveness in settling the West Bank area almost single-handedly. Simcha Ehrlich of the Liberals provides an example of ineffectiveness in policy. Lack of support for his economic plans led to his resignation as finance minister. His unrelenting loyalty to Begin, however, resulted in a further strengthening of his personal position and that of his group of Liberals. Ehrlich's case indicates that policy effectiveness is not the only path to political survival.

PREPAREDNESS TO RULE

The question whether a party is ready to rule is inextricably related to a tradition of alternating parties in power. This tradition was not present in Israel up to 1977, when the Likud relegated Labor to the opposition for the first time since the establishment of the state.

The literature notes a number of tools at the disposal of parties in preparation for governance. Previous experience is, of course, helpful. Specialized task forces were used in the United States by presidents Kennedy, Johnson, and Nixon.[18] Think tanks are another available tool. President Nixon, for example, used people with previous experience in government for these groups. President Kennedy, in his preparations for rule, used people of ideas in his teams. They were expected to facilitate a smooth transition, introducing innovation and change that would transcend the expected incremental pace.[19] In more concrete terms, new U.S. presidents have the power to appoint a long list of top positions in the bureaucracy. A more informal arrangement in the United States gives a new president a period of grace of about 100 days to get organized. In England an institutionalized arrangement, which facilitates a transfer of power, exists in the form of a shadow government, which often replicates the ruling government. It helps in gaining experience and specialized skills.[20]

In 1977 the Likud clearly had a number of people who were groomed for government—Begin as premier, Weizmann as minister of defense, Ehrlich for finance minister. The difference between Labor in 1981 and Likud in 1977, however, was in the degree to which the entire process of preparation was institutionalized. Policy task forces, for example, were practically nonexistent in the Likud. The Likud did appoint one of its Knesset members to lead a task force.[21] It dealt mainly with structural changes in the future government, proposing a lowering of the number of cabinet ministries to enable better management. Coalition requirements, however, prevented this reform, and according to Yehezkiel Flumin, former deputy minister of finance, little was accomplished by the Rom Committee.[22]

Lastly, it should be noted that the Likud gave little attention to the organizational-bureaucratic setting it was likely to face, once in power. This problem was noted in the literature. In his study of the rise of a new party to power in Canada, Lipset attributed the inability to initiate policy changes to bureaucratic opposition and the lack of change among the key public executives, whose ideological inclinations had become an obstacle to change.[23]

The Likud, according to one of its key political figures, suffered from "victory shock." In analyzing whether the Likud was prepared for government, one should exercise a great deal of caution. Task forces, think tanks, or shadow governments do not necessarily assure preparedness to rule. The important dimension of preparedness probably lies in the tradition of change of power, which was lacking in Israel up to 1977. A number of actions may provide an indication as to the Likud's preparedness for rule:

1. The Likud entered the corridors of power cautiously. Fears of mass firing of top personnel were not realized. For example, the important key position of director-general of treasury was retained for over two years by the pre-Likud Labor appointee. Some key positions were occupied by Likud appointments. Generally, however, it was clear that the Likud had opted for a low-keyed transition to power. Even some of the personal staff of Premier Begin had previously served in the Labor government. Inadvertently, the Likud's personnel strategy pointed to a shortage of qualified persons and to a decision to learn about administration and its machinations by establishing a climate of continuity.

2. The retention of many administrators of the previous administrations, which pointed to a policy of continuity, was instrumental in building legitimacy for the Likud's rule. It facilitated the Likud's efforts to confront the overwhelming dominance of Labor in government and the Histadrut (Labor Federation). Changes in top administrative positions were slow but steady. In organizations such as the Lands Authority, the Likud made impressive inroads. This unit is important to the Likud's settlement policy.

3. Perhaps the most dramatic indication of the Likud's desire to rely on the experience of others and to lean on proven and well-known experienced figures was the appointment of Moshe Dayan of the Labor party as foreign minister. This appointment of a key Labor figure created a minor uproar—against Dayan himself, not the Likud. This controversial personality would give the Likud, however, much needed legitimacy in public opinion. Furthermore, Dayan's appointment did not hamstring the Likud. Dayan was famous for his pragmatism. He adjusted his views to changing conditions. His views on peace and security were not that far away, ideologically, from the Likud's—closer, in fact, than to the dovish wing of the Labor party. Dayan's flare for dramatic events and utterances would make him a willing partner to the most dramatic of all changes that occurred in Israel's history—Sadat's and Begin's peace initiative and the subsequent peace treaty between Egypt and Israel.

Preparedness for goveranance should be considered not only according to preelection preparations or by personnel changes and inputs. Observations should also focus on policy outputs and on the extent to which a party is successful in: (1) initiating new policies, (2) modifying past policies, and (3) institutionalizing itself as a future competitor for power from the perspective of both inner party dimensions and the legitimacy with which the public views the party in future elections. The first two items will be considered below in the discussion of the Begin government's social-economic policies and its peace and security policies. Such considerations will be followed with discussions of the entrenchment of the Likud in the Israeli political system.

THE LIKUD AND ITS POLICIES

Introduction

Electoral politics sharpen the differences between competing parties. When an opposition party gains power, it attempts to underscore its uniqueness. New policies, as is well known, are not easily instituted nor are old policies easily changed. The literature on policy and change speaks of incremental changes, earmarked budgets, the inability of governments to overcome established pressure politics, and the modifying effects of various structural and environmental factors.[24] In spite of these difficulties, new parties want change and the Likud was no exception. In order to leave its mark on politics a strategy of dramatic acts and massive public spending was undertaken.

The outcome of these strategies posed a series of paradoxes. Few people in Israel expected the hawkish Likud to be the party that would head the peace negotiations with Egypt. Similarly, few expected this party with its bourgeoisie component, the Liberals ("a party of merchants, landlords, and shopkeepers" as they were often described), to bring the country to an inflation rate of nearly 150 percent per annum.

These unexpected situations in the economic sphere resulted from the inherent conflict between the more populist, socially aware Herut and the economically free-enterprise oriented Liberal wing of the Likud. During the writing of the economic platform for the 1977 elections, these two orientations were present in the background. The Likud document attempted the virtually impossible combination of a public-welfare oriented program together with a free-enterprise capitalistic approach to the economy.

The Economy as an Issue

During the election campaign of 1977 public surveys showed that the public was dissatisfied with the state of the economy. In one poll, 81 percent said that they were dissatisfied with the Alignment's economic management.[25] It was widely believed that the Likud, especially the Liberals, might manage the economy well, eliminate corruption, and implement their election promise to reduce inflation from 29 percent to 15 percent. Clearly, an improvement in the economy was expected to accompany the Likud's rise to power. Anti-Likud feeling following the 1977 elections was related to expectations and hopes that the Likud itself had previously built in the economic sphere among the electorate. By 1979 the public was disenchanted with the Likud management of the economy, and major efforts by the Liberal party's "capitalist" minister of finance to change structural features of the welfare state were not appreciated by the public. Nearly 65 percent thought that the minister of finance ought to resign, and nearly 50 percent thought the entire government should resign.[26] By September 1979, 23 percent preferred a government headed by the Likud, against 36 percent who wanted a Labor government.[27] Only 17 percent of the public thought that the Likud government could manage the economy.[28] The economic situation even affected Begin's popularity. In September, 39 percent expressed satisfaction with Begin and 38 percent dissatisfaction. In December 1979, 28 percent, and in January 1980 only 25 percent, were satisfied with Begin.[29] The culmination of all this was in May 1980 when surveys showed that had the elections been held then, the Likud would have received 26 seats in the Knesset.[30] By September nearly 50 percent of the public thought the government should resign.[31]

The discussion below deals with the manifestations of economic policy and not with economic analysis. The measures used are related to the question raised earlier, namely, to what extent did the Likud initiate new policies and alter previous Labor policies?

Managing the Economy

The economic programs of the Likud were outlined in great detail in the 1977 platform. These were the programs of an opposition party that most likely did not fully believe that it would win. The promises made in the economic sphere were an outline for a normative and structural change in the economy of Israel. Few believed that it was also operational.

A few examples will suffice. The Likud promised to: lower inflation by 50 percent from a level of about 30 percent annual inflation in 1977, retain full employment, balance the budget, increase economic competition, increase the GNP by 5–8 percent annually, introduce new productivity schemes, facilitate worker mobility, and cease public construction of housing. The Likud also planned to sell public corporations, cease the linkage of maturing public bonds to the cost of living index, and reduce government trade in the money market. The Likud had hoped to stop the issuance of linked government bonds. Investment funds would be mobilized through a strengthened stock market.[32]

The more general statements read like a textbook of capitalist economics: "free economy," "efficiency," "initiative," "competition." But, in a section dealing with "social welfare,"[33] one reads a list of programs, supports, and subsidies with which a socialist party could easily be comfortable. For example, the Likud committed itself to subsidizing housing in order to help all those living three persons and more to a room.

The contradictory policies outlined in the economic and social sphere clashed head on with daily realities. Inflation increased by nearly 60 percent in the Likud's first year in power. The linkages to the cost of living index continued. Government bonds were not done away with. Public companies were sold merely to the tune of 3 percent of the government's stock value,[34] while the stock market became a place of wild speculation and served only moderately as a source of investment funds. These gaps between promises and execution are important in order to shed light on the process of adjustment of a new party in power. Notably: (1) observation of the Likud's management of the *economy* indicated a lack of experience in government and gave basis to the assertion that the Likud was somewhat surprised by its ascension to power; (2) the contradictions between the actual social programs and policies and "free economics" rhetoric were sharp and irreconcilable; (3) in the economic and social sphere the Likud paid a heavy toll for its built-in structural paradox: the Liberal capitalist rhetoric, which had to be reconciled with Herut's economic populist orientation. In this confrontation, as in many others, the Liberals lost to the Herut, while the economic indicators worsened.

Efforts of the early Liberal finance minister, Simcha Ehrlich, to cease public subsidies to failing individual plants were aborted. The first test case between the Liberals and Herut laid the foundations for the latter's domination. The test case involved a failing textile plant, which required subsidies in order to continue production. Ehrlich's policy was the first major effort to change previous Labor practices, and it failed. Herut's links to the masses prevented change in the basic welfare state conceptions and policies that were in practice during the previous 29 years of Labor's rule. Indeed, it may be speculated that this dimension of the Likud's rule accounts for its success and the legitimacy it acquired with the masses. This became obvious in the 1981 elections, when a great majority of the population of low socioeconomic status voted Likud.

The Likud government introduced many popular programs, which emerged less as a result of social planning than as an effort to please the masses. It legislated free high school education financed mainly by an increase in national insurance taxes. It provided for a wide physical rehabilitation program of poor neighborhoods and extended it to social rehabilitiation, while also passing an income guarantee law. Although there is presently a debate in Israel about the measure of success of the rehabilitation program, its very initiation is another testament to the basic welfare state orientation of the Likud.

Lastly, mention should be made of the Likud's initiative for a national health plan. This poses yet another paradox of the Likud's rule, where the free-enterprise oriented Likud is set on nationalizing what are essentially voluntary health programs. The Likud's national health plan emerged first as part of its attempt to weaken the sectorial health programs, especially the one dominated by Labor in the Histadrut (Labor Federation). This program and other minor health insurance programs—including one that is linked to the Herut—cover about 85 percent to 90 percent of Israel's Jewish and Arab populations. The Histadrut's health plan alone covers nearly 80 percent of the population.

In the Likud, the Histadrut's sick fund is considered Labor's major stronghold. The Likud argues that once a national health insurance scheme is introduced, the ability of Labor to mobilize members will diminish and the Histadrut will then become a much weaker trade union. Indeed, only a blow to the Histadrut health fund will contribute to setting the Likud on a more equal footing with Labor. The issue has strong symbolic overtones. To the Likud, Labor's nearly 60 years of control over particularistic social programs is a symbol of its advantage in popular mobilization.

Clearly, it was not a lack of health services or programs that stood behind the Likud's health nationalization plan. In fighting the sectorial health plans, especially the Histadrut's Kupat Holim (Sick Fund), the Likud was able to emphasize the issue of sectorial versus national interests. Posing the issue along these lines enabled even the Liberals of the Likud to freely support a national health plan. Lastly, the Democratic Movement, a minor coalition partner of the Likud, was committed to a national health plan. In the 1977 elections, voluntary sectorialism was defined as antistatism and even as a nest of corruption, which drew economic resources for narrow political aims.

The national health plan was not instituted mainly because the National Religious Party opposed it. The party, which is a key coalition partner of the Likud, is composed of a strong central Labor faction. It has a long standing understanding with the Labor movement and the Histadrut Sick Fund. It is, however, conceivable that following the 1981 elections new efforts will be made to institute the national health plan.

In social policies the Likud in power overcame its inexperience, in part, by continuing policies that were ingrained in Israel's political culture. It strengthened what was already entrenched. In the economy, what it could not curtail it supplemented, and this, in great part, resulted in excessive public spending.

Security and Peace

In this policy domain, which was accompanied by much drama, the Likud showed itself at its best. As in other policy domains, however, the paradoxes that accompanied the Likud in power were further underscored. In 1977 the Likud entered the government with an unfriendly public image, which the Likud itself was aware of. Its platform, Section C, states: "It has become clear that the pretentions and promises of the Ma'arach (Labor) as the party of peace and its smears of the Likud as a party of war, are groundless. Bloodshed and five wars beset Israel under the Ma'arach's rule ... a Likud government will be credible in the eyes of all concerned and her chances to bring peace are realistic. ... Negotiations with Egypt and Syria are intended to achieve a peace treaty. ..."[35]

The Likud's role in security and peace, must be understood in a broader context beyond policy. It was a party's efforts to gain general acceptance and public support, which often required action in a manner contrary to its utterances before it attained power. It is in this light that we view the appointment of Dayan to the Foreign Ministry and the continuation of the welfare state.

The peace process itself had its drama, of course. In a well-concocted plot of mystery, cloak-and-dagger type negotiations and surprises, President Sadat's visit to Jerusalem was arranged.

There were various attempts to explain why Begin at the head of the Israeli government was able to make peace with Egypt (after three decades of hostility), and not others. One view suggests an Egyptian apprehension of Begin's war-mongering image.[36] Others, especially in Isreal, offered an historic perspective, pointing to Begin's view about himself as a peacemaker versus that of Ben-Gurion as the founder of the state of Israel. Sadat, it is argued, accurately assessed that Begin and the Herut would make the needed concessions in order to ensure themselves a place in history. The Labor opposition argued that Begin had merely completed a process that had begun with a series of interim agreements Israel had concluded in the mid-1970s under Labor rule. Begin as peacemaker would, no doubt, be placed in Israel's history at the honored side of Ben-Gurion. These interpretations deal with various probabilistic motivations, which are less central here than actual occurrences. Clearly, the Sadat visit brought Begin the immediate widespread support and recognition that he lacked even after his electoral victory in 1977.

In entering the peace negotiations with Sadat, Begin's leadership role would be ascertained. He had to break away from deeply rooted conceptions over the role of territory to the country's security and from specific positions of his own political base. He faced an Egyptian president who openly uttered "traditional" Arab demands and positions regarding the solution to the Arab-Israeli conflict. At the same time Sadat offered Israel what it did not have before—direct negotiations with a major Arab state, i.e. recognition.

The Likud's formal election platform position on peace negotiations was set forth as follows: "Peace negotiations of the Likud government will be ... direct or through a friendly country. Negotiations will be direct (face to face) ... the aim: a peace treaty with no prior conditions ... each side will be free to advance proposals..."[37] The text appears to be the model for the actual negotiations. Differences and positions held by the two states still hover over the negotiations. The key concept in the negotiations, however, linkage between the Sinai agreement with Egypt and the future of the West Bank and the Palestinians, has not yet been resolved (February 1982). The linkage issue will be crucial for Begin during the peace negotiations because it involves the West Bank, which is viewed by the Likud as an integral part of Israel.

Many factors helped in building the necessary political support for the peace treaty. The very opportunity for a breakthrough in relations with the Arab states was an important factor. Peace as an existential Israeli goal was another. The drama surrounding the event was not an unimportant factor. The key factor, however, lies in a basic pattern of behavior of the Begin government, which was, in the case of the peace treaty, to underscore what already had a wide consensus in the nation.

In the case of the Camp David peace agreement, Begin proceeded to build support on the basis of the long standing national Israeli goal of peace. By willingly responding to Sadat's offer for direct negotiations, he actually achieved his own party's formal position and the opposition Labor party's long standing position. Paradoxically, Begin had a majority for the peace agreement in Israel's parliament even without his own political home base—the Herut. But, the Likud, including the Herut, provided him with support and so did the opposition Labor party. Begin's leadership position on peace was unchallenged.

ENTRENCHMENT OF THE LIKUD

The election of June 1981 indicated that the Likud is not an ephemeral phenomenon. Within eight months prior to this election, the Likud rose from a low of 28 seats, which one survey predicted, to a victory of 48 seats in the Knesset. There are many political factors that explain this process. However, adhering to the theme of this chapter, we enquire into three related dimensions: (1) the process of entrenchment (or institutionalization) of the Likud in Israeli politics, (2) the party and its ability to become a competitor for power, and (3) the building of legitimacy of the Likud in public opinion.

It is said that the success of a revolution is not in toppling old regimes, but in its ability to become entrenched in the mind of the people as a legitimate alternative. Ataturk is remembered in Turkey less for his take-over than for his ability to institutionalize his revolution through the establishment of a party and a new way of life. Begin was successful in the entrenchment of the Likud in Israeli politics. By 1981 the party had become a natural political competitor in Israeli politics.

The Likud became an institutionalized party because, as its smaller factions weakened, its core political group, Herut, became dominant, especially through the leadership role of Begin. Indeed, the Likud showed itself to be very Begin-dependent. Furthermore, the party exhibited an extraordinary ability to overcome secessions and its abandonment by key figures.

Theory on factions suggests that the various parts of a factionalized party remain viable when: (1) they have leaders who compete with the party's leadership, (2) they are highly institutionalized, (3) they have identifiable clientele, and (4) they have identifiable policy positions.[38] With the exception of the Liberal party, the other Likud factions and subgroups showed a low level of institutionalization. The salient dimensions about these groups were their leaders. Yigal Hurvitz of La'am became minister of finance. He evolved an economic plan of recovery that involved, for example, less government subsidizing of basic products. This was clearly not popular with the Herut constituency—it adversely affected the less affluent sector in society, among which the Jews of Asian and African origin are a great majority. Their dissatisfaction was shown in opinion surveys. In January 1980, 43 percent of this group claimed dissatisfaction with Hurvitz's economic policy, compared with 41 percent who were satisfied and who belonged to the more affluent sector of European and U.S. origin. Among people of high income, 51 percent were satisfied, while 47 percent of the low income group were dissatisfied. Among those with the lowest education level, 54 percent were dissatisfied and 51 percent of the higher education group were satisfied.[39] Hurvitz tried to introduce an economic policy that was somewhat apolitical and that attempted to disregard Likud constituencies. Hurvitz's policy, however, turned out to be more painful in its rhetoric than in actual implementation. Inflation and public expenditures were not markedly reduced, though the balance of payments improved. Hurvitz admitted to political limits on his ability to cut the budget.[40] The Hurvitz episode indicated that individual personalities played an important role in the Likud. They had helped during the elections and had reached high positions, but they were dispensible (like Dayan and Weizmann). These people had no strong political backing. Some headed factions, but they were no threat to Begin's leadership and apparently had no clearly defined support. Indeed, Hurvitz's faction, La'am, split close to the 1981 elections. Hurvitz ran on a separate list with Dayan. This list received only two seats, and Hurvitz was not elected. The remaining personalities of La'am integrated well into the Likud. So did others such as Ariel Sharon and Ehud Olmert. The resignation of Weizmann from the important post of minister of defense on May 25, 1980 did not affect adversely the Likud's chances in the June 1981 elections. Begin became minister of defense, a role he had hesitated to take on in 1977. The dual position of premier and defense minister apparently brought to mind examples of strong past leaders—Ben-Gurion, for example—who held both positions.

An aid to the entrenchment of the Likud was its ability to overcome conflict such as the secession of the movement for a Greater Israel and two key figures of Herut, Geula Cohen and Shmuel Katz. They opposed the Camp David agreement with Egypt and the withdrawal from all of the Sinai together with the evacuation of the Jewish settlements there. They also attacked Begin's autonomy plan for the Palestinians in the West Bank and Gaza Strip. Ideologically, this was an opposition that touched the very heart of Begin's own beliefs and his party's (Herut) long-held stand, and therefore such acrimony was unusual.

Begin mustered support for the peace agreement in the Knesset and emerged triumphant, not just because of his success over a major policy, but mainly because he had established his leadership role. Begin did not divide the vote on the peace document on the one hand and the removal of Jewish settlements from the Sinai on the other. The package deal he urged upon the Knesset finalized the peace treaty. In August 1981, less than a year before the settlements would have to be evacuated, Begin felt confident enough to blame the Labor party for not separating the vote on peace and the evacuation of settlements. His unique achievement as a leader of a nation was in mobilizing across-the-board support

for peace. In 1981 he attempted to rehabilitate himself ideologically as a traditional Herut leader.

The entrenchment of the Likud in politics was accompanied by a growing
Likud dependence on Begin. Less than a year before the June 1981 elections
Herut controlled the most important government ministries, including finance,
which was previously in the hands of the Liberals. From this post a populist
policy of tax reductions and regulated price cuts was instituted to the delight of
the Likud's constituency.

In managing the entrenchment of the Likud under Herut's dominance,
Begin found in the Liberal party a steadfast partner willing to play second fiddle.
Their leader had no ambition beyond his support for Begin and the Likud. In the
1981 elections Ehrlich hardly appeared in the media. His main contribution was
in retaining the Liberal party intact in the background. After 1977 this party
had undergone severe factional conflict. Its government ministers headed groups
of loyalists who attempted to overthrow Ehrlich. Their formal claim was that
under Herut dominance the Liberals might wither. Ehrlich's reasoning was that
the stronger the Likud under Begin, the better for the Liberals. He was right.
This old professional remained at the Liberal helm, and with the 1981 victory,
factional conflicts ceased—albeit only temporarily. The Liberals received 18 seats
in the Likud and four ministerial posts. The Liberals never again asked to head
the Finance Ministry. They appeared satisfied with secondary posts. They even
supported a resolution that allowed Begin to appoint Likud government ministers. For all practical purposes, this gave Begin the final say over specific ministerial appointments, thus helping to limit factional conflicts in the Likud.

In economic matters they were silent mainly because Hurvitz of La'am
had adopted Liberal-type policies when he replaced Ehrlich as minister of
finance. In matters of security the Liberals were mute and supportive of Begin.
In social legislation that challenged "Liberal" issues such as the anti-abortion
law, the Liberal party claimed it had to support the Likud coalition and religious
parties, thereby enabling the passage of an anti-Liberal law. The Begin government was built on a narrow coalition. Had the Liberals chosen to pursue their
ideology, the government would have fallen. From the latter perspective they
chose well, and the Likud as a whole benefitted from the Liberal choice. In
1981, they were rewarded when Begin personally supported the Liberal claim
for a large share of government positions. To sum up, the outwardly weak
Liberal party strengthened the Likud. This subgroup's retention of internal discipline helped the Likud as a whole in its survival as a party and a government.

Given the above party dimensions one may trace the many varied steps that
led to a high degree of entrenchment of the Likud as a major force in Israeli politics. In 1981 the Likud's growth had contributed to the polarization of the
voters between the two major parties, Likud and Ma'arach (Labor). These two
parties control 95 out of 120 seats in the Israeli Knesset. The third party of
1977, the Democratic Movement for Change, virtually disappeared. Out of its

15 seats, only its rump Shinui (Change) faction now has two seats in the Knesset. Even the National Religious Party was reduced from 12 to six.

The Begin era hastened various dimensions of change in Israeli society. These overlapped with the entrenchment of the Likud in Israeli politics. The Likud's rise to power in 1977 also signified the elements of class politics in Israel correlating with ethnic divisions. These divisions were especially underscored in the 1981 elections. During the Likud's first period in power there was a continuous conflict between the populist wing of the Likud, headed by David Levi of Herut, and the Liberal wing, along with efficiency advocates headed by Yigal Hurvitz of La'am. What appeared in late 1979 to be a government torn by interpersonal and interfactional rift might be, in fact, identified as steps in the Likud's search for identity in actual situations of policy. When the Likud was in opposition little was heard from the party about social policy. This was considered Labor's domain. When in power, the Likud's populist Herut wing seemed to become dominant and was probably a key factor in the Likud's return to power in 1981. In 1981, the Likud relegated Liberal economic ideology to rhetoric, whereas in 1977 it had been the plan of action. All these are causal factors in the entrenchment of the Likud as a mass party. The Likud's social policy was a continuation of the welfare state embellished by capitalistic rhetoric. If one combines Likud's social policy with the homogenous position of the Likud's factions on matters of security and the territories of the West Bank, one will find the factors that led to the regaining of public support for the Likud in 1981.

Finally, in the entrenchment of the Likud in Israeli politics, Begin's role cannot be ignored. Take, for example, the personalities who confronted him in various conflicts. They only contributed to Begin's reassertion as an undisputed leader. Ezer Weizmann's resignation, for example, created a great uproar in the press, but he had no faction or group to lean on. His personal, public popularity was not and could not be translated into political action within the Likud or in the Herut—his political home. Weizmann's resignation can be viewed as Begin's easy removal of an impatient challenger.

CONCLUSION

The Likud's first term in office was characterized by its efforts to consolidate itself as a political party and become entrenched in Israeli politics. Its use of international relations to change policies, and the leadership of Menachem Begin, were instrumental in the acquisition of legitimacy as a ruling party and as a future competitor for power.

The factionalized structure of the Likud and its new experience in government did not enable the party to adopt a program of change in the domestic sphere. Policy changes occurred in foreign relations where autocratic leadership navigated the events.

The apparent policy divergence, which the 1977 Likud platform posed in socioeconomic policies, was overcome by (1) continuation of old policies, (2) rotation of key positions such as the Ministry of Finance, and (3) a program of massive public spending. Thus, up to 1981, the Likud remained a party of paradoxes, where capitalistic rhetoric served as a fig leaf for increased social welfare policies. The expectation that the Likud would improve the economy did not materialize. However, this did not prevent the Likud from removing the stigma of being a perennial opposition party, which the previous Labor government had attempted to attach to it.

Perhaps the most dramatic of all changes that the Likud's rise to power signifies is the change in voter identification and the alliance of the center-right Likud with the masses of voters of low income and of low socioeconomic status.

NOTES

1.   Richard Crossman, *The Diaries of a Cabinet Minister* (New York: Holt, Rinehart and Winston, 1975–1976); S.M. Lipset, "Bureaucracy and Social Reform," in *Complex Organizations: A Sociological Reader,* ed. A. Etzioni (New York: Rinehart and Winston, 1961), pp. 260–67.

2.   Except in 1967–70 in a national unity government.

3.   Examples of this are found during the term of the Franklin D. Roosevelt government in the United States and Winston Churchill in England.

4.   For further discussions, see Efraim Torgovnik, "Party Factions and Election Issues," In *The Elections in Israel 1969,* ed. Asher Arian (Jerusalem: Jerusalem Academic Press, 1972), pp. 21–40.

5.   See Maurice Duverger, *Political Parties* (London: Methuen, 1959); Sigmund Neumann, "Toward a Comparative Study of Political Parties," in *Modern Political Parties,* ed. Sigmund Neumann (Chicago: University of Chicago Press, 1965); R. Rose, *The Problems of Party Government* (London: Macmillan Press, 1974).

6.   There were other generals who also entered politics. Chaim Bar-Lev and Aharon Yariv, for instance, who joined the Labor party, and Shlomo Lahat, who in 1978 won his second term of office as Mayor of Tel Aviv on a Likud ticket.

7.   The case of the mayorality of Tel Aviv shows this clearly. In the past, the Liberal party had one major strength. It provided an impressive array of candidates for the mayorality. Examples are mayors Dizengoff and Rochach of Tel Aviv. There were other good candidates when ex-General Lahat appeared. But, apparently, the dominance of national politics, a loss of confidence or perhaps merely a process of giving into popular images, had overcome the party, making it resort to an ex-general as a candidate. To the Liberal party structure itself this new situation signified a beginning of unrest, a fierce conflict among factions and groups, and most significantly, resentment at the party's secondary position to Begin's Herut within the Likud.

8.   Efraim Torgovnik, "A Movement for Change in a Stable System," in *Israel at the Polls,* ed. H. Penniman (Washington, D.C.: American Enterprise Institute for Public Policy Research, 1979), pp. 147–72.

9. Ibid.

10. *Haaretz*, July 19, 1973.

11. Ibid.

12. *Haaretz*, July 22, 1973.

13. *Haaretz*, July 29, 30, 31, 1973.

14. See Asher Arian, *The Elections in Israel 1977* (Jerusalem: Jerusalem Academic Press, 1980).

15. See Ibid., passim.

16. See *Arian*, 1980.

17. Efraim Torgovnik, "Accepting Camp David the Role of Party Factions in Israel Policy Making," *Middle East Review*, 11 (Winter 1978-79): 18-25.

18. Arthur Schlesinger, Jr., *A Thousand Days: J.F. Kennedy in the White House* (Boston: Houghton Mifflin, 1965), pp. 155-64; Natan Glager, "On Task Forming," *The Public Interest*, 15 (Spring 1969): 40-46.

19. See Aaron Wildavsky, *The Politics of the Budgetary Process* 2nd ed. (Boston: Little, Brown, 1974) and *Speaking Truth to Power* (Boston: Little, Brown, 1979).

20. Interestingly, the Likud victory in 1977 inspired the opposition Labor party to follow methods mentioned above in preparation for the 1981 elections.

21. *The Rom Committee Report*, 1977.

22. Interview with Y. Flumin.

23. See *Lipset* (1961).

24. See *Wildavsky* (1974, 1979).

25. Efraim Torgovnik, "A Movement for Change in a Stable System," in Asher Arian's *The Elections in Israel 1977* (Jerusalem: Jerusalem Academic Press, 1980), pp. 75-100.

26. Results of survey conducted by the Jersualem Institute of Applied Social Research, see *Yediot Acharonot*, August 3, 1979.

27. *Yediot Acharonot*, September 21, 1979.

28. *Haaretz*, September 26, 1979.

29. *Haaretz*, January 30, 1981.

30. Results of surveys conducted by Mina Zemach, *Yediot Acharonot*, May 23, 1980.

31. Survey conducted by Hanoch Smith, *Ma'ariv*, October 3, 1980.

32. Likud *Platform 1977*.

33. Ibid., p. 15.

34. State of Israel, Ministry of Treasury, *Government Corporation Report*, no. 18, Jerusalem, March 1980, p. 60. For a further discussion of the issue of public companies, see pp. 71-72.

35. *Platform 1977*, p. 2.

36. *Ha'aretz*, September 1, 1978.

37. *Platform 1977*, p. 2.

38. Alan Zuckerman, *The Politics of Faction* (New Haven: Yale University Press, 1979).

39. Survey conducted by Pori, *Haaretz*, January 30, 1980.

40. Relayed via interview.

2

Likud in Power:
Divided We Stand

David Pollock

This chapter analyzes the early attrition, subsequent consolidation, and eventual triumph of Begin's Likud-led coalition. In June 1977, Menachem Begin took over as prime minister of Israel for the first time. In October of that year, the addition of the Democratic Movement for Change (DMC) to his coalition raised Begin's majority to a solid 77 in the 120-member Knesset. Over the next three years, however, defections from both the "dovish" and "hawkish" ends of this coalition cut into its numerical strength. Personal rivalries eroded it further. The result was a smaller but somewhat more cohesive coalition—and one more dependent on the religious parties than ever before. New elections in June 1981 left that coalition picture essentially intact.

The government that Begin put together in 1977 included his own Likud party (45 seats), the DMC (15), and the "independent" vote of Foreign Minister Moshe Dayan, plus two religious parties with another 16 seats between them. Likud comprised three main factions: Herut, the Liberals, and La'am. In 1978, the DMC split into separate Democratic and Change factions, the latter moving into opposition. After Camp David, the outspoken Likud deputies defected to found the new right-wing Tehiya (Revival) party. In mid-1980, the rump Democratic party split again, when several members bolted the coalition to form a new faction called Ahvan (Brotherhood). By that time, Dayan and Defense Minister Weizmann had both resigned, and both voted against the government later that year. The final blow to Begin's dwindling Knesset majority was the defection of another Likud splinter—a three-man Rafi group led by Finance Minister Hurvitz—in early 1981.

This chapter will analyze the attrition of these fringe elements from the coalition, the factional infighting among those elements that remained, and the implications of all this for Israel in the Begin era. As much as possible, we will avoid historical or ideological background, which have been treated elsewhere at some length.[1] We will also shun discussion of "purely" religious or security issues, which are the province of other chapters in this book—though some discussion of such overlapping issues is unavoidable here. Instead, we will concentrate on the play of political and personal rivalries among the non-religious coalition parties, led by Menachem Begin's Likud.

The subject is admittedly arcane, but important for Israel's policy, both domestic and foreign. It is especially in need of objective analysis in view of misconceptions in the press: overemphasis on unusual personalities and extremes, on Begin's image problems, and on his government's likely fall for substantive reasons. The Western media focused on the discontents of Weizmann and Dayan, who in fact were isolated figures. We will see that, despite the impression of change, a continuous Likud core was maintained all through Begin's first term. His party was thus poised to pursue its traditional policies—and its traditional infighting—upon winning reelection in 1981.

To preserve a rough chronological order, however, we begin not with Likud itself, but with the defectors from its coalition, beginning in 1978. The first and largest group came from the DMC.

THE DEMOCRATIC MOVEMENT FOR CHANGE:
REVOLT ON BEGIN'S LEFT

Founded in 1977 as the party of internal reform, and headed by renowned "apolitical" archaeologist Yigal Yadin, the DMC began as the second-largest party in Begin's coalition. Its core consisted mainly of middle-class professionals and academics, with many "doves," a sprinkling of (non-Jewish) "minorities," but also some well-known "hawks" within its ranks. Some (like David Golomb and Meir Amit) hailed originally from Labor, others (like Shmuel Tamir, Akiva Nof, and Binyamin Halevi) from Likud. This rather incongruous mixture piled up an astonishing 15 Knesset seats in its first (and last) electoral bid. Most of those votes were taken from Labor and thus played a critical part in Likud's assumption of power.[2]

In October 1977, after protracted negotiations, the DMC joined Begin's coalition and gave the government a much broader parliamentary base. The ostensible catalyst for this decision was Yadin's desire for national unity, in the face of a brief "crisis" in U.S.-Israeli relations over a Geneva Arab-Israeli peace conference and related issues. More important, however, was the imminent expiration of Begin's deadline for holding open cabinet positions for the DMC. In line with the rough ratio applied to each faction's Knesset strength, four cabinet posts were reserved for members of the DMC. On policy issues, however, the party got none of the internal reforms it had demanded. About the only real concession it obtained was the right to appeal cabinet settlement decisions to the Knesset Foreign Affairs and Security Committee, where opposition Labor representatives could be counted on to reinforce Yadin's moderating voice.

Once in power, the DMC underwent a complicated series of defections and splits, which reduced its numbers almost to the vanishing point by the elections of 1981. This section will explain that process, and then assess the impact of the DMC on Begin's coalition as a whole. Minor incidents will be omitted, the better to clarify the main steps in the DMC's precipitous decline.

The party's best-known "hawk," Meir Zorea, was one of the first to go. He resigned his Knesset seat the first time his party appealed a settlement decision, making way for the next candidate on the DMC's electoral list. But the first major split took place a few weeks before Camp David. Seven "dovish" deputies moved into opposition, amid charges that the peace process under Begin was stalled. They took back the name Shinui, or Change, the original title of the group around Amnon Rubinstein that had merged with Yadin's group to form the DMC a year before. Soon after their defection, when Begin returned to the Knesset from Camp David, he could not resist looking out at Shinui's deputies and asking, "Why couldn't you have waited another month?!"[3]

For Shinui, however, there were few regrets. For the next two years and more, the party remained a vocal, albeit small, opposition voice in the Knesset. Its deputies spoke out for fewer settlements and more flexibility in peace negotiations and for social, economic, legal, religious, and electoral reforms.[4] They even attracted a lone new defector from Begin's coalition, Yosi Tamir of the Liberals, for a while. But Shinui was just too small to have much effect. Before the 1981 election, two of its members returned to Labor's fold, and many voters did the same. Other original DMC constituents of 1977 had voted literally just for "change," not necessarily for Liberal or "dovish" positions. In the 1981 election, therefore, only two Shinui candidates—Rubinstein and Mordechai Virshuvski—were returned to the Knesset.

In the meantime, the DMC deputies who stayed with the government after Shinui left were now called simply Democrats (DM). Individual defections by Knesset members Mordechai Elgrabli and Asaf Yaguri, who launched separate one-man factions, further reduced the Democrats' strength. Thus, by mid-1979, there remained only six out of the original 15 DMC members of the Knesset. In the cabinet, the party still held three posts: Yadin as deputy prime minister, Shmuel Tamir at Justice, and Israel Katz, the only one not also serving in the Knesset, at Social Welfare. Even this small group was not united. Its members quarreled publicly, for example, over a cabinet reorganization in November 1979 that created a second deputy prime minister, alongside their own Yadin.[5]

In mid-1980, the rump Democrats' strength was cut in half once more. Two more party backbenchers defected, to found the ill-defined faction called Ahvah (Brotherhood). They cited disapproval of government haggling over settlements and defense spending as reasons for their departure. The two, Shlomo Eliyahu and Shafiq Asad, were soon followed by a third DMC deputy, Akiva Nof. A few weeks later, Justice Minister Tamir resigned, saying that he disagreed with government policy as well. Anyway, Tamir added, it was absurd for his party to have as many cabinet ministers as members in the Knesset.[6] By this time, not surprisingly, the DMC was consistently given a less than 1 percent preference rating in Israeli polls—compared to 12 percent or more at the start of its meteoric career.

Through it all, the party's leader, Yigal Yadin, remained outwardly philosophical and unperturbed. He too was unhappy with the government's performance, Yadin told an interviewer in 1980, but it was better than the Labor alternative. He cited the peace with Egypt, and a pending national health bill, as evidence of his government's achievements in foreign and domestic affairs. Nevertheless, as the 1981 election approached, Yadin announced his retirement from political life.[7] Among the five other Knesset representatives of the Democrats plus Ahvah, only one—Akiva Nof, who rejoined Likud in time—ran for parliament again. Tamir also sought to rejoin Begin's party but was rebuffed. Israel Katz, who had served the DMC in the cabinet but not the Knesset, ran on Dayan's new Telem ticket but failed to win a seat. Hardly anyone even noticed that no DMC ticket was entered on the ballot in 1981.

Yet as long as that party was in Begin's government, it did have some influence on policy, at least in foreign affairs. Yadin's own statements indicate what that influence was: speeding up the treaty with Egypt and slowing down the growth of settlements on the West Bank. As to the former, the DMC leader noted, with the 1981 election near, that "Likud can say what it wants now, but we gave (Begin) his majority for peace."[8] This was an allusion to the fact that half the prime minister's own Herut faction failed to endorse the Camp David accords—though they passed the Knesset plenum by a comfortable margin, including many Labor votes. Parliamentary approval, then, would have been possible even without the DMC, but that party did at least give Begin more backing for Camp David inside the governing coalition.

The settlement issue was more subtle. The DMC, it will be recalled, was guaranteed the right to appeal new projects to a Knesset committee. It exercised this right an average of only once a year, and then it was regularly overruled.[9] In the cabinet itself, party spokesmen were hard pressed to find specific votes where the winning margin was provided by the DMC. Still, as one Likud spokesman privately admitted, the prospect of a divisive cabinet or Knesset confrontation, and the occasional procedural delays even after a decision was announced, did "complicate" settlement policy to some extent.[10]

The most protracted such episode took place in 1980. At stake was a cabinet decision, partly in response to a Palestinian terrorist attack, to repopulate an abandoned Jewish hospital and school in the West Bank city of Hebron. Cabinet approval in principle was reached in February, but the DMC delayed a vote on any specific project until late March. At that time, all three DMC ministers voted against even a scaled-down proposal but were outvoted by their more militant colleagues. The losers then appealed to the Knesset committee, where they found themselves in a minority once more. The Hebron project went ahead.

A month later, when a terrorist ambush there killed six Jewish settlers, Yadin discerned the "original sin" of this whole affair in his government's earlier failure to evict Jewish squatters from the town.[11] The DM, typically, had managed to delay, but not to prevent, a government policy it thought unwise.

In a rather similar fashion, DM opposition helped scuttle, or at least postpone, the transfer of two "hawkish" ministers—Sharon and Moda'i, of whom more later—to head the ministries of Defense and Foreign Affairs. The party also helped keep a 1979 cabinet memorandum, asserting Israel's eventual claim to sovereignty over the West Bank, from being formally presented to Egypt during Palestinian autonomy negotiations. There were "many other such decisions over the years," according to Yadin, that his party was "able to stop or stall," though some of those decisions could not be revealed just yet.[12] Independent observers were not as kind, variously terming the DMC "terribly ineffectual" and "tremendously disappointing."[13] Clearly, the party was able to exert some "moderating" influence on Begin's government. Just as clearly, however, that influence was limited in the extreme, the more so as the party's numbers rapidly diminished. The DMC's major, perhaps unwitting, role was to help Begin take office in the first place—not to keep him there, or change his policies while he served.

Thus the early promise of the DMC—indeed, the party itself—vanished within a few short years. After the 1977 election, some analysts had viewed the rise of this large alternative party as a major structural change. Four years later, analysts saw a shift toward a two-party system instead.

The DMC's fate confirmed an old truth about Israeli politics: new parties, whether personalized (like Dayan's) or more broadly based, are either coopted as factions by the two largest parties or consigned to the margins of political life— if not to complete oblivion. Nevertheless, a tendency toward factionalism persists, as a way of obtaining more bargaining leverage over established leaders.

TEHIYA: REVOLT ON BEGIN'S RIGHT

After Shinui, the next defectors from Begin's coalition came not from the "dovish left" but from the "hawkish right." Worry about such defections had led Begin to quibble over fine print in his 1977 offer to return the Sinai to Egyptian control. Camp David, with its promise to evacuate Sinai settlements and suspend Israel's claim to sovereignty (in favor of Palestinian autonomy) in Gaza and the West Bank, raised the specter of wholesale right-wing desertions. This accounts for Begin's insistence that the vote on Camp David be free of coalition discipline; that way, members of his own party could vote against the agreement without automatically leaving government ranks. When the vote came, fully one-third of Likud abstained or even voted against Camp David.[14] Only two deputies, though, actually switched to opposition—as the new, ultranationalist party of Tehiya (Revival).

The two were Geula Cohen, one of Begin's erstwhile comrades-in-arms, and Moshe Shamir, elected on a Greater Israel platform. After Camp David, these two maintained an isolated but vociferous opposition to Begin's regime. Several times, Cohen disrupted Knesset proceedings with persistent heckling of the "turn-coats" in Likud. Twice in 1980, she tried to force the government's hand by sponsoring bills extending Israel's sovereignty over territories captured in the Six-Day War. Her first try, concerning Jerusalem, was a success. The timing was deliberately provocative, in that it coincided with the approaching "target date" for completion of Palestinian autonomy talks. But so strong was the national consensus on keeping the ancient city as Israel's "eternal and undivided capital," that a solid majority of the Knesset gave Cohen's bill their reluctant assent. The only result, though, was another diplomatic flap with Washington, and another reason for Sadat to suspend the deadlocked autonomy talks.[15]

Cohen's next attempt to embarass Begin's government, on the Golan Heights question, failed. Despite an impressive number of signatures on a supporting petition, a bill effectively annexing that former Syrian territory languished in committee, for want of government support. In November 1980, when Begin barely escaped defeat on an unrelated no-confidence motion, Cohen reportedly offered him Tehiya's two votes—in exchange for his endorsement of the Golan law. Begin refused the deal, and his former comrade resumed her heckling as before.[16] On still another controversial issue, she managed to drive a temporary wedge into the coalition by sponsoring a bill—supported by some Begin loyalists, but strongly opposed by his orthodox allies—mandating "national service" for women exempt from the military on religious grounds.[17]

Moshe Shamir, Cohen's Knesset partner in Tehiya, was more eloquent but restrained. His rhetoric harked back to the "heroic," pioneering days of Zionism, in a manner similarly calculated to embarass the "moderates" of modern times. A typical example was his response in 1980, when Yadin and others suggested that Jews in Hebron might not have been murdered had the government evacuated Jewish squatters from that Arab town. "And if we had evacuated Tel-Hai in 1920," Shimar reported, "then Trumpeldor (an early Zionist hero) would not have been killed!"[18] Likud, he observed sardonically on another occasion, had "devalued everything, from money to Israel's most sacred principles."[19]

Such rhetoric seemed, at first, to bring Tehiya a significant measure of support. Luminaries of the Greater Israel and related Gush Emunim movements—Yuval Ne'eman, Hanan Porat, Gershon Shafat, and Tzvi Shiloah—were observed, according to one Israeli report, coming and going in the Knesset cafeteria as if they already belonged. Tehiya was also, as even its detractors admitted, one of the few Israeli parties that still attracted both secular and orthodox backing—thanks to its association with the heavily orthodox prosettlement lobby of Gush Emunim.[20]

But in the end, despite the early enthusiasm, rousing rhetoric, and parliamentary ploys, right-wing defections caused Begin only minor problems. Once

Tehiya was launched with just two Knesset members on board, the threat of such defections no longer swayed government policy very far. At most, fear that other popular Likud "hawks"–like Knesset leader Moshe Arens, or Defense Minister Ariel Sharon–might join Cohen and Shamir, swelling the right-wing opposition, gave Begin's government a slight extra impetus toward narrow interpretations of autonomy and expanded settlement programs on the West Bank. Though the sentiments symbolized by Tehiya continued to exert a strong pull on many members of Likud, the political impact of this maximalist movement was contained. Its potential converts in the Knesset and among the voters–and even, according to Begin, his own immediate family–largely failed to heed the call.[21]

Before the 1981 election, some observers thought Camp David had "betrayed" Likud ideology enough to alienate the party's traditional base.[22] That prediction did not come true. Hardliners suspected that Tehiya's electoral prospects were slim and feared to strengthen Labor by splitting the Likud. Tehiya won only three seats; while Likud gained just as many, for a new high of 48. The little support that Tehiya did obtain was garnered, according to precinct breakdowns and informal opinion samplings, mostly from the strongholds of the National Religious Party instead of from Likud.[23] Still, the coalition's postelection one-vote majority (without Tehiya) meant that Begin would try not to antagonize Tehiya's three deputies further with too strong a show of "moderation."

THE "CENTER" FOLDS: DAYAN AND WEIZMANN DEFECT

This section, as its title shows, deals with individuals, not organized factions. Foreign Minister Dayan and Defense Minister Weizmann were both strong personalities, and both played a big part in Israeli foreign policy during the first half of Begin's first term. Both later resigned their cabinet posts, for a combination of personal and policy reasons–Dayan in October 1979, Weizmann in May 1980–and both eventually voted in the Knesset to bring Begin's government down. Yet the diplomatic influence they exerted, and certainly the amount of attention they received, was out of proportion to their respective internal political standings. The distinguished duo deserted, yet Begin's ship of state remained afloat. Here the emphasis is again on the domestic rather than the foreign policy implications of these two dramatic defections from Begin's regime.

One month after the 1977 election, Dayan resigned from the Labor party and, as a newly "independent" Knesset member, became Begin's foreign minister. The move was controversial in Israel, if not abroad. Dayan's political fortunes had been in eclipse ever since his resignation as defense minister, after near disaster in the 1973 war. To many Israelis, inside and outside Begin's coalition, the leap to Likud patronage only reinforced Dayan's image as an unprincipled opportunist. Likud purists looked askance at Dayan's willingness to make foreign policy concessions. Nevertheless, the international respect he commanded made Dayan a distinct diplomatic asset for Begin's mostly unknown and untested team. In return, Dayan exacted a price: a commitment to postpone outright annexation of any occupied territories indefinitely, or "so long as there were prospects of peace negotiations."

Dayan did have many government supporters. The DMC was generally favorably inclined, on policy if not on personal grounds. Other backing, inside the Likud, came from the Liberal faction, and from the small but influential Rafi group—once headed by Dayan himself, and now by cousin Yigal Hurvitz. Most important of all was the confidence of Prime Minister Begin, who entrusted sensitive negotiations with U.S., Egyptian, and other interlocutors to Dayan. (Not even Defense Minister Weizmann, for example, was told about Dayan's secret 1977 meetings with Egyptian representatives in Rabat.)[24]

In that capacity, Dayan played a major role in arranging Sadat's first visit to Jerusalem, and all that followed: Camp David and the Egyptian-Israeli peace treaty. But once the treaty was signed, Begin seemed to shunt his foreign minister aside. The Palestinian autonomy team was directed by Interior Minister Burg, administration of the occupied territories by Weizmann, settlement policy by Agriculture Minister Sharon. This left Dayan with the diplomatic duty he claimed to like the least: the cocktail parties!

On matters of substance, too, Dayan no longer saw "eye to eye," as he himself facetiously put it, with Begin. His government, Dayan later charged, just "did not want to implement autonomy," witness its dilatory tactics and overly restrictive definitions.[25] After several months of watching the stalemate from the sidelines, a frustrated Dayan resigned his cabinet post in October 1979. The move made headlines around the world, but in Israel almost nothing changed. Soon afterward, Dayan was replaced as foreign minister by veteran Herut figure (and recent Knesset Speaker) Yitzhak Shamir. Both the coalition and the autonomy negotiations meandered on as before.

After his resignation, Dayan adopted an independent parliamentary posture, variously abstaining, evading, and finally supporting motions to bring the government down. As election time approached, he created a new party called Telem, the Hebrew acronym for National Renewal Movement. At first, polls predicted a respectable showing. In the end, however, Telem picked up only two seats—one for Dayan, and one for his ever-loyal and oft-disappointed friend, Mordechai Ben-Porat. Rafi stalwarts Yigal Hurvitz and Zalman Shoval, who had quit Likud and thrown in their lot with Dayan at the last minute, were left out in the cold.[26]

All in all, Dayan's impact on Begin's domestic (as opposed to diplomatic) fortunes was minimal—certainly far less than media coverage might suggest. He joined the cabinet as a loner and left it the same way. Dayan's departure did weaken the government a bit, as even Begin conceded, especially since economic troubles were coming to a head at the same time. But since Dayan controlled only his own vote, the coalition was free to carry on without him for nearly another two years—and carry on it did. Much the same fate befell Ezer Weizmann, who resigned half a year after Dayan.

Weizmann, unlike Dayan, was not only a crucial cabinet minister, but also a promising political leader of Begin's own faction, Herut. Offsetting his impulsiveness, and relatively late party career, was a combination of attractive personal qualities. He was young, good-humored, a former air force commander, and the effective organizer of Likud's first winning campaign. In the beginning, therefore, Weizmann had many supporters in Likud, especially among the younger generation of leaders like David Levi and Yoram Aridor.

Weizmann's relations with one-time brother-in-law Dayan, on the other hand, were correct but cool. But relations with Sharon, another ex-general, were positively stormy. In mid-1978, the defense minister publicly and successfully opposed Sharon's plan to construct what Weizmann called "dummy settlements" in the Sinai, threatening to resign if construction were not halted right away. It was.[27] Later, during Palestinian autonomy negotiations, Weizmann often sided with the Democrats and other cabinet "moderates" who tried to limit Jewish settlement on the West Bank. In early 1980, for example, he voted with the minority opposing the new Israeli "presence" in Hebron.[28]

As the "target date" for autonomy approached with no agreement in store, Weizmann began voicing increasingly public disenchantment with his government's performance. The prime minister, he charged, was no longer leading the Likud, let alone the nation. Weizmann's restiveness was compounded by his party's abysmal popularity ratings at the time. Meanwhile, in intraparty discussions, the "old guard"—Bader, Shilansky, Dekel, and Stern—were ganging up on the upstart, "pragmatic" defense minister.[29]

The last straw for Weizmann, perhaps just an excuse, was an on-again, off-again budget cutting proposal, which he said made it impossible to plan properly for Israel's defense. In May 1980 he tendered his resignation, and Begin accepted it with no regrets. Weizmann, the prime minister's letter replied, had acted with "shocking frivolity" and "mind-numbing ambition." The defense minister's diatribes against the government at military headquarters, Begin claimed on another occasion, were "morally tantamount to a *coup d'etat.*" In November 1980, the cabinet censured Weizmann for intervening in U.S. politics, on Carter's side. The ultimate insult, to Weizmann's party colleagues, was his vote against the government on a close no-confidence motion later that month. Herut's central committee voted, by a large majority, to oust the former defense minister from his own party.[30]

All this time, Weizmann was testing the chances of leading a new, centrist political party, only to find that neither the Liberals nor the Democrats were interested—nor was either group likely to succeed without Begin. So Weizmann sat out the last election, telling a reporter to call him back in 1985.[31] But unlike

Dayan, who is older, unconnected with Herut, tainted by failure and not all that well,* Weizmann could make a political comeback with Likud. So far, like Dayan, he has made his mark mainly in defense and foreign policy, not in the domestic sphere. In internal Israeli politics, Weizmann's recent career is chiefly significant as another demonstration that talented, ambitious men often seek to escape the bonds of party discipline—and that isolation and political impotence is often their reward, at least temporarily. Now, with our survey of defectors during Begin's first three years completed, we can turn to the large core of Likud supporters who remained.

LIKUD FACTIONALISM: DISTINCTIONS WITHOUT MUCH DIFFERENCE

Likud, as its Hebrew name implies, is a "union" of three factions: Herut, the Liberals, and La'am, in descending size order. (There was also a one-man faction ironically named Ahdut, another Hebrew word for unity.) The two largest components joined forces in 1965, as the Gush (Bloc) Herut-Liberalism—known by its acronym Gahal. The addition of La'am in 1973 formed the Likud, or union of right-wing Israeli political forces.

The combination ran on a joint ticket, with places on the list assigned to each faction in rough proportion to its original size. Knesset candidates were ranked by each faction separately and then inserted more-or-less alternately into the Likud list. Each large faction also had its own executive, conventions, parliamentary leaders, and other paraphernalia. Younger cadres—student leaders, local officials, district organizers, and so on—gained some influence as well, after a flurry of internal reform in 1977.

In that year, when Likud took power for the first time, cabinet ministries and other top positions were assigned according to the factional "key." By that time it was common knowledge that this sytem underrepresented Herut, in relation to its electoral drawing power and campaign activity, compared to the Liberals and La'am. Nevertheless, Begin, the leader of Herut and of Likud as a whole, stuck with the time-honored factional formula for dividing up the spoils. The Liberal partnership, especially, still gave Herut an extra measure of respectability among more middle-class and "moderate" Israeli voters. The Liberals were still strong in Tel Aviv, where both the mayor and his deputy represented that faction. Besides, the leaders of Herut and the Liberals—Menachem Begin and Simcha Ehrlich—were old friends.

On substantive issues, the two factions represented somewhat different combinations of nationalism and other concerns. Herut's first priority is militant nationalism, encompassing the entire "Land of Israel" including the West Bank.

---

*Dayan was to die in October 1981.—ED.

Concerning internal matters, Herut's position has been less clear. It tends to favor a vaguely greater role for Jewish religious tradition and to oppose Labor's socialist edifice in favor of free enterprise garnished with what might be termed "state populism."

It was precisely on such domestic issues, by contrast, that the Liberals—traditionally more "moderate" on foreign policy—generally focused their concerns. This faction stood first for private enterprise, and then for limiting the role of religion in public affairs. On all those issues, the differences from Herut were really matters of degree, and a range of opinion existed even within each faction. La'am, broadly speaking, combined Herut's approach to foreign policy with Liberal predilections on domestic affairs.

In the four years that these factions have exercised power together, as we shall see, the ideological divide among them has become even more blurry than before. By election eve in 1981, this policy convergence—and even more so the political reality of Herut's predominance—wrested an agreement at the party convention to open talks on merger and to abandon factional distinctions in cabinet assignments. Like so much else in politics, however, there was less to this agreement than met the eye. In matters of patronage and political power, and even in some policy debates, many factional distinctions have been preserved. This section will analyze the recent evolution of each main faction in Likud. We will then conclude with a review of their interaction with each other and with other elements in Begin's Likud-led coalition as a whole.

Before proceeding, however, a simple table showing each Likud faction's numerical strength in the Knesset, after the last two Israeli elections, will help keep the "qualitative" analysis in perspective: (see Table 2.1).

TABLE 2.1
Likud Knesset Members, by Faction

	Herut	*Liberals*	*La'am*	*Other*	*Total*
1977	22	14	8	1	45
1981	25	18	4	1	48

HERUT: LEADERSHIP, ORGANIZATION, AND SUCCESSION

Any discussion of the internal politics of Herut (Hebrew for "freedom") begins with Begin. He has headed the party since preindependence days. He led it to victory in 1977 and then again, against all odds, in 1981. He has also survived internal challenges before: Tamir and his Free Center faction in the 1960s, Weizmann and Sharon in the last few years. His personal appeal in Israel brought out throngs of supporters chanting "Begin, King of Israel" during the last campaign.

Of course, the title is misleading. Begin's party won only about 40 percent of the Israeli vote, nearly matched by Labor. But for many Likud supporters, and even more so inside Herut, Begin is indeed king. As of 1981, he remains the undisputed party boss. He shows only a few signs of slowing down, or grooming a successor. Still, even a king has courtiers, ministers, and perhaps pretenders to the throne. This section will examine Herut's internal dynamics and then explain how Begin has manipulated them so far.

Herut's basic organization during Begin's first term was reasonably straightforward and need not detain us long. At the top was the Secretariat, headed by a 15-member Executive Committee. Next were the factions' Directorate and Conference, each with a Steering Committee. Then came an Organization Department (Agaf Irgun), several Knesset caucus chairmen and "whips," and a Local Elections Command (Mateh). These were followed by regional and municipal branches, headed by Herut "Strongmen." There were also influential Herut delegations to affiliated institutions, like the Jewish Agency and Israel's giant labor federation, the Histadrut.[32]

Membership on these bodies was interlocking. Control of key committees could confer considerable clout, as in the case of David Levi, Herut's number one organization man and number two, after Begin, in the faction as a whole. But position in the hierarchy did not necessarily indicate power. For example, once Begin took over as prime minister, chairmanship of the Directorate became a largely ceremonial post. Some big city bosses—Meir Cohen in Haifa, Chaim Corfu, Rabenu Levi, and Yehoshua Matza in Jerusalem—have more power than their nominal superiors, even on a national level. Most important, therefore, is the play of personalities and (to a lesser extent) policy orientations around this lifeless organizational skeleton.

Unfortunately, there is no consistent criterion—generational, positional, or otherwise—for predicting either policy preferences or degree of political power. There are no semiofficial factional distinctions within Herut, as there have long been in other Israeli parties. Thus, the competition for high cabinet posts, and for Begin's succession, revolves primarily around individuals, not ideologies or organized groups. The backdrop is a network of personal alliances and cliques, and sometimes family connections, shifting to meet the expedience of the moment.

One recent and important episode in this endless mosaic will suffice to illustrate the point. It began in 1980, and involved then-Knesset Speaker Yitzhak Shamir, Foreign Affairs Committee Chairman Moshe Arens, Agriculture Minister Ariel Sharon, and party manager Yoram Aridor—all leading members of Herut, and all vying for the posts of foreign minister, defense minister and/or successor to Begin. Arens supported Shamir, the winning aspirant over Aridor, for foreign minister; but Shamir did not support Arens in his quest for the

Defense Ministry, which eventually went to Sharon. Now, in another ironic twist, the supposedly "hawkish" Shamir appears to be supporting "moderate" Aridor (the man he beat to the Foreign Ministry) for unofficial third place within Herut—instead of the "hawkish" Sharon.[33] Apparently, neither policy leanings nor long-term personal loyalties play much part in this game, whose rules are subject to change at any time.

At one time, Weizmann was considered Begin's heir apparent. His resignation in 1980 opened the field to a host of new contenders. The prime minister has hinted that veteran Ya'acov Meridor, newly-appointed chairman of the cabinet economic "superministry," is his personal favorite, without committing himself to an explicit choice. Better placed in terms of party support and life expectancy, however, is Deputy Prime Minister and Housing Minister David Levi. As number two on the Herut election list, he also has the Liberal faction's endorsement to succeed Begin. Levi is followed, unofficially of course, by Defense Minister Sharon. Dark-horse, somewhat less experienced, and less well connected candidates include Arens and Aridor, the latter now finance minister. Each of these men has a personal following: Meridor for his experience and close ties with Begin; Levi for his organizational ability and ethnic (Sephardi) appeal; Sharon for his toughness, charisma, and ties with Gush Emunim; Arens for his combination of militance and careful thought; Aridor for his freshness and intellectual cachet.[34] The final selection, still nowhere in sight, will probably depend less on any domestic or even foreign policy issues than on the partisan alignments of the day.

HERUT: POLICY "CAMPS"

Nevertheless, there seem to be two broad camps, one of "hawks" and one of relative "moderates" on foreign policy issues, within the higher councils of Herut. The former camp is a loose amalgam of the old guard, plus several comparative newcomers and younger party leaders. The old guard, in turn, includes veterans of two different 1940s factions. Veterans of the extreme Lehi ("Stern Gang") faction are represented by Foreign Minister Shamir, and Knesset member (and brother of the late Lehi commander) David Stern. Original Irgun members include old Begin comrades Meridor, Yohanan Bader, and Chaim Landau, along with Knesset members Avraham Schechterman and Mordechai Dekel (the latter now also deputy agriculture minister). The most influential "new" spokesmen for the hawkish camp are Arens, Sharon, and Knesset member (and Begin son-in-law) Roni Milo. It was this camp that started the "dump Weizmann" bandwagon, eventually drumming him out of the party altogether after the defense minister resigned his cabinet post.

By that time, Weizmann had alienated even his friends among the relative "moderates" in Herut. This camp spans a wide cross section of party cadres, led by Levi and Aridor. The largest single group is loosely attached to Levi, and also to relatively "moderate" positions within the spectrum of Herut.[35] Thus, the jockeying for position at the top does have an ideological as well as a personal dimension.

It is not easy to judge the balance between "hawks" and "moderates" in Herut, and even harder to make specific policy predictions on that basis alone. With the departure of Weizmann and the elevation of Shamir and Sharon, the "hawkish" contingent was strengthened. Likud's victory in the general election, without Weizmann and without indirect assistance from the DMC, also strengthened the party's more militant wing. "Hawks" are now in charge of the Foreign Affairs and Defense portfolios, while "moderates" seem to concentrate on internal affairs: Finance, Housing, and the like. The rank and file at party conferences seems also to be moving in a more "hawkish" direction. And in the latest Herut internal elections, leading "hawks" like Arens, and even lesser-known ones like Dov Shilansky, did surprisingly well.[36]

On the other hand, a balanced overall listing on the 1981 ticket was preserved. Arens remains influential in the Knesset, but he did not receive a cabinet post.* Another "hawk," Chaim Landau, relinquished the Transport portfolio due to illness and was replaced by the more "moderate" Chaim Corfu, also of Herut. Shamir and Sharon have both moderated their tone after promotion to higher position. The expanded settlements on the West Bank are "facts," as the Israelis say, but there was little further expansion in the immediate postelection period. And at middle levels in the party, the balance still seems to favor a relatively "moderate" line.[37] Altogether, if the "hawkish" wing has recently strengthened slightly, this does not appear to presage any major internal shakeup or foreign policy change.

To this survey of informal factionalism in Herut, four caveats must be appended. First, as noted, the "hawkish" and "moderate" labels do not do justice to the strange bedfellows that intraparty politics breeds. Personal followings remain more important than policy nuances. Second, the two camps differ largely on tactical grounds. Such differences have mattered in the past, as in debates about conditions for returning the Sinai, "linkage" between the peace treaty and the Palestinians, or land expropriation on the West Bank. Today, there is some divergence on settlement policy, on military operations, on degrees of Palestinian autonomy, and so on.[38] But even the "hawks" have, with some exceptions, accepted the sacrifice of the Sinai as an accomplished fact. At most, they may demand some "compensation" on the West Bank for the painful evacuation of Israeli settlers from the Sinai, which took place in 1982. Conversely, even the "moderates" insist on Israel's right to "Judea and Samaria," that is, the West Bank. Herut's "hawks" and "moderates" are not very far apart right now.

Third, those labels are only a rough guide to individual positions on specific issues, or to trends within the faction as a whole—where circumstances and lead-

---

*He later became Israel's Ambassador to the United States, however.—ED.

ership, particularly Begin's, play a critical role. That, in turn, suggests the fourth and final caveat: talk of succession, or even predominance, in Herut is moot so long as Begin is alive—and healthy, as he was in 1981.

HERUT: BEGIN'S PERSONAL ROLE

It was not always so. In between a stroke in mid-1979 and a heart attack the next year, the prime minister seemed to lose control over the centrifugal forces in his own faction—not to speak of the coalition as a whole. For example, in the struggle to succeed Dayan as foreign minister between Arens and Aridor, Begin took little active role, eventually settling on the compromise selection of Shamir. Half a year later, when Weizmann too resigned, Begin wanted to move Shamir to Defense. He was faced with objections from Sharon, who also wanted the job. Again Begin temporized, appointing nobody, keeping the Defense portfolio himself, and leaving military matters to the discretion of Chief of Staff Rafael Eitan.[39]

Yet just when Begin's fortunes seemed at their lowest ebb, when diverse coalition partners had defected, and the opposition was already squabbling over the spoils—indeed, partly because of that situation—Begin's political comeback began. His sarcastic personal references were suddenly more effective, and his intraparty skills more apparent, than before. He repaid the loyalty of others with his own but waited patiently for party politics to take their "natural" course before conferring his reward. Hence a temporary eclipse, but eventual triumph, of loyalists Meridor, Shamir, and Aridor. By the same token, Begin let others do the dirty work of cutting party troublemakers down to size. Hence the eclipse or even disgrace, at one time or another, of Weizmann and Sharon.

On substantive questions, too, Begin managed to find a middle ground. He did this by postponing—at Camp David, in the 1981 election platform—formal application of Israeli sovereignty in the West Bank, Gaza, and Golan.* To be sure, Begin looked for every loophole in the Palestinian autonomy plan. But Camp David still meant agreement to return the Sinai, to suspend Israel's "eternal" claims on the West Bank, and to negotiate that territory's future with others in a few years' time. This Begin accepted, yet he retained the loyalty of all but a tiny fringe within Herut.

HERUT: THE UPS AND DOWNS OF ARIEL SHARON

Apart from Begin, the personality and past record of Ariel (Arik) Sharon rate special mention. A military hero, Sharon joined Likud in 1973. He tried at

---

*The Golan was to be annexed in December, 1981.—ED.

first to make it live up to its name as a unified opposition by erasing factional distinctions within its ranks. When that did not work, Sharon moved to the opposite extreme. In 1977 he ran a separate party of his own called Sholomzion (Peace of Zion, also a traditional Jewish name), winning two Knesset seats. He rejoined Herut shortly thereafter, assuming the post of minister of agriculture and settlement.

In that capacity, Sharon led a vigorous campaign to expand Jewish settlement in occupied lands. Often he argued his case in the cabinet against the opposition of Weizmann, Yadin, and others. Occasionally he acted before any discussion was possible, as in his doomed 1978 effort to start new Sinai settlements before it was too late. Still, once Sharon was convinced that peace with Egypt depended upon it, he readily assented to remove not just "dummy" but real settlements from Sinai land.

On the West Bank, though, Sharon personally oversaw the tripling of the Jewish population (to about 20,000, excluding Jerusalem) in four years. He pushed for more government land expropriation and took up the cause of unauthorized squatters from Gush Emunim. The work was sometimes stymied by cabinet opposition, by adverse court decisions, or by lack of funds, but it ground slowly on. On the eve of elections in 1981, Sharon organized promotional tours of his handiwork for fully 10 percent of Israel's voting population.[40]

All of this was in line with government policy, for Sharon was only one of several such militants on the settlement question. What distinguished Sharon from the others was not the substance, but the style. This was brusque almost to the point of violence. Sharon engaged in running feuds with fellow coalition members from several different factions at once. He nearly came to blows with Weizmann. He railed at the "insignificant blabberings" of up-and-coming Liberal leader Pesah Gruper. He threatened to strip Yadin naked on the cabinet table. Even Begin was not immune to Sharon's taunts of "charlatanism" and worse. The prime minister, in turn, questioned Sharon's fidelity to democratic procedures.[41]

Under the circumstances, it was not surprising that opposition from all those quarters denied Sharon the defense portfolio after Weizmann resigned. But, despite the histrionics, political realism reconciled Sharon and Begin in time for the 1981 election. When it was over, Sharon got the Defense appointment after all. In the months since then, he has been a model of discretion. On some policy issues, like West Bank military regulations and reportedly also on Israel's bombing of Beirut, Sharon has advocated a "soft" or at least a flexible line.[42] He has also remained on civil terms with most of his colleagues, at least so far.

Sharon is a colorful and forceful figure. Yet his influence derives not so much from personality, or even from outside contacts with Gush Emunim—and certainly not from the professional military establishment or former colleagues on the general staff, with whom he has often been at odds. Rather, Sharon's strength lies in his very fidelity to the principles of Herut. So long as he stays within the party framework, his influence is likely to be strong.

Indeed, Sharon's influence has already excited the envy of potential rivals, including David Levi. In postelection coalition negotiations, Sharon stole a march by arranging to split the Immigration Ministry from Levi's Housing portfolio, in order to satisfy the desire of a religious splinter faction for a cabinet post. Levi had earlier managed to resist similar moves by other rivals, and even by Begin himself, and was now determined to recoup his prestige. He did, by engineering an appointment as deputy prime minister—leaving Sharon to ponder his next move.[43] If the experience of Weizmann, Dayan, and others is any guide, the chances are that a powerful defense minister—especially one without a major party machine—will be checked by a combination of lesser-known intraparty rivals, acting in concert against a common threat.

HERUT: CONTINUITY OR CHANGE?

Through it all, the solid core of Herut, leaders and followers alike, has remained quite stable. At the same time, the party has gradually accommodated promotions from the ranks. Some veteran activists, like Bader, Shechterman, and Eitan Livni, were passed over for good positions in 1977 or 1981. They remained loyal, however, and some even regained a measure of influence in recent years. Other veterans, like Meridor and Shamir, were actually promoted to cabinet posts in 1980-81. Even of those who did not support Camp David, only a tiny fraction left the party. Weizmann excepted, the party's capable "second generation" ministers—Levi, Aridor, and Sharon—all remain in the cabinet as well. Two representatives of the rising Herut generation have just made it to lesser cabinet slots: Chaim Corfu at Transport, and Mordechai Zipori at Communications. Next in line are several other "junior" leaders: Cabinet Secretary Aryeh Naor; Herut caucus chairman, and now deputy finance minister, Chaim Kaufman; party information chief Gidon Gadot. Finally there are the rising young stars, among them Moshe Katzav, Zevulun Shalish, and Michah Reiser. These men serve, in order, as deputy minister, trade union representative, and Jewish agency executive. In the Knesset, the Herut delegation includes a considerable number of new and young faces, many of Sephardi origin. Among them are several locally-elected small-town officials, like David Magen and Moshe Shitrit, thrust onto the national stage—a political rarity, and one that augurs well for Herut's continued grass-roots appeal.[44]

Despite the often advanced age of their superiors, most of these younger men will probably have to wait a while before rising to the very top, given the long "waiting list" already there and Herut's still centralized structure. But the young guard already has an impact, in the way that it divides allegiance among more senior contenders.

On policy issues, the prospect, in sum, is for low-key debate over tactics, with less of the internal squabbling sparked by "extreme moderates" like Weizmann or "superhawks" like Geula Cohen and Moshe Shamir. On issues of political power, the prospect is for similarly low-key but continuous maneuvering for position. Indeed, it was not in Herut but in the smaller Liberal faction of Likud, that the most serious internal power struggle recently took place.

THE LIBERALS: HOW MUCH POLITICAL POWER?

At stake in the Liberal faction was a challenge by Energy Minister Yitzhak Moda'i, still in his mid-40s, to old-time party chairman "Reb" Simcha Ehrlich. In this challenge, other Young Turks among the Liberals—Trade Minister Patt, political organizer Flumin, Jewish Agency Co-Chairman Dulzin—were sometimes partners, more often rivals of Moda'i. Ideology was a secondary issue, though press leaks about cabinet decisions show that Moda'i was more "hawkish" ("resolute," in his phrase) than the others. For example, he abstained on the draft treaty with Egypt and generally favored West Bank settlement expansion.[45]

At first, Moda'i did well. He unilaterally raised demands for preferential access to Egyptian oil, during final peace negotiations in early 1979, yet escaped any cabinet rebuke. Later that year, as inflation hovered in the triple-digit range, Moda'i quietly encouraged pressures on Ehrlich to resign his Finance Ministry. In a secret factional ballot, only four out of 14 Liberal leaders supported their senior minister. Ehrlich was accordingly "kicked upstairs" to deputy prime minister, a largely symbolic post. Inflation continued, but Moda'i had made his point. Finally, at the Liberal convention in mid-1980, Moda'i maneuvered into a new post as party president, effectively replacing Ehrlich's leadership with his own.[46]

The infighting along the way was fierce. Dulzin, too aloof and also too "dovish" for the new climate in his party, abruptly found himself shorn of political allies. "I once was a businessman myself," he mused at the convention, "but in all my life, I never bought and sold human beings!"[47] Moda'i readily admitted his methods. "You cannot get ahead without intrigue and trickery," the new party president explained. "Such practices disgust me, but circumstances force me to adopt them."[48]

But Ehrlich, a consummate political survivor, had the last laugh. He watched in silence while other coalition partners denied Moda'i, the new Liberal standard-bearer, the prestigious foreign minister's slot in a proposed 1980 cabinet shuffle. Over the next year, with his old friend Begin's tacit support, he cut Moda'i back down to size. In a series of carefully orchestrated internal preelection ballots, Ehrlich took back the mantle of Liberal faction leader. After the 1981 election, behind the scenes, he helped deny Moda'i the Trade, Finance, or even Energy ministries, leaving his rival literally the minister without a portfolio.[49] In all this maneuvering, ideology and even Liberal-Herut rivalry took a back seat to personal vindication. Ehrlich himself retains his deputy prime minister's post.

The Liberal faction as a whole, though, did not fare quite so well, in relation to their senior partner in Likud. Before the election, Herut's young guard had charged that the Liberals were overrepresented in the cabinet and Knesset, compared to the number of votes they probably attracted to the ticket. Some also feared that if the Liberals maintained their separate identity, they might bolt from Likud if it lost the election to Labor. Under pressure, the Liberals half-heartedly accepted "unification" of Likud (in Hebrew, Likud Ha-Likud), waiving the right to guaranteed factional posts in government—but only in principle.[50] In practice, the old "formula" for slots on the ticket and ministries in the government remained in effect. Thus, in the Knesset, the Liberals stayed in about the same 2:3 "junior partner" relation to Herut as before. The system of alternating places on the list meant that both factions automatically gained an almost equal number of new seats. In the (expanded) 1981 cabinet, the Liberals have one less ministry than Herut, just as before.

But as always in politics, the numbers do not tell the whole story. Since 1977, Herut has taken over the critical ministries of Foreign Affairs and Finance—the latter at the Liberals' direct expense. A Herut minister has displaced a Liberal at the less important Energy Ministry as well. Ehrlich now shares the deputy prime minister's post, not with the DMC's Yadin, but with yet another minister from Herut. Then there are the deputy ministries—an even dozen, up from only one on election eve. Here too, Herutniks got more and better positions, in terms of patronage and policy control, than did their Liberal allies. Altogether, the Liberals are more in the shadow of Herut than ever, though the suspicion lingers that they are overrepresented even now.

THE LIBERALS: POLICY POSITIONS IN RELATION TO HERUT

On the ideological level, the distinctions between the two factions have faded, in foreign policy and in economic affairs. Through 1980, Liberal ministers were usually still numbered among the "moderates" on security issues—though Moda'i was an important exception even then. Liberal support, for example, helped Begin ignore the trap Geula Cohen set for him on the Golan Heights.[51] But in the latest internal Liberal elections, confirmed "hawks"—led by Moda'i, and including Pesah Gruper, David Shiffman, Pinhas Goldstein, and Dan Tichon— captured one-third of the "safe" spots in their factions list of candidates for the Knesset.[52] Aryeh Dulzin, long a leading "moderate" voice, was out of the running.

There remains a range of Liberal opinion on foreign policy, perhaps best exemplified by Dror Zeigerman—the youngest, and by pure coincidence also the most "moderate," of all the Knesset deputies from Likud. Ironically, but not atypically, Zeigerman got in by aligning himself with Moda'i's "hawkish" grouping.[53] For that group is now the most cohesive one within the faction, and so the line between "moderate" Liberals and "hawkish" Herutniks no longer holds very well. The most that can be said today is that Liberals tend to cluster nearer the "moderate" pole of Likud's spectrum on foreign affairs.

As for the economy, neither faction has a clear-cut program any more. The Liberals, in sum, have gradually shifted to a less distinctive and less powerful position within the councils of Likud. The last four years have witnessed an acceleration of this long-term trend. As a result, the Liberals cannot be expected to exert a major influence, restraining or otherwise, on the Begin government's policy today. There is still one area, however, where the Liberals do represent at least a significantly different shade of opinion on the Likud spectrum, and where their influence may continue to be felt.

On legislative issues involving *halachah,* or traditional Jewish religious law, the Liberals are cooler to orthodox demands. Their reservations were rarely decisive, but they were taken into account, as this issue more than any other distinguished the Liberal faction from Herut. For example, Liberal opposition in committee helped keep some clerical bills from ever reaching the Knesset floor. One such instance concerned a draft amendment defining conversion to Judaism in strictly *halachic* terms; another was a bill to tighten restrictions on the sale of pork. In other cases, the Liberals won a few concessions on bills that eventually passed the Knesset by a very narrow margin. For example, in a law limiting autopsies—generally forbidden by *halachah*—an exception was made for medical necessity during epidemics. A family member's permission could only be challenged by a relative equally close to the deceased.[54]

In many other cases, though, only a few Liberals broke coalition discipline to oppose bills championed by Begin's fundamentalist allies, Agudat Israel. In this category, for instance, was an emotional controversy over limiting abortions in accord with Jewish law. One Liberal member, Shara Doron, spoke out passionately against such a bill on the Knesset floor. Most of her colleagues, however, swallowed their misgivings and voted with the government's majority in favor of the bill. Another such case involved a regulation easing military service exemptions for women on religious grounds.[55]

Just after the 1981 election, another simmering religious dispute boiled to the surface. At stake were archaeological excavations in Jerusalem, on a site the Chief Rabbis claimed was once a Jewish cemetery, and hence not to be profaned. Typically, some Liberal spokesmen—this time with the veteran Ehrlich in the lead—opposed automatic application of a narrowly-construed *halachic* ruling.[56] As of this writing, the outcome of this issue remains unclear, although some makeshift compromise involving concessions to Orthodox requirements will probably be found.

Altogether, the Liberals helped slow the pace of clerical legislation, often with help from the DMC, rather in the way that the DMC helped delay Jewish settlement on the West Bank. The DMC's strength rapidly eroded, while Herut had a more "positive" attitude toward the place in public policy of Jewish religious tradition. Thus, it was mainly the Liberals who moderated the clerical trend of the Begin era and prevented too sharp a break with the previous uneasy status quo. It was in this manner, especially in recent years, that the influence of Herut's "junior" Liberal partner was chiefly felt. We turn now to an even smaller and less distinctive Likud faction, La'am.

LA'AM

The La'am ("For the Nation," in Hebrew) faction had only eight members out of 45 Likudniks in the 1977 Knesset, and it has only four out of 48 today. Small as it is, La'am in 1977 was a composite of even smaller groups: two remnants of mid-1960s splinter parties, Rafi from Labor and the Free Center from Herut, plus Moshe Shamir, of the Greater Israel movement. In foreign policy, there was little to distinguish La'am from Herut; both were somewhat more "hawkish" than the Liberals.

On Camp David, both La'am and Herut deputies divided, with only about half voting for the concessions Begin had offered Sadat. Of the two La'am cabinet ministers, one—Yigal Hurvitz—quit his post in protest. A month later, La'am's remaining minister, Eliezer Shostack, was one of only two in the entire cabinet who abstained on a draft peace treaty. Votes on West Bank settlement issues in 1979 and 1980 followed the same pattern.[57] This half of La'am, in other words, is fully as "hawkish" as any in Herut.

Moshe Shamir was even more "hawkish"; he actually left Likud altogether to found the right-wing opposition party of Tehiya. Three other members of La'am—Hurvitz, Yitzhak Peretz, and Zalman Shoval—reverted to the status of a semi-separate Rafi faction but did not defect. The remaining four—Shostack, and Knesset deputies Amnon Lin, Ehud Olmert, and Yigal Cohen—kept their positions in La'am.

Even within these two minifactions, there was a range of nationalist militance. Lin and Shoval, in particular, were considered the "moderates" of their respective groupings.[58] But it was on economic and not foreign policy issues that La'am's leaders had the most to say.

Barely ten months after resigning his Trade Ministry portfolio in protest against Camp David, Yigal Hurvitz was back, this time to take over the crucial Finance Ministry from Ehrlich's faltering hands. In an attempt to stem the rocketing inflation that had hastened his predecessor's downfall, Hurvitz demanded across-the-board budget cuts. He was immediately met by a volley of opposition, as each minister fought to protect his own turf. Housing Minister Levi, posing as champion of the underprivileged, angrily reminded his new colleague at Finance that "subsidy is not a dirty word." Ehrlich wryly suggested that Hurvitz, a wealthy entrepreneur, should really head a faction with the Hebrew initials Rami, for Roster of Israeli Millionaires—instead of Rafi, for Roster of Israeli

Workers. Moda'i, not to be outdone, withdrew from one of his portfolios in protest against the proposed cuts. Sharon wanted more money for settlements;
Hurvitz told him there was none. Weizmann resisted defense budget cutbacks,
and finally took the occasion to quit the cabinet in a huff. Hurvitz, too, began
threatening to resign again only months after rejoining the cabinet, if his austerity program fell through.[59]

In November 1980, a no-confidence motion on grounds of economic failure
brought Begin within three votes of losing power, his narrowest margin yet. Still,
an internal government showdown was postponed, by improvisation and
compromise, until January 1981. Then it was the turn of Education Minister
Zevulun Hammer, of the National Religious Party, who insisted on a teachers'
pay hike—and threatened to resign if one were not approved. It was. Instead it
was Hurvitz who resigned. He took with him Rafi's two other members, depriving the government of its bare majority in the Knesset, and leading to new elections in the summer of 1981.[60]

In the meantime, Hurvitz was replaced by Yoram Aridor, a young Herut
intellectual, who promptly instituted an Israeli version of supply-side economics
by slashing taxes and import duties. The economic benefits, if any, are still unclear. But the national spending spree that following was of major benefit for
Likud's election prospects, which urgently needed a boost.[61]

Throughout these proceedings, policy and politics intertwined. Economic
difficulties, bureaucratic protectionism, conflicting priorities, and factional rivalry all brought Hurvitz down. He did not have to worry, as Ehrlich did in his
place, about backbiting inside his own faction. He did, however, face the same
problems of near-complete absence of popular support, plus Herut resentment of
his faction's exaggerated importance. In the end, though, Hurvitz's resignation
was precipitated by his own assessment—supported by all the polls in early
1981—that Likud would likely lose the next election and that Rafi would therefore do better to ride someone else's coattails to power.

Needless to say, Hurvitz was wrong. The coattails he picked to ride were
those of his cousin Dayan, who had broken with Begin earlier. But Dayan's new
Telem party won only two seats in 1981, while Hurvitz and fellow Rafi member
Shoval were in places three and four on the list.

The other ex-Rafi Knesset deputy, Yitzhak Peretz, was more fortunate; he
had already rejoined Likud. For by election time, Begin's personal appeal and
militant foreign policy, along with (crowning irony) Aridor's new economic program, had completely turned the polls around.[62]

Today, as a result of all these maneuvers, a truncated La'am is still part of
Likud in power. But the faction is only half the size it reached in 1977, and it is
no more cohesive or distinct in ideological terms. La'am has only four Knesset
members, the same ones who stayed with it through election eve. One, Shostack,
is still minister of health. The faction's power in economic matters has all but
dissipated, and, as a group, it toes Begin's line on foreign affairs. Its four depu-

ties cling to their collective identity only because their ability to grant or with-hold support en masse (if that is the right phrase for so small a group) assures them all "safe" spots on Likud's election ticket, and perhaps a chance for a cabinet post as well. Even more so than for the Liberals, theirs is truly a "distinction without a difference" inside Likud.

CONCLUSION: FACTIONAL INTERACTION AND ITS IMPLICATIONS FOR LIKUD TODAY

Having examined each of the relevant factions in turn, we can now briefly review their interaction during Begin's first term and speculate a bit about their likely evolution after 1981. Factional interaction involved balancing both politics and policy, with the emphasis increasingly on the former. Inside Likud, the Liberals were only slightly more "moderate" on foreign policy than Herut or La'am. Instead, the Liberals focused on internal issues: the economy and, later, religious affairs. On foreign policy issues, DMC "moderates," aided for a while by Weizmann and Dayan, sparred with Herut "hawks." Through 1978, these factional postures made a difference. Weizmann and Dayan, and even the DMC, played a part in the year-long negotiations that produced Camp David—so much so that a Likud splinter group broke off to protest Begin's concessions.

After 1978, however, factional policy posturing became largely futile, with the few exceptions analyzed above. Neither the Liberals nor the Democrats—not to speak of those who moved into opposition—maintained much distinctive influence, on either foreign or domestic policy. The defectors left because their influence was over, and they gained nothing by being in opposition. The loyal elements were precisely those who tended to downgrade ideological divisions in favor of maintaining their common hold on power.

As a result, in the latter half of Begin's first term, personal or partisan rather than policy issues dominated interfactional relations. The key for Begin was to find an acceptable distribution of positions, within and among the coalition's components. Thus, it was for reasons of political balance, as much as policy failure, that each major faction of Likud had a chance at running the Finance Ministry during those years. An Israeli editorial summed up the cabinet shuffle of late 1979:

> Since it is impossible to transfer [Finance Minister] Ehrlich to the Interior Ministry, already occupied by Dr. Burg, Ehrlich must be "promoted" to Deputy Prime Minister—even though that slot, too, is already occupied by Professor Yadin. The law must therefore be amended to allow two deputy prime ministers... And since the Liberals are about to lose the Finance Ministry to Yigal Hurvitz of La'am, they must be pacified by appointing their Minister Without Portfolio, Moshe Nissim, to [a new position].[63]

Later, when the Finance Ministry finally landed with Herut's Aridor, the Liberals were compensated with better representation on a "Ministerial Economic Committee." In the Knesset, similarly, Likud's caucus chairman was a Liberal, while the overall coalition chairman was from Herut.[64]

In short, each faction's prerogatives had to be preserved. This was complicated by infrafactional infighting, even among those elements who stayed with the coalition to the end. The most egregious examples were Moda'i's "subversive" campaign against fellow-Liberal Ehrlich and rivalry within Herut over the vacated foreign and defense ministers' posts. The balancing act resumed as soon as the 1981 election was done.

As director of factional bargaining, Begin was little different from previous prime ministers and more successful than some. His government's policy, and especially its image, were compromised by internal squabbling. But, from the limited perspective of keeping a minimal coalition together, Begin accomplished his goal. Almost from the day that coalition had come together, analysts began predicting that it would quickly come apart. Instead, Begin held on for a full four years, nearly the maximum allowed by law.

During that time, Begin rode a roller coaster of ups and downs in national popularity and in control over his own coalition. The vicissitudes reflected internal and external circumstances, interacting with the prime minister's personal health. In 1977, an initial burst of national enthusiasm gave way to despondency later in the year. It was lifted by the DMC's accession to the government and then by the visit by Sadat. Subsequent stalemate bred "dovish" defections. Camp David and peace with Egypt restored public confidence but at a small cost in "hawkish" defections from Begin's Knesset strength. Then, from late 1979 through early 1981, there followed another stalemate on the Palestinian issue, economic crisis, and two bouts of serious illness for Begin himself. All this led to more defections, factional disarray, and a steep decline in the polls. Finally, in mid-1981, economic pump priming, military action, and domestic political battle reinvigorated Begin enough to close Likud ranks behind a victorious campaign.

Through it all, defectors were accompanied by much media fanfare and opposition wishful thinking about the coalition's imminent demise. In fact, the secret of its longevity was deceptively simple and twofold: first, even after divergent or disaffected elements had gone, there remained a large Likud core who supported Begin's policy—and depended upon him for political power. Second, within that core, Begin was able to balance conflicting group and individual claims.

Today, without the DMC, Begin's coalition is considerably smaller but also more cohesive than it was four years ago. The foreign policy "extremes"—Weizmann, Dayan, and the DMC on the one hand, Tehiya on the other—have gone. Inside Likud, the factions retain their separate identities, but their policies have imperceptibly merged. The Liberals, slowly but surely, have moved toward Herut's position, especially in foreign affairs. Their power is diminished, even if their ratio of Knesset and cabinet members is roughly as before. La'am's Knesset strength has been halved and, thus, its power even more greatly diminished in relation to Herut. The latter's predominance, ideological and political, is therefore assured.

Within Herut itself, "hawks" and "moderates" have tended to coalesce—despite continuing tactical divisions and muted competition for personal power—around a "moderately hawkish" position. Moreover, the coalition is so much smaller, and the cabinet so much larger, that fully half of Begin's Knesset backers are also ministers or deputy ministers today—giving them an added stake in the government's survival. The net effect of all this is a new Likud-led coalition that is very narrow, yet probably stable. The government is now relatively united on foreign policy and no more than usually divided on internal issues of religion and political power.

What of the future? Begin's own unexpected victory in 1977, the surprising comeback in 1981, make prediction hazardous. Much will depend upon internal Israeli opinion, and even more on external circumstances—and both are notoriously volatile. The picture is also incomplete without the religious parties. They have been quite loyal to Begin so far, but it is still barely possible that they might provoke a government split. Then, too, one must recall that Labor now has about the same numerical strength in the Knesset as Likud.*

Still, the preceding analysis suggests that, beneath all the political turmoil of the past four years, Likud has experienced much more continuity than change. This is so, of course, in the sense that Menachem Begin is again prime minister of Israel today. But continuity is also evident in the other personalities, policies, and political structures—inside Likud, and in Israel generally—that made Begin's personal vindication possible. In all those areas, then, the most likely prospect in Israel is more of the same. Whether this sameness signals stability or merely stagnation will depend upon how successfully Likud can "muddle through" the challenges of the next few years—as they have in the past four. Given the size of those challenges, that is not an uninspiring goal.

NOTES

1. See, for example, Rael Jean Isaac, *Israel Divided: Ideological Politics in the Jewish State* (Baltimore: The Johns Hopkins University Press, 1976) and *Party and Politics in Israel: Three Visions of a Jewish State* (New York: Longman, 1981); Howard R. Penniman, ed., *Israel at the Polls: The Knesset Elections*

---

*The entrance of former Laborite Shulamit Aloni and her Citizens Rights Party into the Labor Alignment gave Labor the same number of Knesset seats as Likud.—ED.

of 1977 (Washington: American Enterprise Institute, 1979), especially chapters on "The Likud," by Benjamin Azkin, and on "A Movement for Change in a Stable System," by Efraim Torgovnik.

2. See Torgovnik and Asher Arian, "The Electorate: Israel 1977," in Penniman, ed., *Israel at the Polls.*

3. This episode was related by several Israeli informants: interviews with Yosi Priel, correspondent for *Davar;* Harry Hurvitz, Information Director, Israel Embassy; and another Israeli journalist who preferred to remain anonymous; all in Washington, D.C., September 1981. Mr. Priel was especially informative, for which I am grateful.

4. *Jerusalem Post,* International (Weekly) Edition, November 4–10, 1979; December 14–20, 1980.

5. *Ha'aretz,* September 14, 1979; November 2, 1979.

6. *Washington Star,* June 24, August 4, 1980; *Washington Post,* August 1, 1980.

7. *Jerusalem Post,* June 8–14, 1980; February 1–7, 1981.

8. *Jerusalem Post,* February 22–28, 1981.

9. *Ha'aretz,* September 21, 1979; *Jerusalem Post,* March 30–April 5, 1980; January 25–31, 1981.

10. Interview with Harry Hurvitz, Israel Information Director, Washington, D.C., September 1981.

11. *Washington Star,* August 27, September 6, 1980; *Jerusalem Post,* March 23–29, 1980; May 11–17, 1980.

12. *Jerusalem Post,* June 1–7, 8–14, 1980.

13. Interviews with Israeli correspondents, Washington, D.C., September, 1981.

14. Efraim Torgovnik, "Accepting Camp David: The Role of Party Faction in Israeli Policy Making," *Middle East Review* (Winter 1978/79): 18–25.

15. *New York Times,* August 24, 1980; *Washington Post,* July 2, 28, 31, 1980; *Jerusalem Post,* July 6–12, 1980; *Washington Star,* July 24, October 22, 1980; *Jewish Week* (Washington, D.C.) August 28–September 3, 1980. See page 184 for a discussion of the international effects of this action.

16. *Jerusalem Post,* November 23–29, 1980. The Golan Heights were to be annexed on Begin's initiative in December 1981, an action that also angered the United States.

17. *Jerusalem Post,* January 18–24, 1980.

18. *Jerusalem Post,* May 11–17, 1980.

19. *Washington Post,* November 20, 1980.

20. *Ha'aretz,* October 12, 1979; *Jerusalem Post,* October 14–20, 1979.

21. Dan Margalit, "Let's Begin All Over Again?" (in Hebrew), *Ha'aretz* Magazine, October 19, 1979. Interviews with Israeli correspondents confirmed this report.

22. Isaac, *Party and Politics in Israel,* pp. 13, 211.

23. Interviews with Harry Hurvitz and other Israeli informants, Washington, D.C., September 1981. The NRP lost six seats, or half its Knesset strength. Some apparently went to a breakaway Sepharadi faction called TAMI, others most likely to Tehiya, and still others to some other choice, including Likud itself.

24. Ezer Weizmann, *The Battle for Peace* (New York: Bantam Books, 1981), pp. 117, 191, 312. Cf. *Ha'aretz*, September 14, 1979; *Washington Post*, September 24, 1979.

25. *Washington Star*, October 22, 1979; *Jerusalem Post*, June 21–27, 1981 (interview with Dayan); *Time* Magazine, October 28, 1979. See also Moshe Dayan, *Breakthrough: A Personal Account of the Egypt-Israel Peace Negotiations* (New York: Alfred A. Knopf, 1981).

26. *Jerusalem Post*, October 26–November 1, 1980; March 29–April 4, 1981; April 19–26, 1981.

27. **Weizmann**, *Battle for Peace*, p. 227; cf. *Ha'aretz*, November 2, 9, 1979.

28. *Jerusalem Post*, March 16–22, March 30–April 5, 1980.

29. *Jerusalem Post*, January 13–19, 1980.

30. *Washington Star*, November 24, 1980; *Jerusalem Post*, June 1–7, November 2–8, 1980.

31. *Jerusalem Post*, November 30–December 6, 1980; May 25–31, 1980; March 29–April 4, 1981.

32. *Ha'aretz*, October 12, 1979.

33. *Jerusalem Post*, December 30, 1979–January 5, 1980; September 7–13, 1980; January 25–31, 1981; August 31–September 6, 1981; Dan Margalit, "From Underground to Elite," (in Hebrew), *Ha'aretz* Magazine, September 11, 1979.

34. Interviews with Israeli informants, Washington, D.C., September, 1981; *Jerusalem Post*, July 13–19, 1980; May 24–30, 1981.

35. Margalit, "From Underground to Elite," *Ha'aretz*, October 12, 1979; *Jerusalem Post*, January 13–19, 1980.

36. *Jerusalem Post*, May 24–30, 1981.

37. Interviews with Israeli informants, Washington, D.C., September, 1981. Cf. *Jerusalem Post*, May 24–30, 1981.

38. Interviews with a high-level Israeli intelligence officer and with a senior civil servant in the prime minister's office, Tel Aviv and Jerusalem, July 1979, and with Israeli informants in Washington, D.C., September 1981. Cf. also Weizmann, *Battle for Peace*, especially pp. 111, 386; see also Mattityahu Peled, "The Year of Sadat's Initiative," in *Great Power Intervention in the Middle East*, ed., G. Sheffer and M. Leitenberg, pp. 301–12.

39. *Time* Magazine, July 14, 1980; Weizmann, *Battle for Peace*, pp. 309, 332–33; *Ha'aretz*, October 19, 1979; *Jerusalem Post*, December 30, 1979–January 5, 1980; March 16–22, 1980; September 7–13, 1980.

40. *Jerusalem Post*, October 14–20, 1979.

41. *Washington Post*, August 5, 1981; *Jerusalem Post*, January 27–February 2, 1980; March 10–16, 23–29, 1980; July 13–19, 1980.

42. *Jerusalem Post*, June 21–27, 1981; August 31–September 6, 1981.

43. *Washington Post*, September 24, 1970; *Jerusalem Post*, March 2–8, 1980; May 24–30, 1981; August 16–22, 1981.

44. Interview with Yosi Priel, Washington, D.C., September 1981. Cf. *Ha'aretz*, October 12, 1979; *Jerusalem Post*, February 10–16, 1980; May 3–9, 24–30, 1981; August 16–22, 1981; *Jewish Week*, August 13–19, 1981; *Washington Post*, July 9, 1981.

45. *Jerusalem Post*, May 11–17, 1980.

46. *Ha'aretz*, September 14, October 19, 1979; *Jerusalem Post*, September 30–October 6, October 14–20, 1979.

47. *Jerusalem Post*, May 11–17, 1980.

48. *Jerusalem Post*, June 15–21, 1980.

49. *Jerusalem Post*, June 1–7, 1980; January 18–24, June 21–27, 1981.

50. *Jerusalem Post*, September 30–October 6, 1979; November 2–8, 1980; January 25–31, 1981.

51. *Jerusalem Post*, May 11–17, 1980; November 2–8, 23–29, 1980.

52. *Jerusalem Post*, May 24–30, 1980.

53. Interview with Harry Hurvitz, Washington, D.C., September 1981.

54. *Washington Post*, December 2, 1980; *Jerusalem Post*, November 4–10, 1979; December 30, 1979–January 5, 1980; November 30–December 6, 1980; March 29–April 4, 1981.

55. *Washington Post*, December 18, 1979; *Jerusalem Post*, January 18–24, 1981.

56. Interviews with Israeli informants, Washington, D.C., September 1981; cf. *Washington Post*, August 22, 1981.

57. See, for example, *Washington Post*, October 26, 1978; *Jerusalem Post*, November 2–8, 1980.

58. *Jerusalem Post*, March 30–April 5, 1980.

59. *Washington Post*, June 23, 1980; November 19, 20, 1980; cf. also weekly issues of *Jerusalem Post* for December 1979–March 1980, June 1980, and October 1980–January 1981.

60. *Washington Star*, January 12, 1981; *Jerusalem Post*, January 18–24, 1981.

61. On Hurvitz's calculations, see *Jerusalem Post*, November 2–8, 1980; March 22–28, April 19–26, 1981. On Aridor's economic program, see *Washington Star*, February 2, 1981; *Washington Post*, June 3, 1981; *Jerusalem Post*, May 3–9, 1981.

62. For the fall and rise of Begin in the polls, see *Ha'aretz*, November 2, 1979; *Time* Magazine, July 14, 1980; *Jerusalem Post*, February 10–16, July 6–12, 1980; *Washington Star*, January 4, 25, June 8, 1981; *Washington Post*, July 1, 1981.

63. *Ha'aretz*, November 2, 1979. Cf. similarly *Jerusalem Post*, June 1–7, 1980.

64. For the text of the coalition agreement, see *Jerusalem Post*, August 6, 1981.

3 Changing Domestic Policy 1977-81

Ira Sharkansky and Alex Radian

Menachem Begin's election as prime minister of Israel in May 1977 is interesting not only in its own right, but for the light it sheds on some important questions of political theory. Some of the features that make the election inherently interesting also make it especially interesting to the political scientist. It was the first time ever in the history of Israel that a non-Labor party would dominate the government. It was a victory not only for a party but for an individual. Menachem Begin had campaigned, and lost, at virtually each major point of decision in the history of Israel—both at times of election and at critical points between elections. Now there was an opportunity to see him and his followers in power. Not only could they be tested on the range of issues about which they had spoken repeatedly but also on additional issues where they had no clear public record. Much more than other elections in democratic countries, the Israeli election of 1977 permits an examination of questions basic to the history of political thought: What is the significance of election? What difference does it make for the actions of government when an opposition party comes to power?[1]

The reelection of Prime Minister Begin in June 1981 suggests that 1977 was a turning point in Israeli politics, and not just an isolated event. There may be a new dominant party on the scene or a period of alteration between the parties that dominate coalition governments.

For the purpose of this analysis, the reelection of 1981 provides an opportunity to see a more mature and confident government in action. The Begin coalition of 1981 was better prepared than that of 1977 in concrete plans and available candidates for key administrative posts. This chapter looks both at the first Begin government and the first months of the second Begin government. It deals with the impact of a new government on domestic policy and the advantages enjoyed by the new government when it wins a second term from the voters.

FACTORS THAT DISCOURAGE CHANGE

Sophisticated observers of politics should expect only limited change in the early years of a new government. Governments generally, and democracies in particular, are like supertankers. They can change direction only slowly. Among the features responsible for their inertia are complex structures. Few governments are truly ruled by one person. Even where ministers are members of a single party, there are likely to be disputes about how policy changes will be scheduled and put into effect. Most civil servants carry over in their positions from one government to another, even some in senior positions with roles in the design and implementation of policy. The heads of local authorities may be responsible to their own electorates and resist sweeping changes in policy ordered from the capital city.

Established programs have lives of their own. Clients and staff members tend to oppose too many changes that come too quickly. New decisions usually deal in increments to be added or subtracted from what exists. If major change does occur, it may be apparent only years after the fact, as a result of repeated steps in a certain direction. The first step may be small and deliberately disguised to minimize opposition.

Even if new policies are pursured, the competition that prevails in democratic societies helps to obscure the reality of change. Parties compete on post hoc analyses as well as on campaign promises. Opponents seek to minimize the success of government programs. Complex conditions also frustrate simple assessment. How much of an upturn in an economic indicator is due to the policy of a new government? Or to the groundwork laid by its predecessor? Or to extraneous events in the national or world economies? Seldom are there clear answers to such questions, especially when opposing parties compete with their own experts, data, and interpretations.

ISRAELI FACTORS THAT INHIBIT POLICY CHANGE

Israel exhibits each of these general factors that inhibit policy change after an election, as well as some distinctly its own. The multiple centers of political power in Israel complicate any simple definition of the Israeli state, much less a clear charting of *Who can do what?* after a change in the Knesset. The municipalities, the Histadrut, the Jewish Agency and other international Jewish institutions, all have their say in domestic policy making. The civil service is entrenched and well organized, with a strident sense of its rights and prerogatives. The numerous categories of government workers and the vocal independence of local workers' committees create a special maze for policy makers concerned to elicit the cooperation of the civil service with their programs.

A government led by Prime Minister Begin's Likud movement faced a special problem with respect to the civil service. Senior posts in the ministries had been filled during 30 years of Labor-dominated governments. During the first months after the 1977 elections, only one director general (foreign affairs) resigned on the grounds that he could not work under the new minister. Other senior administrators remained in office, including the director general of the treasury, who was active in the Labor party. Senior officials declared that they were neutral professionals, who would have no difficulty serving a new master. The new ministers generally deferred. Directors general in only six out of 16 ministries changed in the first year of the new government. Rather than insist on bringing in their own professionals, several ministers chose to emphasize the neutrality of the civil service. Even if the new ministers wanted to staff senior posts with their own people, they would have been hard pressed to quickly find suitable candidates. Having been always in opposition and gaining power with little forewarning, Likud had few people prepared for key positions. The bulk of the civil service remains tenured and, in the eyes of Likud supporters, a source of Labor party influence on policy implementation that will take years to overcome.

The ideological cast of Israeli politics, the numerous parties, and the inevitability of coalition government put other barriers in the way of dramatic policy change. One feature of ideological politics prepares an observer to see sharp change in policy. Each party and faction has a stake in the application of its own distinctive program. But another feature of the same condition works to create stability in established policies. The status quo benefits when ideologues dig in their heels against their rivals' programs. Coalition government gives to several parties a role in policy formulation and gives *compromise in support of the status quo* an edge over acceptance of a rival's program. Coalitions water down the reality of the new government's program, even if they do not temper the verbiage of a party newly in power.

The lack of priority given to domestic programs is another Israeli factor that works to inhibit change. This is a condition evident in the careers of many prime ministers, and especially Menachem Begin. Quite in contrast with the publics in other democracies, Israelis concern themselves more often with foreign than with domestic policy. The explanation is obvious, given the beleaguered nature of the country. The result is low priority for issues of domestic reform. National leaders focus on relations with the great powers or with Arab neighbors, or on matters of military resources and strategic planning. There is little time or energy for the detailed problems of education, health programming, road building, or environmental protection. These fields attract the attention of people who are not at the center of the political stage. Policy making in these areas is less glamorous, more painstaking, and often a scene of small movement.

The early marriage between Zionism and socialism made economic policy a main topic of party ideology in Israel. Yet there is much about the Israeli condition that makes economic policy dependent on what happens elsewhere. The prices of imports and exports reflects more what occurs outside the country than what occurs inside. Wage settlements in the United States, Europe, or Japan, together with international prices for energy, weigh heavily on the cost of imports. Israel's agricultural exports depend partly on its own weather and partly on conditions in countries that compete with its fruits and vegetables. The fortunes of the tourist industry vary with prosperity in Europe and North America. Israel's arms exports depend on the international position of those countries willing to buy war material from Israel and—in the case of products equipped with U.S. components—the willingness of the United States government to permit sales. A sizeable amount of Israel's capital comes from outsiders in the form of voluntary contributions. These depend partly on the mood and prosperity in Jewish communities throughout the diaspora, as well as on the policies of their own national governments toward the export of capital to Israel.

Israel's economy is heavily managed, but not solely by the government. The Histadrut is the largest employer in the public sector. Its various companies and cooperatives account for some 23 percent of all workers. Government departments employ 7 percent, and government companies employ another 5 percent of the work force. Even when the Labor Alignment controlled both the Histadrut and the government there was conflict and something of a standoff between the two powers in matters of wages, prices, taxes, subsidies, and cost of living. Now with Likud dominant in the government and Labor in the Histadrut, there is the added stimulus of party competition to keep the two powers at odds on economic policy.

SINCE THE 1977 ELECTION

Likud came to power in 1977 as the first non-Labor government in the history of Israel. Yet the underlying conditions that have discouraged change in domestic programs did not merely continue. During the 1977-81 period they increased in intensity.

Politicians and the public of Israel were not simply preoccupied with issues of foreign and security policy. They were obsessed with these issues. The ups and downs of Israeli-Egyptian contacts and the maneuverings of domestic groups with a stake in the negotiations—ranging from Peace Now to Gush Emunim—all but monopolized the front pages of the daily press, the top of the government's agenda, and the public's attention.

The Begin government, like all its predecessors, did not escape the need to coalesce with partners who were uneasy with each other. Six parties joined the Begin coalition during complex negotiations that extended several months beyond the 1977 election. They brought explicit strains between the overtly secular Democratic Movement for Change (DMC) and the stridently religious

Agudat Israel. Several coalition partners were affected by internal changes during the first Begin government. Pressures of international negotiations led the DMC first to split into two movements. One segment of the original DMC left the government early in Begin's first term. The other segment of the DMC disappeared at the beginning of the 1981 election campaign. Its leader—Yigal Yadin—announced that he was leaving politics. Squabbles over issues of policy and leadership afflicted Herut and Liberal members of the Likud. Several members of Herut voted against the government on key issues. Begin's first minister of finance—the leader of the Liberal party—fired his deputy and party colleague when the deputy openly challenged the minister's authority within the party. A senior member of the La'am faction of Likud resigned from his post as minister of industry and tourism as a protest against the Camp David agreements, only to return later as Begin's second minister of finance. This minister himself resigned from the ministry of finance late in Begin's first term and joined an opposition party for the 1981 election campaign. Ministers of foreign affairs and defense resigned in moves that received international attention. More than once the prime minister admitted publicly that the cabinet was not functioning smoothly and promised time and effort to put it in shape. Resignations forced frequent reshuffling of ministerial posts with some appointments held back by lengthy negotiations to maintain the relative weight of each coalition partner.

Those who predicted wrangling between the government and the Histadrut were not disappointed. Many municipalities continued to assert their independence. Despite a party link between Tel Aviv's mayor and the prime minister, that city embarassed the government with theater performances on the Sabbath. The Jerusalem municipality, led by Labor party member Teddy Kollek, tweaked the government by general moans of poverty, explicit charges that the government was behind in fulfilling its financial commitments, and—in a repeat of a tactic that had proved successful in an earlier budget tussle—it turned off the lights on its most impressive tourist attractions.

The situation of the second Begin government was both more problematical and more promising than the first. The government was more finely balanced after 1981, with a narrow margin of two votes over the combined opposition. A vote of confidence that came in early December 1981 required the hasty recall of ministers from missions to the United States and Latin America and the transfer of the prime minister from a hospital bed to the Knesset.

On the other hand, the government began the 1981 term with more experience and a narrower range of coalition partners making policy demands. Gone was the Democratic Movement for Change, whose own newly established wide ranging group of academics and other professionals offered ambitious but amorphous demands for change. In its place as prominent stimulus for the government was Agudat Israel, a religious party of long experience in the politics of Israel and international Jewry. Its demands may be no less radical than those of the Democratic Movement for Change, but those of the Agudah were more sharply defined and offered by a party more disciplined and skilled in the politics of policy making. The government was also more in control of senior administrative appointments. Virtually all directors-general had been replaced since 1977. A prominent exception was the director-general of the interior. He was closely identified with the National Religious Party, which has been a partner of every Israeli coalition from the very first. He also had the confidence of the prime minister and assumed important policy making tasks for the Begin movement. If the test of government is the extent of domestic policy changes—leaving aside judgments about the *quality* of those changes—the prospect at the end of 1981 was for a second Begin government more successful than the first.

POLICY INITIATIVES

Government continues, it does not start. Change is normally gradual and evolutionary. Only rarely are new ideas quickly implemented with a sharp break from past practices. The question "What policies did the Begin government initiate?" seems simple. It may be difficult, however, to distinguish between a policy change continuing from the past and an initiative that is entirely new. Some events are described as significant by partisans of the government, while its opponents will trace their lineage to action taken by former governments.

Some things changed early in the first Begin term. Statements more stridently nationalistic than in the past emanated from the prime minister, other ministers, and the ambassador to the United Nations. The minister of education—for the first time a member of the National Religious Party—made public statements and some internal appointments that increased the concern of Israelis fearful of too great an emphasis on religious doctrine. The government announced that it would reduce its involvement in economic management. Should these events be taken as the sign of changes in policy? The answer depends largely on one's sensitivity to symbols, on the one hand, or on one's insistence that policy changes be marked with tangible changes in the distribution of services or resources, on the other. Israel has long been a noisy society, with some political leaders in every generation stirring up emotions with sharp statements about matters of security, concessions in relations with Israel's neighbors, or the role of religion in state policy.

NEW ECONOMIC POLICY

A significant change in economic policy seemed to occur with the abolition of foreign currency control in November 1977. Officially, the value of the Israeli pound would be determined by the forces of supply and demand. Israeli citizens were allowed to hold unlimited amounts of foreign currency in accounts. Some restrictions on purchasing and withdrawing cash from the accounts were established and later (in February 1980) tightened. This seemed to be a policy tailormade by a Liberal party finance minister, yet a major part of it was designed earlier by the Labor government. In part, it was a continuation of previous policy with a new set of tools. The Bank of Israel continued the government's heavy involvement in the currency market, buying and selling currencies with the explicit goal of affecting the value of the Israeli pound.

With the announcement of free currency conversion, the government indicated that the new rate would begin at 15.5 pounds to the U.S. dollar, which represented a devaluation of some 43 percent from the previous rate. It is difficult to escape the conclusion that the Begin government did not depart from the policy of continuing small devaluations, plus occasional large ones, that has been followed since the autumn of 1974. The mechanism of devaluation changed in 1977 from explicit government decision to currency trading by the central bank. From late 1974 to late 1981, the value of the Israeli pound has declined from about U.S. $0.24 to about U.S. $0.006, taking account of the replacement of the pound by the shekel as the unit of currency.

That a big devaluation was coming after the 1977 election was widely anticipated, no matter which party won. The Labor government slowed the rate of devaluation in the months before the election, as part of a campaign to improve the image of the economy and to temper the wage demands that flooded in from one group of workers after another. When the "New Economic Policy" did come in November 1977, it was announced by the Likud's finance minister, but it had been prepared with the active cooperation of the Bank of Israel governor, who had been appointed in the final months of the Labor government. Along with the devaluation of 43 percent, there was a cost of living spurt of about 12 percent in less than one month. The move came in the same month as President Sadat's visit to Jerusalem when the economic issues could not dominate the headlines. The national mood of ecstasy over the prospect of peace faced the fury of Histadrut leaders and calmed their desire to call out the workers in general protest over the new surge of inflation. Skeptics saw the label of "New Economic Policy" and the symbol of free dealing in foreign currency as *sweetners* for the principal action of massive devaluation. Cynics saw them as *disguises* for the devaluation.

THE SALE OF GOVERNMENT COMPANIES

A prominent component of the "New Economic Policy" was to be the sale of government companies. Free enterprise was the theme, with the deputy finance minister in charge.

Ever since its earliest years, the state of Israel has been heavily involved in the ownership of limited liability companies. Government companies are prominent in the fields of energy production, banking, transportation, minerals, water, manufacturing, and tourism. Some government companies—like the Israel Electric Company, El-Al airlines, and Israel Aircraft Industries—were established to serve important functions of economic viability or national security. Others, like the Housing and Development Company, Israel Chemical, and special purpose banks were set up to meet social goals, to provide employment in certain regions, and/or to spur economic development. Still others, like the Government Corporation for Coins and Medals, appeared when a public sector entrepreneur convinced a cabinet committee that the state had an opportunity to make some money.

Despite the prominence of government companies in the Israeli economy, it is not entirely clear just what they are, how many government companies exist, or what they are worth. For one thing, there are competing definitions of a government company. One law assigns to the Government Companies Authority—a unit in the Finance Ministry—jurisdiction over companies where the government's share of stock ownership or of the board of directors is at least 50 percent. Another law assigns to the state comptroller—a unit responsible to the Knesset—responsibility over all companies in which the government has *some* share (but not necessarily a majority) in ownership or control. According to a recent *Annual Report*, the Government Companies Authority counts 105 government companies according to its definition. The state comptroller has not recently recorded how many companies he finds within his jurisdiction. Neither the Government Companies Authority nor the state comptroller has a complete list of the subsidiaries owned by government companies, or the joint ventures owned by government companies as partners with firms owned by the municipalities, the Histadrut, the Jewish Agency, the universities or other "public" or private investors. This collection of joint venture and second tier government companies may number more than several thousand.

In keeping with the pragmatism that pervades the Israeli public sector, there has been a fair amount of government trading in company shares. The government buys shares to help a company in trouble, to spur growth in a sector of the economy defined as important, or in the hope of making some money for the state. Government shares are sold—or government companies are allowed to issue new shares—as private investors appear interested, to realize profits that can be employed elsewhere in the government's annual planning, or simply to reduce the size of an annual budget deficit. The *Reports* of the Government Companies Authority for 1976/77 and 1975/76 reveal share acquisitions amounting to 143 million Israeli lira (IL) and IL111 million and sales of IL4 million and IL9 million. Between 1975/76 and 1976/77 the number of companies having a majority of government shareholdership or control declined from 116 to 105.

Against this background, the accomplishment of the Likud government with respect to the sale of government companies appears modest. By the middle of 1978, a list of 48 companies to be sold was compiled. Implementation proved difficult. The country's socialists—including people of that persuasion in some parties aligned with the Begin government—did not want to lessen the state's role in vital sectors of the economy. Private investors seemed unwilling to help the state rid itself of investments in expensive or risky ventures, where there had been a dearth of private money in the first instance. The small size of the Israeli economy made it impractical to put too many shares on the stock market at any one time. There may have been foreign money to buy certain companies, but other opposition rose at the prospect of selling important pieces of the public's holdings overseas.

Three banks and a handful of small companies were sold. The deputy minister of finance, who led the program in the beginning, is no longer in office. He was ousted in a power struggle with his minister and Liberal party colleague Simcha Ehrlich, who himself is no longer finance minister. No major sales were made in 1979, 1980, or 1981. In November 1981, the government appointed a new committee to oversee the sale of companies, but to date little progress had been made. Despite the Begin government's emphasis on reducing the extent of government intervention in the economy, it may have sold less of its company shares than the previous Labor governments sold routinely in comparable periods. The policy of selling government companies now seems relegated to the back burner. The number of companies with a majority of their shares owned by the government increased to 137 in 1980—up from 105 in 1977.

SUBSIDIES AND TRANSFER PAYMENTS

As part of its noninterventionist strategy, the Begin government sought to cut back on subsidies and transfer payments. Its first two finance ministers expressed the sentiment that real prices (unsupported by subsidies) should help to create an attitude of living within one's means. They also objected to the benefits that middle and upper income people derived from subsidies and across the board transfer payments like child support. If the Begin government was to help the needy, the finance ministers wanted to do so without spillovers that helped the well-to-do.

Pressure for cuts in subsidies and transfer payments also came as much from necessity—i.e., budget pressures—as from ideology. Cutbacks in subsidies were also initiated by the former government. Thus, it is as difficult to distinguish between continuity and initiative as between necessity and ideology in the efforts of the Begin government with respect to subsidies.

The first two finance ministers did reduce or eliminate subsidies, despite much clamor and some street disturbances. Prices for milk and its by-products, bread, cooking oil, sugar, rice, frozen poultry, and public transportation increased substantially. However, both ministers failed to hold the line against pressures. It was not possible to cut subsidies (allowing prices to rise sharply) and to resist demands for wage increases with an inflation rate of more than 100 percent. The third finance minister—Yoram Aridor—approaches subsidies with pragmatism. Indeed, subsidies are among the tools he has used for economic and political leverage. He has avoided dramatic reductions in the subsidies of individual items. All told, expenditures for subsidies have increased since Aridor came to office.

Early announcements with respect to transfer payments also suffered from less than clear accomplishment. Finance Minister Ehrlich attempted on a number of occasions to limit the payment of child allowances to families with three or more children. The child allowance is paid to parents regardless of their income. The minister argued that small families with one or two children could do without the allowance. Among the voices raised successfully in opposition was that of the National Insurance Institute, an agency associated with the Ministry of Labor and Welfare, which pays the child allowance.

TAX POLICY

Taxation is a classic battleground between liberals and socialists. For years Labor governments were criticized for high tax rates that were said to stifle individual initiative and encourage evasion. The Begin government came to power while several major tax reforms introduced by the former government were being implemented, including a reduced rate structure, self-assessment of income tax, universal compulsory bookkeeping, new definitions of taxable income, and the introduction of a value added tax. An observer could conclude that the previous Labor government anticipated its successor with liberal tax reforms. The Begin government continued a policy of simplifying the tax structure. The value added tax rate increased, while a number of smaller nuisance taxes were eliminated.

Two tax items provided some excitement early in Begin's first term: taxation of the kibbutzim and a tax amnesty. For many years, Liberal and Herut party members charged that the kibbutzim—which provide most of their votes to socialist parties—escaped the heavy tax burdens imposed on other enterprises. Liberal party leader Simcha Ehrlich picked up the old charge during the 1977 election campaign and promised to change things if the Likud won the election. The idea had some support. The traditional image of the kibbutz member as hard working and committed to a simple life had given way to the realization that most kibbutznikim enjoy the amenities of the urban middle class.

Ehrlich took action immediately following the election. He appointed a commission to study the taxation of the kibbutzim and to propose changes to bring their taxes up to par with the rest of the economy. Commission members included representatives of the kibbutz sector, and it was headed by the president of the certified accountants association.

Contrary to expectations, the commission reported that kibbutzim were paying more, not less, than other economic enterprises at comparable levels of income. It found that regulations pertaining to them took a stricter than usual interpretation of the tax code. This put an end to Liberal hopes for a change in the policy toward kibbutzim.

Tax amnesty was a campaign promise directed at the self-employed core of Liberal party voters. Proponents of the amnesty explained that large scale evasion developed when tax rates were high and administrative enforcement low. Though tax rates were lowered in the 1974 reform, many self-employed continued to evade. A tax amnesty, which would remove penalties from those who had evaded taxes in the past, would make it possible to start afresh. Rates were now more reasonable, and there would be no backlog of past evaders to consume the resources of the Tax Department.

The public debate was heated. Opponents accused the Liberals of legitimizing tax evasion and making a gift to their political supporters. The issue reached the prime minister, who met with leading economics professors and took the issue off the government's agenda. Two earlier tax amnesties had been implemented by Labor governments. When Labor proposed amnesty, it encountered little opposition from the Liberals. The center of opposition to amnesty is within the Labor movement itself. When the initiative came from Liberals, pragmatists within the Labor movement, who might otherwise support amnesty, joined the opposition. The Histadrut might have tolerated a Labor-inspired move, but it rallied against a Liberal party amnesty.

There was, however, a tax change late in Begin's first term that seemed tailor-made for the reelection campaign. In February 1981, Finance Minister Aridor reduced a number of customs duties and sales taxes, most prominently on expensive consumer items like appliances and automobiles.

CHANGING EMPHASIS IN ECONOMIC POLICY

Any review of economic policy efforts and accomplishments of the Begin government must take account of changes in finance ministers and the policies they pursued. Like most prime ministers before him, Menachem Begin relegated economic policy initiatives to the minister in charge. He involved himself only when public pressures turned a significant portion of the cabinet against economic policies and the pains they caused. The first two of Begin's finance ministers resigned under a combination of public and internal government pressure. Both called for austerity and worked in the tradition of finance ministers who say "no" to requests for tax cuts, subsidies, and service improvements. The third finance minister—Yoram Aridor—came to office when the standing of the Begin government was at its nadir in public opinion polls and when the 1981 election loomed ominously near. Aridor projected the image of a good fellow who enjoyed handing out goodies to the masses. He cut import duties on a number of items and prompted buying sprees of color television sets and automobiles. He held the line against price increases for gasoline, bus tickets, and other items for months at a time, even when the value of the shekel continued to drop. He thereby recreated a policy of subsidies. He sought to steal the initiatives of the Labor party and the Histadrut by proposing 100 percent cost of living adjustments to wages, with the adjustments to be made monthly instead of every three months. Aridor's adversaries in the Labor party soundly condemned him for buying the voters and predicted sharp increases in taxes and prices after the election. To date (December 1981), it is true that controlled prices have increased, but gradually. There have been no sharp increases in major taxes.

NATIONALIZATION OF HEALTH CARE

The nationalization of health care is an old issue in Israel. In the long historical view, it is part of the state's accumulation of vital services, which had been performed by public bodies in the prestate days of the *yishuv*. The first confrontation—in the 1940s—came over the nationalization of the armed forces. This did not occur without actual firing between those who stood for a nationalized army and those who stood for the continued autonomy of prestate forces. Menachem Begin was among those against nationalization at the time. The second confrontation occurred over the nationalization of primary and secondary education, putting into the hands of the Education Ministry and local authorities schools that had been run by political parties and religious bodies. This was not accomplished without a severe crisis in which Prime Minister Ben-Gurion resigned in the face of an expected no-confidence vote in the Knesset. Yet to be finalized is the nationalization of health care. Several Labor governments raised the issue but backed off in the face of sharp opposition from party colleagues in control of the Histadrut. With the election of the Likud government, proponents of nationalization saw their best chance of success. Ideological purists in other lands might blink at the scenario. Economic liberals in favor of free enterprise sought to nationalize health care, against the strong opposition of the labor federation that backs health delivery by its own Sick Fund and a number of other private bodies.

Like other policy initiatives considered here, the nationalization of health care could not occur on a clean slate. Thirty years of state history, plus several earlier decades of the *yishuv* impose inevitable complications. Not only was Likud picking up proposals that had circulated for years, but there was an active committee of inquiry created under the previous Labor government. Its report helped set the stage for Likud's own actions in support of nationalization. If nationalization is accomplished under Likud, the Begin government could claim to have implemented a policy that was long under consideration. To date, however, the nationalization of health care remains stalled.

The existing system of health care in Israel is heavily socialized, even while it relies on nonstate bodies for most services. The principal unit is the Sick Fund of the Histadrut, which provides comprehensive care via its own clinics, hospitals, pharmacies, and rest homes. Some four-fifths of the population belong to this Sick Fund, and it employs the majority of health care professionals. Its support comes partly from members' dues and partly from government subsidies. The remaining population belongs to smaller sick funds or subscribes to private insurance. Most new immigrants and indigents are enrolled in the Histadrut Sick Fund at the government's expense.

Prior to the 1977 election, most arguments for nationalizing health care dealt with the merits of a single system, more comprehensive planning, coordination, and efficient use of resources. After 1977, issues of organizational conflict have been closer to the surface. Without the Sick Fund, the Histadrut would lose one of its best attractions for membership. The Labor party would also suffer along with the Histadrut. Both Herut and the Liberals have their own sick funds, but they are small compared to the Histadrut's.

On the one side of nationalization are countless stories of petty bureaucracy in the Histadrut Sick Fund. Clients wait forever in disorderly queues to visit a physician or to receive medicine, held up by those who are waiting for an excuse from a day of work or for prescriptions for band-aids or aspirin. Every visit to a specialist must first be approved by a general practitioner, forcing patients to wait twice in queues. Other complaints focus on the quality of the medical care, lessened by physicians working under the pressure of long lines. Also, studies have shown duplication of sophisticated services and medical equipment in certain areas and less than minimal standards elsewhere.

The complaints were joined by scandal. The chief executive of the Histadrut Sick Fund, Asher Yadlin, was jailed in early 1977 for dealing in bribes and kickbacks with respect to land purchases and building contracts. The case was made spectacular by Yadlin's high position in the Labor party. He had already been nominated by Prime Minister Rabin as the next governor of the Bank of Israel when the police announced an investigation in its final stages.

Despite the problems of the Histadrut's Sick Fund, the government found few friends for its plan of nationalizing health care. The public remained generally unconcerned. Beyond the limited circle of health professionals, few seemed to comprehend the government's plan. The Histadrut warned that nationalization would add IL4 billion to the government's budget. Members and operators of smaller sick funds joined the opposition to a single national scheme.

The government position has yet to prevail after more than four years in office. A few months before the 1981 elections, the government succeeded in moving a proposed bill through the first reading in the Knesset and sending it to a committee. There it seems to lie undisturbed. What appeared to be a cakewalk when Likud and its coalition partners defeated the Labor Alignment now seems to be continued stalemate and another victory for the status quo. Party discipline and a majority in the Knesset have not been sufficient to enable the government to push legislation against the opposition the plan encountered.[2]

PENSION FUNDS

The Begin government also moved to introduce a national pension law during its first term but was not up to the competition offered by the Histadrut. The case resembles the conflict over national health care. A large segment of the working population contributes to pension funds established in the framework of Histadrut enterprises. These are important to the Histadrut as sources of capital for its industrial and commercial enterprises. With control of the Knesset in the hands of the Likud (still the minority party in the Histadrut), there came a proposal to develop a national pension scheme that would remove one of the prime sources of Histadrut funding. At the same time, two of the largest banks—Bank Leumi and Bank Discount—moved to develop private pension schemes to compete with those of the Histadrut. The third giant in Israeli banking—Bank Hapoalim (the Workers' Bank)—remained in the Histadrut fold and refrained from entering the competition.

The Histadrut prevailed against both the government's scheme and those of the two large banks. The advantage of the Histadrut was its large existing base in the pension field. The Histadrut would not make it easy to transfer credit for prior contributions to new pension funds. The Histadrut added to its leverage in the course of 1981 with an agreement with the Industrialists Association. According to this agreement, all members of the organization—an extensive segment of the Israeli economy—became obligated to enroll their employees in Histadrut pension schemes. Unlike the case of the Sick Fund, there was no mass feeling of discontent that opponents of the Histadrut could use against its pension fund. Bank Leumi and Bank Discount dropped their own new pension schemes in 1981, partly in realization that the Histadrut already controlled much of the potential market, and partly under a Histadrut inducement to channel certain deposits through their banks. The government's pension plan withered for lack of support.

PROJECT RENEWAL

Shortly after the 1977 election, Prime Minister Begin announced that housing in poor neighborhoods would be a major target of his government. He personally went on a campaign to raise funds for the program among Jewish communities abroad. It is unusual for the prime minister to involve himself in the details of a domestic program, but this was an appropriate gesture to repay the poor Oriental neighborhoods that had provided much of Likud's support.

It is not easy at this stage to evaluate Project Renewal as an initiative of the Begin government. For one thing, it was composed in large part of ideas and ongoing programs already apparent in the Housing Ministry and other units of the previous Labor government. Without doubt, the programs expanded in substance and concept and increased in funding and attention during the Begin years. This condition presents a second problem of evaluation. The program has been overloaded with numerous goals. Aspirations for the new program ranged widely over issues of substance and procedure. Neighborhoods selected for renewal were to be upgraded both physically and in programs to enrich the educational qualifications, cultural lives, and leadership capacity of neighborhood residents. Decision making for the project was to involve representatives of several national ministries (Housing, Education and Culture, Labor and Welfare, Finance, the office of the prime minister) plus the Israel Lands Authority, the Jewish Agency, the municipalities, neighborhood representatives, and the overseas donor communities. Much work has been accomplished. At the same time, the Project has been a fertile field for representatives of the various interests involved to assert that their own interests have not been given due weight. Reports of the Israel State Comptroller have faulted procedural and substantive features of the complex program. They have found a lack of central control mechanisms sufficient to coordinate the various aspects of projects, or to assemble information sufficient to monitor resource use and program accomplishments.

EDUCATION

When it became known that the Ministry of Education would go to the National Religious Party, many took seriously Knesset member Shulamit Aloni's prediction that religious education would expand in place of secular studies, and that children would be indoctrinated. However, it may take years to assess the impact that Minister Zevulun Hammer will have on education. To date, no overt moves seem to have been initiated with respect to the religious content in secular education. As senior posts in the ministry have been vacated, however, the minister has filled them with NRP candidates.

Certain policy moves with respect to government support of religious education and institutions came at the initiative of another religious party, Agudat Israel. These occurred most prominently after the 1981 election, and they represent an issue distinct from the religious content in secular schools. They will be treated below in the section on religious policy.

The most prominent overt policy change of the first term of the Begin government was the extension of free education to all four years of high school.

However, this was not a new idea. The former government had begun moving towards this goal by instituting free education through the first two years of high school.

ELECTORAL REFORM

What may have been the most explicit and prominent of domestic pledges made in the 1977 election campaign has disappeared, despite its party's initial appearance as the second largest partner in the Begin coalition of 1977-81. The Democratic Movement for Change emerged in 1977. It appealed primarily to well-educated middle and upper income Israelis of European extraction, many of whom were disaffected by the lack of meaningful changes being pursued by the Labor Alignment. Yigal Yadin—a national personality, first as military chief of staff in the 1950s and later as a world renowned archaeologist—assumed its leadership. The label of the new party signalled its principal mission. It promised change in the political system of Israel, to make it more thoroughly democratic.

Such a mission seems odd from one perspective. The Israeli electoral process is already among the most democratic in the world. Polling is by proportional representation with voters choosing which of several parties to support. In the one nationwide constituency, each party receives a percentage of Knesset seats very close to their percentage of the vote. From another perspective, however, Israelis are at arms length from the selection of their representatives. The composition of party lists comes from internal nominating procedures that have not been open to mass participation. The voters cannot choose the *individuals* to represent them. They choose only the party whose lists of nominees will sit in the Knesset according to the percentage of the total vote received.

The Democratic Movement for Change promised more open elections and greater discretion for the voters. Its own procedures for choosing candidates and defining its platform were explicitly participatory, with elaborate procedures to allow each party member to share in the formulation of the party list. If victorious, the DMC promised above all else to work for the direct election of Knesset members.

The DMC did well in the election of 1977. Its 15 seats in the Knesset came as a result of winning 11.6 percent of the popular vote. But the party did not have the strength to dictate terms in the new government. From the beginning of negotiations, its leadership was in the classic quandary of the party not powerful enough to impose its principles: *Should it accept a role in government at the expense of its principles or stick by its principles at the expense of power?* When the leaders accepted a role in the Begin government, they claimed to be preserving the most basic of their principles. Internal tensions were apparent then, however, and they surfaced periodically in the face of tough decisions. The DMC split openly in the fall of 1978 over the negotiations with Egypt. While a major faction of the movement left the government, Yigal Yadin remained as deputy prime minister. Yadin himself exited from politics in 1981. He did not run in the election and the DMC disbanded. Its proposal to reform the electoral system did not appear in the 1981 campaign or in the policy commitments of the second Begin government.[3]

RELIGION

The Begin election of 1977 was the first occasion of change in the dominant party of Israel and the first time for the most orthodox of the religious parties, Agudat Israel, to join the government.[4] The Agudah did not request ministerial appointments. Its emphasis was on changes in law and administration in conformance with its interpretation of religious law. Its accomplishments during the Begin government were impressive. In summary fashion they:

1. Strengthened government policy against abortion.
2. Strengthened control over archaeological digs that disturb ancient Jewish gravesites.
3. Strengthened policy against the activity of missionaries who seek converts away from Judaism.
4. Strengthened policy against postmortem analysis.
5. Forbade swearing in the name of God in court proceedings.
6. Facilitated the excusing of Orthodox women from military service.
7. Required separate swimming beaches for men and women.
8. Facilitated the avoidance of summer daylight savings time.
9. Strengthened policy against work on the Sabbath and religious holidays.

The Agudah assumed an even stronger position at the beginning of the second Begin term. It held four votes in the governing coalition that had a margin of only two votes over the opposition parties. Its weight appeared quantitatively in the formal agreement between the partners in the coalition. Thirty of the 83 points in the agreement dealt with religious issues. The Agudah won recognition for several general demands and a number of specifics. Several themes continued from its concerns in the 1977–81 period. It stressed the observance of religious law by public institutions and, to some extent, by all Jewish residents of Israel. There would be further limitations of work on the Sabbath and religious holidays, prohibition against the sale of pork and other nonkosher food, increased concern for the role of religious law in marriage and population registration, increased concern for the privileges of religious Jews in the framework of military service, and greater concern to prevent archaeologists from disturbing Jewish burial sites. In the second Begin term, there would be greater emphasis on the distribution of financial resources to religious education and other religious institutions. Also, the Agudah demanded key personnel appointments for its supporters, i.e., senior policy level posts in a number of ministries.

It is too early to judge the policy success of the religious bloc in the second term of Prime Minister Begin. Not all of the 30 religious points in the coalition agreement are commitments on the same level of assurance with respect to implementation. On several points, the agreement commits the government to operate in certain ways. On other points, however, there is only a commitment that the government concern itself with the measures at stake. Points dealing with financial support for religious institutions tend not to set explicit monetary targets or deadlines. The agreement gives considerable freedom to the prime minister to define the priorities and the timing of implementation.

Looking to the near future, the lack of specificity in the coalition agreement can work two ways. On the one hand, it can provide flexibility to the prime minister, allowing him to delay on delicate policy steps toward the religious community in the light of other considerations. On the other hand, the lack of specificity allows the Agudah to be the judge of its own success. On any point, its Knesset members may decide that they are not achieving enough and that they must use their critical four-vote leverage against the government.

CONCLUSIONS

There have been changes in both the symbols and the substance of domestic policy since the first Begin election of 1977. However, changes came slowly. Even now, some four and a half years after the first Begin election, and a half year into his second government, the changes on the domestic scene are less than thorough. From this experience, it may be possible to extract several lessons of general application. There are few cases of a first change in party control several decades into the history of new democracies. The special conditions of Israel add other barriers to facile generalization. Nonetheless, some thoughts emerge from this record that relate to the general problems of opposition political parties in democracies as they aspire to gain control of government and define public policy.

1. Change is not likely to be dramatic and extensive. Instead, it is delayed and comes piecemeal. A party coming to power after years in opposition must build an infrastructure of key personnel, information, and concrete plans. Before then, its leaders can speak freely and change the symbols uttered by the government. Only with an infrastructure in place can a new government embark on concrete proposals that differ significantly from its predecessor's policies.

2. Many new ventures appear to be more innovative than they in fact are. Much that is advertised as new will be extensions, embellishments, or repackaging of previous activities. A new government can boost the resources given to an existing program and change its scope or its name far more readily than it can develop a program that is genuinely new.

3. Contending institutions outside the government framework will remain strong, with an incentive to counter government proposals. In Israel, the Histadrut remains a potent force, with a firm grasp on fields such as health care and pension funds. So far it has been more than a match for government efforts to challenge its domain.

4. Ventures that do attract massive amounts of government attention and resources—like Project Renewal—may have their own problems of starting. Perhaps the grander the vision and the greater the resources, the more extensive and diffuse will be the goals and—along with these traits—greater problems in realizing accomplishments in the short term.

5. Accomplishments may depend as much on the evolution of circumstances as on the formal plans or priorities of the new governing party. Among the most prominent of changes in policy since the first Begin election have been alterations in law reflecting the demands of Agudat Israel and the wave of populistic changes in import duties and purchase taxes that came on the scene with the elevation of Yoram Aridor to the Finance Ministry. Both trends crystallized only when the Begin government was well under way. The wave of religious legislation may have benefitted from the diminished weight of the secular Democratic Movement for Change and the greater leverage of the Agudat Israel in the first and then the second Begin governments. The wave of populistic tax changes came only in the last half year of the first Begin government, with Begin's third finance minister, and with an eye toward the government's need for a boost in public support.

6. Domestic policy change must compete with other interests of the government. Israelis generally, and the prime minister in particular, have been heavily involved with foreign policy issues since 1977. The peace process with Egypt continues with periods of relative quiet and storm. Other incidents have included the law defining all of Jerusalem as the capital of Israel, tension on the northern border, Syrian missiles in Lebanon, the AWACS and F-15 deals between the United States and Saudi Arabia, and the extension of Israeli law to the Golan Heights.

The promise of the present government is that it can make peace, led by old warrior Menachem Begin as prime minister. If the peace process continues, however, it will continue to preempt the resources and energies that could otherwise be devoted to such domestic matters as economic reform or Project Renewal. It is neither simple nor cheap to relocate the military and civilian installations of the Sinai. It could be even costlier to accommodate the decision that may come with respect to the West Bank and Gaza. For the Begin government to have a maximum impact on domestic policy, it may require several more years in office plus a benign international setting such as no Israeli government has yet experienced.

NOTES

1.   This paper, initially presented to the Conference on Israel in the Begin Era at the Baltimore Hebrew College in May 1979, was revised for publication in the Winter 1981 *Jerusalem Quarterly* and has been expanded and updated further for publication in this volume.

2.   The political dynamics of the Sick Fund debate are discussed in Chapter 1 (see pp. 19–20).

3.   A discussion of the DMC and its problems is found in Chapter 2 (see pp. 29–32).

4.   A more detailed discussion of Agudat Israel is found in Chapter 5 (see pp. 111–14).

4   The Labor Party in Opposition

Myron J. Aronoff

INTRODUCTION: THE DECLINE AND FALL OF THE LABOR PARTY

In evaluating the performance of the Labor party in the opposition, it is essential to understand how it came to be there. But first it must be understood how it came to dominate Israeli politics for almost 50 years. The formative period during which the most important institutions of the political system were created determined to a significant extent the character and relations of power within the system for decades thereafter. The period between the creation of the Histadrut in 1920, through the creation of Mapai in 1930, to Mapai's capturing of the dominant position in the Executive Committee of the Jewish Agency a few years later witnessed the creation by the Labor movement of the system's major institutions. Labor came to dominate most of them in the remaining years prior to independence. Yosef Gorni attributes the high degree of legitimacy of the leadership of the Labor movement during this period to their successful articulation and implementation of the ideology to which their followers adhered.[1] Yonatan Shapiro balances the picture by showing the pragmaticism of the leaders in building strong and centralized political organizations.[2]

Some of the main characteristics of emergent Labor rule during this period that became dominant in later periods but that also contributed to the decline in responsiveness of the party include: (1) the emergence of a top group of national leaders supported by a secondary echelon of leaders who controlled the party and the Histadrut, a development that ensured that political goals dominated economic ones; (2) a system of indirect elections to party and to Histadrut institutions (and later to the Knesset) through oligarchic appointments committees, which guaranteed elite domination of these institutions; (3) dependence on the elite was reinforced by the predominance of functionaries of the party and Histadrut bureaucracies on the forementioned institutions; (4) certain categories and groups (particularly those most supportive of the leadership) were overrepresented on them; recruitment and mobility were primarily through patron-client relationships; (5) democratic procedures and the party constitution were frequently ignored or put aside for reasons of expediency; (6) criticism of and/or opposition to the elite was suppressed; and (7) there were isolated cases of corruption in the misuse of public funds, which were suppressed—although these were minor in their scope and impact compared with the public scandals that rocked the party 50 years later.

With independence, many of the important functions and services previously carried out by the Histadrut and other voluntary agencies were taken over by the state, e.g., defense, education, and employment exchanges. Ben–Gurion's articulation of *Mamlachtiut* (literally, statism) attempted to give ideological legitimacy to this process. However, it created strains within the Labor movement. Among other consequences, this process led to the lessening of the citizen's dependence on the political movements. With the mass immigration of immigrants from Islamic countries, Mapai increasingly relied on material inducements to mobilize their support. Ideology became increasingly irrelevant. Party machines developed in the major cities with smaller versions in the periphery. Support was organized through an elaborate system of patronage, which the leaders of the machine effectively employed to guarantee unquestioned support for the top leaders and their policies.

A number of increasingly serious internal party struggles, starting with the Lavon Affair, and including an involved struggle between the Young Guard and the leaders of the dominant party machine, culminated in a major leadership struggle, which led to the split of the Ben-Gurion-led Rafi from Mapai in 1965. As Medding aptly summarized the outcome of the 1965 election: "Organization triumphed over charisma and institutional power over prophetic morality."[3] Unlike previous party splits, ideology played a secondary role, as it was overshadowed by the struggle for power. The decline in the role of ideology corresponded to a parallel rise in the importance of the party machine. In the ensuing years internal unity decreased, feelings of political inefficacy increased, and party institutions became increasingly less effective. The net result was the decline in the party's responsiveness to demands that were being articulated as a result of the dynamic changes that were taking place in the society.

The period between the 1967 and 1973 wars was one of political *immobilism*. Ideology was restricted to ritual discourse. Power and the resources of the party dominated institutions; inertia, the conservatism of the electorate, and the ineffectiveness of the opposition maintained Labor's rule. Party activists generally felt powerless and ineffectual but were severely constrained from expressing criticism of the top leaders and their policies. Control of the nominations process perpetuated the domination of the party by the elite and their clients. The issue agenda and decision making were effectively controlled by the elite, and controversial issues were suppressed. The ritualization of important aspects of politics contributed significantly to the further erosion of the responsiveness and effectiveness of the party. Although marginal improvements were made, the pattern of unequal representation of various groups in the party continued. However, in answering the demands of various groups for representation on party institutions, the institutions were simply expanded. This made them both easier to control and less effective deliberative bodies. Consequently, decisions were made by informal gatherings of the elite. This expanded the growing gaps between them and the party and the general public. The cumulative effect of this process crystalized in the catalytic "earthquake" of the Yom Kippur War.

The new period that followed was characterized by a major crisis of confidence in the credibility of the national party leadership and the Labor party as a whole. The combination of mass public protests and internal criticism led to the resignation of Golda Meir and to the changing of the guard at the helm of the party and of the nation. The succession of Yitzhak Rabin essentially left the party, if not the nation, leaderless. In spite of his attempts to build a new coalition, desperate attempts to bring back Golda Meir to help revive the party, and other tactics, the party and its major bodies atrophied from lack of use under Rabin's rule. Whereas a number of organizational reforms were undertaken to make the party more democratic and responsive, they were insufficiently effective to convince even those involved in them, much less the wider public, that the party had sufficiently reformed itself to merit their confidence. These efforts could be simply summarized as having been too little and too late.

Besides these cumulative long-range factors, there were many more specific immediate causes for Labor's defeat. The more important factors included the decision to hold the Knesset elections prior to the Histadrut elections and the decision to separate Knesset election day from that of local elections, two major departures from tradition that cost the party dearly at the polls. Similarly, Rabin's decision to force the NRP out of the government was hardly a politically astute one.

The public scandals that rocked the party, including the Asher Yadlin "affair," Avraham Ofer's suicide, and Prime Minister Rabin's resignation over his wife's foreign currency account conviction, further undermined public morale and confidence in the Labor party. President Carter's statements about a Palestinian homeland hardly helped Labor's cause either. Severe economic hardships, spiraling inflation, devaluations, and severe labor strife contributed to the growing social *malaise*, which was symbolized by the decrease in immigration to, and the increase in emigration from, Israel. Labor, as the dominant party, was blamed for all these ills and many more.[4]

With the newly-gained respectability and legitimacy of the Likud, and the idealistic appeal of the promising Democratic Movement for Change (DMC), there were for the first time serious alternatives to disenchanted Labor supporters.[5] Long-range demographic trends relating to age, ethnicity, and class further undermined Labor's traditional base of electoral support.[6] In sum, a complex combination of long-term and short-range factors contributed to the public's loss of confidence in the Labor party.

The leaders of the Labor party temporarily recovered from their respective states of shock, disbelief, dismay, and demoralization to desperately contest the elections to the Histadrut. They were able to prevent the calamity of defeat in this important institution through the infusion of masses of kibbutz volunteer workers sent by the agricultural movements. The kibbutzim were shocked out of their complacency and frightened by the clear and present danger to them of a Likud dominated government hostile to their interests possibly gaining control of the last bastion of Labor influence. The fact that many voters felt that Labor had been sufficiently punished by their loss of governmental power, the likelihood that some former Labor supporters were having second thoughts as to the wisdom of their Knesset votes or abstentions, and the rationale of others that it would not be a bad idea if the government and the Histadrut were controlled by different parties undoubtedly aided Labor in maintaining its narrow margin of ascendency in the Histadrut.

CONTINUITY AND CHANGE: THE INTERNAL PARTY DIMENSION

There is a genuine difficulty in accommodating the real ideological diversity and conflicting interests of the varied groups within the Labor party. The need for consensus and a semblance of party unity is reinforced by the potential explosiveness of serious policy differences within the party, particularly in such areas as peace, security, and territories. Clearly this is not new. It has been one of the dominant characteristics of the party since it was formed. The real question is: Has there been any change in the manner in which the "consensus" is reached? Are alternatives raised and are they seriously considered? What groups are represented in the decision-making processes that set party policy? Are they responsive to the constituencies they represent? In short, how much has the Labor party really changed? I shall attempt to give at least tentative answers to these and related questions.

The central role and importance of the Histadrut, both its central office and its labor councils, to the party after Labor's loss of government office and patronage is obvious. In the case of communities where Labor lost control of the municipality, the officials of the local Histadrut labor councils gained political ascendancy in the local party branches. Similarly, the national leaders of Histadrut, Yorucham Meshel, Israel Caesar, Aharon Harel, and Nava Arad, among others, who retain control over the considerable resources of the Histadrut, have grown in relative stature and importance. Consequently, they exercise their power with much less direction from the party than they and their predecessors had done in the past. Because the party was considerably weakened by its defeat in 1977 and the aftermath of this defeat, the relative position of power of the Histadrut has been strengthened.

The relative importance and power of the kibbutz movements also grew after 1977 and will undoubtedly grow even more once their recent merger is

fully implemented and consolidated.[7] Since they provided the personnel and resources that saved the Histadrut for Labor, helped save the party from financial
bankruptcy, and replaced, with their own volunteers, a significant proportion of
the functionaries of the party bureaucracy who were laid off after the party's
defeat, the kibbutz movements pressed for greater influence commensurate with
their increased activities.

Dramatic changes have taken place at the central party headquarters on 110
Hayarkon Street in Tel Aviv. The few remaining professional party functionaries
are now outnumbered by the young volunteers sent by the kibbutz movement
to man the party bureaucracy. They partly account for Rabin's place as number
four on the Knesset list. Motivated by the antikibbutz propaganda of the Likud,
they moved in to fill the political vacuum created by the disintegration of the
old political alignments and machines. Two of the most important departments
of the party were taken over by these new men of the kibbutz movements—
the Organization Department and the Information Department. Mussah Harif,*
former secretary of the Ichud Kibbutz movements, and Danny Rosolio, former
secretary of the Kibbutz Hameuchad movement, are among the group representing this important power base in the party.

However, the increasing involvement and power of the kibbutz movements
is not seen as a universal blessing. Clearly, those whose power was based on the
big city machines of Tel Aviv, Jerusalem, and Haifa could not be expected to
remain content with the erosion of their bases of power and the growing power
of the kibbutzim. There has been an interesting rise in the status of the eight
regional branch councils created during the political vacuum that accompanied
the changing of the guard at the top of the party in 1974. In order to attempt to
retain the influence they gained through the competition between Peres and
Rabin (as was reflected in the list to the Knesset), they are likely to align with a
nascent Tel Aviv-based group (see below). Since they can potentially provide
channels for more responsive representation in the party of groups that the party
must attract in order to make a strong political comeback, e.g., the Orientals in
the development towns and poorer areas of the main cities, the competition between those new urban alignments and the kibbutzim in the party has serious
sociopolitical implications.

For example, in order to increase their own political influence, members of
the kibbutz movements are taking part in the establishment of new regional
labor councils (of the Histadrut). Designed by Labor to counter the growing
power of the Likud, these councils will unite a number of urban labor councils
with kibbutzim in the area. Unless there are strong regional party branch councils, this could lead to the domination of the development towns and other

---

*Mussa Harif was to die unexpectedly on January 16, 1982 before he could
rise higher in the hierarchy.—ED.

smaller urban communities by the kibbutzim. Since the kibbutzim are predominantly Ashkenazi and the development towns are predominantly Oriental, this could result in reversing some of the gains that the Orientals have made in recent years in gaining greater political representation and influence in the party. Not only do the kibbutzim represent different economic and political interests than the urban branches, given the differences in ethnic composition between them and the development towns, there is a grave danger of the reappearance of a new form of political paternalism, which characterized the party in earlier years.[8]

Dov Ben-Meir, secretary of the powerful Tel Aviv Labor Council, estimates that approximately 70 of the previous 814-man Central Committee (of which only around 200 bothered attending meetings) were the bases for tactical coalitions that swayed party decisions.[9] This group could be ranked hierarchically with Peres at the apex, but is actually the first among a ruling group that includes former Foreign Minister Abba Eban, and the secretary-general of the party, Chaim Bar-Lev who was designated to become defense minister (before Peres and Rabin made a last minute deal prior to the election). Yitzhak Rabin retains considerable stature and is again showing signs that he may make another bid to regain the party leadership. The rest of the former Labor ministers, the present members of the Knesset, and the members of the party executive Leadership Bureau form the respectively wider circles that constitute the top and secondary echelons of party leadership. They are tied to one another, and to lower ranking party activists, through links of patron-client relations and of more ramified sociopolitical networks.

There is an amorphous middle-aged stratum of party activists who constituted the reportedly now defunct *Shiluv* Circle. Many of them were involved in the group organized to back Peres in his struggle with Rabin over the party leadership. Most reports indicate the dissolution of the temporary factions built around the support of the two candidates. Many of the members of this category are linked into the above-mentioned patron-client ties and more extended sociopolitical networks. There appears to be a potentially powerful alliance emerging between the leadership of Tel Aviv, the moshav movement, Haifa, and the urban sector of the former Achdut Ha'avoda faction. This nascent alliance might potentially become a new "Gush" under the leadership of Tel Aviv strongman Eliahu Speiser.[10]

During the period under discussion two new informal party groupings were formed. The Beit Berl group (named after the party's ideological institute where they met) included among its more prominent participants: Ya'acov Levinson (the party's leading economic expert), the late Mussa Harif who was at the time the secretary of the Ichud Kibbutz Federation (formerly affiliated with Mapai), Uzzi Baram who served as secretary of the Jerusalem district, and the official leadership of the Haifa district. The image which emerged of this group was predominantly Ashkenazi (European), liberal, intellectual, and moderately dovish. Although this group supported Shimon Peres against the challenge of Yitzhak

Rabin (who was backed by the Kibbutz Hameuchad and urban supporters of the former Achdut Ha'avoda), it clashed with Yahdav, another group which also backed Peres.

The Yahdav group (named after the party clubhouse where they met) was led by the two top party Tel Aviv officials, Eliahu Speiser, secretary of the Tel Aviv District, and Dov Ben-Meir, secretary of the powerful Tel Aviv Workers' Council of the Histadrut. The group included Histadrut and trade union officials, e.g., Aharon Harel; leaders of the moshav movement; leaders of the opposition to the official party leadership in Haifa, e.g., Wertman, and in Jerusalem, e.g., former Police Minister Shlomo Hillel. The image this group projected was less elitist than the Beit Berl group, more trade union and Histadrut oriented, more Oriental, and more hawkish. Although their leaders claimed his sponsorship, Peres never officially adopted this group. The combined support of the Beit Berl and the Yahdav groups helped Peres to defeat Rabin's challenge to his leadership.

Before the elections, Peres promised to support Eliahu Speiser's candidacy in the race for party secretary-general but agreed to postpone the contest for party secretary until after the national election at the request of Uzzi Baram, the leader of the Beit Berl group who also desired the post. At the time Peres was convinced that Labor would be returned to power and the present party secretary-general, Chaim Bar-Lev, would receive a senior cabinet post. Facing a challenge to his leadership of the party after its failure to regain power in the election, Peres is desperately trying to keep Bar-Lev in his post. He fears that if Speiser successfully challenges Bar-Lev, Peres' own standing as party leader would be imperiled. Speiser, an Ashkenazi, has attracted the enthusiastic support of most of the party's Oriental activists in his own constituency, Tel Aviv, in the development towns and the moshavim throughout the country who argue he is Labor's answer to Begin. Speiser has made overtures to the urban members of Rabin's camp, and if he succeeds in bringing them into his nascent group it might well swing the balance of power in the party.

The category of intellectuals, academics, or as they were traditionally called, "the working intelligentsia," include a group of university professors called Group 77, who demonstratively joined the party in its worst moments after defeat. They have figured most prominently in the efforts to reform both party structure and ideology as a prelude to its return to power. They have attempted to link up with the kibbutz groups, which share this penchant for ideological politics. Although both groups share a propensity for ideology, their views differ on important issues: the professors tending towards the dovish end of the ideological continuum, and the kibutniks by-and-large tending toward the hawkish end with some notable exceptions like Yitzhak Ben-Aharon. While most observers agree that the party under Peres is far more hospitable to intellectuals than in the past, there are markedly different estimates of the influence of this group.

Closely linked ideologically are the members of the Young Guard (including members up to the age of 35), who in many cases are the students or former students of the aforementioned professors. Traditionally, they are players of the roles of "enfants terrible," proponents of party reform, and most particularly of the need to democratize the party's representative institutions and decision-making processes, because they have so little influence on these institutions.

Bar-Kedma quotes party Secretary-General Bar-Lev at length and uncritically about the "new momentum" in the party, the commission to investigate the party structure to make recommendations for reforms, the new form of leadership slowly emerging, and the 40 new members of the Central Committee and three new members that were added to the Leadership Bureau.[11] The latter were the retiring chief of staff of Zahal, Mordechai Gur; the retiring ambassador to the United Nations, Chaim Hertzog; and the former chairman of Bank Hapoalim, Ya'acov Levinson. Unfortunately, for those who hoped for democratic reform, they were "parachuted" from above (co-opted) by oligarchic appointment to the top party executive. This is yet another indication of continuity of traditional practices, which contributed directly to Labor's decline. Clearly, the Labor party did not learn all there was to learn from its 1977 defeat. Although there were some promising moves in the right direction, e.g., in the breaking up of the centralized oligarchy, fundamental structure changes and renewal of basic principles did not take place to a meaningful extent.

What can be concluded about the nature of continuity and change in the Labor party during the Begin era? Certain things are obvious. There is no single, strong, and cohesively united elite that dominates the Labor party. Nor is there a single major party machine, like the Gush when it was led by Netzer, the new machine dominated by Sapir, or even the coalition based on the big city machines on which Rabin had depended for support. At this stage the situation appears to be somewhat in flux. Peres has clearly established a position of pre-eminence, but not of absolute dominance. He has gathered around him most of his generation of former ministers and high-ranking personnel, with the exclusion of Rabin and his closest supporters. There is the possibility of a split in the group that centered around Rabin. The Kibbutz Hameuchad has merged with the Ichud in the newly united Kibbutz Federation. Rabin's urban supporters are likely to collaborate with the Speiser-led group.

Clearly, there have been significant changes in the relative positions of power, not only of individuals, but more importantly of groups within the party. The Histadrut leadership and the kibbutz movements appear to have been the biggest gainers as a result of the reversal of party fortunes. The major city machines are rebuilding to recoup their losses. Tel Aviv is the most successful, having made strategic alliances with the moshav movement and the branches in the outlying areas, which had only recently made gains through their organization into districts. It is not yet clear how stable these new alignments are and what their relative positions of power are within the party. New groups like the university professors, which have traditionally not been particularly active or influential in the party, have been recruited and at least potentially might be influential in some policy areas. They, and their allies in the Young Guard, are pressing for major structural reforms and ideological rejuvenation. However, their gains in these areas appear to have been limited to symbolic gestures and minor reforms.

In terms of the major party institutions, their membership, methods of nomination, size, and functions, there have been no significant changes. There has been no attempt to curtail the size of the respective institutions to make them capable of functioning more efficiently. On the contrary, both the party's new executive and the new Central Committee are larger than those that preceded them. This can hardly be seen as a harbinger of the democratic reforms that have been called for by those who view such reforms as essential to making the party worthy of regaining public confidence.

Given the new openness that characterizes the party today, it is most unlikely that there will be the type of ritualized decision making that took place when the party was led by Golda Meir and Pinchas Sapir. On the other hand, if the various proposals of the members of the new task forces are not really taken seriously, then they run the risk of being the new ritual-like formats in which the intellectuals are allowed to play at formulating party policy without having any real influence. There is the real possibility, although not certainty, that this could happen. This problem is aggravated by the sharp differences in policy represented by the new groups, such as the professors and the intellectuals, older groups that have made gains in their positions, such as the kibbutzim, and those groups that are presently aligning around the different urban branches, e.g., Speiser's new Tel Aviv-based "Gush."

The problems created by the reversals in relative positions of power within the party were manifested in the power struggles over the new party institutions, from the taking of a new party census (which involved the struggle over "real" as opposed to "fictitious" members), the election of delegates to the new party conference, and the selection of the membership of the other important party institutions. Whereas these proceedings were more open and democratic than in the past, there was considerable continuity of the old oligarchic practices. For example, Knesset members who had served two terms were required to receive the support of 60 percent of the Central Committee to stand for a third term. Half of the names for the Knesset list were chosen by a nominating committee of five members, which was appointed by the party's Political Bureau. As a democratic concession, the other half were chosen by the party branches. The ordering of the names on the list was done by a special committee, and this determined who had a realistic chance to be elected. The committee consisted of Peres and the leaders of the two kibbutz movements, the moshav movement, and the three major cities—Tel Aviv, Haifa, and Jerusalem. Most of the actual work of the committee was done by Speiser (Tel Aviv) and Baram (Jerusalem). The first 20 names on the list were mainly national leaders, the following ten were mostly the leaders of the districts, and the next ten were a mixture of both. Therefore, while the nomination process through which members of Knesset are chosen and ranked remained an oligarchic one controlled by the party bosses, it gave greater representation to the leaders of the larger regional branches.

Most of the changes that took place in the party after 1977 were the consequences of the calamity of Labor's defeat, rather than having been part of any well considered or purposeful plan. Although among the party ideologues and intellectuals there were those who understood the long-term and deeply-rooted causes for Labor's decline and defeat, most of the leaders—many of whom are intellectually impressive individuals—gave far more superficial explanations. The weakest explanation of all the leaders was that of Yitzhak Rabin whose memoirs indicate his inability to comprehend or explain his own downfall or the decline of the party.[12] According to Rabin, he was brought down by personal intrigues against him. Abba Eban published his autobiography shortly after the fall of Labor. Although it was obviously added on to an already complete manuscript, this does not excuse the superficiality of the analysis from someone of Eban's intellect. He attributes Labor's defeat to a badly organized election campaign and "a sharp swing toward political militance and social conservatism in Israel."[13] Peres' views, which shall be discussed below, while more sophisticated than the above mentioned accounts, were still an inadequate explanation, which failed to take into account the long-range reasons for Labor's decline and defeat. From among the top leaders, Chaim Bar-Lev, who as secretary-general of the party commissioned more scientific analyses of the party's 1977 defeat, offered the most sophisticated explanations.[14] But even his analysis lacked a deeper historical and structural perspective.

Since the top leaders of the Labor party failed to comprehend the full causes and significance of their party's defeat in 1977, they failed to press for the more fundamental structural reforms that would have been required to democratize the party and make it more responsive to the party membership and wider public. They also failed to press for more open discussions of the wide range of policy options and the kind of ideological changes and rejuvenation that such discussions would have required. In order to reverse its defeat of 1977 in 1981, Labor had to convince the Israeli public that it had drawn the proper conclusions from its punishment by the voters and had undergone a fundamental change of attitude and heart. David Krivine, prophetically before the election, ventured the opinion that, "The expected change of heart did not take place. Perhaps the Alignment is not chastened enough by its once-only defeat at the polls. Perhaps it is too sure of victory next time. Perhaps it will have a nasty surprise when next time comes around."[15]

OPPOSITION BEHAVIOR: THE PUBLIC DIMENSION

First Phase

With the partial exception of the Histadrut campaign, the Labor party was characterized, from its defeat in May 1977 until approximately the middle of February 1978, by a general state of disarray. The defeat was followed by a long series of bitter recriminations as different individuals (and factors) were singled out as scapegoats on whom blame could be laid for the party's misfortunes. The public was "treated" to a spectacle of a party airing its dirty linens in public, a fact that did little to improve its already besmirched public image. The head of the party's campaign committee, Chaim Bar-Lev, and individuals in charge of various aspects of the propaganda campaign, such as Yossi Sarid, were subjected to particularly severe criticism. Former Premier Yitzhak Rabin published (in *Haaretz* and later in his memoirs) a particularly bitter attack on Shimon Peres, whom he blamed for his downfall. Peres reciprocated with a more indirect attack on Rabin, stressing the tremendous difficulties imposed on the party by Rabin's resignation as premier and party leader only six weeks before election day.

In an interview in the *Jerusalem Post* Peres said, "The Likud did not bring us down, it was the Democratic Movement for Change that did it. We fell because of our internal weaknesses and failings in office, not because of the Likud's unassailable appeal.... Our way was not proven wrong, it was our conduct that caused our ruin."[16] He claimed that the scandals that engulfed the party leadership (another oblique swipe at Rabin), combined with raging inflation and the rash of strikes, caused Labor's defeat.

During this period, Labor spoke with more than one voice as various leaders, particularly Peres, Rabin, Allon, Eban, Bar-Lev, and others criticized the Likud government and proposed variations of Labor's approaches to a peace settlement. However, during this period a fairly consistent line evolved, and it was most frequently and most forcefully articulated by Shimon Peres. Peres adamantly rejected Begin's (and later Weizmann's) proposals that Labor join in a Government of National Unity. Instead, he stressed the differences in Labor's approach, particularly the need for territorial compromise in Judea and Samaria with a close link to Jordan. Peres criticized Begin's plan for West Bank autonomy as being "worse than the Rogers' Plan." In the meantime, Rabin and Bar-Lev stressed the strategic importance of the Sinai bases and led the attack on Begin's eventual relinquishment of them.

Organizationally, the Labor Party was visibly in a chaotic state of disarray. Even the traditionally pro-Labor *Jerusalem Post* editorialized about "Labour in Decay."[17] The fact that Labor continued to employ its traditional oligarchic nominations process is clear evidence that those in power failed to either recognize or give sufficient importance to the claim that such undemocratic procedures contributed directly to the lack of responsiveness of the party and its leadership to public demands, which led to its defeat. For example, the fact that the executive forum remained at the inflated number of 61 ensured the likelihood of the emergence of a smaller informal elite group to fulfill this function in traditional Mapai/Labor style.

Second Phase

The second period of the development of Labor in the opposition (which lasted from approximately mid-February 1978 through September 1978) began with Shimon Peres' participation in the conference of the Socialist International in Vienna, Austria, where he also held discussions with President Sadat. This gave Peres the needed image of a leader with international recognition, capable of dealing with Sadat—and, as it appeared to many, apparently more likely to be able to come to terms with him than was the prime minister at the time. Labor stepped up its attacks on Begin for contributing to the impasse in the peace talks and pushed with greater force and clarity its own policies, which offered greater willingness to make territorial concessions on the West Bank. In various forums, Labor spokesmen led by Peres and including Rabin, Eban, Professor Shlomo Avineri (former director-general of the Foreign Office), and others launched an increasingly more effective campaign.

Clearly, Begin's political honeymoon was over, and he was losing considerable popularity at home, a development that added to the growing confidence of Labor, whose leaders were moving on to the offense. Infighting within Begin's cabinet was growing and was constantly publicized in the media. Increasing wildcat strikes and a runaway inflationary situation made clear that the government had neglected vexing domestic issues. Many began to perceive that the government's shift toward a free-market economy was not benefitting the average wage earner. At the same time, public euphoria, which had been precipitated by Sadat's visit to Jerusalem (November 9, 1977) had been replaced by a pall of depression as the peace talks bogged down, and many felt that there was some justice in Labor's charge that Begin bore a share of the blame for the stalemate. This is best exemplified by the spontaneous popular support that arose from the letter of 350 reservists to Begin, which led to the Peace Now Movement and its series of successful mass demonstrations and rallies. Dovish Labor M.K. Yossi Sarid is reliably reported to have helped in the drafting of this famous letter, and Mapam's Kibbutz Artzi is known to have given considerable backing in resources and manpower to the Peace Now movement. Peres met with the movement's leaders and declared they made a favorable impression on him. Many of Labor's more prominent doves gave them more enthusiastic support, although some party hawks opposed the movement.

More importantly, Labor's renewed attack on the Begin government coincided with the independently run Peace Now campaign for greater flexibility in government policy. In April, Peres launched a particularly sharp attack on the Begin government's handling of the peace negotiations, and particularly his interpretation of Resolution 242 in a manner that precluded the return of territory in Judea and Samaria. This campaign apparently struck a particularly responsive chord in Israel as well as abroad. Signs of growing popular discontent with the government, and signs of renewed support for Labor, such as the very successful May Day celebrations sponsored by the Histadrut, convinced Peres that the Likud could not last out its term of office.

The publication of Peres' fourth book, *Ka'et Mahar (At This Time Tomorrow)*, in which he outlined Israel's tasks and goals symbolized the beginning of the forthcoming election campaign. He revealed in June 1978 that in his well publicized "friendly" talks with Sadat, the Egyptian president had agreed to Israel retaining military strongholds on the West Bank. They also unofficially agreed to President Carter's "Aswan formula" as guidelines for a statement of principles, something the Begin government had rejected. In addition, Austrian Chancellor Kreisky and Willy Brandt, chairman of the German Social Democrat party, (with the behind-the-scenes help of Abba Eban it was later revealed) introduced a similar draft and recommended its acceptance as the Socialist International's Middle East policy statement. All of this infuriated Begin and his supporters, who contended that Peres was attempting to thrust himself into the political limelight and undercut Begin at a time of delicate diplomatic maneuverings to revive direct contacts with Egypt.

Begin so resented this episode that he vented his displeasure in such an uncharacteristically unparliamentary manner that certain Labor leaders questioned his physical and psychological fitness to remain in office. This precipitated one of the most acrimonious periods of hostility between an Israeli government and the opposition in recent history. The Laborites charge that Begin was unfit to rule was made in a meeting of the Labor party's Political Committee, and resulted in a statement from Begin's personal physician, denying that the prime minister was in any manner incapacitated. The accusations were called "slanderous" by Begin, who clashed bitterly with Peres in the next meeting of the Knesset. The ensuing acrimonious interchanges were accompanied by decisions of the cabinet to curb meetings of opposition leaders with foreign leaders, and specifically the refusal of Begin to give permission to Peres to meet with King Hussein (at Hussein's initiative).

It was clear that by now the government's period of grace was over, and its domestic and foreign policies were increasingly under attack. Increasingly, serious cabinet infighting became common public knowledge. The combination of growing international and domestic criticism for what was perceived as the government's hardline stand in negotiating with the Egyptians, the demonstrations of Peace Now, and equally strong internal criticism of the government's economic policy, gave Labor plenty of ammunition to fire at the Likud government. The internal frictions within the government only aggravated its plight and tended to give credence to Peres' view that the Likud was helping Labor to return to power.

Third Phase

Given this political climate, President Carter's invitation to Premier Begin to attend the Camp David summit conference with President Sadat was almost a providential way out of an extremely difficult political situation. This led to a change in tactics of the Labor party during this new phase, which lasted approximately a year, extending from the Camp David summit conference in September 1978 through the signing of the peace treaty between Israel and Egypt on March 26, 1979 and its subsequent ratification. Labor had already been severely criticized for having gone too far in its questioning of Begin's fitness to rule by many groups within Israel and abroad, who were not linked in a partisan way to the Likud government. These reactions were warnings that immoderate criticism of the government could be counterproductive by causing groups Labor was eager to attract to support the government. A second factor was the traditional closing of ranks behind the leader when the country is being subjected to pressures that are perceived to threaten the security of the nation. A third factor was the unexpected flexibility Begin demonstrated at critical stages in the Camp David talks, which took the wind out of the sails of Labor criticism, temporarily at least, on the critical occasions when such spurts of flexibility led to concrete political achievements. Clearly, the leadership of the Labor party was far too responsible to oppose the first peace treaty Israel had ever had a chance to reach with any of its Arab neighbors, particularly since it was with the largest and most politically significant and militarily powerful of its Arab neighbors—Egypt. A fourth factor that constrained Labor's campaign against the government was the increasingly divisive nature of the internal struggle within the party between its own doves and hawks.

Labor's questioning of Begin's fitness to govern drew a strong reaction from several U.S. Jewish groups, which constituted an almost unprecedented intervention on their part in internal Israeli political conflicts. For example, the Anti-Defamation League of the B'nai B'rith in the United States and the World Council of Synagogues and the United Synagogue of America (the conservative movement) strongly criticized Labor party leaders for their personal attacks on Prime Minister Begin. They claimed that such attacks crippled the U.S. Jewish community's information efforts and damaged Israel's image. Labor received a clear and unambiguous message to moderate its attacks on the government or else it might jeopardize the goodwill of important nonpartisan groups at home and abroad.

Prime Minister Begin expertly exploited the strong tendency of the Israeli people, including opposition politicans, to rally around the leader at times of crisis. He was thus able to weaken opposition within his own party and government as well as that of the Labor party in the Knesset. Furthermore, when his tactics—balanced by what appeared to be considerable flexibility—succeeded in actually producing a peace treaty, Labor could do little else but congratulate the prime minister and give the treaty their political support while claiming that they would have negotiated a better one. However, the increasingly divisive ideological disputes between Labor party doves and hawks, which were related to internal power struggles, set additional constraints, which limited the effectiveness of the opposition during this period.

All of the various Labor spokesmen were most critical of Begin's having sacrificed the strategically important air bases and the major naval base in the Sinai. They were also extremely critical of Begin's autonomy plan, which Peres labeled "a mine-laden course." In addition to the traditional hawks in the Labor party, the late Yigal Allon, who had generally appeared to have been dovish, strongly opposed the Camp David agreement. New hawkish voices were added to the top executive body of the Labor party in the forms of the newly retired chief of staff of the army, Mordechai Gur (who announced his eventual aspirations to the premiership) and some of the representatives of the increasingly influential kibbutz movements.

Alarmed by the increasingly hawkish tones of Labor spokesmen, the party doves called a meeting at the end of December 1978, which they were forced to cancel because of the strong opposition of the party chief, Peres. Obviously, Peres regarded with suspicion the makeup of the dovish group, which was viewed as too closely paralleling the old Mapai group, especially since it was led by some of his arch rivals, e.g., Yitzhak Rabin and Yehoshua Rabinowitz. The power of these individuals and the old Mapai machine they lead had been seriously undermined with the ascension of Peres to leadership, the debacle of the 1977 election, and the rise in the influence of the kibbutz movements with their disciplined bloc of 10,000 active members. The concern of many Labor doves was expressed by former party Secretary-General "Lova" Eliav (who left the party) who said, "Some voices in the Labor Party are once again becoming louder in trying to outflank Begin on the right."[18]

While Labor's political support of the government in the two critical Knesset votes (the first in support of the Camp David accord and the second in support of the Israel-Egypt peace treaty), along with its vocal articulation of serious reservations about both, received the most attention of the foreign media, the less well-publicized attack of Labor on the government's economic policies was probably, in the long range, of greater internal political significance. In the forefront of this campaign has been the Histadrut, led by its Secretary-General Yorucham Meshel. Meshel, who worked his way up through the ranks of the trade union movement, has an exceptional knack for teamwork, which has aided him in achieving an unchallenged position of leadership in the Histadrut and in the Labor party. Clearly, the Likud's weak domestic performance considerably helped to fortify both the authority of the Histadrut and of Meshel. The Histadrut's campaign in opposition to Finance Minister Ehrlich's economic policies culminated in a half-day general strike at the end of March 1979 in protest against price rises in basic foods and the government's failure to control inflation. A million workers were reported to have participated in the strike. Ehrlich resigned his post as finance minister shortly thereafter.

Fourth Phase

The fourth phase was ushered in with the resignation of Moshe Dayan as foreign minister in October 1979, witnessed the resignation of Ezer Weizmann as defense minister at the end of May 1980, and culminated with public opinion polls predicting an unprecedented absolute majority of 61 seats in the Knesset for Labor (to the Likud's 29 seats) in October 1980. Never before had an Israeli government suffered the resignation of the three most important ministers after the prime minister, i.e., the ministers of defense, treasury, and foreign affairs. Nor had any Israeli political party ever received an absolute majority in a public opinion poll forecasting a Knesset vote; although, to be sure, the unprecedentedly high proportion of undecided voters qualified the implications of the results of this poll. Likewise, no Israeli cabinet had ever had three different finance ministers during its tenure of office; but then, Israel had never had triple digit inflation before either. During this period Israel passed Argentina to lead the world in inflation. For the first time in the history of the Knesset it was asked four times to lift the parliamentary immunities of three of its members—all of whom were associated with the ruling coalition—at the request of the attorney-general. Given the grim record of the Begin government, the Labor party had little to do but get its own house in order to topple the weak and wobbling Likud coalition cabinet.

Party Chairman Shimon Peres labored diligently, traveling long hours to practically every branch in the country to rebuild the party. In so doing he won the respect, if not the affection, of a broad spectrum and cross section of the party rank and file and activists. The grass-roots reconstruction of the party appeared to be paying off in terms of a resurgence of labor morale, self-confidence, and even a semblance of long-lost unity. With the apparent debacle of the Begin government, and the rising popularity of Labor (even taking into consideration the large proportion of undecided voters), the return of Labor to power began to appear to be a foregone conclusion. The main question seemed to be whether a vote of nonconfidence would bring down the government, or whether the government would determine the date for early elections. This was the peak of Labor strength, unity, and popularity in the opposition.

Fifth and Final Phase

The final phase was ushered in with former Prime Minister Yitzhak Rabin's formal announcement that he would challenge Shimon Peres for the party's candidacy for prime minister. Rabin had narrowly defeated challenges by Peres for leadership of the party in 1974 (after Golda Meir resigned) and in 1977 only to have to resign the party leadership to Peres when the prime minister's wife's illegal foreign currency account was made public. This challenge represented the third major confrontation between the two leaders. Originally, Rabin had supported Yigal Allon's candidacy in contesting the party's nomination for the Premiership. However, with the death of Yigal Allon (in February 1980), Rabin (who had served as Allon's deputy commander of the Palmach before it was disbanded in 1948) assumed the leadership of the group centered around the Kibbutz Hameuchad which challenged Peres' leadership of the Labor party. Rabin reveals in his memoirs that his bitter conflicts with Shimon Peres and Moshe Dayan began in the early 1950s, a development he claims slowed his rise to chief of staff (which he became in 1964).[19] Tension between them intensified in the period preceding the outbreak of the war in June 1967 and resurfaced later in Rabin's cabinet. Although his campaign actually began a year before, Rabin did not formally announce his candidacy for the top party spot until October 1980. The publication of Rabin's memoirs, in which he made numerous accusations against Peres, set the bitter, personally antagonistic tone of the competition for the Labor party leadership. For example, a few days before the election to the party conference, the French weekly *L'Express* published a false charge that Lea Rabin's fine for maintaining an illegal foreign currency account in Washington, D.C. had been paid by a reputed underworld figure. Rabin immediately denied the charges and accused the Peres camp of responsibility. Several months later *L'Express* retracted its story, claiming that it had been given false information by "persons known as Shimon Peres' friends." Peres, who had condemned the original report, denied having anything to do with it. The obsessive hatred Rabin and Peres have for each other caused organizers to carefully schedule their speeches so as to avoid the possibility of the two candidates meeting. As was the case four years previously, their competition did little to raise the level of debate over the most outstanding issues, the morale of the party, or its public image.

The intensely bitter personal leadership struggle considerably weakened the party at a time when it desperately needed to maximize its unity and strength. The intemperate public attacks that constituted the Rabin/Peres campaign of mutual recrimination was particularly senseless given the lack of significant ideological or policy differences between them. Ultimately, the Rabin supporters were unable to convince more than a minority of the party members that the differences between Rabin and Peres was sufficiently significant to warrant the terribly divisive campaign. Also as a *party* politician Rabin was no match for Peres. To be sure, Peres had the advantage of being the formal leader of the party appartus during the contest, and he proved his skill in knowing how to use the position to his advantage. Even his critics grant Peres credit for having devoted tremendous time and effort in rebuilding the party after its destructive defeat. His efforts to rebuild the party from the local branch level up were largely successful, although he did it within the frame of reference of the Labor party as it had been previously constituted in its traditional oligarchic form, albeit with minor changes.

No significant reforms were initiated under the leadership of Peres. In fact, he rebuilt the party and his power in it in traditional Mapai/Labor style. The national membership drive, the internal party election of candidates to the national party conference, the preparation and control of the conference, and the election of the party's candidate for prime minister were, according to all reports, almost identical to the processes that took place in previous conferences. The most tangible differences were the absence (mostly due to death) of a few of the actors and the appearance of a very few new actors to take their places. Of course, as far as Peres was concerned, the most important difference between the party's second and third national conferences was the outcome of the election of the party's candidate for prime minister. Whereas Rabin had narrowly defeated Peres in their previous contest, this time around Peres soundly defeated Rabin with slightly more than 70 percent (2,123 votes) of the 3,028 votes cast.

The conference was very much Shimon Peres' show. It was his reward for three and a half years of arduous and painstaking labor and preparation. He played it for all it was worth. Leading European socialist leaders attended the conference, which was addressed by Francois Mitterand, head of the French Socialist party, vice-chairman of the Socialist International, and subsequently President of France. The Egyptians also sent a high-level delegation. Peres, as party chairman, delivered the main address, which was timed to make the prime time television news. After the election results were announced (in a different session of the conference), Rabin made a less than magnanimous concession speech. Peres immediately capitalized on this by prefacing his victory speech by a dramatically demonstrative shaking of Rabin's hand and announcing, "I want every delegate who voted for Yitzhak Rabin to know that I feel as if I have just shaken each of your hands as well."[20] This is reported to have brought the house down.

However, the second most important event after the nomination of the party's candidate for the premiership, the election of the new central committee, did not take place at the conference as had been planned. Sharp rivalries between the different groups fighting for representation on the central committee, particularly a last ditch fight by Rabin's supporters to insure representation proportionate to their strength necessitated the postponement of this decision to the convention's second session in February 1981. Indeed, the party had been thrown into turmoil the day before the conference opened when the Tel Aviv District Court accepted the Rabin camp's challenge to the party election results in Rehovot and disqualified that city's 39 conference delegates.

A controversial resolution sponsored by a group of hawkish kibbutz members that would have amended the party platform to support the annexation of the Golan Heights was hotly opposed by party doves who threatened to break up the meeting over the issue. The traditional technique of postponing a decision on the proposal by referring it to the new central committee succeeded in temporarily defusing the issue. Similarly, the perenially controversial plank of the party platform on religion and the state ended up after a hot debate as a carefully worded compromise on the coexistence of the Orthodox, Conservative, and Reform trends in Judaism.

Peres delivered another severe blow to the demoralized and disintegrating Rabin camp by excluding Rabin from his shadow cabinet. However, he was careful to assure the leadership of the Kibbutz Hameuchad group, Israel Galili, Ya'acov Tzur, M.K. Danny Rosolio and Mulla Cohen (who had originally supported Allon and, subsequently, Rabin) that their interests would be represented and taken into consideration. In fact the jockeying for positions in the shadow cabinet occupied a good deal of the time and attention of the top leadership of the party in the ensuing several months after the party conference. One of the most serious of several errors made by Shimon Peres after his resounding defeat of Rabin was his handling of the drafting of a shadow finance minister. It was widely publicized that Ya'acov Levinson, who was then chairman of the board of directors of the Histadrut's Bank Hapoalim, was Peres' first choice for finance minister. The consensus of conference delegates appeared to be that Levinson was the star of the second session of the conference as Peres had been at the first session. Levinson presented the main economic platform for the renewal of the Israeli economy. When Peres refused to guarantee Levinson the considerable power of economic matters, which he demanded as a condition for accepting the post offered to him, Levinson declined the offer.

After refusing to give Levinson the guarantees he demanded, Peres turned to Professor Chaim Ben-Shahar, President of Tel Aviv University, to serve as shadow finance minister. Whereas Ben-Shahar is a respected economist, he lacks the political experience, backing, and stature within the party that Levinson has. To compensate for this, Peres announced that Ben-Shahar would head an economic "troika," which would include veteran Knesset member and Peres supporter Gad Ya'acobi as shadow minister of industry, trade, and tourism and Naftali Blumenthal (a former protegé of Levinson), head of the Histadrut industrial conglomerate—Koor—as shadow deputy finance minister. It is well known that a troika is a most difficult vehicle to drive, since the horses tend to pull in slightly different directions. Given the composition of Labor's economic troika and the extreme economic problems facing Israel, Peres' team did not inspire the public confidence that a powerful candidate like Levinson might have done. Ben-Shahar was not even given a realistic position on the Labor party's Knesset list.

Meanwhile, Labor had lapsed into a state of lethargic overconfidence at the very time that the public opinion polls showed that the party was losing its commanding lead over the Likud. Yigal Hurwitz had resigned in January 1981 (after slightly more than a year in office), which led to the scheduling of early elections in June 1981. Evidently precipitated by the new Finance Minister Yoram Aridor's tactical reduction of taxes on luxury items (including color television sets and cars), the Likud began to steadily regain popularity. In addition to the mishandling of the drafting of Ya'acov Levinson, Peres was widely criticized for the publicity surrounding his meeting with the brother of King Hassan II of Morocco. In an editorial comment on March 31, 1981 the *Jerusalem Post* commented: "While the polls flash their warning signals, the party bigwigs sit around, happily quarrelling over the division of the spoils of an imagined triumph. The wages of Labour's nonchalance and lethargy will be paid in full in June. For that is when the chickens come home to roost."

The results of the April election to the Histadrut were interpreted by both Labor and the Likud as victories. Although party optimists had predicted 70 percent of the vote, the Labor Alignment (which includes Mapam) received 62.9 percent of the vote, compared with 57.1 percent in 1977. However, in 1977

Labor had to contend with a promising new Democratic Movement for Change, which attracted many of its supporters. By 1981 the DMC was defunct and therefore was not a factor in the Histadrut election. Whereas support for the Likud declined from 28.1 percent in 1977 to 26.3 percent in the 1981 Histadrut election, after accounting for the votes for Rafi, which ran as part of the Likud list in 1977 and independently in 1981, the Likud held its own. Perhaps the most significant result of the Histadrut election was the fact that only slightly more than half of the eligible Histadrut members bothered to vote. The nonvoters reflected roughly the same proportion of the electorate that the public opinion polls indicated was undecided.

Rather than demonstrating party unity and the disciplined subordination of private and group interests to the public good, the Labor party continued to display the opposite image. Although the fight for the top position was the most spectacular and well publicized of the divisive conflicts, the jockeying for position in the shadow cabinet and on the Knesset list was no less intense. For example, the last minute public reconciliation (three days before the election) between Peres and Rabin resulted in Rabin's being made shadow defense minister, a post that had been promised to Bar-Lev. There was even a major fight over the post of secretary-general of the party between Uzzi Baram (supported by the Jerusalem branch and the Beit Berl group) and Eliahu Speiser (head of the Yahdav group and a leader of the Tel Aviv branch). Although there had been a major decline in the relevance of the old factions based on the parties that merged in 1968 to form the Labor party, there was no lack of factional competition based on a combination of traditional and newly emergent groups within the party.

CONCLUSION: WHY LABOR FAILED TO RETURN TO POWER

The failure of the leaders of the Labor party to fully understand the reasons for the defeat of their party in 1977 and their failure to undertake the necessary structural and ideological changes an appreciation of these reasons would have required constituted their most serious strategic mistake. They also made many costly tactical errors as well. I have already discussed many of them, e.g., Labor's overconfidence, the bitterly divisive contest between Rabin and Peres, the failure to co-opt Ya'acov Levinson as shadow finance minister, the power struggle between various groups within the party, the inability to reconcile serious ideological divisions and antagonisms between various groups in the party, and Shimon Peres' having become too involved in the minutia of these petty party squabbles. In addition, the Labor party made many more mistakes on which the Likud successfully capitalized.

There were a number of serious problems with the way that the Labor election campaign was run. First of all, the constant feuding between the two party officials who were appointed to head the campaign staff, Aharon Harel and

Michael Bar-Zohar, seriously impaired the effectiveness of the staff. Second, the election staff headquarters (unlike previous campaigns) was moved from the main party headquarters, a development that made communication between officials involved in the campaign more cumbersome. Third, there was no meaningful coordination between the official party campaign staff and the Citizens for Peres campaign staff. The latter was run by associates of Peres from his tenure as defense minister who, as a nonpartisan group, were able to obtain funds that were not under the audit of the controller general as were the government supplied election funds provided to the political parties. In short, the Labor campaign was poorly organized and run.

Clearly, Prime Minister Begin's handling of the Syrian missle crisis in Lebanon and the Israeli bombing of the Iraqi nuclear reactor successfully shifted the focus of public opinion from domestic economic issues, which hurt the Likud, to security issues, which tended to rally public support around the incumbent government.[21] Peres handled the last issue particularly poorly. Peres' and Labor's failure to keep public attention focused on the Likud's horrendous domestic record, particularly the unprecedented perilous state of the economy, was probably the most significant tactical failure of the campaign.

However, it is difficult to persuade an electorate, and particularly the less sophisticated sectors of it, that the economic situation is as bad as it really is when salaries are linked to a cost of living index and when a propitious cut in luxury taxes allowed the voters to buy such eagerly sought items as color television sets and automobiles at "bargain" prices shortly before the election. When everyday business and life go on as normal, and people adapt as well to living with an extreme inflationary spiral as well as they adapt to living with terrorism, the public tends to ignore the dangerous long-range consequences of present economic policy.

Labor conspicuously failed to counter the effects of long-term demographic trends, which deprived them of the support of many young native-born Israeli voters and a significant proportion of Oriental voters. The general decline of political commitment to political parties, expressed in the enormous floating vote, was particularly critical for Labor among these categories. "Continuing public-opinion polls commissioned by Labour have shown that the major factor coloring the attitudes of large numbers of Sephardi (Oriental) voters towards the leading political parties is the religious and traditional symbolism their leaders project."[22] There are three analytically separate, but empirically related, aspects of these research findings: (1) the relative appeal of the various parties to Oriental voters, (2) the appeal of religious and traditional symbolism to these voters, and (3) the ability of party leaders to successfully communicate to the Oriental voters (and others) in an appropriate symbolic style to evoke their support.

No contemporary Israeli party leader, and certainly not Peres, can even begin to approach Prime Minister Begin's mastery of rhetorical style, which is rich in religious and traditional symbolism. Style, the relation between form and content in political rhetoric, has not been given sufficiently serious treatment in the study of politics. Too frequently inappropriately used concepts such as charisma are used to account for the effectiveness of politicians in communicating with, and mobilizing the support of, various constituencies. More careful and systematic analysis of political rhetoric reveals that the successful mastery of such techniques as argument by *enthymeme,* in which propositions are left implicit or assumed, enable a politician to mobilize shared sentiments having a high emotional charge.[23] Although it would take systematic research on the subject to document such conclusions, my impression is that Begin was far more effective in appealing to the Oriental voters in their own "code" and in organizing their experiences through his symbolic appeals than was Peres. Begin, who is personally religiously observant, succeeded in projecting his image as a "proud Jew."[24] In fact, he has frequently been called Israel's first "Jewish" prime minister since none of the previous Labor prime ministers were religiously observant. In addition to respect for Jewish tradition and Oriental culture, another important aspect of Begin's public persona is that he appears to be a humble man without pretensions, i.e., a man of the common people. He has managed to maintain his populist antiestablishment image even while he was prime minister.

The public image of Labor's leading figures among many Israelis, particularly, but not exclusively, among Orientals, is that they form an elitist, arrogant, secular, Ashkenazi "establishment," which tends to be condescending and paternalistic. Not only are none of the top leading Labor leaders personally religious, some give the impression that they are unsympathetic, if not actually hostile, towards Jewish religious tradition. Ever since Yitzhak Rabin broke the historic partnership between Labor and the National Religious Party by forcing the NRP out of the cabinet (which brought down his government), the gap between the two former allies has widened to an almost unbridgeable chasm. To be sure, that is not entirely due to the actions of the Labor leaders alone. The shift in power in the NRP has brought the party under the control of the Young Guard led by Zevulun Hammer, the present minister of education and culture. The leaders of this group, many of whom are identified with the "Gush Emunim" and who are more militant on religious issues and more adamant than most of the older party leaders about the need to retain territories, find Begin's Likud to be a much more desirable and accommodating coalition partner than Labor. Labor's support for the recognition of the conservative and reform movements in Israel and its co-optation of former Laborite Shulamit Aloni and her Citizens Rights Movement into the Labor Alignment after the election make Labor less attractive to the religious voters and less attractive as potential coalition partners to the religious parties. Although Labor made appreciable gains over its performance in 1977 and received nearly as many Knesset mandates as did the Likud, the strong preference of the religious parties for a coalition with the Likud kept Labor in the opposition.

Prior to the election, Labor party Secretary-General Chaim Bar-Lev claimed that the central problem facing the party was, "to reach the sons of Salach Shabati."[25] The reference is to Efraim Kishon's satirical film, which deals with the trials and tribulations (or to use the Israeli perferred term, the "absorption" problems) of a large family of new immigrants from Morocco in the early days of Israeli independence. Kishon aims his satirical barbs at the general cultural arrogance, intolerance, condescension, and paternalism displayed by the Ashkenazi veteran officials toward the new immigrants, most of whom were from Islamic countries. These officials representing the kibbutzim, public agencies such as the Jewish Agency and the Histadrut, the bureaucracy of the state, and the various political parties, literally controlled the lives of the new immigrants in the early stages of their settlement. Since the Labor party was the dominant party during this period, it was associated with the aforementioned characteristics of the veteran elite in their relationships with the dependent immigrants. Consequently, Labor continues to be the target of frustration and resentment, which have evolved and festered over the years, e.g., the friction between development towns and neighboring kibbutzim, the negative image of unresponsive bureaucrats, the underrepresentation of Orientals in the higher echelons of power, and the correlation between class and ethnicity.

Kishon's film also highlighted the manner in which the political parties attempted to mobilize the votes of the new immigrants almost entirely through material inducements, which led to the development of party machines and patronage systems. The political education this system gave to new citizens who were unfamiliar with democratic party politics emphasized (by implication) the importance of personal and/or particularistic familial/ethnic interests in a bargaining situation that traded political support for the largess of the highest bidder. The trend towards a decline in the sense of more generally public or communal political obligation and in widespread commitment to political movements and parties can be traced to this period. Labor's relative failure to attract the support of the sons of Salach Shabati can be seen as the consequence of its earlier attitudes and policies and its failure to convince a significant portion of this constituency that it had turned over a new leaf.

Another example of the general erosion of wider units of political obligation and commitment in Israeli society are the trade unions. Whereas the Histadrut formerly maintained a disciplined and solidly pro-Labor political constituency, the Likud has made considerable inroads in this last bastion of Labor supremacy. Both local union shops and major national trade union units, e.g., the electric corporation workers, transportation workers, maritime sailors, El-Al maintenance workers, etc., have exerted much greater independence in terms of collective bargaining agreements and in terms of political allegiance than ever before in the past. This, of course, has adversely affected the Labor party but has implications far beyond the partisan interests of Labor.

I have attempted to demonstrate in this chapter that the behavior of the Labor party in the opposition over the past four years, and the reason why it has remained the opposition after the election in 1981, can best be explained by examining the causes for its being in the opposition in the first place. I contend that the leaders of the Labor party failed to comprehend the fundamental cumulative factors that led to the party's decline and defeat. They therefore failed to initiate fundamental structural or ideological changes that would have been necessary to regain public confidence in the party and its leadership. The present coalition of the Likud and the religious parties is a shaky one and is not likely to last out its full term of office. However, rather than taking advantage of this situation by uniting its ranks, the Labor party continues to fight its old fights. Rabin has indicated he may again challenge Peres, and Speiser is grooming his forces for a major bid for power. Labor may return to power by default, i.e., through the failure of the present government. However, if it is to regain the leadership position it once enjoyed in Israeli society, it will have to undergo more fundamental reforms and changes than the present leadership has indicated that it is willing to initiate.

NOTES

An earlier and briefer version of this chapter, entitled "Defeat and After: An Analysis of the Labor Party's First Two Years in Opposition," was published in the *Jewish Frontier,* XLVI (August/September 1979): 10-18. My thanks to the editor, Mitchell Cohen, for his helpful editorial suggestions as well as permission to reprint portions of this essay. I am also grateful to Dr. Yosef Beilin and Dr. David Somer for their helpful comments on this essay.

1.   Yosef Gorni, *Achdut Ha'avoda 1919-1930: Hayesodot Haraayonim Veha-Shita* (Achdut Ha'avoda 1919-1930: The Ideological Principles and the Political System) (Ramat Gan: Hakibbutz Hameuchad Publishing House, 1973).

2.   Yonatan Shapiro, *The Formative Years of the Israeli Labour Party: The Organization of Power* (London and Beverly Hills: Sage, 1976).

3.   Peter Y. Medding, *Mapai in Israel: Political Organization and Government in a New Society* (Cambridge: Cambridge University Press, 1972).

4.   For more detailed analyses of these and related points see: Myron J. Aronoff, *Power and Ritual in the Israel Labor Party: A Study in Political Anthropology* (Amsterdam and Assen: Van Gorcum, 1977) and Myron J. Aronoff, "The Decline of the Israeli Labor Party: Causes and Significance," in *Israel at the Polls: The Knesset Elections of 1977,* ed. Howard R. Penniman (Washington, D.C.: The American Enterprise Institute Studies in Political and Social Processes, 1979), pp. 115-45. I note that these earlier accounts are based primarily on my own first-hand participant observation of events, whereas I am limited to published accounts and reports to me by participants in the events discussed for this essay. Therefore conclusions in this analysis are more tentative than those in my earlier publications on the Labor party.

5.   For an analysis of the legitimation of the Likud see: Ariel Levite and Sidney Tarrow, "Delegitimation and Legitimation in Dominant Party Systems: The Cases of Israel and Italy," prepared for delivery at the 1981 Annual Meeting

of the American Political Science Association, New York, Hilton Hotel, September 3–6, 1981; and for an analysis of the Democratic Movement for Change see: Efraim Torgovnik "A Movement for Change in a Stable System," in *Israel at the Polls* pp. 147–71.

6.   Asher Arian, "The Electorate: Israel 1977," in *Israel at the Polls,* pp. 59–89.

7.   The two kibbutz movements affiliated with the Israel Labor party were divided in their support of the two candidates for prime minister. Most of the Ichud tended to support Peres, whereas the majority of the Kibbutz Hameuchad supported Rabin. Therefore, their merger, which formed the Tnua Kibbutzit Hameuchedet (United Kibbutz Movement), was delayed until after the competition was resolved in the national party conference. Subsequently, the newly elected leaders of both movements, Zamir of Kibbutz Hameuchad and Perlmuter of the Ichud, have been working to close the political gap between the two federations. If the newly emerging Tel Aviv-based urban alliance (with links to the moshav movement) succeeds it will be an even greater impetus for the newly united kibbutz movement to consolidate and strengthen itself through unity. Sharp criticism of the kibbutz movement by the prime minister, and from within the party by Eliahu Speiser have provided additional incentives for the leaders of the kibbutz movement to forget their past differences, and to unite to protect their common interests and ideology.

8.   See Sammy Smooha, *Israel: Pluralism and Conflict* (Berkeley and Los Angeles: University of California Press, 1978). The Likud successfully exploited the resentment of the kibbutzim by many people in the development towns. In one case, local Likud leaders adapted a cartoon that originally had depicted Arab terrorists threatening Kiryat Shmona. The cartoon was relabeled, "The Kibbutz Mafia—quiet they are coming!" It depicted a subhuman, gorillalike thug labeled "Kibbutz Movement—Alignment" and a pack of rapacious wolves bearing the names of neighboring kibbutzim descending on Kiryat Shmona. For more details see Helga Dudman, "Collective Resentment," *Jerusalem Post*, International Edition, July 19–25, 1981, p. 14.

9.   Yosef Goell, "The Labours of Labour," *Jerusalem Post*, International Edition, June 13, 1978.

10.   See Sarah Honig, "Strongman of Labour," *Jerusalem Post*, International Edition, August 30–September 5, 1981, p. 10.

11.   See Emanuel Bar-Kedma (assisted by Danny Karman), "Ha'avoda: Oz l'tmura l'achar poranute?" ("Labor: The Courage to Change After the Calamity?") *Yediot Achronot*, February 9, 1979.

12.   See Joshua Sinai, "Review of *The Rabin Memoirs,*" *Jewish Frontier*, January 1980, pp. 28–29.

13.   Abba Eban, *Abba Eban: An Autobiography* (New York: Random House, 1977).

14.   See Yosef Goell, "Commentary: The general who turned Labour Party boss," *Jerusalem Post*, International Edition, January 4–10, 1981, p. 12.

15.   David Krivine, "Dissonance in Labor," *Jerusalem Post*, International Edition, April 26–May 2, 1981, p. 11.

16. *Jerusalem Post*, International Edition, September 12, 1977.

17. Editorial "Labour in Decay," *Jerusalem Post*, International Edition, January 18, 1978.

18. Cited in *Jerusalem Post*, International Edition, January 28-February 3, 1979.

19. Yitzhak Rabin, *The Rabin Memoirs* (Boston: Little, Brown, 1979).

20. David Twersky, "Labor Prepares for Battle," *Jewish Frontier*, March 1981, pp. 4-7.

21. These crises are discussed in Chapter 7 (see pp. 185-88).

22. Yosef Goell, "The Labours of Labour," *Jerusalem Post*, International Edition, June 13, 1978.

23. See Robert Paine, "When Saying is Doing," in *Politically Speaking: Cross-Cultural Studies of Rhetoric*, ed. Robert Paine (Philadelphia: Institute for the Study of Human Issues, 1981), pp. 9-23.

24. This point is discussed in detail in Chapter 5 (see pp. 111-14).

25. Emanuel Bar-Kedma, "Ha'avoda."

5 Religious Parties and Politics in the Begin Era

Daniel J. Elazar

THE SETTING

Formally, Israel is a secular democratic state, more so than any other state in the Middle East except Turkey. Israel has no established religion, nor any provisions in its laws requiring a particular religious affiliation, belief, or commitment—Jewish or other—as a requirement for holding office, a requirement that is quite common in other Middle Eastern constitutions, most of which provide that only Muslims can hold certain offices.[1] On the other hand, the place of religion in Israeli society very much follows the pattern of the Middle East, which means there is a close interconnection between religious communities and the state, where religions are held to have a claim upon the resources of the state to support their legitimate activities. Any religious community can apply for and receive official recognition in Israel and receive state support. Israel's Ministry of Religions is the ministry of *religions* and not of one religion only. This is to say, it is a ministry that serves Jews, Muslims, Druze, various Christian denominations, and others.

Informally, Israel's society and policy are permeated with Judaism and Jewishness, just as the other countries in the Middle East are permeated by Islam and Islamic sectarianism in one form or another. People from outside the region may not see or understand this characteristic element of the region, and even people living within it may not perceive just how much Israel's character as a "Jewish state" is closely parallel to similar phenomena among its neighbors.[2]

Increasingly, Jewish religion has become an important element in Israel's civic culture. The transition in this direction in the past 30 years is very noticeable indeed. When Israel's Declaration of Independence was issued in 1948—a document that addresses itself to the secular democratic character as well as to the Jewish character of the state—a strong secularist bloc opposed any mention of the Deity. The compromise was to use a traditional phrase, "Rock of

Israel," which in traditional circles is used as a synonym for God, but which could also be interpreted by atheists or agnostics in some other way. Contrast that with the scene that took place after the Entebbe raid in 1976, when the Knesset special commemorative session was opened by the late Yisrael Yeshay-ahu, then its Speaker, taking out a skullcap from his pocket, ceremoniously placing it upon his head and reading from the Psalms.

FIVE FORMS OF RELIGIOUS EXPRESSION

Relations between religion and politics in Israel can be understood only by understanding the five forms of religious expression influential in the state today. First, there is Orthodox Judaism as reflected by the established organs linked to the state. These include the chief rabbinate, the local religious councils, the rabbinical courts, and the state religious educational system. For the most part this is the religion represented by the National Religious Party, which has been a coalition partner in every government since the state was established, and even before. In that role, it has exercised a predominant, though by no means exclusive, influence over the public expression of religion in Israel.

Then there is the popular religion of the broad public, a combination of residual folk traditions, commonly accepted Jewish practices, and elements of emerging civil religion (of which more below). Even though only a quarter of Israelis define themselves as *dati* or "religious" (which in the Israeli context means Orthodox), probably the largest single body of Israelis—the estimates are around 40 to 50 percent—define themselves as *masorati* or "traditional." For the Israelis, "traditional" is an umbrella term that includes people who are highly observant by any standards, those who simply maintain certain home customs, and those who observe virtually nothing but consider themselves believers. Even among the 25 percent who define themselves as *hiloni* or "secular," many retain a very substantial element of folk religion in their own lives—certain Sabbath observances in the home, avoidance of overt mixing of meat and milk, and the like—though they will define themselves as secular because, for them, these represent a comfortable kind of "Jewishness" rather than manifestations of religious belief. Popular religion is well rooted in Israel, in almost every quarter. It is undergoing radical change right now, because of the transformation of most of the 55 percent or so of Israelis who come from Afro-Asian backgrounds, who are in the midst of a process of detraditionalization, to a greater degree than the Jews who came from European backgrounds, most of whom started that process a generation or two earlier.

The third element is civil religion, which is in the process of rapid development in Israel today.[3] In a sense, civil religion represents the point of intersection between establishment and popular religion. The transformation mentioned above from the use of the term "Rock of Israel" to the reading of the

Psalms in a neo-traditional manner in the Knesset reflects the emergence of a civil religion in Israel that is grounded in traditional Judaism but that is not traditional Judaism. Elsewhere I have suggested that it reflects the reemergence in new ways of Sadducean Judaism, the civil religion that existed in Israel prior to the destruction of the Second Commonwealth and the great Jewish dispersion. In this respect it is different from the Talmudic or Pharisaic Judaism embodied by Israel's establishment religion, and which was the dominant mode of Jewish religious expression for at least 1600 years. This neo-Sadduceanism is based on the centrality of Jewish public life for the expression of Judaism. The evolving civil religion in Israel seeks to sacralize expressions of Jewish moralistic nationalism connected with the state and to infuse into those expressions traditional religious forms.[4]

There was always a degree of this, even when the most secularist halutzim took Jewish festivals and reinterpreted them along lines that gave expression to the values of the Zionist revival.[5] One could see the beginnings of the present civil religion in those efforts. In recent years, celebrations that once were entirely secular even when they relied upon adaptations of traditional Jewish forms are being infused with Jewish religious symbolism and modes of behavior.

For example, Israeli Independence Day has increasingly taken on the elements of a religious holiday. It is expected that the president of the state and prime minister will go to evening and morning religious services on that day. Those services, parts of the regular daily prayer cycle, now include recitation of traditional prayers of praise and thanksgiving for Israel's independence. In addition, the religious establishment is trying to develop some kind of appropriate recognition of Israel Independence Day as a holiday that can be institutionalized in the Jewish calendar. Jerusalem Day, the anniversary of the liberation of the old city according to the Jewish calendar, is also acquiring the characteristics of a quasi-religious holiday.

Fourth, there is ultra-Orthodox religion, so-called because it is even more extreme in its expression of classical Talmudic Judaism than establishment religion. Included in this category are the people who make the headlines by throwing stones at autos that travel through or near their neighborhoods on the Sabbath, who protest the immodesty of women dressed in modern fashion, and the like. But it also includes the Agudath Israel and the various Hassidic sects who hold ultra-Orthodox views but express them moderately. The extremist activists are small in numbers, consisting of at most a few thousand by the broadest definition. The bulk of the ultra-Orthodox community, consisting of several hundred thousand people, are numbered among the moderates. Both constitute a state within a state, and it is accepted that they will be. They maintain their own schools, institutions, rabbinical courts, and the like. There are points of intersection between them and the larger polity, but generally the policy of the latter is to try to leave them alone, to give them the same state support as every other group, but in order to get them to leave the state alone.

This is an uneasy relationship that usually leads to sporadic conflict when the intersection between the two communities occurs around certain critical issues, but this should not obscure the degree of routine cooperation that exists between them at other times.

Finally, there is an emergent nonestablishment Judaism in the form of the *M'sorati* (Conservative) and *Yahadut Mitkademet* (Reform) movements, which, taken together, are approaching 50 congregations in strength. With M'sorati congregations now being formed in all parts of the country, a Reform kibbutz on the land, and the first Reform rabbi recently ordained in Israel, it is reasonable to conclude that these nonestablishment movements are in the country to stay. While they remain formally unrecognized, there are increasingly contacts between them and the authorities in the course of their daily activities and, in some respects, they have gained a certain tacit recognition. For example, the Ministry of Education has supported the establishment of M'sorati schools within the framework of the state educational system. Under a minister of education from the National Religious Party (NRP or, in Hebrew, MAFDAL), their number has grown from one to three schools, and more are being established as the demand appears. Various congregations have obtained land for buildings from the municipal authorities, and occasionally M'sorati rabbis have been authorized to perform marriages.

What are we to conclude from all this? It is vitally important to understand that the government of Israel does not control or seek to control the religious establishment in the state. Rather, the various religious communities and groups utilize state instrumentalities to further their own ends.

Various headline grabbing events notwithstanding, relations between religious and nonreligious in Israel are probably better than ever. There is widespread understanding of the differences between the perhaps 20,000 fanatically Orthodox, who are the source of most of the conflicts between the two elements, and the great bulk of the religious quarter of the population, which numbers in the vicinity of three-quarters of a million people.

THE RELIGIOUS PARTIES IN ISRAELI POLITICS

Given the pervasiveness of religious expression—and often concern—in Israel, it is not surprising that most of the foregoing groupings or positions find political expression through the party system. Where the need for political expression is reinforced by the desire to gain benefits from the instrumentalities of the state—whether institutional control, financial support, recognition of legitimacy, or state enforcement of religious norms, or any combination of the above—the likelihood of acting through a political party is greatly increased.

The party system, which Israel inherited from the prestate Zionist movement and has since maintained, with its ideological camps and coalition politics, adds to the likelihood of giving political expression to religious interests through religious parties (or parties identified with particular religious trends) by making the effort worthwhile. Today, as in the past, the country divides into three "camps": *labor,* civil or liberal (the Hebrew term is *ezrahi*), and *religious.* Contrary to the conventional wisdom, the three camps do not relate to each other on a left-right continuum but stand in something like a triangular relationship to one another as portrayed in Figure 5.1. For a long time, preoccupation with European modes of political thought prevented students of Israeli politics from seeing this, even though there never was a time when Israel did not operate on that basis. Thus for certain purposes, each of the camps is more to the left or more to the right than any of the others. What each has staked out for itself is a particular vision of what the Zionist enterprise and its creation, the Jewish state, are all about. At times that vision has taken on ideological form, and at times it has been nonideological.

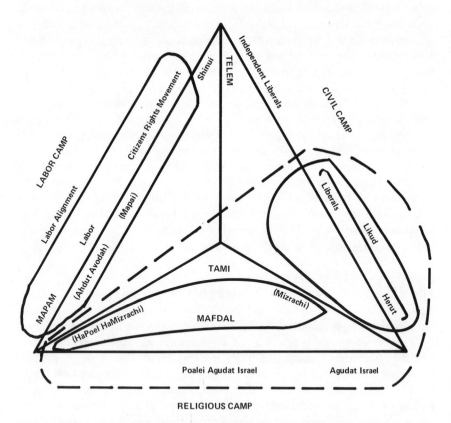

Figure 5.1.   The three Zionist camps.

Note: The circled areas indicate the present major party alignments and coalitions.

The camps themselves divide into parties, some of which are quite antagonistic to one another within the same camp (it is within the camps that left-right divisions can exist). The size of each camp is not fixed, either in relation to the total Jewish population or in relation to one another, but whatever the fluctuations, the camps themselves persist. Their persistence is reflected in the Knesset elections in Israel, in the division of offices within the World Zionist Movement, and in the various other organizations and associations within Israel.

An examination of the results of the elections to the Knesset since 1949 reveals that a governing coalition is formed when major shares of two of the camps can be combined. Until the most recent elections, coalitions generally consisted of some two-thirds of the labor camp plus two-thirds of the religious camp, plus a small crossover element from the civil camp. In the Begin-led coalition, the same principle was observed but in reverse. Virtually the entire civil camp, except for independent Liberal Gideon Hausner, linked with the entire religious camp. This, more than any mathematical formula, explains the basis for coalition formation in Israeli politics.[6]

The shift toward greater concern for Jewish tradition on the part of pacesetting elements of Israeli society is a reflection of at least two factors: the perennial search for meaning which is characteristic of Jews, including Israeli Jews, and the concern for the Jewish future of Israel. These factors are mutually reinforcing and both are appropriate in a world where religious concern is on the rise.

THE RISE AND FALL OF THE MAFDAL

The religious camp is divided into the MAFDAL (National Religious Party or NRP), which, as we have noted, is the party of the dominant religious establishment in Israel, Agudat Israel, and Poalei Agudat Israel, the latter two parties representing ultra-Orthodoxy within the Zionist framework. Bitter rivals for decades, their negative attitude towards one another had the intensity to be expected of advocates of different expressions of the same vision. The NRP is the product of a union between the Mizrachi and the HaPoel HaMizrachi, the two religious Zionist parties of the prestate era.

The Mizrachi was founded in 1902 to provide a basis for the articulation of a religious Zionist vision within the World Zionist Organization. Because it was opposed by many leading Orthodox rabbis at the time, who saw in Zionism an antireligious effort to hasten the messianic era by exclusively human activity, the Mizrachi movement developed a strong anticlerical streak, emphasizing the role of the laity in Jewish religion and keeping rabbinical intervention in party and other political affairs to a minimum. Over the course of time, the party came to be dominated by a social democratic faction and outlook, which brought it into easy alliance with Mapai, the dominant party in the labor camp. This alliance persisted for 50 years, from the formation of the communal auton- omy of the Jewish *yishuv* in 1928 until 1977, and was considered the bedrock of Israeli politics, enabling Labor-NRP coalitions to unite majorities of two of the three camps so as to form governments.

After the Six-Day War in 1967, a Young Guard faction developed within the NRP that challenged virtually all of the premises upon which that coalition had been built, sometimes by taking the opposite position from the dominant fac- tion and sometimes by carrying party premises to an extreme. Thus, for example, the religious Zionist synthesis upon which the Mizrachi movement was founded, was transformed among the Young Guard into a linkage between religion and nationalism, which expressed itself in the effort to retain the entire land of Israel west of the Jordan—this while the other party factions followed the Labor government's policy of being open to a territorial compromise. So, too, was the Young Guard willing to turn to the chief rabbinate (an NRP-linked institution, as we have noted) and involve them in party affairs in opposition to the party's traditional anticlerical position.

By 1977, the Young Guard had become the dominant faction in the NRP and was able to lead it into coalition with the Likud, breaking the 50 year link- age with Labor for one with which it was more comfortable and that offered the religious community more tangible rewards—which not incidentally also strength- ened the Young Guard's position within its party.

In the 1977 elections, the NRP emerged with 12 seats, a gain of two seats over the 1973 elections, which, in the context of the narrowly balanced Israeli political scene, encouraged the new leadership of the party greatly. Indeed, a kind of triumphalism became manifest in their ranks and was clearly visible in their election campaign. In the aftermath of the election, as the new Likud government seemed to be floundering and unable to find a proper cadre of leaders to assume the government positions now under its control, the new young leadership of the NRP began to reassess the appropriate role of their party in Israeli politics.

Until then, the NRP was only concerned with maintaining its position as a balance wheel in coalition politics so that it could protect the interests of that part of the religious community identified with it within Israel. It had no aspira- tions to seek power beyond that. Suddenly the opportunity seemed to present itself for the NRP to step forward to begin building toward the possibility of offering itself as a contender for the leading role in a governing coalition. Its young leadership was attractive and saw itself as at least as competent as those holding the key positions in the Begin government. Public support for the NRP was at an all time high and seemed to be growing, and much of the new support garnered by the party seemed to be coming from people who were not otherwise identified with the religious camp but who were concerned about the problem of the Jewishness of the Jewish state and saw in the strengthening of religious education and religious Zionism a means for coping with that problem, especially in connection with the younger generation.

The first step taken by the Young Guard was to try to bring the NRP to take policy positions outside of narrowly religious interests. At the same time, Zevulun Hammer, the leader of the Young Guard who became minister of education in 1977, was building a highly successful record in his ministry as the best incumbent in more than a decade. Interested as he was in promoting more Jewish content in the Israeli school curriculum, he was equally open to promoting a variety of Jewish expressions within the schools. His success was particularly notable in view of the hysterical expressions of the Labor party when he received the education portfolio that he would turn the entire school system into an instrument of religious Orthodoxy.

About mid-term during the first Begin government, sentiment began to grow within the NRP to open up the party to religiously traditional but non-Orthodox elements and to move it in the direction of the European Christian Democratic parties—in other words, to make it a broader based party that would be able to gain the requisite number of seats to compete for control of the government. This expression began very tentatively because it posed very real problems for the NRP, given the character of establishment religion in Israel and the character of the NRP as its principal voice. Certainly Yosef Burg, as the head of the other major faction in the party, did not see such an opening as viable, assessing the constraints of Orthodoxy to be such that the non-Orthodox, no matter how traditional, would simply not be able to find a serious place within the party ranks without alienating the Orthodox faithful. Nevertheless, the NRP did entertain a delegation from the Christian Democratic Union (the "international" of the European Christian Democratic parties) and made plans to send a delegation to visit those parties in Europe in return.[7]

In the meantime, however, other stresses and strains emerged within the party that prevented any serious movement in the direction of broadening the party's base. Quite to the contrary, the NRP found itself in a struggle to survive the hardline religious nationalists associated with Gush Emunim, who dug in their heels and made great demands upon the party leadership. One serious stress point was between hardliners with regard to retaining Judea, Samaria, Gaza, and the Sinai versus those who were prepared to make territorial compromises. While the leadership of the Young Guard was initially numbered among the hardliners, as they assumed governmental responsibility, they also moderated their position, supporting Begin and the government with regard to the peace treaty with Egypt and somewhat backing off from the more extreme positions of Gush Emunim. As a result, they were challenged by the hardliners who suggested that they might break off to join Tehiya, the new party of the Land of Israel Movement.

In an effort to keep their right wing intact, the party leadership threw the dovish wing to the winds, purging the party list of the principal doves for the

1981 elections. As it turned out, they did not succeed in proving their bonafides to many of those traditional NRP voters who accepted the hardline position and who shifted to Tehiya in any case. They also lost support among moderates.

If that were not enough, the scandal surrounding NRP Minister of Religions Aharon Abuhatzeira brought an open split in its wake. Abuhatzeira, accused of misuse of funds as minister of religions, was tried and found innocent. He charged that the other NRP factions had instigated the whole business and, with the backing of Nessim Gaon, the multimillionaire president of the World Sephardi Federation who resides in Geneva, broke away from the NRP to establish his own party, TAMI (*T'nua Masoratit Yisraelit*—the movement for a traditional Israel), which was essentially a communal list designed to appeal to North African Jews (Abuhatzeira comes from a noted North African rabbinical family).

Abuhatzeira had presided over the one faction in the NRP which had included significant numbers of Sephardic Jews in positions of importance, led, of course, by Abuhatzeira himself. The party's other two factions, Lamifneh headed by Burg and the Young Guard headed by Hammer and Yehuda Ben-Meir, were notably laggard in that respect. At the same time, it was authoritatively reported that 70 percent of the party cardholders were Sephardim who were increasingly smarting under the lack of representation in the party councils and on the party list. The NRP's concessions to the hardliners—in the eyes of the Sephardim, simply another Ashkenazi faction—and the breakaway of Abuhatzeira further alienated them. Many joined the defectors in the voting booth on election day.

Finally, the closeness of the race between Likud and Labor led many of the MAFDAL voters who wanted Begin to retain power to vote directly for him through the Likud. All these factors together led to an NRP debacle. The party's representation dropped from 12 to six seats. While the whole party was stunned, the Young Guard leadership was stunned most of all. Israelis were treated to the spectacle of once supremely confident Zevulun Hammer hardly able to express himself on television as the voting results came in. His shock continued for months after the election.

Dreams of an expanded NRP competing for a leading position in the government evaporated as the party leadership turned to evaluate how to keep their party alive. The only bright spot for them was that the near tie between Likud and Labor left them in at least as strong if not a stronger position as a balance wheel in the coalition negotiations, so that they were able to retain the positions gained in the 1977 election and even add to them.

In the meantime, the Sephardim in the party have begun to organize a forum through which to express their demands more forcefully in light of the party's weakness and greater dependence upon them. This forum is still in its early stages of development, but, given the tendency in Israeli politics as a whole for Sephardim who have reached second echelon leadership positions to begin to demand their rightful places at the top, it certainly should be a factor in determining the direction of the party over the next several years.

THE "NEW" AGUDAT ISRAEL

If the NRP passed through the first four years of the Begin government and the second Begin electoral victory by turning success into failure, Agudat Israel has had a very different experience. The history of its emergence as a force on the Israeli political scene during the past five years is a classic illustration of some of the vagaries and contraditions of Israeli politics.

Agudat Israel was founded in Europe in 1912 to unite non- and anti-Zionist Orthodox elements in the struggle against the Zionist effort to "conquer the communities"—that is to say, to become the dominant force in the diaspora. Except for a common religious orthodoxy, its ideology and character were the reverse of the NRP. Ideologically opposed to Zionism and any expression of Judaism through the vehicles of modern nationalism, from the first the movement relied upon recognized rabbinical leaders to give it guidance. The supreme decision-making body of Agudat Israel then as now was the Council of Torah Sages, great rabbinic authorities of the age who identified themselves with the movement and indeed took over its leadership. The political leaders in Agudat Israel were definitely considered to be subordinate figures, indeed somewhat tainted by being sent out into the world to engage in the rough and tumble of politics in contradistinction to the Torah Sages who concentrated on matters of transcendent importance. This understanding of the relationship between the political and spiritual remains as strong today within Agudat Israel as it ever was.

Agudat Israel soon became a worldwide movement and, in the first of many paradoxes that mark its history, developed a great center of strength in Eretz Israel after World War I when it became the vehicle through which the Ashkenazic members of the old *yishuv* (those who settled in Israel either before or outside of the framework of the Zionist movement) struggled to preserve their own way of life and to resist Zionist pressures. By the mid-1920s, Agudat Israel had become the dominant party of the Ashkenazic old *yishuv*. As such, it refused to enter any coalitions with the Zionist parties and looked upon the NRP as a traitor to the Jewish way of life because of its Zionism.

Nevertheless, because it had a substantial presence in Eretz Israel, it did have political interests. So its leaders were dragged into the political game despite themselves, and certainly in the face of their movement's ideology. After the Holocaust, Eretz Israel was left as the principal center of Agudat Israel, making it even more important in the movement. Thus, despite its formal anti-Zionism, Agudat Israel participated in the declaration of Israel's independence and in the wall-to-wall coalition government established at that time.

Subsequently, however, it abandoned active participation in the governing coalition and merely negotiated a modus vivendi with Mapai and its successors, which gave it control over its own school system (known as the *Hinuch Atzmai*, or the independent schools), exemptions from military service for students in yeshivot, exemption from the authority of the chief rabbinate, along with the right to establish its own rabbinical courts and other similar devices designed to give it the status of an independent community within the framework of the state. While some state funding was involved in these efforts, for the most part the state and Agudat Israel reached an agreement to allow the latter to go its own way more than to provide extensive state subsidization for its institutions. The movement, now a political party in Israel, settled into a rather stable routine of winning four seats in the Knesset time after time and functioning in a kind of limbo, neither Zionist nor anti-Zionist.

After 1967, the differences between Agudat Israel and the NRP became pronounced in yet another way, with AI generally taking a much more moderate and compromising position with regard to the future of the administered territories and not at all supporting Gush Emunim. Thus, it was an even greater irony when after the 1977 elections, Agudat Israel suddenly agreed to become a mainstay of the Likud's governing coalition—of course with the approval of the Council of Torah Sages without whose consent the party leaders would never have ventured to change their longstanding position. Agudat Israel agreed to support the Begin government, although it would not take seats in the cabinet. In return, it transformed its relationship with the state institutions into a far more positive one, particularly in the matter of funding. That, indeed, was the price of Agudat Israel's participation. The party demanded major support for Agudat Israel institutions, coupled with certain government concessions with regard to the maintenance of Jewish religious principles in the state as a whole.

Agudat Israel was willing to enter into this arrangement because it had reached the point where it felt that it needed state support in order to accommodate the growing population of the ultra-Orthodox community. Members of that community tend to have larger families and to have at least some members of those families engaged in full-time study as adults instead of entering the labor market. Thus, they need extra sources of support. The Likud was willing to pay the price—to provide financial support and to support legislation that would come closer to the AI position with regard to abortions, public observance of the Sabbath, easier exemption of presumably religious girls from military service, and various other state regulated activities where halachic norms had not been enforced sufficiently according to ultra-Orthodox expectations.

Thus Agudat Israel suddenly became visible on the Israeli political scene. Perhaps more surprising, it was perceived by most Israelis in a more positive than negative way. First of all, except for hardline secularists, much of the population simply appreciated the skill of their leaders in negotiating a good deal for their constituency. Second, in the wake of the crisis of Israeli morale after the 1973 war and a turn towards a more sympathetic appreciation for believing Jews, even on the part of doubters and many nonbelievers, AI was received with greater sympathy than it would have been at any time in the past. If relatively few Israelis wished to live the ultra-Orthodox way, many did not at all object to having such a presence in their midst.

The one point of continued disagreement between AI and the overwhelming majority of Israelis was in connection with army service for women and yeshiva students. AI insisted on exemptions and indeed has consistently tried to broaden the base for such exemptions, while the rest of the Israeli public, very much including the NRP, is strongly opposed to such exemptions and views them as either parasitic or traitorous.

The statesmanlike qualities displayed by the Agudat Israel leadership during the first four years of the Begin era stood them in good stead in the 1981 elections. While they did not win any additional seats—their constituency is fairly well fixed—the closeness of the result put them in an even more strategic position in the coalition bargaining. Once again, they displayed both skill and statesmanship, making clear-cut demands for more support, and presenting other demands for changes in state laws, such as the definition of who is a Jew under the Law of Return, from which they were willing to retreat for a price. In all, they displayed great skill in knowing when to retreat and when to accept compromises. Leadership of the Agudat Israel Knesset faction passed into the hands of a new figure on the political scene, industrialist Avraham Shapiro, a long-time member of Agudat Israel who had built a major industrial base in Israel giving employment to many people in development towns and providing a ready source of funds for AI institutions, a man who had acquired a strong reputation for good humor, good sense, and fair play.

While some of Agudat Israel's demands continued to be repellent to the vast majority of Israelis, particularly when it came to more exemptions from military service for those in the yeshivot and a greater effort to prevent women from serving in the defense forces, whether religious or not, by and large on the Israeli scene Agudat Israel has managed to raise its image considerably and at the same time gather support for what is clearly a long-term strategy of growth. It is not unreasonable to assume that the AI leadership is looking well into the future when the growth of their population will make them an even more formidable force on the Israeli scene. Hence, they are willing to sacrifice symbolic issues of an immediate character for institutional support that will enable them to foster large families, many yeshiva students, and the like. This is a price the Begin government not only must pay but is willing to pay, at least relative to the other demands.

In the meantime, the Council of Torah Sages, which once was an extraordinarily secretive body, has allowed itself to become much more visible. Its members now give interviews to the press, allow some coverage of their meetings, and even make public pronouncements on policy issues. With regard to the territories and foreign affairs, the council remains essentially dovish. For example, in December 1981 it came out in opposition to the extension of Israeli law and jurisdiction over the Golan Heights. Yet the party remains faithful to the Begin coalition, and indeed its four seats keep the present government in power.

In the aftermath of the formation of the second Begin government, admiration for Agudat Israel diminished somewhat as its price for joining the coalition became known and as it was pulled into the conflict surrounding the archaeological excavation of the City of David adjacent to the Temple Mount in Jerusalem. The issue of exempting yeshiva students from the Israel Defense Forces (IDF) continues to rankle the overwhelming majority of Israelis, including those associated with the "national religious" movement persuasion (e.g., Mafdal). Agudat Israel's attempt to widen the list of exempted people only exacerbated that feeling. A clear interference on the part of Agudat Israel with IDF efforts to conscript women, whether religiously observant or not, also added to public dissatisfaction. Finally, while Agudat Israel was not originally involved in the opposition of the religious zealots to the archaeological excavations at the City of David site, as it and the Moetzet Gedolei HaTorah were pulled in the fray, AI's image was further tarnished.

With the possible exception of the latter issue, none of these represented a departure from the traditional stance of the AI. In the latter case, what was originally started by a small group of extremists (to the right of AI), who managed to drag Ashkenazic Chief Rabbi Shlomo Goren into the middle of it, brought an involvement that the Agudat Israel political leadership actually sought to avoid. Thus, inevitably, the feelings of the Israeli public toward Agudat Israel remain distinctly mixed, even if more positive than in the past.

Parallel to Agudat Israel is the miniscule party of Poalei Agudat Israel, based essentially on the rural settlements established by Agudat Israel members. Depending on the election, PAI either joins in an alignment with AI or tries to go it alone. This time they tried to go it alone and failed to win even one seat, a reflection of their decline within the context of an increasingly urbanized environment in which they did not have the tools to attract a constituency.

TAMI: SEPHARDIC OR TRADITIONALIST?

The breakaway of the Abuhatzeira faction from the NRP and its reconstitution as a separate party, TAMI, represents in one sense the addition of another party to the religious camp. More important, it is a sign that the religious camp, which more than any other had retained its integrity in Israel's postideological years, was also capable of being frayed at its edges. TAMI, which from the first was a party dominated by Jews of North African origin, drew in non-Orthodox as well as Orthodox members in its effort to build a broad base, the first party growing out of the religious camp to do so.

Whatever the problematics of its birth, emerging as it did out of the Abuhatzeira trial and the special character of its constituency, emphasizing as it does communal divisions within the state, the formal premise behind TAMI—namely, that there is a large body of Jews in Israel who want a state that maintains Jewish tradition and a public that is committed to the maintenance of that tradition—was a stroke of genius. Since Sephardic Jews are at the forefront of this particular tendency, it only shows how TAMI's leaders have their fingers on the pulse of their constituency. TAMI's own somewhat perverse origins may prevent it from fulfilling the potential inherent in that idea, although that is by no means certain. It made a good beginning by gaining three seats, all at the expense of the NRP, and does have apparently unlimited funding from Geneva-based Nessim Gaon, president of the World Sephardi Federation, who has entered into an alliance with Abuhatzeira and TAMI to build an Israeli base.

TAMI's vote came almost exclusively from Jews of North African background. Hence, it is being touted as the first "ethnic" party to succeed on the Israeli scene since the early 1950s. This charge is, of course, made by Ashkenazim who do not see groups like the Citizens Rights Movement, which appeals well-nigh exclusively to Ashkenazim, or the Independent Liberals whose voters are almost all from central Europe (and which has been declining as that population dies out) in the same light. Like those parties, TAMI did not present itself as being exclusively for one group on the Israeli scene but rather as the champion of some central idea, one which, as we have noted, has great drawing power, drawing as it does on the popular religion so widespread in the country, particularly among Sephardim who are comfortable giving it expression through Orthodox forms rather than seeking other frameworks such as Conservatism or Reform, which demand reinterpretation or formal alteration of halachic requirements.

Setting aside the narrow aspects of its appeal to Jews of North African origin, TAMI in essence appeals to the population the NRP would have had to mobilize in order to become a broad-based party. However, the NRP is dominated by the Ashkenazic Orthodox establishment and consequently is unable to make the compromises with pure Orthodox behavior required to reach out to that population, which TAMI obviously can. Whether this appeal to popular religion can sustain even a small political party is as yet unclear. TAMI's combination of that appeal plus jobs for the faithful reminds the observer more of a machine style party serving immigrant outsiders than of a major contender in the political process, and there is every likelihood that TAMI will turn out to be just that. In the meantime, the price of its participation in the coalition government that Begin formed after the 1981 elections has been strictly jobs and funds with which to support and reward its adherents.

THE LIKUD: AN EXPRESSION OF THE NEW CIVIL RELIGION

It would be easy to gather from all this that the Begin coalition is merely based upon a division of spoils among special interests. It is clearly more than that, however, not only with regard to the prime minister's sense of mission to preserve the Israeli hold on all of Eretz Israel occupied in 1967 but also in terms of fostering a kind of Jewishness in the Jewish state, which is quite different from the secular socialist Zionism of the labor camp. In this respect, Begin has become the embodiment of the official expression of Israel's civil religion and the transformation of that civil religion into one that draws heavily upon Jewish religious expression in its traditional form.

Following the approach developed by his mentor, Zeev (Vladimir) Jabotinsky, Begin has actively cultivated the synthesis between nationalist politics and Jewish religion to develop a civil religion that draws heavily from traditional Judaism. In this he is ahead of his party activists (except for the Sephardim) and certainly far ahead of the Liberal party partners in the Likud who were traditionally secularists. But he is very close to his constituency and has found a common language with his closest potential coalition partners. No doubt part of the reason that voters who previously supported MAFDAL were able to vote for Likud in 1981 was because they felt that Begin has a properly positive attitude toward religion and religious tradition.

There is no doubt that Begin's constituency was drawn heavily from among those who are deeply rooted in the popular religion, the Sephardic *shomrei masoret* (observers of the tradition) and their Ashkenazic counterparts. Outsiders have raised the question of how Begin—in so many respects the quintessential Polish Jew—manages to appeal to the Sephardim. I would suggest that part of the answer lies precisely in this sharing of a common popular religion to which he gives expression in both his official and private capacities. For them, he is an authentic Jew, even if one whose customs are different from theirs, unlike the Labor party leadership who impress them as being not very "Jewish" at all, since they seem to have no links with Jewish religious tradition. If Begin is able to implant his approach within the Likud, it will undoubtedly strengthen its hold on a majority of the voters in Israel and secure its emerging role as the dominant party in the country. In this respect, the religious dimension affects politics beyond the limits of the religious parties.

RELIGION AND PARTY: THE PRESENT ALIGNMENT

To recapitulate, four of the five forms of religious expression discussed at the beginning of this chapter are represented in the political process by political parties, as indicated in Table 5.1. Establishment religion has the MAFDAL; popular religion, TAMI; ultra-Orthodox religion, Agudat Israel; and civil religion, the Likud, at least under Begin's leadership. Only nonestablishment Judaism remains unrepresented in the political sphere, in great part because of its character as an expression of Western, particularly American, ideas about the relationship between religion and state and the need to maintain separation between them. Those views are reinforced by their own interests in Israel, which would require a separation between establishment religion and politics in order for nonestablishment Judaism to gain the full recognition that it seeks.

On the other hand, there is a growing minority among the nonestablishment leadership that has come to understand that the situation in Israel is inevitably

TABLE 5.1
Religious Expression and Party Alignment

Religious Expression	Political Party
Establishment religion	MAFDAL (National Religious Party)
Popular religion	TAMI
Civil religion	Likud
Ultra-Orthodox religion	Agudat Israel
Nonestablishment religion	(Citizens Rights Movement)

different from that in the United States and that for nonestablishment religion to get its share of the pie, it must have some representation in the political arena. This minority has worked in two directions. Some have tried to form an alliance with the Labor Alignment to get Labor to endorse the full recognition of the movements of nonestablishment Judaism. At one point in the 1981 campaign, this group seemed to be gaining a measure of success. When the Labor Alignment thought that it was really going to win an absolute majority of seats in the Knesset, they were willing to endorse such a stance following intensive lobbying by leaders of Reform Judaism in Israel. This was at the period when Labor was actively alienating its former coalition partners from the religious camp. However, once it became apparent that Labor would not win that majority and, indeed, was in a struggle for its very political life, its leaders tried to back away from that position—unsuccessfully as it turned out since they had become identified in the minds of Orthodox and non-Orthodox alike as essentially committed to secularism (see below).

The other element that has sought to link nonestablishment Judaism with Israeli politics consists of people who have become actively involved in the parties of the sabra reform movement, including the short-lived Democratic Movement (CRM). The CRM, indeed, has offered them a certain hospitality, perhaps because of Aloni's intense hostility towards Orthodoxy. It would be premature to suggest that the CRM has become the political expression of nonestablishment Judaism. But it, more than any other party on the scene, has the potential for being that if its leaders overcome their strong hostility towards religion in general and if the movements of nonestablishment Judaism overcome their great reluctance to accept the linkages between religion and politics, which are part and parcel of the Israeli scene.

LABOR IN LEFT FIELD

What of the Labor Alignment in all of this? What the foregoing analysis suggests is that they are left out, and as their behavior over the past two years has suggested, they have even sought to be left out. Whether as a result of a nostalgia for the great days of socialist Zionism before the establishment of the state, or because they draw so heavily from the 25 percent of the population that considers itself secular, the parties of the Labor Alignment have become secular parties with minimal ties to any of the five forms of religious expression abroad in the land. Even their approach to civil religion has not made the leap from the old attempt to infuse secular content into traditional forms to the new condition of linking traditional content with civil norms, and they have little connection with the popular religion of the person in the street. Given the fact that religious expression through one or another of these forms is prevalent among the Israeli population, this is another way in which Labor is rendering itself increasingly irrelevant to the contemporary Israeli scene and less likely to be a compelling force in Israeli politics.

There are voices in Labor who realize this, who castigated their party for breaking off their links with the religious camp. But even these voices essentially rely upon their instinctive perception of the need to align with the majorities of at least two of the three camps in order to form a government. They do not seem to perceive the new role of Judaism among the Israeli Jewish public who are searching for ways to manifest the Jewish authenticity of their state.

Despite the expectations of some Zionists that the reestablishment of the Jewish commonwealth would lead to a kind of normalcy for the Jewish people in which they would be no different than the French or Italians, in the sense of taking their nationality and homeland for granted, Jews remain more like the Americans and people from other new societies who must be moved by a shared vision in order to feel comfortable in their national identity. For Jews, it seems that this vision must come from Judaism and, indeed, must have a religious component since every effort to secularize Judaism to date has failed to move more than small groups of Jews. Given all of this, Labor's detachment from any form of viable expression of Judaism within the Jewish state is a tremendous disadvantage to it in Israeli politics.

CONCLUSION

What, then, has continued in the relationship between religion, parties, and politics in the Begin era and what has changed? The major point of continuity has been the continuing division of the political parties in Israel into three camps and the necessity for the governing coalition to embrace majorities in at least two of the three. Indeed, the Likud government for all intents and purposes embraces two camps in their totality.

On the other hand, there is a clear weakening of the camps qua camps. This weakening was first apparent in the labor and civil camps but with the emergence of TAMI is even becoming apparent in the religious camp. In politics, the camps are less hermetically sealed from one another than ever before and are more likely to overlap at the fringes and to attract at least a small segment of the electorate that will swing from camp to camp, something that did not occur before 1969 and occurred for the first time with regard to the religious camp in 1981.

The obverse of this is the spread of elements of religious expression into the civil camp. If the religious camp is no longer hermetically sealed, and it was perhaps the most hermetically sealed in the past, the civil camp is increasingly committing itself to express some combination of civil and popular religion. It is in this development that such new trends as may be in the offing are becoming manifested in Israeli politics. It bears watching closely because, rather than following the "modernization" model that many U.S. political scientists have posited with regard to the future of Israeli politics, namely, that as Israel's population becomes "modernized," Israeli politics will move towards the U.S. model of separation of church and state or at least greater secularization, there is every sign that we are witnessing the opposite. As Israel becomes further removed from its founding generation, its Jewish majority is even more concerned about the state's Jewish authenticity and is looking for ways to link the state to appropriate forms of Jewish religious expression that will reaffirm and strengthen that authenticity.

At the time of the Second Jewish Commonwealth, over 2,000 years ago, the Jewish people were also divided into three camps: Sadducees, Pharisees, and Essenes. The former were the party of Jewish statehood in the sense that their Jewishness was principally expressed through the political institutions of the state and those religious institutions, such as the Temple and its priesthood, that were bound up with statehood. The Pharisees, on the other hand, emphasized individual internalization of Jewish norms and a system of religious behavior designed to give those norms expression independently of the formal institutions of statehood. For them, the state was an important convenience but not the central focus of Judaism. The Essenes sought their salvation in the religious life of the commune. It seems that, for Jews, normalization is the restoration of these three camps as modes of Jewish expression. Pharisaic Judaism, solely dominant for 1,800 years or more, is continued through the Orthodox minority in Israel. The so-called secular Zionists are neo-Sadducees, while the kibbutzim have revived the Essene vision in semisecular form.

The growth in the number of Jews who are "traditional"—that is to say, who mix secular and religious norms, is bringing the neo-Sadducean camp more into line with its earlier counterpart. The civil religion that is emerging in Israel is essentially Sadducean in character. That is to say, the religious forms are designed to bolster ties with the state and its institutions rather than treating the state and its institutions as handmaidens of the Jewish religious vision. That, indeed, is what separates the civil religion from the religious camp when push comes to shove. But, since the religious camp itself places a high value on the state and its institutions as instruments to achieve the religious vision, in practice the difference often becomes irrelevant. Menachem Begin is the fullest expression to date of neo-Sadduceanism handled in such a way as to be a bridging rather than a divisive force. The Labor leadership are also neo-Sadduccees, but their expression of that tendency emphasizes its divisive side. It is that perception that enables Begin's version of the civil religion to be as bridging as it has proved to be to date.

NOTES

1. For an up-to-date review of the situation in the contemporary Middle East see Michael Curtis, ed., *Religion and Politics in the Middle East* (Boulder, Colo: Westview Press, 1981).

2. Two general overviews of the relationship between religion and state in Israel, from diametrically opposed perspectives, are S.Z. Abramov, *Perpetual Dilemma* (New York: Associated University Presses, 1976) and Zvi Yaron, "Religion in Israel," *American Jewish Year Book* (New York: American Jewish Committee and Philadelphia: Jewish Publication Society of America, 1975), pp. 174–223.

3. The definitive study of Israel's civil religion to date is that of Charles S. Liebman and Eliezer Don-Yehiya, *The Civil Religion of Israel: Tradition, Judaism and Political Culture in the Jewish State* (forthcoming). The two have published the following articles drawn from their forthcoming book: "Symbol System of Zionist Socialism: An Aspect of Israeli Civil Religion," *Modern Judaism* 1 (September 1981): 121–48 and "Zionist Ultranationalism and Its Attitude Toward Religion," *Journal of Church and State* 23 (Spring 1981): 259–64.

4. See Daniel J. Elazar, "The New Sadduccees," *Midstream* 24 (August/ September 1978): 20–25.

5. Eliezer Don-Yehiya, "Secularization, Negation and Integration: Concept of Traditional Judaism in Zionist Socialism," (in Hebrew) *Kivunim* 8 (Summer 1980): 29–46.

6. For further discussion of the three camps, see Daniel J. Elazar, "Toward a Renewed Zionist Vision," *Forum* 26 (1977): 52–69.

7. See Shmuel Sandler, "The National Religious Party: Israel's Third Party," *Jerusalem Letter* No. 24 (October 28, 1979).

6 Israel's Arab Minority in the Begin Era

Ian Lustick

INTRODUCTION

Ever since Israel's establishment in 1948 Jewish attitudes toward Arab citizens of the state have been strongly colored by the chronic state of siege within which Israel has struggled to survive. In view of the natural affinities between Israel's Arab minority of approximately 14 percent and the hostile Arab populations on Israel's borders, and with no clear role for non-Jews in the upbuilding of the Jewish homeland, it would be strange if Israeli Arabs were not feared and distrusted by the Jewish majority and the Israeli government. Indeed they have been. Yet in striking contrast to the political strain caused by discontented ethnic and national minorities in other countries, the demands of Israel's Arab citizens have only intermittently disturbed Israel's domestic tranquility and have never constituted an issue of sustained central concern to the government or the Jewish public. Nor have Israeli Arabs acted as a fifth column in time of war. But in certain important respects the pressures emanating from this growing and strongly dissatisfied proportion of Israel's population have intensified in recent years, partly due to the policies of the Likud government. It would appear that the Arab minority problem will loom increasingly large in coming years in ways that may not only disturb Israel's domestic tranquility but also complicate the peace process.

POLICIES TOWARD ARABS IN ISRAEL: 1948-77

An Arab population of 160,000 remained within Israel's borders following the 1948 war. These were the Palestinian Arabs who, through accident, fortune, or tenacity, did not become refugees.[1] Arabs in Israel were concentrated in western and central Galilee, in a strip of land, known as the "little triangle," border-

121

ing the Jordanian controlled West Bank, in the Negev desert, and in small neighborhoods within the large cities. Except for the Negev, these were among the areas slated to have become part of a Palestinian Arab state under the terms of the United Nations partition plan.

From 1948 to 1966, 85 percent of Israeli Arabs lived within the jurisdiction of a military government (*memshal tzvai*). The original purpose of military rule in the Arab areas was to establish order and regularized contact with Arab civilians in the midst of the fighting. In 1949 the war ended, but the military government remained in place for another 17 years. In addition to providing security in frontier areas threatened by armed infiltrators, it proved to be a convenient instrument for transforming "occupied territories," which were almost totally devoid of a Jewish presence, into integral parts of Israel. At very little cost to the society as a whole, the military government was not only able to prevent the severe discontent of Israel's Arab citizens from affecting the allocation of scarce resources, but was also able to facilitate the use of Arab economic resources (housing, land, and labor) for the satisfaction of Jewish needs. However, mainly as a result of political abuses by successive Labor party governments, the system was reformed and eventually abolished in December 1966.[2]

The disappearance of the military government did not entail a substantial change in the relationship of the Arab minority to Jewish-Israeli society. Responsibility for supervision of the Arab sector had, at any rate, gradually shifted to Jewish specialists in Arab affairs (Arabists) appointed as directors of the Arab departments of government ministries, the Labor party, and the Histadrut (the Israeli federation of trade unions). Drawn heavily from the security services, these individuals were the highest officials of the state to which Arab citizens could gain access. Overall responsibility for maintaining the political quiescence of the Arab minority, including coordination of the activities of the various Arab departments with those of the security services, has been the assignment of the office of the adviser to the prime minister on Arab affairs.

From 1966 to 1977 the Arab affairs adviser was Shmuel Toledano. Toledano's entire career, until his appointment to this post, had been spent in the security services. His long tenure in office, under five different Labor governments, reflected his success in maintaining the low salience of the Arab minority problem for the Israeli political system, and the essentially peripheral nature of the tasks he was delegated to perform—peripheral from the point of view of successive prime ministers and their cabinets. Also contributing to the low profile of the problem during Toledano's reign as "king of the Arabs" was the occupation of the West Bank and the Gaza Strip. Following June 1967 what attention the political leadership focused on internal Arab affairs was devoted to the bureaucratically very separate problem of controlling the more than one million Palestinian Arabs in those territories.[3]

But pressures within the Israeli Arab community were building, and by the mid-1970s many Arabists were warning of impending disturbances if more systematic attention and more substantial resources were not devoted to the control of the Arab population in Israel itself. These pressures were generated by three basic trends. Modernization and erosion in the position of traditional patriarchs, sheiks, and notables accompanied the emergence of large numbers of educated young Arabs whose behavior was less readily monitored and influenced by co-opted traditional elites than had been the case in the 1950s and 1960s. The development of stronger and more inclusive "Arab" and "Palestinian" identities made it increasingly difficult for the authorities to use religious, kinship, and other parochial loyalties to keep the Israeli Arab population divided. Finally, the crystallization of more effective frameworks for the expression of discontent—most importantly the growing significance of Rakah (the Israeli Communist party)—gave educated and aware young Arabs increasing opportunities to express their anger and their new identities while providing alternatives to regime sponsored frameworks for the acquisition of status and a sense of political efficacy.[4]

However, cabinet-level decision makers proved unresponsive to the Arabists' warnings. In March 1976 Rakah organized a countrywide general strike among Israeli Arabs to protest land expropriation in the Galilee. The absence of 20-25 percent of Arab workers from their jobs at Jewish farms, factories, and construction sites represented the most successful act of organized dissent in the Arab sector since 1948. Last minute efforts by the adviser's office to avert the strike were fruitless and embarrassing to the government. The dispatch of unprepared troops to many Arab villages and the declaration of rigid curfews sparked clashes during which six Arabs in the Galilee and the little triangle were killed, 70 injured, and 300 arrested.

"Land Day" and the violence in Arab villages made the discontent of Israeli Arabs front page news in the international press (including the *New York Times*) for the first time since the creation of the state. The events of March 30, 1976 triggered the first cabinet discussions of the Arab minority problem since the 1966 decision to abolish the military government. The debate over policy toward Israeli Arabs that ensued is important for an understanding of the options available to the Likud government, upon taking power in April 1977, and the choices in this sphere that were (and are) being made.

In the year preceding his resignation as Arab affairs advisor in February 1977, Toledano came under fire for being too tolerant of Arab dissent and too anxious to achieve quiescence by pushing for changes in public policies and attitudes that affected the minority. Among the most important of his critics were Amnon Lin, former director of the Labor party's Arab department, now a Likud member of Knesset, and Israel Koenig, the Interior Ministry's district commissioner for the Galilee. Lin had long been known for his opposition to Toledano's policy of encouraging Arabs to maintain a low political profile while minimizing the use of strong-arm methods. Lin's position has been that all Israeli Arabs should, like the Druze, be called upon to demonstrate their loyalty by service to the state and by offering positive, active proof of their identification with Israel and its Jewish-Zionist vocation. For those Arabs unwilling to adopt this posture Lin has favored tough measures and more overtly discriminatory policies. A detailed discussion of how and why such a "strong-arm" approach should be implemented was contained in a confidential memorandum submitted to the cabinet by Israel Koenig (published in full by a left-wing Zionist newspaper in September 1976) several months after Land Day. Koenig's proposals included stepped up land expropriations, smear campaigns against Rakah activists, expulsions, blacklisting, administrative detention, and specific techniques for reducing the economic security of the Arab community, and increasing emigration, especially of educated Arabs.

Although agreeing that a more systematic reward and punishment of "positive" and "negative" Arabs was needed, Toledano argued that it was unrealistic to demand a pro-Zionist posture from most Israeli Arabs and that their dependence on the Jewish economy and institutionalized isolation from vital centers of decision making would prevent any threatening deterioration in the control relationship. Despite unrest, all could be well if only more resources were made available for the satisfaction of real employment and development needs in Arab villages and the co-optation of traditional and younger, more educated elites. Toledano was supported in his stance by the Histadrut's Arab department, which published its own report and recommendations in October 1976.

POLICIES OF THE BEGIN GOVERNMENT TOWARD ISRAELI ARABS: 1977-81

Upon assuming power in May 1977, the Begin government gave no firm signals as to its intentions toward Israeli Arabs. Benjamin Gur-Aryeh, Toledano's deputy, was kept on as acting Arab affairs adviser. Begin's only explicit campaign commitment regarding Israeli Arabs, a promise to allow the Biram and Ikrit villagers to return to their homes, was referred to a ministerial committee for further study.[5] In September Moshe Sharon, a professor of Islamic studies at Bar Ilan University who had virtually no prior experience with Israeli Arabs, was named as adviser to the prime minister on Arab affairs. A Herut party stalwart, Sharon had formerly served as a military governor on the West Bank.

During the first eight months of his tenure as Arab affairs adviser, Moshe Sharon concerned himself primarily with reforms in the administration of the Muslim Waqf (charitable endowment), the award of scholarships to Arab university students, the management of the government supported Arabic language newspaper *Al-Anba,* and attempts to settle disputes over land expropriation between Arabs and various public institutions. By the fall of 1978 he submitted recommendations to the prime minister that government efforts toward satisfying the economic and social demands of Arabs be substantially increased, that his advisory post be abolished, and that coordination and implementation of policy toward Israeli Arabs be delegated to a cabinet minister with executive authority, a staff, and resources equal to 1 percent of the national budget. These recommendations reflect an analysis of the Arab problem and the opportunities available to the government for reversing dissident trends in the Arab sector that is very similar to that of Shmuel Toledano and the Histadrut's Arab department. His proposals were not accepted. Early in 1979 he resigned, indicating he was frustrated by the indifference of Prime Minister Begin to the problems of the Arab sector, the powerlessness of his "advisory" position, and the tendency of officials close to the prime minister to consider an "eruption of the Arab minority ... unavoidable ... and an opportunity to throw the Arabs out."[6]

Meanwhile Amnon Lin kept up a drum beat of criticism of government policy toward the Arab minority. In June 1980 he submitted to the cabinet a detailed comprehensive analysis of the Arab problem in the Galilee, prepared by "The Movement for Haifa and the North," a political lobby group founded by Lin, warning of the need for swift action to avoid "radicalization among Arab circles hostile to Israel which could reach the proportions of a civil war."[7] In March 1981, he sharply criticized the government for failing to formulate a clear policy toward Israeli Arabs, for providing insufficient protection to "loyal" Arabs, and for ignoring his organization's proposals.[8]

Following Moshe Sharon's resignation in early 1979, Benjamin Gur-Aryeh was renamed acting Arab affairs adviser. Several months later the word "acting" was removed from his title. Although Lin was again passed over for the post, his approach has been partially mirrored in Gur-Aryeh's tougher line against dissent in the Arab sector, his emphasis on security concerns over economic and social problems, and his inclination to work closely with the army, the police, and the security services in the suppression of demonstrations in Arab villages and the imposition of restrictions on the movement of scores of communists and other radical Arab activists. Described as a man who "eats and breathes security," Gur-Aryeh worked in the security services and the military government before joining the staff of the adviser's office.[9] His public statements reflect greater optimism about the willingness of the majority of the Arab population to "adapt" to their position in a Jewish state and about the government's ability to control Arab dissent cheaply than those of either Toledano and Moshe Sharon, or Amnon Lin.

The low profile of the adviser's office under Gur-Aryeh means that policy toward Israeli Arabs is not formulated in its own right so much as it results from the general disposition of government officials and their efforts to achieve objectives that happen to intersect with the resources and presence of the Arab minority. Thus, in spite of the appearance of "minority affairs" in the list of minor responsibilities assigned to Simcha Ehrlich after his resignation as finance minister, the most authoritative statements and consequential decisions concerning Israeli Arabs have been those made on an ad hoc, decentralized basis in reaction to instances of Arab unrest or in relation to the specific concerns of individual ministers or army commanders. The actions and comments of these men naturally reflect the more nationalistic and explicitly anti-Arab stance of the Begin government, as compared with previous labor governments. Of particular importance, in terms of its impact on the Arab minority's sense of security and its future relations with the Jewish majority, has been the repeated characterization by high ranking officials of Israeli Arabs as alien to the country and possibly subject to mass expulsion. In August 1977, in the first significant public statement by a Begin government minister concerning Israeli Arabs, Minister of Agriculture Arik Sharon characterized Israeli Arabs as "foreigners" whose theft of "national land" by means of squatting and building on disputed plots would soon be halted.[10] In January 1979, Foreign Minister Moshe Dayan reacted to expressions of support for the PLO by a group of radical Arab university students by warning Israeli Arabs that "if they will not be satisfied and if they don't want to live together with us, then they will have to pay for it very dearly." Dayan went on to remind Israel's Arabs of "what happened with the Arab people" in the 1948 war. "They had a chance to live with us in peace, not to have a war. So they find themselves now, some of them, as refugees in Lebanon. And that should serve as a lesson."[11] Speaking to a large group of Knesset deputies in August 1979, General Avigdor Ben-Gal, military commander of Israel's northern region, labeled the Arabs of Galilee a

> cancer in the heart of the State ... (who) identify with the PLO, receive support from it and from the Arab countries and they consider themselves the taskforce of the Arab national forces, and they are waiting in order to "screw" us ....[12]

Following a cabinet decision to ban a Rakah sponsored "Congress of the Arab Masses" in Nazareth in December 1980, Arik Sharon told a Jewish audience that:

> We have no intention of evicting the Arab citizens in Galilee, but I would advise the Arab citizens in the region not to radicalize their positions, in order not to bring on another tragedy like the one which struck the Palestinian people in 1948. Even if we do not want this, it could repeat itself.[13]

Justifying the government's decision to ban the Nazareth congress, Minister of Industry, Trade, and Tourism Gideon Patt declared that:

> Any member of the Arab minority who doesn't like living here can take a taxi and be elsewhere within a half hour, where we shall see how they will permit him to fulfill his national desire. He can cross over the bridge, we will even wave goodbye to him.[14]

These references to mass expulsion, combined with government toleration of right-wing Jewish student violence toward Arab student groups,[15] the repeated use of violence to quell demonstrations in Arab villages, coercive policies toward Negev Bedouin, and regular references by Gur-Aryeh to the possibility of uncontrollable Jewish outbursts against Arabs, suggest that intimidation, more than demand satisfaction or collaborative "anti-subversive activists"[16] (as Lin has proposed), is being used to maintain Arab political quiescence.

ISRAELI ARABS 1977-81

Changes in the experience, attitudes, and behavior of Israeli Arabs during the four years of Likud rule are, of course, not only a function of the policies implemented by the Begin government, but also of regional and international developments, and of longstanding social, economic, and political trends within the Arab community itself. Analysis of these changes may most conveniently be presented by focusing, first, on patterns of social and economic change and the levels of discontent associated with those trends. This will be followed by discussion of changes in the political and cultural identification of Israeli Arabs and, finally, by analysis of changing patterns of political mobilization and participation in the Arab sector.

Social and Economic Trends

The rapid growth of the Arab population of Israel, the transformation of small and medium sized villages into large towns and small cities, the enrollment in and completion of higher levels of education by larger numbers of Arab children, the increasing role of younger, educated men in local affairs, and the wider availability of electricity and medical care in the Arab sector are trends that have continued apace over the last four years. From December 1976 to December 1980 the Arab population of Israel, excluding East Jerusalem, grew 15 percent, from 459,000 to 530,000.[17] As a percentage of Israeli citizens, Arabs increased, during this same four-year period, from 13.2 percent to 14.2 percent. If East Jerusalem Arabs, classified as "permanent residents" following the incorporation of Arab East Jerusalem into Israel in 1967, are included (as they are by government statisticians), Israel's non-Jewish population was 637,000 at the end of 1980, or 16.2 percent of its total population.[18] Aside from 9.2 percent of Israeli Arabs who, in 1979, lived in Tel-Aviv—Jaffa, Haifa, Ramle, Lod, (West) Jerusalem, and Acre, most Israeli Arabs live in more than 135 purely Arab communities. The rapidly increasing size and density of many of these villages are reflected in the fact that whereas, in 1976, 18 of Israel's 82 localities numbering more than 5,000 inhabitants were purely Arab, in 1979, 25 of 92 such communities were Arab. While, in 1976, 92,500 Arabs lived in five purely Arab localities with populations over 10,000, in 1979, 134,000 Arabs lived in eight such municipalities.[19]

By 1979, 34.9 percent of Israeli Arabs had received more than eight years of schooling, up from 26.2 percent in 1975, while, in 1979, 7.8 percent had received at least some post-high school instruction, compared to 4.5 percent in 1975.[20] In the academic year 1979/80, approximately 31 percent of all Arabs in Israel were enrolled in some sort of educational institution, up 18.7 percent from 1975/76.[21] In 1979, 22.5 percent of all Arab household heads had more than eight years of schooling, compared with 14.0 percent in 1976.[22]

By 1979, virtually all sizeable Arab villages were connected to the national power grid, while more than 65 percent of Israeli Arabs had access to medical care in their communities, compared to 41 percent in 1974.[23]

It can be presumed, though reliable data is difficult to come by in this sphere, that associated with movement in these demographic, education, and infrastructural indices there has been continued, though gradual, replacement of traditional patriarchal norms with more universalistic "achievement oriented" expectations and behavior, as well as an equally gradual erosion in the centrality of kinship loyalties and authority relations. That this is the case is indirectly suggested in a number of ways. Increasingly, individual Arabs are inclined to approach government offices on their own, without the services of a traditional "go between" or *wasta.*[24] Reported trends toward nuclear family living arrangements and widespread substitution of the extended family for the larger clan (*hamula*) as locus of economic decision making is partly evidenced by an increase in the proportion of Arab households headed by someone less than 35 years of age, from 38.9 percent in 1976 to 42.6 percent in 1979.[25] Erosion in traditional life styles and norms is also apparent in a noticeable drop in the fertility rates of Arab women, from 6.86 children per woman in 1976 to 5.94 in 1979, in a 65 percent jump in the number of employed Arab women during the same period, and in the small but growing number of Arab women studying in Israeli universities.[26]

On the other hand, the abiding strength of traditional social structures and norms is reflected in the young and stable median age of Arab brides, the still low rate and extremely restricted pattern of participation by Arab women in the general labor force, and the continued dominance of *hamula* organized lists of candidates in local elections. From 1975 to 1978, slightly more than 58 percent of all Arab women marrying for the first time did so before the age of 19. During the same period the proportion of Israeli Jewish women marrying for the first time, who did so below the age of 19, dropped from 29.6 percent to 26.7 percent.[27] Although the number of employed Arab women rose from 11,300 in 1976 to 18,800 in 1979, the proportion of Arab women age 14 and over that were employed was still only 5.7 percent, compared with 42.9 percent of Israeli Jewish women.[28] In local council elections held in 51 Arab cities, towns, and villages in 1978, 82 percent of the lists of candidates competing for seats on the councils were sponsored locally, the overwhelming majority of these by *hamulas.*[29]

Nor has the higher level of educational attainment among Israeli Arabs been reflected in substantial shifts in their occupational distribution toward white collar jobs and higher incomes, or toward greater control of capital resources. In 1977, 4.4 percent of all Arab workers were employed under categories described by the Central Bureau of Statistics as "administrators and managers" and "clerical and related workers." In 1979, 6.5 percent of Arab workers were so employed. Among Jews the proportion was 24.2 percent in 1977 and 23.6 percent in 1979. In 1977, 22.9 percent of Arabs were employed in construction; 21.6 percent were so employed in 1979. Among Jews the corresponding percentages for 1977 and 1979 were 5.7 percent and 5.1 percent.[30] During this same period the average income of an urban Arab family fell from 92.3 percent of the average income of urban families to 78.4 percent.[31] The chronic absence of investment and industry in the Arab sector is reflected in the steadily increasing percentage of Arabs who work outside their localities of residence. In 1979, 52.3 percent of employed Arabs worked away from their towns and villages, compared with 43.7 percent in 1976.[32] In 1976/77 Arab farmers received 2.25 percent of water used for irrigation in Israel, though they cultivated approximately 20 percent of the crop area. In 1978/79 they received 2.5 percent of water used for irrigation.[33]

In general these trends and the basic socioeconomic profile of Israeli Arabs have been unaffected by Likud government policies. Although the Likud government did continue the relatively intensive efforts of the previous Labor government, beginning in 1974, to expand the hook up of Arab villages to the national electricity grid, the increase in medical facilities in Arab villages has largely been a consequence of actions of the Histadrut-sponsored Kupat Holim medical care and insurance organization. The Likud government has accelerated the rate of sedentarization of Bedouin in the Negev and the Galilee, but for the most part the demographic, social, and institutional processes at work are too basic to reflect changes in government policies, especially over such a short time. On the other hand, the Begin government's rejection of the Rabin government's recommendations to increase economic development aid to the Arab sector, as well as the generally depressed state of the Israeli economy as a whole, have done nothing to reverse the economic stagnation of the Arab community. Instead, four more years have been added to the frustration and resentment accumulating within it.

Arab Discontent and Likud Policies

The specific issues over which Arab discontent has been expressed most strongly and most consistently during the last four years have been:

- Problems of land expropriation from the Negev Bedouin.
- Opposition to the government's intensified efforts to "Judaize the Galilee."
- Shortages of housing and classrooms in the Arab sector.
- Low levels of government aid to Arab local councils for the maintenance and development of public services.

Only 20 percent of the Bedouin who had inhabited the Negev desert remained in Israel following the first Arab-Israeli war in 1948. The military government concentrated these 13,000 Bedouin within a reservation of approximately 300,000 acres in the northeastern Negev. Following Ariel Sharon's appointment as agriculture minister in the first Likud government in 1977, armed representatives of the agriculture ministry and the Nature Reserves Authority, known as the "Green Patrol," have engaged in a systematic, determined, and sometimes brutal effort to bring an end to the nomadic life style of the now 35,000–40,000 Negev Bedouin, even within their reservation, and to transfer effective control over the lands used by the Bedouin to the Israel Lands Authority (ILA).[34]

In the fall of 1977 Sharon and his personal and political associate, Avraham Yoffe, head of the Nature Reserves Authority, embarked on a series of sudden demolitions of Bedouin dwellings built without permits and evictions of their inhabitants. These houses were among the 800 Bedouin structures against which demolition orders have been issued. Such actions, which have continued sporadically since 1977, have been accompanied by a campaign in the press to portray the Bedouin as disloyal, as a threat to the desert environment, and as engaged in the theft of "national land." According to Alon Galili, head of the Green Patrol,

> Stretches of land which the Israeli nation bought with blood and money are slipping away from us. They are slipping through our fingers as a result of this Bedouin conquest of the land which is being carried out with deliberate cunning. The Israeli people have so little land. Why shouldn't we protect it?[35]

In November 1977, the Finance Ministry announced the expropriation of 12,000 acres of Bedouin-claimed land. Beginning in early 1978, the "Black Goat Law," passed in 1950 but never applied in practice, was strictly enforced. A large proportion of Bedouin herds consist of the animals whose husbandry the law prohibits. An announcement by the Nature Reserve Authority that 375,000 acres in the northeastern Negev was to be turned into a nature preserve was accompanied by a declaration that within it Bedouin would no longer be allowed to live, graze their flocks, or cultivate land. Leasing of land by Bedouin from the ILA for extensive agriculture became more difficult, and the length of those leases granted was shortened. In July 1978, the Green Patrol ordered Kibbutz Sde Boker to stop supplying nearby Bedouin with their traditional allotment of water. Following the signing of the Camp David accords in September 1978, 6,000 Bedouin were told that they would have to evacuate 20,000 acres at Tel-Malhata, east of Beersheva, since one of the new airbases to replace those to be evacuated in the Sinai would be constructed there. Additional Bedouin lands were expropriated southeast of Beersheva in connection with the expansion of a military training base.[36]

The anger of the Bedouin has been directed not only at the fact of the expropriations, but also at the government's refusal to recognize even the reduced Bedouin claims to land ownership in the Negev, from more than 500,000 acres throughout the whole southern part of the country to 100,000 in the northeastern corner of the Negev. Bitter resentment, especially among Bedouin army veterans (many have volunteered to serve as scouts in the Israeli Defense Forces) and their families has also been caused by the harsh methods employed by the Green Patrol, the low levels of compensation offered by the government for relocation, the derogation of the Bedouin in the eyes of the Israeli public as disloyal and dangerous, and the fear of being turned into wage laborers by sedentarization policies that make no provision for Bedouin husbandry or agriculture.

In 1981 the government did offer substantial compensation for the relocation of the Bedouin evacuated from the airbase site at Tel-Malhata, but the Bedouin resented the absence of funding for the construction of infrastructural facilities in the six new villages established for them. Though difficulties in the evacuation of the Bedouin have developed, the government's campaign to sedentarize all Negev Bedouin continues.

Among Arabs in central and northern Israel the expropriation of land, per se, has not been a major problem during the last four years. Most Arab agricultural land was expropriated in the Galilee and the little triangle in the 1950s and 1960s. The last substantial expropriations in the Galilee were carried out in 1976.[37] Still Arab demands, as in the case of Ikrit and Biram villages, to return to homes and lands from which they have been evicted, for recognition of Arab ownership, for claims of parcels also claimed by the state, for approval of master zoning plans that would permit expansion of and legal construction in Arab localities, and for an end to the threatened demolition of thousands of dwellings built without permits have kept alive the bitterness surrounding the whole issue of land expropriation since 1948. In this context the policy of the Likud government that has disturbed Israeli Arabs most has been its intensified effort to "Judaize the Galilee" (*Yehud HaGalil*).

After years of predictions that high Arab birth rates and a prolonged outmigration of Jews were endangering the existence of a Jewish majority in the Galilee, an Arab majority was admitted to have become a reality in 1978.[38] After the successive failure of attempts by Labor governments to induce Jewish migration to the Galilee from the coastal plain, the Likud government adopted a new tack. Instead of trying to establish full fledged settlements in the area, the Jewish Agency Land Settlement Department, the Agriculture Ministry, the

Israel Lands Administration, and the Jewish National Fund announced plans in 1978 to establish 30 *mitzpim* (observation post settlements) on hills overlooking Arab villages. By December 1980, construction of 28 of the outposts had been completed, with at least four more scheduled for 1981. Inhabited by only small numbers of Jewish settlers, the *mitzpim* nonetheless serve a number of purposes, including the establishment of a Jewish presence in otherwise overwhelmingly Arab areas, the acquisition of parcels of land adjacent to Arab villages for future expansion of Jewish settlement, the more effective assertion of government claims to scattered parcels within adjacent Arab localities, the prevention of illegal building of Arab homes and shops on lands claimed by the authorities, and the creation of fait accomplis to discourage the growth of Arab nationalist and secessionist sentiment and bolster the morale of Galilee Jews.

Arab opposition to the *mitzpim* has been intense and has resulted in clashes with police and construction crews, demonstrations, roadblocks, and an embitterment of relations between Jews and Arabs in the Galilee. Writing in December 1979, a well-known Israeli journalist and long-time observer of Arab-Jewish relations commented that "since the establishment of the state of Israel the relationship between Jews and Arabs in the Galilee has never been so tense as it is at present."[39] While previous Labor governments were careful, at least since the early 1970s, to refer to activities in this sphere as efforts to "develop" or "populate" the Galilee, in principle on behalf of both its Jews and Arab inhabitants, the Likud government, expressing a more forthright and militant perspective, has much more explicitly justified its efforts as a Jewish-Zionist enterprise. The Likud government's inclination to abandon even the rhetoric of mutual development has increased Arab frustration by removing what officially-sanctioned grounds for criticism of discriminatory policies had existed. Fearing for their future in the Jewish state, but also emboldened by their growing numbers, and the example set by Palestinian protests in the West Bank, Galilee Arabs now commonly chant slogans such as "With our spirit and our blood we will liberate the Galilee." But Arab emigration is also on the increase.[40] Meanwhile, Galilee Jews have expressed, in increasingly hostile terms, their opposition to Arabs living in Jewish towns, their suspicion of Israeli Arab participation in arson and economic sabotage, and their fear of the expansion of the Arab population and the growth of Arab radicalism.

An important focus of this sharpening conflict in the Galilee has been the Interior Ministry's commissioner for the Galilee, Israel Koenig, author of the controversial memorandum, described above, that urged the Rabin government to adopt a much harsher set of policies toward Israeli Arabs. Though Israeli Arabs have repeatedly called for his dismissal, Koenig, a member of the National Religious Party, has remained in office and has assumed a leading role in the formulation and implementation of the Likud government's policies in the Arab sector. Indirect encouragement of Arab emigration, housing demolitions, reinforcement of police and security units stationed in Arab localities, construction

of *mitzpim,* vigorous assertions of state and Jewish National Fund land ownership claims, and other measures put into practice during the last four years were
among the recommendations contained in his memorandum. In January 1980
the chairmen of Jewish local councils in the Galilee inscribed Koenig's name in
the "Golden Book" of the Jewish National Fund to honor his contribution to
Zionism and the Judaization of the Galilee.[41]

Combined with a population explosion in Arab villages (spurred by a rate
of natural increase that is more than twice as high as that among Jews), the
scarcity of land in the Arab sector has aggravated very serious shortages of housing and schools. In 1979, 37.4 percent of Israeli Arab households had an average
density of three or more persons per room, compared with 1.9 percent of Israeli
Jewish households.[42] According to a report submitted to the government in
December 1980 by a joint commission sponsored by the Ministry of Education
and a group of Arab local councils, 1,200 or 39 percent of all classes in Arab
villages were not held in schools but in rented rooms in private homes. The difficulties caused by this shortage, as well as shortfalls in funds for teachers'
salaries and the general absence of auxiliary school services and equipment, are
reflected in the poor performance of Arab students on national matriculation
examinations and the relatively small size of the Arab university and vocational
school populations. Protested regularly and vociferously by the Association of
Arab Local Council Chairmen, these conditions triggered student strikes and
teachers strikes in a number of Arab villages in 1980.

Although increases in the number of classrooms built in the Arab sector in
recent years, promises to build more, and Gur-Aryeh's November 1980 announcement that two additional stories would be allowed on Arab dwellings reflect a
willingness of government ministries to be somewhat responsive in these spheres,
shortages of housing and schoolrooms are still particularly significant as sources
of Arab discontent because they are so intimately linked to the land problem
and the continued reluctance of the interior Ministry to grant planning authority
to local zoning boards in the Arab sector. Long delays (up to 15 years) in the
processing and approval of zoning plans result from the government's hesitation
to extend official recognition to Arab land ownership claims and to the per-
manence of buildings constructed by Arabs in lieu of the plans. Also, in the
absence of approved plans and authorized local zoning boards, the Interior
Ministry enjoys wide discretion to grant or withhold building permits and to
enforce or refrain from enforcing thousands of fines and demolition orders
levied on or issued against permitless dwellings. This gives the Israel Lands Administration and other agencies important leverage in their efforts to convince
Arabs to accept compensation for previously expropriated land, or to trade parcels of agricultural or vacant land for small building plots controlled by the
ILA.[43] In September 1980, 85 percent of Arab localities were still without
zoning plans, and by January 1981 only five local Arab planning boards had
been approved in all of Israel.[44] Demolition of illegal dwellings in at least nine

Arab villages in 1979 and 1980 resulted in violent demonstrations and scores of arrests. In 1981, efforts were being made to sue the Interior Ministry for failing to comply with the 1965 law requiring the approval of zoning plans in all localities within three years.

Aside from questions pertaining to land, schools, and housing, specific issues that have fueled Arab dissatisfaction over the past four years have included discrepancies in the size of government loans and grants available to Arab, as opposed to Jewish, localities; deterioration in or absence of sewer systems and waterworks in the Arab sector; discrimination in the provision of food subsidies, aid to large families, and social welfare benefits stemming from legislated preferences for relatives of army veterans or from the simple exercise of administrative discretion. Many strikes by municipal workers in the Arab sector, especially in Nazareth, have been called in the last two years. The last several years have indeed been extremely difficult for Jewish municipalities as well, but it is estimated that grants and loans extended to Jewish localities exceed those made available to Arab towns and villages by a factor of 8:1 on a per capita basis. Partly this reflects the lower tax base of Arab villages, and thus the lower tax revenues (and matching funds) available. However, it also appears that as Rakah has taken charge of more local councils, ministerial Arabists have more frequently prevented the transfer of budgeted funds to those municipalities.[45]

Most of these complaints, however, predate the Likud government, and there is no evidence that these chronic problems have dramatically worsened in the last four years. Indeed, in terms of employment, Arabs have been significantly less prominent in the ranks of the unemployed than Jews during the recession marking Likud's tenure in office. This is partly due to the absorption of unemployed Arabs as temporary workers on family agriculture plots but is primarily due to the concentration of Arabs in menial occupations. White collar employment for educated Arabs continues to be in short supply, pushing Arab graduates into blue collar and local teaching jobs.

Changing Identities among Israeli Arabs

Since 1948 regional and international developments, changing conditions of life within Israel, the ambiguities involved in living as theoretically equal "Israeli" citizens in an explicitly Jewish-Zionist state, and the cultural and psychological adjustments associated with social modernization have contributed to a striking fluidity in the identities felt, cherished, and/or discarded by Israeli Arabs. In 1948 the most important source of political identification and loyalty was the *hamula,* followed by village and sect (Muslim, Christian, Druze). The rise of Pan-Arabism, and especially the unification of Syria and Egypt under Gamal Nasser from 1958–61, strengthened Israeli Arab feelings of identification as "Arabs" that cut across kinship and communal lines. With the collapse of many attempts at Pan-Arab unity, Israel's defeat of the Arab states in 1967, and Nasser's death in 1970, Israeli Arab attachment to the Arab nation as a whole lost much of its emotive power. On the other hand, with the rise of the Palestine Liberation Organization in the late 1960s, the protracted Israeli occupation of the West Bank and Gaza and the contact with the inhabitants of those areas that the occupation made possible, and the international legitimacy and prominence accorded the Palestinian movement following the October war of 1973, Israeli Arabs developed a stronger sense of themselves as Palestinians.

Meanwhile, Israeli Arabs learned that life within Israel, though often difficult, was possible and that Israel was an established and most likely permanent fact. Their rights as Israeli citizens and the modern and successful examples set by the Israeli economy and social system added an "Israeli" dimension to their identity. Thus, in an opinion survey conducted in 1976, "Israeli," "Palestinian," and "Arab" were all highly salient terms of self-reference. Arab responses to the six alternatives provided were as follows: Israeli, 3.6 percent; Israeli Arab, 37.8 percent; Arab, 12.3 percent; Israeli Palestinian, 12.6 percent; Palestinian Arab, 27.3 percent; Palestinian, 6.5 percent. Not surprisingly, self-identification as "Israeli" was most common among the Druze, while appellations including the term "Arab" were most popular among Christians, and those including "Palestinian" tended to be preferred by Muslims.[46] In general, however, religion, per se, as a focus for loyalty, identity, and belief seemed to fade rapidly in the 1960s and 1970s. Though family and local loyalties loosened somewhat, they have always remained very strong.

The plasticity of Israeli Arab identity has been shown dramatically during the last four years by a relatively sudden intensification in religious orientation, particularly among Muslims, who comprise 78 percent of Israeli Arabs. Beginning in the homogeneously Muslim little triangle, and spreading also to heavily Muslim villages of the Galilee, and even to the Negev Bedouin, the revival of interest among young Arabs in Islam corresponds to a movement of Islamic revivalism in the Middle East as a whole, and in the West Bank and Gaza Strip in particular. Encouraged by visiting sheiks and holy men from these areas, by post-1967 opportunities to make the traditional pilgrimage to Mecca, by the appearance, for the first time since the creation of Israel, of native graduates of theological seminaries in the West Bank, and spurred by the spectacular success of Khomeini's Islamic revolution in Iran, young Israeli Arabs who had scoffed at tradition and religious ritual, began joining in daily prayers with their grandfathers, rebuilding mosques, growing beards, fasting during the holy month of Ramadan, and quoting from the Koran. While for many educated young people such involvement may prove to have been a fad, or a convenient facade for less acceptable political activity, it is clear that for many return to Islam has alleviated serious anxieties caused by deep-seated feelings of frustration and alienation.[47]

Indeed, associated with the Likud's distant to hostile stance toward Israeli Arabs, has been a trend toward alienation of Israeli Arabs from an identity as "Israelis" that many had begun to acquire. While previous Labor governments at least spoke vigorously about the "full integration of the minorities in all the paths of life of the state," and while Labor party and Histadrut spokesmen often use notions of "partnership" between Israeli Jews and Israeli Arabs, the most common references to them made by leading ministers of the Begin government have been as "foreigners" or "strangers," or as "the Arabs of the Land of Israel" —a formulation whose context often suggests its application to West Bank and Gaza Arabs, but which, from the Likud's perspective, and certainly to the ears of Israeli Arabs, connotes Arab citizens of Israel as well. This formal, if implicit, placement of Arab citizens in the same category as Arabs living under Israeli military occupation both expresses and reinforces what has been the most important trend in the political identity of Israeli Arabs over the last four years— the strengthening of its Palestinian dimension and the coalescence of a stronger sense of solidarity with the Arabs of the West Bank and Gaza.

With the prolongation of the occupation, the lives of Israeli Arabs have become more and more intertwined with those of the inhabitants of the occupied territories. In addition to important religious influences and loyalties, several hundred marriages between (mostly) Israeli Arab men and West Bank women have taken place. Ties of kinship and friendship, interrupted by the armistice line in 1949, have been invigorated. There have even been reports of substantial numbers of West Bank Arabs, mostly refugees from 1948, who have drifted across the green line to establish permanent, if unofficial, residence in the little triangle and the Galilee. Many Israeli Arabs serve as contractors for Arab laborers from the territories, while the inhabitants of towns and villages in the West Bank, along the green line, have become accustomed to shopping, working, and relaxing, along with Israeli Arabs, in the cities and on the beaches of the coastal plain.[48]

Aside from its mere continuation, the Likud government's stepped-up policies of land expropriation and settlement on the West Bank have increased the significance of the occupation as an issue, which affects Israeli Arabs directly. The diversion of settlers and limited financial resources to the West Bank, for example, is what lay behind the government's accelerated program to Judaize the Galilee by establishing small and inexpensive, but highly salient, *mitzpim* near Israeli Arab villages. Attempts to camouflage Jewish settlement in the West Bank have also included the establishment of a number of new settlements in heavily Arab areas in Israel proper adjacent to the West Bank, which can eventually be expanded into that area.[49]

Israeli Arab identification with the struggle of Palestinians in the occupied territories to resist land expropriation and settlement is encouraged by the similarity of the tactics used by the authorities there to those used to transfer the property of Arabs in Israel to Jewish control. Thus, a large proportion of the attorneys representing Arab landowners in the West Bank before military government tribunals and the Israeli High Court of Justice have either been Israeli Arabs themselves or Jewish lawyers with long experience in cases involving Israeli Arab lands. Though the original focus of "Land Day," on March 30,

1976, was the problem of land expropriation from Israeli Arabs, in the demonstrations and rallies that have been held annually in the Arab sector since 1976, expressions of solidarity with Palestinians in the occupied territories and protests against land expropriation and settlement on the West Bank have been increasingly prominent themes. West Bank Palestinians have reciprocated with commercial strikes and demonstrations, which in 1981 assumed larger proportions than the observance of Land Day in Israel itself.

The Likud government's public commitment to the permanent incorporation of "Judea, Samaria, and the Gaza district" into Israel and the "iron fist" policies it has pursued toward dissident activity in those areas have affected Israeli Arabs in other ways. Military crackdowns and closures of universities on the West Bank, where a score of Israeli Arab academics are employed, have triggered increasingly explicit expressions of Arab university student support for the Palestinians in the occupied territories and for the PLO, and have inspired waves of right-wing Jewish student violence against Arab students on Israeli campuses. The vigilante activity of Jewish settlers in the West Bank, following the murder of a settler in Hebron in February 1980 and of six more in May, contributed to a polarization of relations between Jews and Arabs within Israel itself, aggravated by high-level statements threatening expulsion of Israeli Arabs (see above). The annexation of East Jerusalem, by depriving the military government of jurisdiction over the city's 115,000 intensely nationalistic Palestinians, has pushed the government toward the passage of laws to control pro-PLO political activity, which of course then apply to all Israelis, but most significantly to Arab Israelis. Thus, in 1980, Justice Minister Shmuel Tamir introduced legislation, which the Knesset passed, banning the use of Palestinian symbols, slogans, and songs and giving the interior minister the power to deprive Israelis of their citizenship for acts he interprets as "constituting disloyalty to the state of Israel."[50]

Another factor that has strengthened Israeli Arab identification with the Palestinian struggle and increased their organized and expressive support for the PLO has been the changing attitude PLO officials have displayed in recent years toward Arabs inside of Israel proper. Partly due to the sheer bulk of the Israeli-Arab community (it constitutes more than one-eighth of all Palestinians and almost one-third of those still in Palestine) and party due to its increasingly visible militance, the PLO has shifted from a tendency to ignore it in the late 1960s and early 1970s, to regular, if restrained, references to its role in the overall Palestinian struggle. In the political statement and program issued at the conclusion of the Palestinian National Council (PNC) meeting in June 1974, no mention at all was made of the Arabs in Israel.[51] However, since 1977, and in 1980 and 1981 in particular, the PLO has directed increasing amounts of explicit attention and support to Israeli (Palestinian) Arabs. The political program approved by the fourth conference of Fatah, in May 1980, placed "special emphasis on strengthening links with our Palestinian masses in the territory occupied since 1948 in order to enable them to confront the plans aimed at disintegrating their unity and obliterating their Arab character."[52] According to a leading member of Fatah, one of the most important recommendations endorsed by the PNC, at its April 1981 meeting, was "doubling material aid to our people in the occupied lands and giving material support to our people in the Galilee and the Negev, where they are facing continuous pressure to force them to sell or desert their land."[53] In the concluding statement of this, its most recent session, the PNC "saluted the heroic struggle of our people in the Galilee, the triangle, and the Negev as well as in Jerusalem, the West Bank and the Gaza Strip against the Zionist designs that aim at expanding the settlements, Judaization, and the destruction of the national economy and education and the holy places."[54]

Thus political developments, religious influences, economic interest, and social ties have all strengthened the identification of Israeli Arabs with the Palestinians, and the Palestinians of the West Bank and Gaza in particular. But the Likud government's inclination to place all Arabs under Israeli jurisdiction in the same category has also made most Israeli Arabs more aware than before of the importance of preserving the dual distinction between their national identification as "Palestinian" and their legal status as "Israelis," and between their rights as Arab citizens of Israel, inside the green line, and the more circumscribed status of Palestinians in the occupied West Bank and Gaza. In this context discussions of autonomy for the inhabitants of the West Bank and Gaza raise delicate questions. Implementation of autonomy could provide a formula for Israel's relations with "Arabs of the Land of Israel," that if extended to Israel's Arabs could reduce their rights as citizens of Israel. On the other hand, autonomy could also be used as a slogan in support of separatist movements in overwhelmingly Arab areas of Israel, should a Palestinian political entity emerge on the other side of the green line.

Trends in the Political Mobilization of Israeli Arabs

In response to delicate political circumstances and the forces impinging upon them from inside and outside the borders of Israel, most Israeli Arabs have continued to maintain a low political profile, especially with respect to regional and international issues. Yet their voices are increasingly heard. Some prominent personalities with close ties to the government or the Labor party have endorsed the Camp David accords and the Israel-Egypt peace treaty. Radical groups of villagers and university students, at the other extreme, have issued declarations of support for the rejectionist wing of the PLO. Most significant, however, has been an unprecedented series of declarations and resolutions, sponsored by various front organizations of Rakah, but signed by large numbers of Arab mayors, local council members, educators, professionals, and politicos. In the text of these manifestos there has been a careful effort to express the growing solidarity of Israeli Arabs with the inhabitants of the occupied territories and the

Palestinian people as a whole, without surrendering their claims to equal treatment as loyal Israeli citizens.

In January 1979, 28 chairmen of Arab local councils (more than half of all Arab mayors in Israel) along with 100 members of the Rakah sponsored "Committee for the Defense of Arab Lands" passed a resolution "welcoming the struggle of their fellows in the West Bank and Gaza Strip against the occupation, annexation and colonialist settlements and (expressing) their solidarity with the struggle of the Palestinian people under the leadership of the PLO to establish its independent state."[55] This was the first time that such a large and representative group of Israeli Arabs expressed opinions that identified themselves as Palestinians, supported the establishment of a Palestinian state, and endorsed the PLO as the leadership of the Palestinian people. A statement issued in preparation for a follow-up conference of the same group in February defended the right of Israeli Arabs to participate in the debate over the occupation and the Palestinian problem, arguing that "the struggle for just peace has become an integral part of Israel's Arab residents' struggle for their existence, their lands and their right to equality."[56]

In the spring of 1980 an already tense situation on the West Bank deteriorated rapidly. Extensive new land expropriations, increasingly sophisticated Palestinian political activity, punishment curfews, and spiraling cycles of violence and retribution climaxed in the deportation of the mayors of Hebron and Halhul in May and bomb attacks on the mayors of Nablus, Ramallah, and El-Bireh on June 2. On June 6, the Arabic language newspaper of Rakah, *Al-Ittihad*, published a statement bearing the names of 186 signatories, including 11 Arab mayors and a variety of public personalities associated with Rakah or its front organizations. It protested the government's "iron fist policy in the occupied territories," condemned the attacks on the mayors and expulsions, and noted the contribution of the deteriorating situation on the West Bank to the increasingly hostile attitude of the government to Arabs inside the green line. It went on to declare that Arabs in Israel "are a living, conscious and active part of the Palestinian people." Emphasizing the need for "joint Arab-Jewish democratic struggle inside Israel" and its desire for a peace settlement "which will ensure the establishment of the independent Palestinian state on Palestinian soil next to the state of Israel, and guarantee peaceful coexistence between the two," the manifesto included a call for a representative congress of Israeli Arabs to be held to sustain a political struggle consistent with the terms and objectives it had outlined.[57] Additional signatures were solicited and published in subsequent issues of the newspaper. By July, 4,000 signatures had been attached to the manifesto.[58]

On September 6, a preparatory meeting, including 25 Arab mayors, was held in the Arab town of Shfaram to draw up plans for the congress. In addition to Rakah leaders, the executive committee formed at Shfaram included Mohammad Abu Rabia, a Negev Bedouin sheik elected to the Knesset in 1977 on a list affiliated to the Labor party, and the mayors of eight of the ten largest Arab municipalities and towns in Israel. Shaykh Hubayshi, the Muslim Qadi of Acre and Haifa, attended the meeting, but not as a member of the Executive Committee.[59] The platform approved at Shfaram for the congress, to be held in Nazareth in December, declared that Israel Arabs have:

> no other homeland but this. [H]istorically part of the Palestinian people, and being citizens of Israel, ... [i]t is our right to live as citizens with equal national and civil rights which are inalienable. We demand to realize these rights and the liquidation of all forms of oppression and racist discrimination against the Arab population of Israel.[60]

The specific demands listed in what the Executive Committee labeled as the "Sixth of June Charter" were headed by a call for the Arab population to be accorded official recognition as a "national minority." The bulk of the demands concerned land expropriation, economic development, discrimination against Arab localities, and discrimination in employment and education. The "Charter" also protested oppression of Palestinians in the occupied territories, called for a peace settlement based on a West Bank/Gaza Strip Palestinian state, and called for Israeli recognition of the PLO as the representative of the Palestinians. The organizers of the congress subsequently claimed that 10,000 Israeli Arabs had signed the Charter and that 500 elected Arab delegates (one per 1,000 Arab inhabitants) along with Jewish observers would attend the congress.

The unsuccessful struggle of the executive committee formed in Shfaram to defend itself against attacks from the government, in the Hebrew press, and from more militant, radical Arabs reveals an enormous amount about patterns and problems of Israeli Arab political mobilization. From the radical extreme, the attack on the Nazareth Congress, and on Rakah, the moving force behind the Sixth of June Charter and the Shfaram preparatory conference, came from two groups—*Ibna el-Balad* (Sons of the Village) and the Progressive National Movement (PNM). Comprised of small groups of intellectuals and some workers, *Ibna el-Balad* began in the early 1970s in Um el Fahm, the largest village in the little triangle, as an expression of local resentment against the authorities' manipulation of traditional kinship loyalties and rivalries to sustain effective control over village affairs. Eschewing an integrated countrywide organization, *Ibna el-Balad* groups emerged in several triangle villages and some Galilee villages as well. Although non-Marxist, these groups express a basically more radical position than Rakah in their rejection of alliances with "progressive and democratic forces" among the Jewish majority, their stress on the principle of self-determination as fully applicable to the Arabs of Israel, and their support of the program of rejectionist groups within the PLO calling for a single Palestinian state to include both the territories occupied by Israel in 1967 and Israel itself.

The orientation and objectives of the PNM are much the same as *Ibna el-Balad*, but its organizational base is among Arab university students, especially at the Hebrew University in Jerusalem. In January 1979, six Hebrew University student members of the PNM were banished to their villages for circulating a leaflet entitled "The Conscience of the Conquered Land: To Comrades of the Palestinian Path." The leaflet was in the form of an open letter to the national council of the PLO, identifying PNM members as "an integral part of the Arab masses who are suffering under the occupation of all of Palestine and who openly reject this entity." The leaflet denounced Rakah as an "obstacle to the struggles of the Arab Palestinians people," derided the Camp David accords, and called for the overthrow of the Egyptian, Jordanian, and Iranian regimes.[61] A bitter struggle has been waged between the PNM and Rakah on Israeli campuses for control of the Arab university student organizations.

In February 1981, the PNM gained control of the Arab student organization at the Hebrew University by a margin of 55 percent to 45 percent for Rakah. Rakah retained its majority at Beersheva University by a narrow margin, while also keeping control of the Tel Aviv and Haifa Arab student organizations and the national organization of Arab students. Both PNM and *Ibna el-Balad* supporters have disrupted Rakah-sponsored observances of "Land Day" in recent years, calling for general strikes and other more militant actions and condemning Rakah's association with Jewish and leftist-Zionist groups. Although these groups demanded that they be allowed to send two representatives to speak to the congress on behalf of their organization and to participate in decision making, at the same time they rejected the platform of the planned congress "because," according to a PNM spokesman, "it does not take into consideration the right of self-determination of the Palestinian masses inside the 1948 borders."[62]

Spokesman for the planned congress responded that only individuals who accepted the program approved at Shfaram would be welcome. Consistent with their characterization of *Ibna el-Balad* and the PNM over the previous several years, Rakah leaders associated with the congress condemned them as "childish" and as "chauvinist extremists" and their tactics and objectives as "pretexts to the government to incite against the Arab population in Israel, as if they were striving for a separatist movement, working to dismember areas from the State of Israel, or for the elimination of the state."[63] Attacking the "nationalist" groups as instruments of the government in its efforts to divide the Arab minority, Emile Habibi, editor of *Al-Ittihad*, also stressed that Rakah members "are the most faithful national patriots, and they sacrifice more than any others and they have much experience in nationalistic struggles."[64] Before its Arab and, increasingly, Palestinian oriented constituency, Rakah emphasized its Palestinian credentials by trumpeting all references or endorsements, whether direct or indirect, by the PLO. Thus, great prominence is given in Rakah publications to contacts with PLO representatives, such as that which occurred during a meeting of the "International Peace Parliament" in Bulgaria in September 1980, when a delegation from the Democratic Front for Peace and Equality met with Yasir Arafat. Lavish references have also been made to a brief article in the February 23, 1981 issue of *Al-Thawra*, a Fatah publication, which indirectly urged Israeli

Arabs to support the Rakah sponsored front in the upcoming Histadrut and Knesset elections.[65]

But the ideological and rhetorical formulations used to defend the convenors of the Nazareth Congress on their radical flank, e.g., that Israeli Arabs are an "inseparable part of the Palestinian nation" and that the PLO is the "sole legitimate representative of the Palestinian people," exposed Rakah and its allies to attacks from the government and the Hebrew press characterizing the Shfaram program and the planned congress as subversive acts, designed to mobilize Israeli Arabs to accept the leadership of the PLO in its political and military struggle against the state. The most salient charge was that the Arab minority was being organized to demand plebiscites in heavily Arab areas of the Galilee and little triangle, when, following the establishment of a Palestinian state on the West Bank and Gaza, such areas could secede and attach themselves to it.[66] Speaking to the "Arab-Israeli Association," an Arab group with close ties to Amnon Lin, and to the Histadrut's "Good Neighborhood Circle" in western Galilee, Benjamin Gur-Aryeh reacted to the planned Nazareth Congress by defending government policies in the Arab sector, stressing educational advances made by the Arab population, and promising accelerated efforts to approve master zoning plans for Arab villages, aid for young Arab couples in need of housing, and the construction of mosques. Gur-Aryeh went on to warn, however, that the efforts of Rakah to convene the Nazareth Congress as the representative organization of Israeli Arabs, and its promulgation of a PLO-style "national covenant," brought Israeli Arabs to a "crossroads":

> "I want to warn my Arab friends that the Jews are not angels and if the violence has reached the university as a result of the extremism of the students, there is a danger that it will also reach the markets and work places".[67]

Emil Tuma, a veteran Rakah leader named as the coordinator of the Nazareth Congress, responded to these attacks on the Shfaram program and the congress by arguing that although Israeli Arabs were Palestinians, and though the Palestinians' leadership was the PLO, that only applied to Palestinians whose rights to self-determination were not being respected. Since Israeli Arabs, according to the Shfaram program, accept Israel as their homeland, they do not see the PLO as their leadership.[68] Such convoluted reasoning was a rather ineffective means of mollifying the fears of Israeli Jews at the spectre of an organized and possibly separatist Palestinian Arab minority. On December 1, Prime Minister Begin, in his capacity as acting defense minister, banned the Nazareth Congress and declared illegal any meetings or organizations aimed at convening the congress. Defending the measure, Justice Minister Moshe Nissim labeled the congress "an attempt to promote separatism" and said that "the promoters of the conference hoped to establish a separate Arab entity in Israel, and to set up a permanent forum that would eventually become the representative Arab body and serve as an 'address' for the PLO when it attempted to harness the Israeli Arabs to its cause."[69]

The banning of the Nazareth Congress was the first act of its kind since the declaration of *El-Ard,* a small group of radical intellectuals, as illegal in 1964. Late in December the government also moved against a clandestine Islamic fundamentalist group spread through four large villages in the little triangle. Approximately 70 members of a Muslim Brotherhood-type organization calling itself *Usrat al-Jihad* (the "Jihad Family") were arrested, and guns, maps, photographs, and 160 grenades were seized.[70] Drawing inspiration from Muslim religious leaders from the West Bank and Gaza, the "Jihad Family" was apparently responsible for a rash of arson incidents in forests and Jewish farms, as well as attacks on Arab communists and the secularist intellectuals of *Ibna el-Balad.* In April another Israeli Arab organization, the guns, maps, photographs, and 160 grenades were seized.[70] Drawing inspiration from Muslim religious leaders from the West Bank and Gaza, the "Jihad Family" was apparently responsible for a rash of arson incidents in forests and Jewish farms, as well as attacks on Arab communists and the secularist intellectuals of *Ibna el-Balad.* In April another Israeli Arab organization, the "National Coordination Committee" (NCC), was declared an "outlawed organization." The NCC was an attempt to unite nine different anti-Rakah radical Arab groups, including the PNM, *Ibna el-Balad,* and an Arabic publishing house in Nazareth, within a single organizational framework. Representatives of approximately 100 activists from these groups met in February 1981 in the village of Taiybe to approve a document known as the "Um el Fahm Charter," drawn up at an earlier meeting in Um el Fahm. The Um el Fahm Charter of the NCC differed from the Sixth of June Charter, on the basis of which the Nazareth Congress was to have been held, in its characterization of a West Bank Palestinian state as "but the beginning of the fundamental solution of the Palestinian problem," its explicit avowal of loyalty to the PLO as the only representative of the Palestinians, including Israeli Arabs, and its declaration of the legitimate national rights of the Palestinians as including "self-determination on the whole of its national soil."[71] Modeling themselves on the National Guidance Committee of mayors and political activists in the West Bank and Gaza, the organizers of the NCC also differed from Rakah and its front organizations in their rejection of Knesset elections as a meaningful arena for political struggle by Israeli Arabs and their emphasis on leadership chosen at the local level as the genuine representative of and crucial link between Palestinian Arabs living inside Israel and those outside its borders.[72]

THE OUTCOME OF THE JUNE 1981 KNESSET ELECTIONS IN THE ARAB SECTOR AND PROSPECTS FOR THE ARAB MINORITY DURING THE SECOND BEGIN GOVERNMENT

Just as the efforts of Rakah to mobilize the vast majority of Israeli Arabs around its program of identification and support for moderate Palestinian demands and equality for Arabs in Israel were caught between the millstones of rejectionist sentiment and government oppostion, so too was Rakah's electoral front—the Democratic Front for Peace and Equality (DPFE)—unable to capitalize on the mass support its substantive positions have among Israeli Arabs to increase, or even maintain, its Knesset representation. For in June 1981, in addition to overcoming the fundamental unattractiveness of communist rhetoric, the DPFE also had to contend with the fervent desire of Israeli Arabs to prevent the Likud from retaining power (even if that meant voting for the Labor party) and with an election boycott called by *Ibna el-Balad* and the PNM.

In past elections Arabs voted for Rakah or the DPFE, not for instrumental reasons, but to register their protest against the policies of a Labor party government whose continuation was assumed. In the extremely close race between the Labor party and Likud in 1981, however, Israeli Arab voters believed that their votes might help determine the composition of the government. Thus, in spite of the Labor party's neglect of the Arab minority in its years out of power, the failure of the Histadrut to implement its 1976 decision to foster the industrialization of Arab villages, and the confusion marking the Labor party's campaign in the Arab sector,[73] the proportion of Arabs voting for the Labor party or the list traditionally associated with it increased for the first time since 1951, jumping from 27 percent in 1977 to 36 percent in 1981.[74] On the other hand, the boycott called by the radical Arab groups also had its effect. For the first time a smaller percentage of eligible Arab voters than eligible Jewish voters voted— approximately 69 percent, down from what was until 1981 a record low of 74 percent in 1977. The result was that Rakah's share of the Arab vote, both in absolute and percentage terms, dropped for the first time since 1961, from 71,700 (49 percent) in 1977 to 59,000 (36 percent) in 1981.[75]

In the months following Likud's second electoral victory, there have been no signs of a change in policy toward Arab Israelis. While the Likud, by focusing on land and the national-political aspects of the internal Arab problem, is likely to continue to ignore what potential for improvement in Arab-Jewish relations in Israel does exist, the Labor party's emphasis is much more likely to be on the cultivation of educated Arab elites, assuring them that their concerns for economic development, improved housing and education, and satisfying employment opportunities will be addressed. If the Labor party learns from its mistakes in the 1981 campaign, it should have a good chance to expand its presence and influence in the Arab sector and even increase the proportion of Arab votes it receives in the next Knesset elections. Out of frustration with Rakah's inability to elicit positive changes in government policies, and their antipathy toward the Likud government, several thousand Arabs have joined the Labor party in recent years. The 1981 elections were, in fact, the first time that an Arab, chosen by representatives of Arab Labor party members, was elected to the Knesset. In his postmortem on the June election, Labor party chairman Shimon Peres indicated his belief that the encouragement of splinter Arab lists, rather than more strenuous efforts to elicit Arab votes for the Labor party itself, might have cost the party a plurality in the Knesset.[76]

But while the Labor party may increase its electoral strength in the Arab sector, it will not maintain a dominant political position there unless it embraces and moves to implement the formula of "partnership" between Jewish and Arab Israelis that some of its spokesmen currently espouse. Much more likely, in view of the fundamental reorientation toward the character of the state, which implementation of such a "binational" approach would entail, is that the Labor party, upon returning to power, would also return to the policies of control and benign neglect pursued by previous Labor governments. This would be accompanied by the return of Arab protest votes to Rakah.

For Israeli Arabs, Rakah's substantive policy line, that though Palestinians, they should see their future within an Israeli state that should grant them equal rights and opportunities, has great appeal. However, though Rakah's importance as a vehicle for Arab protest will remain, and increase if either Likud or Labor assumes the kind of consistent tenure in office enjoyed by the Labor party before 1977, and though increasing numbers of Israeli Arabs can be expected to turn to clandestine political and terrorist action, the prospects for mass dissident political mobilization of Israeli Arabs are dim. The current government is quite willing to run risks of bad international publicity by simply banning groups organized on a mass countrywide basis. Domestically, Rakah's isolation, as a pro-Soviet Communist party, from the Jewish majority also keeps its political initiatives vulnerable to harassment and suppression by the government. Meanwhile Rakah's deeply entrenched organization in the Arab sector militates against the mobilization of masses of Arabs by other dissident elements, whether more extremist or more moderate.

Nor is the PLO particularly interested in mobilizing Israeli Arabs into a highly visible spearhead of the Palestinian struggle against Israel, at least not at this stage. Within the PLO public discussion of the problem of Arabs in Israel is an extremely sensitive issue, over which a bitter confrontation could easily erupt. While too little attention paid to this group of Palestinians risks forsaking a potentially large and ideologically important constituency, too much prominence accorded to them, and their presumptive rights to be included in a Palestinian Arab state, would weaken the credibility of the PLO's diplomatic efforts toward a West Bank–Gaza Palestinian state.

But even if they remain unmobilized, as long as the de facto process of incorporation of the West Bank and Gaza into the Jewish state continues, Arabs in Israel are more likely to find themselves identified in Jewish eyes as part of a dangerous Palestinian population than as a potential partner in the development and governance of the country. With the Likud in power this propensity is strengthened by official policies designed to blur and eventually erase the green line between Israel and the territories. Ironically, however, Israeli withdrawal from the West Bank and Gaza, as unlikely as that may now appear, could have profoundly negative consequences for Jewish-Arab relations in Israel itself. The stability of Jewish control over Arabs has already been jeopardized by the social, demographic, and political trends described above. If, to compensate for the "sacrifice" of "Judea and Samaria" to the Palestinians, Israel were to commit itself even more wholeheartedly to the "Judaization" and "Zionization" of "little Israel," and if to support that effort the settlement energies and resources now flowing into the occupied territories were diverted to the Galilee and the little triangle, the political conflict between Jewish and Arab Israelis, especially over land, would escalate sharply.

Fundamental changes in the position of Arabs in Israel that would provide a nonantagonistic basis for Jewish-Arab coexistence and mutual development require not only settlement of the Arab-Israeli dispute, but also a sea change in the image that Israel's Jewish majority has of the country. That kind of basic reorientation is rare in the history of nations, and even more difficult to envision in light of prevailing cultural and demographic trends among Israeli Jews, and the embitterment of growing numbers of Israeli Arabs with the very existence of the state. Thus, evolution in the status of Arabs in the Jewish state, unless interrupted by mass expulsions, is likely to proceed slowly and within the narrow bounds of a superordinate-subordinate relationship.

NOTES

1.   This represents approximately 20 percent of the prewar Arab population of the territory that became Israel as defined by the 1949 armistice agreements. The remainder became refugees, concentrated in the West Bank, under Jordanian control, the Gaza Strip, held by the Egyptians, and in Syria and Lebanon.

2.   For a description of the function and operation of the military government see Ian Lustick, *Arabs in the Jewish State: Israel's Control of a National Minority* (Austin: University of Texas Press, 1980), pp. 52–53, 123–48.

3.   For a comprehensive analysis of the structural and institutional contexts within which policies designed to achieve control over Arabs could do so at low cost, see Lustick, *Arabs in the Jewish State.*

4.   Ibid., chapter VII.

5.   The recommendation of the committee, chaired by Agriculture Minister Ariel (Arik) Sharon, and made public by the government in January 1979, was that the villagers would not be allowed to return. *Jerusalem Post*, January 18, 1979.

6.   *Jerusalem Post* Magazine, March 2, 1979.

7.   *Yediot Acharonot*, March 4, 1981.

8.   Ibid.

9.   Yair Kotler, in *Maariv*, April 24, 1981.

10.   *Jerusalem Post*, August 8, 1977.

11.   *New York Times*, January 24, 1979.

12. *Haaretz,* August 10, 1979.

13. *Haaretz,* December 2, 1980.

14. *Haaretz,* December 4, 1980.

15. Over the last several years militantly anti-Arab right-wing political groups have become increasingly prominent on Israeli campuses. Violent outbreaks by Jewish students against Arab demonstrations and disruptions of rallies held by Arab and sympathetic Jewish students have become common. Although four Jewish students were arrested following a midnight knife attack on Arab students in a dormitory in Haifa, the reaction of the authorities to incidents of disruption and intimidation has been extremely lax. See *Haaretz,* December 14, 1979; June 4, 1980; June 20, 1980; June 24, 1980; June 26, 1980; June 27, 1980; *Davar,* December 16, 1979; *Jerusalem Post,* May 15, 1980; May 30, 1980; February 11, 1981.

16. Lin has expressed his belief that fewer than a score of paid and protected Arab "anti-subversive activists" in each Arab village could provide the government with the capability to identify and suppress negative elements.

17. Calculated based on the following sources: *Statistical Abstract of Israel* 28(1977): 23, 31(1980); 31; *Haaretz,* December 2, 1980; *Jerusalem Post,* June 1, 1981.

18. *Haaretz,* December 2, 1980. These figures are of course exclusive of Arab inhabitants of the West Bank, Golan Heights, Gaza Strip, and Sinai, occupied by Israel, along with East Jerusalem, in June 1967.

19. *Statistical Abstract of Israel* 28(1977): 36–37, 31(1980): 48–49.

20. *Statistical Abstract of Israel* 30(1979): 618, 31(1980): 578.

21. *Statistical Abstract of Israel* 31(1980): 587, 30(1979): 587, 28(1977): 602; Uri Stendel, *Minorities in Israel* (Hebrew) (Jerusalem: Information Centre and the Office of the Adviser to the Prime Minister on Arab Affairs, 1971), p. 12. This is slightly higher than the percentage of Israeli Jews enrolled in educational institutions, reflecting the markedly younger age profile of the Israeli Arab population.

22. *Statistical Abstract of Israel* 31(1980): 66, 28(1977): 55.

23. Stendel, *Minorities in Israel,* p. 10; Yechiel Harari, *Arabs of Israel in 1978* (Hebrew) (Givat Haviva, Israel: Institute for Arab Studies, 1980), No. 30, pp. 40, 53–56.

24. Stendel, *Minorities in Israel,* p. 11.

25. *Statistical Abstract of Israel* 28(1977): 54, 31(1980): 65.

26. *Statistical Abstract of Israel* 28(1977): 81, 31(1980): 91, 312–13.

27. *Statistical Abstract of Israel* 31(1980): 81–82.

28. Calculated from data provided in *Statistical Abstract of Israel* 28(1977): 322–23, 31(1980): 312–13, 324–25.

29. Yechiel Harari, *The Municipal Elections in the Arab Sector–1978* (Hebrew) (Givat Haviva, Israel: Institute for Arab Studies, n.d.), pp. 6, 8–9.

30. *Statistical Abstract of Israel* 31(1980): 313, 316–17, 328–29; 29(1978): 354; Lustick, *Arabs in the Jewish State,* pp. 261–63.

31. *Statistical Abstract of Israel* 31(1980): 275. During this same period urban Arab family incomes fell from 105.7 percent of that of urban Jews born in Asia and Africa to 90.4 percent. The definitions of "urban" used by Israel's

Central Bureau of Statistics includes all Jewish localities with populations greater than 2,000 but excludes all Arab localities with populations less than 5,000. This excludes the smaller, and by and large poorer, Arab villages from the population described by these statistics.

32. *Statistical Abstract of Israel* 31(1980): 313, 28(1977): 313.

33. *Statistical Abstract of Israel* 27(1976): 360, 31(1980): 430.

34. The ILA is charged with supervising the use of 93 percent of Israel's land area, virtually all property that is not privately owned, and is jointly run by the Agriculture Ministry and the Jewish National Fund, the land acquisition and development arm of the World Zionist Organization. The Nature Reserves Authority is an agency of the Agriculture Ministry.

On one level the struggle of the Bedouin against central government efforts to encourage sedentarization and wage labor is similar to such struggles that have taken place throughout the Middle East. Only in Israel, however, has the issue been cast in such starkly nationalist-political terms.

35. *Jerusalem Post,* June 6, 1978.

36. On the problems of the Negev Bedouin, see Attalah Mansour, "The Green Patrol and the Black Goats," *Haaretz,* March 13, 1978; *Israleft: Biweekly News Service,* No. 147, April 15, 1979, pp. 1–4; *Zoo Haderech,* April 4, 1979; April 9, 1979; May 13, 1981; August 10, 1980; Yitzhak Baili, "The Black Goat Law," *Haaretz,* October 19, 1980.

37. See Lustick, *Arabs in the Jewish State,* pp. 170–82, 246.

38. *Haaretz,* November 18, 1980; *Maariv,* December 20, 1978.

39. Amos Elon, "The Galilee of Arabs and Jews: the Sight from Dado's Square and Back," *Haaretz,* December 2, 1979.

40. The difference between the number of Arab Israelis leaving Israel compared to the number arriving increased from 931 in 1976 to 1,805 in 1979. *Statistical Abstract of Israel* 31(1980): 117.

41. *Jerusalem Post,* January 23, 1980.

42. *Statistical Abstract of Israel* 31(1980): 283. See also *Zoo Haderech,* January 10, 1979 for background and the findings of a public report on the land and housing shortage in Arab villages.

43. For examples of how this leverage is used see Avshalom Ginat, "A Barrel of Gunpowder" and "Villages under Siege," *Al-Hamishmar,* September 5, 1980; September 16, 1980, respectively.

44. *Davar,* September 28, 1980; January 7, 1981; *Yediot Acharonot,* October 5, 1980.

45. See Joan Borsten, "The Case of the Druse," *Jerusalem Post,* March 1, 1979; and *Zoo Haderech,* March 7, 1979; January 16, 1980; April 2, 1980. On July 7, 1981, Arab local councils staged a one day shutdown of most municipal services as a protest against low budgets. *Zoo Haderech,* August 5, 1981.

46. Sammy Smooha, *The Orientation and Politicization of the Arab Minority in Israel* (Haifa: Institute for Middle East Studies, 1980), Occasional Papers on the Middle East, No. 2, pp. 59, 166. Although the Likud government has in certain respects favored the Druze, as had previous Labor governments, a draft resistance movement among the Druse, encouraged by a Rakah front organization—the Druse Initiative Committee—has gathered strength. See Gabi Zohar, "The Draft Dodgers," *Al Hamishmar,* March 6, 1981.

47.   On the Islamic revival among Israeli Arabs see *Davar,* November 24, 1980; Yosef Tzuriel, "Will You be Prepared for the Holy War?", *Maariv,* January 30, 1981;*Jerusalem Post,* February 27, 1981;*Maariv,* March 12, 1981.

48.   Ilan Sh'hori, *Haaretz,* December 19, 1980; Kassem Zeid, "Our Part of the National Pie was too Small: The Red Line for Israeli Arabs," *Al-Hamishmar,* August 15, 1980. For an argument stressing the continuing differences between Israeli Arabs and the inhabitants of the occupied territories, see a series of articles on the subject by Attalah Mansour, *Haaretz,* August 1, 1980; August 3, 1980; August 5, 1980.

49.   Concerning three settlements under construction near the green line in the little triangle, see *Maariv,* February 17, 1981. These settlements are conceived as part of the "Reihan Bloc" of new settlements that spans the green line between Wadi Ara and the northwest corner of the West Bank. Regarding similar projects on both sides of the green line west of Hebron, see *Maariv,* January 6, 1981.

50.   *Zoo Haderech,* August 6, 1980. See also *Haaretz* editorial, July 31, 1980.

51.   *Journal of Palestine Studies* (Summer 1974): 224.

52.   Foreign Broadcast Information Service, *Daily Report: Middle East and North Africa,* June 5, 1980, p. A5.

53.   Foreign Broadcast Information Service, April 21, 1981, p. A1.

54.   Foreign Broadcast Information Service, April 22, 1981, p. A2.

55.   *Jerusalem Post,* January 21, 1979.

56.   *Israleft: Bi-weekly News Service,* No. 144, March 1, 1979, p. 4.

57.   *Middle East International,* No. 128, July 4, 1980, p. 14.

58.   *Zoo Haderech,* July 9, 1981.

59.   *Davar,* December 3, 1980;*Haaretz,* September 23, 1980.

60.   *Israleft: Bi-weekly News Service,* No. 179, December 21, 1980, p. 6.

61.   *Israleft: Bi-weekly News Service,* No. 143, February 15, 1979, p. 1.

62.   *Al-Fajr* (English Language Weekly), January 25–31, 1981; Attalah Mansour, *Haaretz,* April 23, 1981.

63.   See the remarks of Toufik Toubi, a Rakah member of Knesset, in *Haaretz,* September 7, 1980; Kassem Zeid, "Rakah Sanctifies the Means," *Al-Hamishmar,* November 21, 1980.

64.   Kassem Zeid, "Rakah Sanctifies the Means," *Al-Hamishmar,* November 21, 1980.

65.   *Zoo Haderech,* May 9, 1979; September 29, 1980; April 1, 1981.

66.   Zeev Schiff, *Haaretz,* November 21, 1980; Hagai Eshed, "The Nazareth Congress against the Moderates," *Davar,* December 5, 1980.

67.   *Haaretz,* December 1, 1980.

68.   Attalah Mansour, "Rakah Seeks to Replace the PLO," *Haaretz,* November 30, 1980.

69.   *Jerusalem Post Weekly,* December 7–13, 1980.

70.   Yaakov Habakuk, "The Jihad Family," *Haaretz,* March 6, 1981.

71.   Moshe Sharon, "When Free Speech Runs Amok," *Jerusalem Post Weekly,* May 17–23, 1981.

72.   See Khalil Nakhleh, "Reassessing the Struggle Inside," *Arab Perspectives* 2(April 1981): 4–9. For Rakah's response to Nakhleh's argument see Emil

Tuma, "Reply to Nakhleh's 'Liberation Mentality,'" *New Outlook* (June 1981): 30–33.

73.   In the final weeks of the campaign the Labor party declared it was not supporting the United Arab List, its traditional affiliated list of Arab notables, but only the Labor party-Mapam list, including one Mapam and one Labor party Arab in realistic places. In early May, however, Raanan Cohen, director of the Labor party's Arab department, had said that the Labor party would promote, as in the past, an affiliated Arab list. *Davar,* May 3, 1981. See also *Davar,* March 23, 1981.

74.   Ehud Yaari, "Contradictory Trends among Arabs," *Davar,* June 3, 1977; *New York Times,* July 16, 1981. While the number of Arabs voting for the Labor party itself more than tripled, 1981 was the first time that lists traditionally affiliated with the Labor party failed to win representation in the Knesset. *Jerusalem Post Weekly,* July 5–11, 1981.

75.   Yechiel Harari, *The Elections in the Arab Sector—1977* (Hebrew), No. 6, (Givat Haviva, Israel: Institute for Arab Studies, 1978), pp. 10, 14, 18; *Zoo Haderech,* July 29, 1981; *New York Times,* July 16, 1981, *Yediot Acharonot,* July 10, 1981.

76.   Foreign Broadcast Information Service, August 14, 1981, p. 18.

7 Moscow, Jerusalem, and Washington in the Begin Era

Robert O. Freedman

In order to understand the position taken by the leaders of the Soviet Union toward Israel in the period since Menachem Begin became Israel's prime minister in May 1977, and the role of the Israeli-U.S. relationship in Soviet strategy, one must first examine the Soviet Union's overall strategy in the Middle East, because Soviet policy toward Israel and the Arab-Israeli conflict has been only a part—albeit a very important part—of overall Soviet strategy toward the region.[1] Soviet strategy toward the Middle East has gone through two stages since World War II. In the late 1940s and 1950s, it was essentially defensive since at that time the primary Soviet goal was to prevent the region's being used as a base of attack against itself. By the mid-1960s, however, the Soviet goal had shifted to an offensive one as the Soviet leadership sought to oust the West from its positions of military, political, and economic influence in the region and replace Western influence with Soviet influence. In each period, Soviet policy toward the Arab-Israeli conflict was part of Moscow's larger regional policy, and this essay will seek to show how Soviet policy toward Israel and the Arab-Israeli conflict has changed as the Soviet leaders' perception of their regional and global interests changed. In addition, the chapter will seek to demonstrate that the advent of Menachem Begin has had relatively little effect on overall Soviet policy, either toward Israel or toward the Arab-Israeli conflict, other than to give Moscow far more ammunition for its propaganda efforts than it had prior to 1977.

SOVIET POLICY TOWARD ISRAEL BEFORE THE BEGIN ELECTION

The Stalin Era

In the aftermath of World War II, the Soviet Union, under Stalin's leadership, sought to consolidate its security through the acquisition, either directly or by proxy, of regions contiguous to its borders. Thus, the Soviet Union took hold of Eastern Europe, strengthened its position in Outer Mongolia, and endeavored to control China's Sinkiang and Manchurian territories. The latter two areas, however, were lost to Soviet control when the Chinese Communists secured power in late 1949. The Middle East, another area contiguous to the Soviet Union did not escape Soviet efforts at control, as the Soviet Union sought military bases and territory from Turkey, and a section of northwest Iran as well. As in the case of Sinkiang and Manchuria, however, the Soviet Middle East efforts proved abortive. Indeed, to overall Soviet policy, they may be seen as counterproductive in that they helped precipitate the Truman Doctrine and the Turkish-U.S. and Iranian-U.S. alignments.

The British were also highly apprehensive at the Soviet territorial demands in the Middle East, a region England sought as its sphere of influence in the postwar period, and the newly-elected Labor government sought to create a bloc of pro-British Moslem Arab states, stretching from Egypt to Iraq, to both block Soviet penetration of the region and to enhance the British position there. With military bases in Egypt, Jordan, Palestine, and Iraq, the British evidently hoped to establish a sphere of influence of their own at a time when East and West Europe were being divided between the two superpowers. Although most Arab states were far from enthusiastic about the British scheme, the primary regional opponent of the British plans was the Jewish community of Palestine, which by this time was actively opposing British efforts to curb Jewish immigration to Palestine from the Holocaust-devastated Jewish communities of Europe. Similarly opposed to the British plan was the Soviet Union, which, cognizant of the tremendous development of military technology during World War II, saw the British base system in the Middle East as posing a threat against the Soviet Union. A coincidence of interests, therefore, placed the Soviet Union and the Jewish community of Palestine on the same side during the diplomatic activity at the United Nations in 1947 and the Arab-Israeli war of 1948–49. Indeed, while the United States was taking what might be called today an "evenhanded" (if not vacillating) position toward the Arab-Israeli conflict during this period,[2] the Soviet Union actively aided Israel by sending it extensive military aid (via Czechoslovakia) and giving it diplomatic support as well. Indeed, in light of current Soviet policy toward Israel, it is most interesting to read the Soviet press during this period as it strongly condemned the Arabs for invading Israel, while praising the newly-established Jewish state. Thus, on May 30, 1948, two weeks after the Arab invasion of Israel, *Pravda* stated:

> The Arab states in attacking the State of Israel, have entered a path fraught with dangerous consequences. The unprovoked aggression against the young Jewish state will encounter the harshest judgment of the people of the Soviet Union and progressive peoples of the whole world.

Stalin's decision to aid in the establishment of the state of Israel and to grant the young state both diplomatic and military support would appear to have been based on his evaluation of the geopolitics of the region. An independent Jewish state would split the bloc of Muslim Arab states the British were seeking to establish while also depriving the British of the excellent harbor at Haifa and of bases in the Negev desert. Indeed, an examination of the material in the archives of the Jewish Agency in Jerusalem indicates that this was the primary Soviet concern, as the only element the Soviets seemed to want as a quid pro quo for their support of Israel was that the Israelis would not grant military bases to any foreign power.[3] While there may well have been other, more secondary, Soviet motivations in deciding to aid the Israelis in the 1947–49 period, the available information indicates that strategic considerations played the most important part.[4] In any case by the early 1950s, the Soviet-Israeli relationship had cooled considerably, in part because of international political developments and in part because of Stalin's severe persecution of Soviet Jews in the 1949–53 period.

The Khrushchev Era

The Soviet turn to the Arab side of the Arab-Israeli conflict in the mid-1950s seems to have been motivated by considerations similar to Stalin's decision to aid Israel almost a decade earlier. By the mid-1950s, Soviet interest had shifted to Egypt, whose leader, Gamal Nasser, had adopted an anti-British posture much as the Israelis had done in the late 1940s. Once again the British were seeking to establish an anti-Soviet military alliance in the Middle East, this time with U.S. support. This alliance, known as the Baghdad Pact, came into being in early 1955 and soon became a target of both Soviet and Egyptian attack. The Soviets, as might be expected, were unhappy with the Baghdad Pact, since it sought to link the anti-Soviet NATO and SEATO alliances. For his part, Nasser opposed the Baghdad Pact because he saw it as bringing the British back into the Arab world—a region Nasser sought for Egyptian influence—after they had agreed to leave Egypt following the signing of the Anglo-Egyptian Treaty of July 1954. Once again, as in the case of Soviet aid to Israel in the 1947–49 period, there was a commonality of interest, and once again the Soviet Union responded to a regional power's requests for diplomatic support and military aid.[5] Nasser's acquisition of Soviet arms, however, posed a strategic threat to the Israelis, and one of the goals of the Israeli attack on Egypt on October 29, 1956 (which was joined by Britain and France for their own reasons) was to prevent Nasser, in his championing of the Arab cause, from using his newly acquired Soviet arsenal against Israel. The Soviet leaders, burdened at the time with a serious problem of their own (the revolt in Hungary) played a relatively small role in the crisis, as their threats against Britain, France, and Israel and their offer of Soviet "volunteers" came at a time when the crisis had already subsided. In the aftermath of the fighting, however, Moscow sought to take credit for forcing the withdrawal of Britain, France, and Israel from Egypt (in reality is was primarily U.S. pressure that accomplished this objective), and the Soviet Union later sought to capitalize on the Eisenhower Doctrine and the growing conflict between Egyptian and U.S. policy in the Arab world to enhance Soviet influence. The Soviets, however, were soon to find themselves on the horns of a dilemma as they sought to extend their influence in the region following the overthrow of the pro-British Nuri Said government in Iraq in July 1958. The conflict for leadership in the Arab world that soon erupted between the new Iraqi leader, General Qasim, and Nasser posed a difficult problem of choice for the Soviets, one that was to be a recurrent problem for them in their Middle East policies, and their decision to side with the new Iraqi leader led to a temporary reconciliation between Egypt and the United States.[6] In any case, for the remainder of Khrushchev's rule (until October 1964), the Middle East was not a center point of Soviet diplomacy, as the Soviets sought gains elsewhere in the Third World while at the same time facing difficult problems in areas more central to Soviet interest (i.e., the Berlin crises of 1958 and 1961, the Cuban missile crisis of 1962, and the escalation of the Sino-Soviet conflict from 1960 through 1964). Essentially, Soviet policy in the Middle East remained defensive during this period, and the Arab-Israeli conflict, which had flared into war in 1956, remained relatively dormant.

The Brezhnev Era

The Soviet Union's defensive stance in the Middle East was to change with the advent of the Brezhnev-Kosygin regime to power in October 1964. Having suffered serious reverses elsewhere in the Third World in countries such as Indonesia and Ghana, and perceiving new opportunities for extending Soviet influence into the Middle East, the new Soviet leadership soon decided to make the region the primary focus of Soviet efforts in the Third World.[7] At the time, the region looked particularly promising for the Soviet Union. In the first place, Egyptian-U.S. relations had hit a new low, and the once proud Nasser was bogged down in a war in Yemen. Second, England had announced in February 1966 that it was going to pull out of Aden, and there was increasing talk of the British pulling out of all of their holdings on the oil-rich Arabian peninsula. Third, a left-wing government had come to power in Syria in February 1966, which openly advocated improved relations with the Soviet Union and which invited Khalid Bakdash, an exiled communist leader, to return to Syria in an apparent gesture of goodwill to the Soviet Union. In addition, the world political situation seemed propitious for a more active Soviet role in the Middle East. The United States was bogged down in the Vietnamese War, and its growing troop commitment in Southeast Asia was helping the Soviet Union to contain China—now a central Soviet goal. For their part, the Chinese Communists had become bogged down in their so-called "cultural revolution" and could be expected to provide little opposition to Soviet policy in the Middle East.

The end result of this situation was that in May 1966, with Kosygin's visit to Cairo, Moscow embarked on a new policy in the Middle East, this time an offensive one. Apparently seeing that the time was ripe to begin to push western influence out of the Middle East (it was already weakened as a result of Britain's forthcoming pullout from Aden and the deterioration of relations between the United States and Egypt, the Arab world's most militarily powerful state), Moscow made its move. During his visit, Kosygin urged the unity of the "progressive forces" of the Arab world and, in particular, an alignment between Egypt and Syria. In coming out explicitly for this strategy, the Soviet leaders sought to solve a number of problems that had hitherto plagued them in their efforts to secure influence in the Middle East. These obstacles included the intra-Arab competition for leadership where, as in the case of the Nasser-Qasim feud, where if the Soviets backed one side, they risked alienating the other; intrastate conflicts such as the ones between Syria and Egypt, and Egypt and Iraq; and the dilemma of the Arab Communist parties, which were perceived as potential or actual competitors for leadership by the one-party Arab regimes in the region.[8] The Soviet leaders evidently hoped that these differences and conflicts could be subsumed in a larger Arab alignment against "imperialism" and what the Soviet leaders termed "imperialism's linchpin" in the Middle East—Israel. Interestingly enough, however, for the Soviet strategy to be successful Israel had to exist, and Soviet strategy required the continuation of Israeli existence, both for this reason and because Moscow did not wish to unduly alienate either the United States, or U.S. Jewry, by calling for Israel's destruction.[9] Yet, by focusing Arab efforts against Israel, by supplying both Egypt and Syria with advanced Soviet weapons, and by actively supporting Arab diplomatic efforts against Israel, the Soviet leaders may have given such Arab leaders as Egypt's Nasser and Syria's Salah Jedid the impression that the Soviet Union would give them support should a conflict with Israel result from the growing Arab-Israeli tension.

In any case, the Syrian government, emboldened by both Soviet military aid and by an alliance with Egypt in August 1966, stepped up its guerrilla attacks against Israel, only to be met by increasingly severe Israeli retaliation. Fearing that Syria's pro-Soviet, albeit weakly-based, regime might fall, both as a result of its internal problems and Israeli attacks, Moscow supplied false information to Egypt that Israel was preparing to attack Syria. Nasser, acting on this information, moved his troops into the Sinai in mid-May 1967, then ousted the United Nations forces there, and announced a blockade of the Straits of Tiran to Israeli shipping.[10] These moves, together with the adhesion of Jordan to the Syrian-Egyptian alliance at the end of May, helped precipitate the Six-Day War. While the Soviet leaders seemed to have grasped the potential consequences of their actions in late May, they were ineffectual in arresting the trend of events as Israel decided to attack Egypt on June 5 and quickly defeated all three of its Arab opponents, capturing in the process the Sinai Peninsula, the West Bank and Gaza regions, and the Golan Heights.

The major Israeli victory seemed at first to be a significant defeat for the Soviet drive for influence in the Middle East. Soviet military equipment and training had proved of little value, and the Soviet leaders' failure to aid their client states while they were being soundly defeated also served to lower Soviet prestige in the Arab world. Yet, paradoxically, the aftermath of the war was to see major Soviet gains in the region, although they were to prove temporary. One of the major results of the war was further radicalization of the Arab world and a concomitant weakening of the U.S. position in the area. Egypt, Syria, Algeria, and Iraq all broke diplomatic relations with the United States because of alleged U.S. aid to Israel during the war, and in 1969 there was a further deterioration of the U.S. position, as a left-wing regime came to power in the Sudan and the pro-Western regime of Libya's King Idris was overthrown.

Meanwhile, by quickly resupplying Egypt and Syria with the weaponry that restored their military credibility, and championing Arab demands at the United Nations, the Soviet Union was able to restore its position in the Arab world. Nonetheless, the Soviet position was not without its problems, since the Arab-Israeli conflict, which had been relatively subdued in the 1957–66 period, now became a central issue not only in the Middle East, but also in world politics. In selecting its policy for this now highly salient issue, the Soviet leadership was faced with a dilemma. On the one hand, they wanted to continue to weaken Western influence in the Arab world while enhancing Soviet influence. On the other hand, however, with the main Arab interest now in regaining the lands lost to Israel in the 1967 war, the Soviet Union risked the possibility of direct confrontation with the United States, which by now was sending Israel advanced weaponry (hitherto France had been Israel's main supplier) and had taken a more overtly pro-Israeli position. The dilemma may have appeared particularly serious for the Soviets after the March 1969 border clashes with China signaled a further escalation of the Sino-Soviet conflict.

Yet another Soviet dilemma lay in the fact that, given the previous history of U.S. success in securing Israeli withdrawal from conquered Arab territory, the Soviet leadership had to be concerned with a possible turn by the Arab leaders toward the United States. Therefore, after neither U.N. Resolution 242 of November 1967 nor the two-power or four-power talks that followed it had succeeded in getting an Israeli withdrawal, which would have enabled the Soviet Union to demonstrate its ability to champion the Arab cause, Moscow decided to back Nasser as he launched his war of attrition against the Israelis in the spring of 1969.[11] The Soviet leadership followed up its decision by sending Soviet pilots and surface-to-air missile crews to Egypt in early 1970, when the war of attrition led to major Israeli retaliatory strikes against Egypt's heartland. Having gained control over a number of Egyptian military and air bases in the process, the Soviet leaders evidently considered the strategic gains worth the political risks, particularly when the Nixon administration, immersed in the Vietnamese War and a new conflict in Cambodia in the spring of 1970, took little action to prevent the consolidation of the Soviet position in Egypt. While the Soviet leaders were later to endorse Nasser's agreement to the U.S. cease-fire efforts in the summer of 1970, their move seemed primarily aimed at completing the emplacement of surface-to-air missiles along the canal at no further loss of Egyptian (or Soviet) lives. The subsequent Soviet/Egyptian violation of the cease-fire agreement, by moving more missiles up to the canal, further underlined both the Soviet commitment to Egypt and the Soviet Union's willingness to enhance Egyptian military strength against Israel, since the emplacement of the missiles gave Egypt the capability of launching an attack against Israel using the missiles as an umbrella against Israeli air attacks—as, indeed, it was to do in October 1973.[12]

Aiding Egypt in its war of attrition, however, was not the same as assisting the Arabs in a full-scale attack on Israel—something the Russians saw at the time as beyond the Arabs' military capability. While Nasser had mortgaged a good deal of Egypt's sovereignty to the Soviet Union in the form of bases in return for rebuilding his army following the debacle of 1967, his successor, Anwar Sadat, who came to power in October 1970 after Nasser's death, was to adopt a different policy. When diplomatic efforts to bring about a Middle East peace plan stagnated, Sadat became increasingly disenchanted with the Soviets, whom he saw as unable to get the Israelis to withdraw by diplomatic means, unwilling to use military force for this purpose, and hesitant to supply the Arab states with the weaponry they needed to fight effectively.

The Soviet reluctance, which became increasingly evident during the 1971–72 period, may have resulted from three factors. In the first place, the strong U.S. reaction to what was at least a tacitly Soviet-supported Syrian invasion of Jordan in September 1970 seems to have indicated to the Soviets that the United States was more willing to take action in the Middle East than it had been in January 1970, at the time when the Soviet Union sent its pilots and missile crews to Egypt and became actively involved in Nasser's war of attrition. Second, the long-feared Sino-U.S. entente against the Soviet Union seemed suddenly on the horizon following Kissinger's surprise trip to Peking in July 1971 and the subsequent announcement of Nixon's visit to the Chinese capital. Finally, the long-delayed strategic arms talks, the centerpiece of Soviet-U.S. detente, were nearing conclusion. In sum, the Soviet leaders clearly did not wish—at that time—to jeopardize the benefits of detente to aid a rather fickle Arab ally such as Sadat, who had not only openly flirted with the Americans (U.S. Secretary of State Rodgers was invited to Cairo in May 1971), but who had also opposed Soviet policy in the Sudan as well, particularly at a time when the United States, after the events in Jordan, was significantly strengthening its relationship with Israel.[13] For his part, Sadat saw the emerging Soviet-U.S.

detente as taking place at Arab expense, and soon after the Soviet-U.S. summit of May 1972 in Moscow, the Egyptian leader expelled the Soviet military advisers from his country while also ending Soviet control over Egyptian air, naval, and army bases. While the Egyptian action was a serious blow to the Soviet Unions's strategic position in the eastern Mediterranean, the subsequent Soviet pullout, not only of advisers but also pilots and missile crews, lessened the chances of any direct Soviet involvement in a future Egyptian-Israeli war, and this factor must have softened the impact of the exodus, which was clearly a major blow to the Soviet Union's Middle East position.[14]

While Sadat may have hoped that his ouster of the Soviets would lead to action from the United States in the form of pressure on Israel to withdraw from the Sinai, such pressure was not to be forthcoming—at least, not for more than a year and a half. Therefore, having sought to mobilize both U.S. and Soviet support for his policies, and having failed in both quests, Sadat moved to rally the Arabs, and particularly oil-rich Saudi Arabia, to his cause. By the spring of 1973 he had also secured a resumption in the flow of Soviet weapons, enough to enable him to launch a limited war against Israel, and by September he had achieved a general coordination of military planning with Syria. While the Soviet Union almost certainly knew about Sadat's plans for war, they did little to prevent it, and once both Egypt and Syria had demonstrated their military ability in the first days of the war, the Soviet leadership reinforced the Arab war effort with a major airlift and sealift of weaponry, as well as diplomatic support in the United Nations.[15] In taking such actions, the Soviet Union was stepping back from its policy of supporting detente, which had reached its highest point at the time of the Moscow summit of 1972, and which seemed to be reconfirmed by the Washington summit of June 1973. The change in Soviet behavior may be explained by several factors. In the first place, the Sino-U.S. entente, which the Soviet Union had initially feared, had not come to fruition. Second, the Nixon administration was now badly beset by Watergate and other scandals and was in a weakened position vis-á-vis the Soviet Union. Indeed, by this time, one of the few positive achievements the Nixon administration could show was detente with the Soviet Union—a policy to which the administration was now wedded. These factors combined to give the Soviet Union more leverage vis-á-vis the United States in its relationship because the Nixon administration, in a reverse of the 1972 situation, was now in the position of needing the Soviet Union more than the Soviets needed it, and the Soviet leadership was not slow in taking advantage of the situation.[16]

The Arab coalition that Sadat had formed on the eve of the 1973 war fit very nicely into the overall Soviet plan of forming an "anti-imperialist" alliance of Arab states to confront both Israel and the United States. The fact that this Arab coalition included not only such "progressive" Arab states as Syria and Iraq but also such conservative ones as Kuwait and Saudi Arabia may have been perceived as an added bonus for the Soviets, because the oil embargo imposed by these countries against the United States and its NATO allies seemed to be a major step on the road to ousting Western influence from the Arab world— the Soviet goal since the mid-1960s—as well as weakening the overall Western position in the world balance of power.

Unfortunately for the Soviets, however, the aftermath of the war was to see not only the collapse of the "anti-imperialist" Arab coalition they had so warmly endorsed but also a serious deterioration of the Soviet position in the Arab world—despite all the military and diplomatic support the Soviet Union had given the Arab cause during the war. While the Arab-Israeli conflict remained the most salient issue in Middle East politics, it was the United States that was to take an active role in working toward a diplomatic settlement, earning for itself in the process a greatly enhanced status in the Arab world. Under the mediating efforts of U.S. Secretary of State Henry Kissinger, Egypt and Israel reached a disengagement agreement in January 1974 that led to the withdrawal of Israeli forces from both banks of the Suez Canal. Then, at the end of May 1974, Kissinger secured a disengagement agreement between Syria and Israel that led to a withdrawal of Israeli forces not only from territories captured in 1973 but also from the city of Kuneitra, which had been captured in 1967. Yet another disengagement agreement was reached in late August 1975 between Israel and Egypt whereby the Israelis withdrew to the Gitla and Middi passes in the Sinai Desert.[17]

While the United States was taking these diplomatic initiatives, the Soviet Union was, essentially, sitting on the sidelines, although in the aftermath of the 1973 war a Geneva peace conference was convened under the cochairmanship of the United States and the Soviet Union. It was quickly adjourned, however, and Kissinger, not the Geneva Conference, became the main instrument in working toward a settlement of the Arab-Israeli conflict. For their part, the Soviet leadership was clearly unhappy with the disengagement agreements—particularly the Sinai II agreement of 1975, which the Soviets loudly denounced—but they proved incapable of influencing the course of events.

In an effort to directly affect the diplomacy surrounding the Arab-Israeli conflict in the aftermath of the 1973 war, the Soviet leadership tried a variety of tactics. Thus, at the Geneva Conference, Gromyko made a point of underlining the Soviet Union's support of Israel's right to exist and met privately with the Israeli representative, Foreign Minister Abba Eban, to suggest their willingness to reestablish diplomatic relations with Israel once an Arab-Israeli settlement was reached.[18] Several months later, however, in the face of the first Egyptian-Israeli disengagement agreement and Kissinger's efforts to work out a similar agreement between Syria and Israel, Moscow took the opposite course by sending arms to Syria and supporting the war of attrition Syria was waging with Israel on the Golan Heights.[19] In taking this action, the Soviet leadership may have hoped to torpedo the negotiations or, at least, prevent the lifting of the oil embargo that was then under consideration by the oil-rich Arab states. At the very minimum, the Soviets may have felt that their aid would strengthen Syria's hand in the bargaining process and thereby preserve the Soviet position in Syria and prevent its slipping into the pro-U.S. camp as Egypt appeared to have done by the spring of 1974.

Another tactic used by the Soviet leadership during the Kissinger disengagement process was to urge the rapid reconvening of the Geneva Conference, although the Soviet calls did not meet with success. Even during the period from March to May 1975 when the Kissinger shuttle had been temporarily derailed and U.S. Middle East policy was going through one of its periodic "reappraisals," the Soviet Union's efforts to seize the diplomatic initiative proved ineffectual. Despite dispatching Kosygin to Libya and Tunisia, and sending a number of signals to Israel of continued Soviet support of the Jewish state's existence (these included sending several Soviet officials to Israel), the Soviet leadership proved unable to even coordinate Arab positions on a settlement let alone work out the details of an Arab-Israeli agreement.[20] A fourth tactic used by the Soviet Union, as Middle Eastern developments began to move in a way unfavorable to Soviet interests in the aftermath of the 1973 war, was a fundamental policy change toward the Palestinians. With Egypt moving toward the U.S. camp, and with the Saudi Arabian-Egyptian axis, tacitly supported by the Shah's Iran, now the dominant one in Arab politics, and with Syria wavering despite large amounts of Soviet military aid, the Soviet leaders began to openly back the concept of an independent Palestinian state in the West Bank and Gaza regions. Given the probable hostile relations between such a state and both Israel and the Hussein regime in Jordan, Moscow evidently hoped that a Palestinian state led by the PLO would turn to the Soviet Union for support.[21]

Following the Sinai II agreement of September 1, 1975, and a U.N. meeting between Gromyko and Israel's new Foreign Minister Yigal Allon on September 24, 1975, Soviet plans for an overall settlement of the Arab-Israeli conflict, one facet of which would include an independent Palestinian state, became increasingly explicit, and proposals were published, amid great fanfare, in April and October 1976. The plans included three major elements. In the first place, a total Israeli withdrawal from all territories captured in the 1967 war. Second, the establishment of a Palestinian state in the West Bank and Gaza areas. Finally, an acknowledgement of the right to exist of all states in the Middle East. In their statements, the Soviets also came out for the immediate reconvening of the Geneva Conference with the full participation of the PLO, but this ploy proved ineffectual since neither Israel nor the United States would accept the PLO as a negotiating partner so long as it continued to openly call for Israel's destruction. In addition to U.S. and Israeli opposition, the Soviet peace proposals, which included offers of Soviet guarantees, were not greeted with much enthusiasm by the Arabs, and the growing civil war in Lebanon further reduced the efficacy of the Soviet plan.[22]

Indeed, the civil war in Lebanon while temporarily sidelining both U.S. and Soviet efforts to settle the Arab-Israeli conflict also posed a very serious problem for Soviet diplomacy. By June 1976 Syria had mounted a major invasion of Lebanon, and battles took place between Syrian and PLO forces. Since the PLO, despite its disparate elements, was now a close ally of the Soviet Union in the Middle East, while Syria remained the key swing country the Soviets wanted to prevent from joining the Egyptian-Saudi Arabian axis, it was inevitable that the Soviet Union's relations with one or both would suffer no matter which position the Soviets took toward the Lebanese fighting. The end result was that the PLO complained about insufficient Soviet aid, while Syria was clearly unhappy with both the negative Soviet comments about Syrian policy in Lebanon and a slowdown in Soviet arms deliveries. Nonetheless, the Soviets were saved further diplomatic embarassment when a settlement of the civil war was reached in October 1976 that preserved the PLO as an independent force in Lebanon, although the fact that the settlement had been worked out under Saudi Arabian mediation and that it also included a reconciliation between Syria and Egypt could not have been happily received in the Kremlin, which continued to fear the adhesion of Syria to the Egyptian-Saudi axis.[23]

In the aftermath of the Lebanese civil war came the U.S. presidential elections. With a new U.S. president in office, albeit one relatively inexperienced in foreign affairs, all sides expected new U.S. initiatives to bring about a Middle East settlement. The Soviets, whose relations with the United States had hit a new low as a result of their involvement in Angola, but who hoped for a new SALT agreement and new trade agreements nevertheless, sent a number of signals to the incoming Carter administration that it would be willing to cooperate with the United States in bringing about a Middle East settlement.[24] The Soviet reasoning appeared to be that given the sharp diminution of Soviet influence in the Arab world due to U.S. diplomatic successes and the establishment of a large pro-U.S. camp in the Arab world (the only strongly pro-Soviet elements at this time were Iraq, Libya, Algeria, and South Yemen—countries with relatively little influence in the area), Moscow would do well to have an overall settlement to consolidate the Soviet position in the region, even if the Soviets were not yet at the point where they could resume their offensive efforts to weaken and ultimately eliminate Western influence.

The Carter administration, however, was not yet willing to join the Soviet Union in working out a settlement, although it did share one important policy principle with the Soviets—that the time had come to end the step-by-step diplomacy and move toward an overall agreement. Convinced that Kissinger's step-by-step approach was no longer viable, the Carter administration was also thinking in terms of a general settlement, to be reached at Geneva, although the elements of the Carter administration's peace plan differed considerably from the Soviet's. In addition to advocating trade, tourism, and diplomatic relations between Israel and her Arab neighbors, Carter also came out publicly in a speech to visiting Israeli Prime Minister Yitzhak Rabin in early March 1977 for "defensible borders" for Israel that might extend beyond the "permanent and recognized" borders reached in a peace settlement.[25] While this statement made the Israelis happy, they were to be confounded only one week later when Carter came out with the second part of his plan, a "homeland" for the Palestinians—the first time a U.S. president had ever publicly mentioned the concept.[26]

The Israelis were not the only ones stunned by Carter's move.[27] While on the surface it appeared to be similar to the Soviet call for a Palestinian state, (although Carter was careful not to use the word "state") the Soviets were quick to object to the plan because it was linked to the idea, put forth by Sadat and Syrian President Hafiz Asad and tacitly endorsed by King Hussein, that a political connection should exist between a West Bank-Gaza Palestinian "entity" and Jordan. The Russians, who were hoping for an independent Palestinian state under their influence, strongly opposed this idea, since any Palestinian entity linked to Jordan would, most likely, come under the influence of the then pro-Western Jordanian monarch. Yet another Middle Eastern problem facing Moscow at the time was the rapidly escalating war in the Horn of Africa between Ethiopia and Somalia, the latter country a member of the Arab League. The war was to lead to the ouster of the Soviets from their military bases in Somalia, as the Soviet Union, confronted once again by the dilemma of having to choose sides in a regional conflict when they wished to maintain good relations with both parties, opted for non-Arab Ethiopia—thus incurring the wrath of the Arab states who were backing Somalia.[28]

While Soviet-Arab relations were increasingly disturbed by Soviet aid to Ethiopia, the Soviets were soon to capitalize on the results of the Israeli election, which took place on May 17, to try to reverse the situation and rebuild their position in the Arab world.

SOVIET-ISRAELI RELATIONS IN THE BEGIN ERA

From Begin's Election to the Soviet-U.S. Statement

The coming to power of the Likud party led by Menachem Begin came as a major surprise to most foreign observers, but the Soviet media lost little time in trying to exploit the election and the new Israeli prime minister's statements, which included calling the West Bank and Gaza "liberated" rather than "occupied" territories and pledging the construction of more settlements in the West Bank,[29] to try to rally the Arabs away from the United States and create the "anti-imperialist" Arab bloc Moscow wanted. The first major opportunity for the Russians came in June when Egyptian Foreign Minister Ismail Fahmy journeyed to Moscow for talks. Soviet-Egyptian relations were at a new low at the time of his visit, but the Soviets, if one is to believe Sadat's account of the trip, lost the opportunity to improve Soviet-Egyptian ties by badly overplaying the leverage over Egypt they thought they had obtained because of Begin's coming to power. According to Sadat, the Soviets "behaved rudely and adopted a very hard line."[30] In addition to demanding that Egypt sign a new political agreement (the Soviet-Egyptian Treaty of Friendship and Cooperation had been abrogated by Sadat in 1976), the Soviets warned Egypt not to exclude them from the Middle East peace-making process—demands that Sadat rejected. As if to underline Sadat's rejection of Soviet policy, Egyptian forces proceeded to pound the Libyan army in a brief border war (Egypt had long accused the Soviet North African client of subversion and sabotage) three days after Sadat had openly announced the failure of the Fahmy visit.

If the Soviet Union had no success in regaining the allegiance of Egypt, the United States was also facing major problems in its Middle East policy, since it became increasingly clear that it would be difficult to coordinate the U.S. peace plan with Israeli actions, and the Soviet media was quick to exploit the situation. Thus, while the United States was coming out for a West Bank-Jordan link in a peace settlement, the Begin government was giving every indication that for both religious/historical and security reasons it was planning to hold onto the West Bank. Despite the Begin government's actions, which included legalizing three hitherto illegal Israeli settlements on the West Bank and planning others, the United States continued to grant military aid to Israel, thereby providing Moscow with ammunition for its anti-U.S. propaganda.[31] Nonetheless, in the face of the strain in U.S.-Israeli relations caused by Begin's policies (Soviet propaganda sought to minimize the differences in the two nations' positions), President Carter sent Cyrus Vance on a visit to the Middle East in early August to try to expedite the peace process. Perhaps naively, Vance said at the time that the Soviet leaders had indicated a willingness to "use their influence" with some of the parties to "encourage flexibility."[32] It is difficult to know, of course, whether Vance took the Soviet leaders seriously as to their "willingness to encourage flexibility" because, at least from Soviet media statements during the Vance trip, it appeared as if the Soviets were openly trying to disparage Vance's diplomatic efforts.[33] In any case, even without Soviet obstruction, Vance had a most difficult task to accomplish. The crucial question was how the Palestinians could be represented at the Geneva talks, with Israel opposing PLO representation and the Arabs supporting it. Egypt, eager to get the talks started, proposed that Arab-Israeli working groups meet in the United States prior to Geneva. Israel endorsed the idea, which appeared to be a way of avoiding dealing with the Palestinian issue until a later stage in the negotiations. Syria, however, rejected Sadat's plan, proposing instead a unified Arab delegation at Geneva—something the PLO rejected almost as rapidly as the Sadat proposal.

Given the stalemate, President Carter then moved once again to try to elicit sufficient moderation from the PLO to make the organization a possible negotiating partner at Geneva. In both a *Time* magazine interview and a news con-

ference timed to coincide with the Vance Middle East mission, Carter told the
PLO that if they recognized the applicability of U.N. Resolution 242, this would
give the United States the possibility "to start discussions with them."[34] The
Carter call for moderation among the Palestinians failed, however, as a PLO
Central Council meeting in late August announced it would not change its charter (calling for Israel's destruction) and would not accept U.N. Resolution 242.[35]
Meanwhile, the Begin government, angered at U.S. flirtation with the PLO
(which was in violation of the written understanding between the United States
and Israel made at the time of the Sinai II agreement) set up three additional
settlements in the West Bank and announced the implementation of Israeli
welfare laws there—further signs that the Begin government appeared to be moving to annex the region.

As the Middle East peace process reached an impasse, PLO leader Yasir
Arafat journeyed to Moscow to coordinate strategy. While the primary concern
of both the Soviet Union and the PLO appeared to be how to avoid exclusion
from the U.S.-directed peace effort,[36] the Soviet leaders utilized Arafat's visit to
emphasize Soviet-Arab solidarity and disparage the U.S. peace efforts. Zuheir
Mohsen, a Palestinian leader who accompanied Arafat to Moscow, later stated
that "the Soviet Union warned us both, Arafat and myself, not to have any trust
in American promises."[37] If the Saiqa leader was quoted correctly, his statement
would seem to put in question Vance's assertion of early August that the Soviet
leaders had indicated a willingness to "use their influence to encourage flexibility," at least insofar as the PLO was concerned.

Nonetheless, the Carter administration was not yet persuaded of the Soviet
Union's unwillingness to play a positive role in Middle East peace negotiations.
Throughout the month of September there were secret Soviet-U.S. negotiations, which resulted in a joint Soviet-U.S. statement, based on a Soviet draft, on
the principles of a Middle East peace settlement (see Appendix A). The joint
statement was made public on October 1, 1977 and transformed, albeit only
temporarily, the pattern of Middle East diplomacy.

The Soviet-U.S. Joint Statement and Its Aftermath

An examination of the joint statement indicates concessions by both sides
from previous positions on a Middle East peace settlement, although the Soviet
concessions soon proved to be merely paper ones, and the United States was also
to pull back from concessions it made in the document.

The Soviet concessions were fourfold in nature. In the first place, the document called only for Israeli withdrawal from territories occupied in 1967 (not
all the territories); second, it made no specific mention of the need to establish
a Palestinian state; third, there was no mention of the Palestine Liberation Organization; and finally, it called for the establishment of "normal peaceful relations"—a term that appeared to reverse the previous Soviet position, emphasized
by a *New Times* editorial of early September 1977, which opposed the concept

of "open borders" because "it would make Tel Aviv the center of a huge neo-colonialist empire in the Middle East."[38] For its part, the United States also made four concessions. The first and most important was its agreement to the term "the legitimate *rights* of the Palestinians" (hitherto the United States had spoken only of the "legitimate *interests* of the Palestinians"—emphasis mine). Second, the document made no mention of either U.N. Resolutions 242 or 338, hitherto the only documents agreed upon by the Geneva participants. Third, the United States came out for a comprehensive settlement, thus publicly ending the step-by-step strategy and appearing to eliminate the possibility of another Egyptian-Israeli separate agreement. Finally, by calling for the resumption of the Geneva Conference "no larger than December 1977," the United States guaranteed the Soviet Union a major role in the Middle East peace-making process as a coequal, since the United States had never before set a specific date for the reconvening of Geneva.

The United States reasoning in bringing the Soviet Union back into the peace-making process would appear to have been based on two assumptions. In the first place, the Carter administration seemed set on an overall peace settlement and saw Geneva as the only way to bring such an overall settlement about. Therefore, it felt, in the words of President Carter, it was better not "to have a co-chairman who might be publicly and privately opposing any peaceful solution."[39] Perhaps more importantly, after the lack of success of the Vance mission in August (reportedly, Vance got the idea for the joint statement after his Middle East trip),[40] and realizing that both Syria and the PLO had to be brought into a settlement, the administration apparently believed the Soviet Union both could and would use its influence to make both Syria and the PLO agree to a peace settlement.[41] If these, indeed, were the U.S. assumptions—and the latter, at least, was a highly debatable one—subsequent Soviet behavior might have raised a few questions about administration reasoning. Within a few days of the Soviet-U.S. statement, the Soviet Union had backtracked from a number of its concessions and returned to its prestatement position on a Middle East peace settlement. Thus, in an Arabic language broadcast on October 3, Radio Moscow interpreted the statement as calling for the *complete* withdrawal of Israeli forces from lands captured in 1967.[42] On the same day, in another Arabic language broadcast, Radio Moscow broadcast the statement of the PLO leader in Moscow, Mohammed Shaer, in which he stated that the term "legitimate rights" of the Palestinian Arab people meant their legitimate national rights to establish their own national state.[43] Soviet radio broadcasts reversing the joint statement "concessions" continued throughout October, and in the last week of the month, Oleg Trayanovsky, the Soviet Union's permanent U.N. representative, made a statement in the Security Council debate on the Middle East supporting the establishment of a Palestinian state and reaffirming Soviet support for the PLO as the sole lawful representative of the Palestinian people.[44] Several days later, in a major *Pravda* article on October 29, Pavel Demchenko called for the total withdrawal of Israeli troops from all occupied territories and again endorsed the right of the Palestinians to their own state.[45] Finally, in early November, a feature article in *New Times* once again attacked the "open borders" concept, thereby calling into question Moscow's interpretation of the "normalization" of Arab-Israeli relations.[46]

While the Soviet Union was backtracking from its concessions in the joint statement, the Carter administration was coming under very severe pressure for having signed the statement at all. Israel, its friends in Congress, the American Jewish community, AFL-CIO leader George Meany, and a host of other people berated the administration for its concessions to the Soviet Union and for taking steps to impose a Middle East solution with the Soviet Union.[47] Indeed, the pressure on the Carter administration grew so heavy that the president, faced with major problems with the Congress over energy and the Panama Canal, and with his position weakened as a result of the resignation of his close friend, Bert Lance, quickly moved to placate his critics. Thus, in his U.N. speech on October 4, Carter emphasized the continued importance of U.N. Resolutions 242 and 338 and stated that the United States was not seeking to impose a peace settlement. In addition, he again came out for a peace settlement with trade, tourism, and diplomatic relations as component parts and restated his commitment to recognized and secure borders for Israel, although he also mentioned "the legitimate rights of the Palestinians."[48] The president took even a stronger step toward placating his critics two days later when, after a lengthy session with Israeli Foreign Minister Dayan, in which a joint working paper was worked out, he told the Israeli leader that Israel would not be required to agree to the wording of the joint Soviet-U.S. statement as a prerequisite for Geneva and that U.N. Resolutions 242 and 338 would remain the basis for the resumption of the Geneva talks.[49]

As might be expected, the Soviet Union, which had warmly welcomed the joint Soviet-U.S. statement as a means of reentering the center of Middle East diplomacy and moving toward the creation of a Palestinian state, lost little time in attacking the U.S.-Israeli working paper and urging the Arabs to reject it.[50] For their part the Arabs showed little enthusiasm about the joint paper, with the PLO rejecting it totally and Syria strongly supporting the PLO. Meanwhile, fighting between Israeli-backed Christian Arabs and PLO forces in Lebanon had begun to escalate, with Israeli settlements in northern Israel coming under fire on November 6 and 8. The Israelis retaliated with a major air strike against PLO positions in southern Lebanon on November 9, and it appeared that not only had the process toward on Arab-Israeli peace settlement reached a halt but that the chances for war had begun to increase. It was in this situation that Anwar Sadat, who, together with Menachem Begin, took a very dim view of the joint Soviet-U.S. statement, made his spectacular offer to come to Jerusalem to end the Middle East peace impasse.[51] It soon became clear that Sadat was setting a new course in Arab-Israeli relations, one with major implications for Soviet policy in the Middle East.

From the Sadat Visit to Camp David

The Sadat visit to Jerusalem came at a particularly difficult time for the Soviet Union's position in the Middle East. Soviet aid to Ethiopia had finally proved to be too much for Somali leader Siad Barré, who, in mid-November, expelled his Soviet advisors, ousted the Soviets from their Somali bases, and renounced the Soviet-Somali Friendship Treaty.[52] In addition to suffering the loss of key bases in Somalia, a development that weakened the Soviet position in the Horn of Africa, the Soviet Union's position in the Indian Ocean had also deteriorated. Not only did the United States unquestionably have the largest and most formidable base in the region on Diego Garcia, but the overall geopolitical balance in the region had also shifted against the Soviets because of the sudden change of government in India, in which Indira Gandhi, who had been quite sympathetic to the Soviet Union, was ousted by popular vote and replaced by Moraji DeSai, who appeared to take a much more neutral position in the Soviet-U.S. struggle for influence in the Third World and who moved toward a reconciliation with China as well.[53] Thus, the overall deterioration of their position in the Horn of Africa and in the Indian Ocean must have concerned the Soviet leaders as they sought to deal with an even more serious problem—Sadat's visit to Jerusalem and its implications for Soviet policy in the core area of the Middle East.

Essentially, Sadat's decision to go to Jerusalem presented the Soviet leadership with both a danger and an opportunity. On the one hand, were Sadat and Begin to successfully negotiate a peace settlement, there was the possibility that Jordan, Syria, and moderate Palestinian elements both within and outside the PLO might follow suit, thus leaving the Soviet Union isolated in the Middle East with only radical Libya and Iraq (whom virtually all the other Arab states distrusted) as backers of Soviet policy, along with radical rejectionists within the PLO, and Algeria and South Yemen as well, although the latter two Arab states were too far removed from the core of the Arab world to count very much.[54] On the other hand, however, should the Egyptian-Israeli talks fail to achieve an agreement to which Syria could adhere, there was the possibility that Syria, together with Jordan (which at that time was closely aligned with Syria), Syria's dependency Lebanon, and its own PLO force, Saiqa, might be drawn to join the "rejectionists," thereby isolating Sadat in the Arab world as the sole Arab leader willing to make peace with Israel . Such a development might well hasten Sadat's ouster or, at the minimum, lead to the formation of large "anti-imperialist" bloc of Arab states, which could be expected to be supportive of Soviet policy in its zero-sum game competition with the United States for influence in the Arab world. Finally, should the Egyptian-Israeli talks fail, Sadat would be discredited, and the United States might feel constrained to push for the immediate reconvening of the Geneva Conference, where the Soviet Union would play a major role as cochairman.

As the Soviet leaders were contemplating their response to the Sadat peace initiative, Sadat was being warmly received in Israel, and when he returned to

Egypt, he received a hero's welcome. The reaction in the other Arab states, however, was considerably cooler. Saudi Arabia, Egypt's main Arab ally, gave at best grudging support for his visit, while Jordan's reaction was also noncommittal. At the same time, Syria, Libya, the PLO, Iraq, Algeria, and South Yemen denounced Sadat's trip, with only the Sudan, Morocco, and Oman strongly supporting it. For its part the Soviet Union strongly criticized the Sadat visit as a legitimization of Israeli occupation of Arab lands and an effort to isolate both the PLO and the Soviet Union.[55]

In part as a result of Soviet opposition to the Sadat initiative, the Carter administration reexamined its attitude toward the Soviet role in a Middle East peace settlement and also changed its position on the dynamics of a Middle East peace settlement, jettisoning its earlier plan for an overall settlement in Geneva. The new U.S. policy appeared to be a "peace by concentric circles" system in which the final step would be a Geneva Conference to ratify earlier agreements. Speaking on the ABC television program *Issues and Answers* in mid-December, Zbigniew Brzezinski, President Carter's national security advisor, articulated the new U.S. strategy of "three concentric circles."[56] The first circle, stated Brzezinski, would include Egypt, Israel, and the United States, "because they want us to be there." The second circle would bring in the "moderate Arabs"—the moderate Palestinians and the Jordanians—to negotiate the issues of Gaza and the West Bank. Finally, Brzezinski said, there is the concentric circle "which involves the Soviet Union and the Syrians, if they choose not to become engaged sooner, and that clearly is Geneva." Interestingly enough, however, Brzezinski denied that the new U.S. strategy in any way changed the U.S. view of the Soviet role in the Middle East peace-making process. Moscow, however, took another view, claiming that the U.S. plan, as outlined "quite frankly" by Brzezinski, was aimed at urging Israel and Egypt to conclude a separate agreement, thus "breaking up Arab unity, keeping Israel as the U.S. strike force in the Middle East and bringing the Arab countries into line one by one."[57]

While the United States was altering its approach to a Middle East peace settlement in response to the peace initiative undertaken by Sadat, the Soviet Union was also responding to the peace initiative and the change in U.S. policy that resulted from it. Essentially, the Soviet response was threefold in nature: (1) a major airlift and sealift to Ethiopia to aid the hard-pressed Mengistu regime; (2) an attempt to reinforce, through military aid and diplomatic support, the anti-Sadat Arab rejectionist front that had sprung up as a result of Sadat's visit to Jerusalem; and (3) continued deprecation of both Sadat's initiative and U.S. efforts to bring about a Middle East peace settlement.

The first item on the Soviet agenda after the Sadat visit to Jerusalem was a massive resupply effort for the Ethiopian government, which was in deep trouble because of major Somali inroads into the Ethiopian heartland and Eritrean successes against Ethiopian troops. On November 26, 1977, less than a week after Sadat's visit, the Soviet Union mounted a huge airlift of military equipment and Cuban troops, which soon succeeded in turning the tide of battle. The Soviet goals in moving to aid the Ethiopian regime seem clear. Moscow feared that Sadat's visit might lead to a Western-supported peace settlement that could effectively isolate the Soviet Union in the region. By aiding Ethiopia, the Soviet Union sought to assure itself of at least a political—and possibly a military—base at the junction of the Middle East and Black Africa, one that commanded a large section of Red Sea coastline. In addition, an Ethiopian victory would prevent the Red Sea being transformed into an "Arab lake" controlled by pro-Western Arab regimes.

In addition to mounting a major airlift and sealift to Ethiopia, the second major Soviet response to the Sadat peace initiative was to try to isolate Sadat and reinforce the anti-Sadat coalition of Arab states that had come into being as a result of the Egyptian president's visit to Jerusalem. Soon after Sadat's return from Israel, a parade of Arab leaders visited Moscow. They included PLO political department chief Farouk Kaddoumi (November 24), Syrian Foreign Minister Abdel Khaddam (November 29), Tariq Aziz, the special representative of Iraqi President Hassan Al Bakr (December 3), Algerian President Houari Boumadienne (January 12), South Yemeni Prime Minster Ali Nasser Mohammed (February 1), Libyan Foreign Minister Abdul Jalloud (February 14), Syrian President Hafiz Asad (February 21) and PLO leader Yasir Arafat (March 9). The Soviet leaders seem to have entertained two goals in inviting the Arab leaders to Moscow. First, it was a good opportunity to reinforce Soviet ties with each Arab opponent of Sadat, and Western intelligence reports indicated a sharp increase in Soviet military aid for a number of the "rejectionist" states, especially Syria, South Yemen, and Libya following the visits.[58] A second goal of the plethora of visits to Moscow may well have been the coordination of the policies of the anti-Sadat forces and their forging into a cohesive "anti-imperialist" front. The Soviets therefore exhibited great satisfaction with the fact that five Arab states (Syria, Libya, Iraq, South Yemen, and Algeria), together with the PLO organized a "rejectionist" conference at the beginning of December 1977 in Tripoli, Libya to take action against Sadat's peace initiative. Unfortunately for the Soviets, however, the Tripoli Conference was severely damaged by a new eruption of the Syrian-Iraqi conflict, as the Iraqi delegation walked out of the conference, claiming that Syria was insisting on a "capitulatory course."[59] Nonetheless, the remaining members signed the "Tripoli Declaration," which condemned Sadat's visit to Jerusalem, "froze" political and diplomatic relations with Egypt, called on the Arabs to give military and political aid to Syria and the PLO, and announced the formation of a Pan-Arab front of "Steadfastness and Confrontation" to "confront the Zionist enemy and combat the imperialist plot."[60] The front was to be open to other Arab states to join, and its members also agreed to consider aggression against any one of them as aggression against all members.

The Soviet leadership gave a strong endorsement to the decisions of the Tripoli Conference, even with the nonparticipation of Iraq in the final declaration, evidently hoping that the Pan-Arab front created by the conference would be the strong nucleus of the "anti-imperialist" Arab unity the Soviet Union had sought for so long.[61] In its early stages, however, the front was not only unable to attract additional members, but also lacked the cohesion necessary to be an effective organization. Thus at the second meeting of the "rejectionist" forces in February, Iraq failed to attend at all, while Libyan leader Muammar Kaddafi arrived late—reportedly because of a disagreement with Iraq over the activities of the conference.[62] The real test of the front, however, came in March following the Israeli invasion of southern Lebanon, which was precipitated by a particularly savage PLO terrorist attack along the Haifa-Tel Aviv highway.[63] Despite PLO calls for help and Syrian President Asad's announcement that he was opening Syria's borders and airspace to anyone willing to fight Israel, the only help that arrived was a few hundred Iraqis, whose purpose appeared to be more to embarass the Syrians than to fight the Israelis. The Soviet Union itself did little to aid its PLO ally in the face of the Israeli assault other than to refrain from vetoing (at "Lebanese request") a U.S. resolution that set up a U.N. force to police southern Lebanon and that called for an Israeli withdrawal.[64] Moscow did, however, seek to make some propaganda gains out of the invasion, blaming the Israeli-Egyptian talks for being a cover for the Israeli move and the United States for backing it.[65]

In sum, while no other Arab state joined the Egyptians in talking peace with Israel—and for this the Soviet leadership must have been thankful—neither did the anti-Sadat front become the major force for "anti-imperialist" Arab unity that the Soviet Union had desired. Indeed, an Arab summit took place at the end of March (without the "rejectionist" states, but with Egypt and a PLO observer), which condemned the "aggressive acts" by foreign forces in the Horn of Africa, a clear reference to the Soviet Union and Cuba.[66] The summit was an indication to the Soviets that Sadat was not as isolated as they might have hoped, and subsequent Soviet propaganda warned of Egyptian infiltration of "imperialist and reactionary nationalist influence" into states adopting progressive positions under the guise of references to their national interest being threatened by the "Communist peril."[67]

While the Soviet leadership was working, albeit without too much success, to solidify the anti-Sadat Arab forces into a cohesive and powerful "anti-imperialist" front, they were also working to undermine the U.S. position in the Arab world by deprecating U.S. moves to expedite the pace of Egyptian-Israeli negotiations, which had become bogged down less than a month and a half after Sadat's visit to Jerusalem.

The steady drumfire of Soviet criticism over the Sadat peace initiative was highlighted by Brezhnev's *Pravda* interview on December 24, 1977, in which the Soviet leader severely criticized the Begin-Sadat talks and warned that the Geneva Conference could not be used as a cover for separate deals. These Soviet propaganda attacks continued as Begin went to Washington to present his West Bank-Gaza autonomy plan[68] and Carter journeyed to the Middle East early in

January, where he was accused by Moscow of trying to get the Arabs to agree to "unilateral concessions" to Israel.[69] Following the recall of an Egyptian negotiating delegation from Israel in mid-January,[70] the Soviets termed the bilateral Egyptian-Israeli talks a failure and called for a return to Geneva, once again emphasizing that the conference could not be used as a screen for separate deals with Israel.[71] Sadat's visit to the United States in early February was also branded by Moscow as a failure since he was unable to get U.S. pressure on Israel to change its position (although he did get promises of economic assistance).[72] The Soviet Union kept up its criticism of Egypt in the latter part of the month, as *Pravda* condemned the Egyptians for their attempted rescue of hostages in Cyprus.[73] Meanwhile, as a result of Soviet activity in the Horn of Africa, and attempts by members of the Carter administration to link the Soviet actions to the SALT talks, Soviet-U.S. relations began to deteriorate sharply, and Soviet criticism of the United States mounted. In addition to attacking the United States for its aid to Israel, and minimizing the differences between the Begin and Carter administrations on Middle East policy (there had been a serious clash between Begin and Carter during the Israeli prime minister's visit to Washington in March),[74] the Soviet leadership also attacked the United States for its plan to sell advanced aircraft to Saudi Arabia and Egypt as well as Israel. Indeed, *Pravda* commentator Yuri Zhukov went so far as to call this a "profound political change of course":

> At present, the U.S. government has embarked on a profound political change of course, from exclusive support of Israel, its sole ally in the Middle East to the present time, to reliance on a group of states with reactionary regimes...on Saudi Arabia...and certain other Arab states.[75]

Meanwhile, although Soviet-U.S. relations deteriorated as a result of the African events, a slowdown in the SALT negotiations, a warming of relations between China and the United States, and the mistreatment of Soviet dissidents and Americans working in the Soviet Union, the two powers continued to talk about the Middle East, although little was accomplished. Vance journeyed to Moscow on April 20, 1978 for discussions with Gromyko on SALT and the Middle East, and the Soviet description of the talks referred to an "exchange of views on the Middle East"—the usual Soviet code words for disagreement.[76] Then, in early May, possibly under Soviet prodding or possibly because the Palestinian position in Lebanon was more and more untenable as the PLO came under increasing Syrian control as a result of the Israeli invasion, Arafat gave an interview to the *New York Times* in which he stated that the Soviet-U.S. joint statement of October 1, 1977, "could become a firm foundation for a realistic settlement."[77] The PLO leader also called on both the Soviet Union and the United States to provide guarantees for the existence of Israel and a Palestinian state. The fact that *Pravda,* on May 3, cited the interview appeared to be tacit support for Arafat's statements, which were very close to the Soviet peace plan of May 1977. Nothing came of the Arafat interview, however, nor of the Carter-Gromyko talks later in the month, and the Egyptian-Israeli peace talks remained stalemated through June and July despite a meeting of the Egyptian and Israeli foreign ministers in England and despite U.S. efforts to expedite the peace process.[78] Thus, by August, more than eight months after the Sadat initiative, the Soviet leadership must have viewed their position in the Middle East as a perplexing one. On the one hand, the Egyptian-Israeli talks had not succeeded and Egypt had become somewhat isolated in the Arab world because of Sadat's peace initiative. On the other hand, however, the anti-Sadat front had not proven cohesive, and Sadat remained in power, while the Carter administration, for its part, continued to seek a way to bring the Israeli-Egyptian negotiations to a successful conclusion, making a final major effort in early September when Carter invited Begin and Sadat to a summit conference at Camp David, the president's mountain retreat near Washington.

From Camp David to the Signing of the Egyptian-Israeli Treaty

As might be expected, Soviet concerns about a possible Egyptian-Israeli agreement mounted during the Camp David summit.[79] In addition, the Soviet media emphasized what had now become a familiar theme since the U.S. tripartite arms deal with Israel, Egypt, and Saudi Arabia in May—that the United States was seeking to create a new Middle Eastern military organization, with Israel joining the Egyptian-Saudi-Iranian axis. The Soviet leadership seemed particularly concerned that the United States would secure military bases from such a development, with *Pravda* on September 10, 1978 going so far as to warn:

> Anyone who nurtures plans for a U.S. military presence in the Middle East must take into account that this region is in immediate proximity to the borders of the USSR and other countries of the Socialist commonwealth, who are by no means indifferent to the future development of events there.

While the outcome of the Camp David discussions did not provide for a U.S. military base in either Israel or Egypt, it was clear that the United States, by virtue of its mediating efforts between Egypt and Israel and its promises to them of economic and military aid, was becoming even more involved in both countries, and the Soviet Union may have sensed that a more formal military relationship might not be far off. There were two agreements signed at Camp David: the rather vague "Framework for Peace in the Middle East," which called for Palestinian autonomy in the West Bank and Gaza (with due regard for Israeli security), with Egypt, Jordan, and Israel helping to arrange the autonomy; and the far more specific "Framework for the Conclusion of a Peace Treaty between Egypt and Israel," which called for: the total evacuation by Israel of the Sinai Peninsula including the airfields and Israeli settlements (two major Israeli concessions)[80] in return for Egypt's agreement to station only limited forces there; the establishment of a U.N. force between Israel and Egypt, which could be removed only by the unanimous vote of the five permanent members of the United Nations Security Council; and the establishment of full diplomatic relations between the two countries along with trade and tourism—just the type of peace that Israel had long been advocating. Finally, Egypt and Israel pledged to complete the signing of a formal Egyptian-Israeli treaty within three months.[81] (See Appendix B for the text of the Camp David agreements.)

Not unexpectedly, the Soviet Union greeted the Camp David agreements with hostility. In a major speech at Baku on September 24, Brezhnev denounced what he termed the U.S. attempt to "split the Arab ranks" and force the Arabs to accept Israeli peace terms. In addition, he returned to the old three-part Soviet peace plan, emphasizing that Israel had to withdraw totally from all territory captured in the 1967 war and agree to the establishment of a Palestinian state in the West Bank and Gaza. Brezhnev also repeated the Soviet call for a return to the Geneva Conference, with full participation of the PLO. Interestingly enough, perhaps to balance the U.S. success at Camp David, Brezhnev hailed events in Afghanistan in his Baku speech, emphasizing that the new left-wing government, which had seized power in that country in April, had embarked on the road to socialism.[82]

If the Soviet reaction to Camp David was hostile, the reaction of most of the Arab states was not much warmer. While President Carter dispatched a series of administration representatives to try to sell the agreement to such key Arab states as Saudi Arabia (a major financial supporter of Egypt), Jordan (which was supposed to play a major role in working out the West Bank-Gaza autonomy plan, but which raised a number of very sharp questions about the Camp David agreements),[83] and Syria, they met with little success. Indeed, only three days after the announcement of the Camp David agreements, the Front of Steadfastness and Confrontation met in Damascus. Not only did it condemn Camp David, which it termed "illegal," and reaffirm the role of the PLO as the sole representative of the Palestinian people, it also decided on the need to "develop and strengthen friendly relations with the Socialist community led by the USSR."[84] Reinforcing Soviet satisfaction with this development, PLO Moscow representative Mohammed Shaer stated that the Front of Steadfastness and Confrontation was "the core of a future broad pan-Arab anti-imperialist front."[85]

The Soviet Union, for its part, moved once again to reinforce its ties with key members of the "rejectionist" front as first Asad, then Henri Boumadienne of Algeria, and then Arafat of the PLO visited Moscow in October. The Soviet media hailed the visit of Asad, who, it was noted, came as a representative of the Steadfastness Front; and one result of the meeting, besides the joint denunciation of Camp David and of attempts "to undermine Soviet-Arab friendship," was a Soviet decision to "further strengthen Syria's defense potential."[86]

While the visit of Asad to Moscow could be considered a success for the Soviet Union in its efforts to prevent the Camp David agreement from acquiring further Arab support, the Syrian leader's subsequent move toward a reconciliation with Iraq was even more warmly endorsed by the Soviet Union. The Syrian-Iraqi conflict had long bedeviled Soviet attempts to create a unified "anti-imperialist" bloc of Arab states, and, therefore, when Assad announced he had accepted an invitation to visit Iraq, the Soviet leadership must have seen this as a major step toward creating the long-sought "anti-imperialist" Arab bloc. While many observers saw Asad's visit as a tactical ploy to strengthen Syria's position in the face of the projected Israeli-Egyptian treaty, the Soviet Union was effusive in its praise, with Moscow Radio calling it "an event of truly enormous importance which has considerably strengthened the position of those forces that decisively reject the capitulatory plans for a settlement drawn up at Camp David."[87]

While the Syrian-Iraqi reconciliation can be considered the most positive Arab development from the Soviet point of view to flow from Camp David, the limited rapprochement between the PLO and Jordan was also deemed a favorable development by the Soviet Union, since it further reduced the chances of Jordanian participation in the Camp David accords and brought Jordan closer to an alignment with the anti-Sadat forces in the Arab world. The Soviet Union, itself, was moving to tighten its relations with the PLO as Arafat visited the Soviet Union in the latter part of October, and the Soviet Union, for the first time, formally recognized the PLO as the sole legitimate representative of the Palestinian people. The communique issued by the two sides after the Moscow talks emphasized the "urgent task to rally and activize all the forces opposing anti-Arab separate deals."[88]

The general opposition of the Arab world to Camp David, the reconciliations between the PLO and Jordan, and between Syria and Iraq, and the announcement of an Arab summit conference (without Egypt) in Baghdad to react to Camp David, all served to further isolate Egypt in the Arab world—a development desired neither by Sadat nor Carter. Indeed, as the Arab world began to move toward an anti-Camp David position, Egypt felt the necessity of demonstrating that it had not "sold out" the Arabs by signing a separate agreement with Israel. Thus, when negotiations began on October 12, Egypt called for a formal linkage between the two Camp David agreements, although no such linkage was part of the accords.[89] While Egypt was making this demand, the United States found itself hard put to maintain the position of "evenhanded" mediator that it had demonstrated at Camp David. It had long been the hope of the Carter administration to draw Jordan, moderate Palestinians (if not the PLO), and Syria, as well as Egypt, into a comprehensive peace settlement with Israel. Having initially sought—and failed—to achieve this objective by means of the Geneva Peace Conference, the United States at Camp David had changed its technique, but not its final goal. Indeed, once it became clear that Jordan, Syria, Saudi Arabia, and the West Bank Palestinian Arabs opposed the Camp David accords, U.S. officials sought to interpret Camp David to these Arabs in such a way that it appeared as if Israel was far more yielding on the ultimate future of Jerusalem and the West Bank than the Camp David accords actually stipulated. The apparent U.S. goal in this effort was to persuade at least the moderate Arabs who were initially opposed to the accords to go along with them. Unfortunately, U.S. efforts in this direction had a counterproductive effect in Israel, where Begin's opponents, both inside and outside his ruling coalition, seized on U.S. statements to prove that Begin had undermined Israeli security at Camp David.

Indeed, Begin's domestic problems began almost as soon as he had returned to Jerusalem from Camp David. His opponents, many of whom were long-time allies in the Herut faction of his Likud party, attacked the prime minister for his willingness to cede the entire Sinai to Egypt, including the settlements that Israel had established in the strategic Rafiah Salient. This, they claimed, was only the first step toward also yielding the entire West Bank (and the West Bank settlements), which Israel needed for its security.[90] Nonetheless, despite a number of opposing votes and abstentions from his own Likud party, Begin, with the help of the opposition Labor party, was able to get the Israeli parliament to approve the Camp David accords (84 to 19, with 17 abstentions).[91] The domestic pressure on Begin increased in mid-October when Egypt began to demand a formal link between the two Camp David agreements. Then, when United States Assistant Secretary of State Harold Saunders, in his visit to the Middle East in late October with the Carter administration's answers to Jordanian King Hussein's questions about Camp David, appeared to give the impression that Israel would ultimately yield the entire West Bank, Begin felt compelled to take action.[92] While Saunders may have hoped with his comments to lessen Arab opposition to Camp David and strengthen Egypt's position in the Arab world on the eve of the Baghdad Conference, his words had the opposite effect, as Begin, now under heightened domestic pressure (and with local elections only a few days away), announced the enlarging of existing West Bank settlements as an answer to Saunders' comments.[93] This in turn further undermined Sadat's position (and that of the United States) just as the Baghdad Conference began.

Soviet commentary prior to the Baghdad Conference was split as to the expected results. Pavel Demchenko recalled that heretofore the lack of Arab unity had "aided the imperialists" and stated that while it was to be hoped that at Baghdad the Arabs, meeting without Egypt, would unify against Camp David, "it should be taken into consideration that the composition of the Baghdad Conference participants are not uniform sociopolitically"[94] —Soviet code words to describe the presence of such pro-Western Arab states as Saudi Arabia, the Sudan, North Yemen, and Oman. Vladimir Kudravstev, usually a more optimistic Soviet observer, stated that while Egypt's breakaway was a grave loss to the Arab world, the Arabs were "capable of compensating for it by strengthening their unity."[95]

Given the rather hesitant Soviet comments prior to the conference, the Soviet leaders could only have been pleased by its results. Not only were the Camp David agreements condemned, with even Saudi Arabia participating in the condemnation, but a joint PLO-Jordanian commission was established, an event that appeared to foreshadow further cooperation between these two erstwhile enemies. In addition, the Arab League headquarters was to be removed from Cairo, and economic sanctions were planned against Egypt should Sadat go ahead with the signing of the treaty. Finally, the Soviet Union must have been pleased by the Baghdad Conference's formula for a "just peace" in the Middle East: Israeli withdrawal from the territories captured in 1967 and the "right of the Palestinian people to establish an independent state on their national soil."[96] While the latter phrase was open to differing interpretations, the juxtaposition of the two statements seemed to indicate that even such radical states as Iraq and Libya were for the first time willing to grudgingly accept Israel's existence. Although the Baghdad statement on peace was far from the trade, tourism, and normal diplomatic relations wanted by the Israelis, it was very close to the peace formula that had been advocated by the Soviet Union since 1976. In sum, the Soviet leadership was undoubtedly pleased with the results of the Baghdad summit, with one Soviet commentator deeming it "a final blow to imperialist intentions aimed at dissolving Arab unity and pressuring other Arabs to join Camp David."[97] An editorial in *New Times* emphasized Soviet satisfaction with the Arab response to Camp David even more clearly:

> Contrary to the prediction of some skeptics, Baghdad marked a transition from mere verbal avowals of solidarity to practical efforts to overcome differences between the Arab countries and to coordinate their actions. . . . Indicative are the meetings of representatives of Syria and Iraq held to discuss close unity of action between these two countries that used to be at loggerheads with each other. And could it be expected only a few months ago that an official delegation from the Palesine Liberation Organization would be received in the Royal Palace in Amman with all honors?[98]

Following the Baghdad Conference, the United States redoubled its efforts to bring about a Middle East settlement. Intense diplomatic bargaining in Washington between Israel and Egypt took place in November, with the United States participating actively. The negotiations stalled, however, as Egypt demanded that Israel agree to a timetable for implementing Palestinian self-rule. Israel, for its part, rejected the timetable, stating that given the lack of support for Camp David on the West Bank and Gaza, it was unwilling to make one agreement conditional on the other. At this point, Sadat withdrew his chief negotiator from Washington and the talks reached another impasse. It seemed clear that after Baghdad Sadat was seeking to demonstrate to the Arab world that he had not sold out the general Arab cause.[99]

In an effort to speed up the negotiations, U.S. Secretary of State Cyrus Vance was dispatched to the Middle East on December 10, the date on which Sadat and Begin were scheduled to receive their Nobel Peace Prizes, and only one week before the target date for completing the treaty. While the atmosphere in Oslo, where the Nobel Prizes were awarded, was positive, it soon became evident in Cairo that Sadat (who, unlike Begin, did not attend the Oslo cere- monies) was unwilling to change his position on the peace treaty. It appeared as if Sadat was escalating his demands during his talks with Vance, seeking, in addition to a timetable: (1) the review of security arrangements after five years, (2) the exchange of ambassadors between Israel and Egypt being made condi- tional upon the establishment of an autonomous administration at least in the Gaza region, and (3) the subordination of Egypt's treaty with Israel to Egypt's military obligations toward the other Arab states in case of a war between them and Israel.[100]

In pressing these demands, it appears as if Sadat was attempting not only to demonstrate to the other Arab states that Egypt was faithfully upholding the Arab cause, but was also trying to get the United States to accept the Egyptian demands, so that the United States would exert pressure on Israel to make con- cessions, so that a treaty would be signed by the December 17 deadline. The Carter administration, beset by serious domestic problems, could thereby claim a major success. Although the United States, mindful of the approaching dead- line, was to endorse Sadat's demands, once again, as in the case of Harold Saun- ders' comments in late October, the United States' action proved counter- productive. Having undergone intense U.S. pressure since October, Begin decided to reject the Egyptian-U.S. proposals, and in doing so he received support not only from hardline Likud members, but also from such "doves" as former For- eign Minister Abba Eban and opposition Labor party leader Shimon Peres, indi- viduals who earlier had been highly critical of Begin's foreign policies.[101] The end result was a collapse in the talks and recrimination between Washington and Jerusalem.

Overshadowing the collapse of the Egyptian-Israeli peace talks were develop- ments in Iran. Since the Nixon era, the United States had depended upon Iran to be its "policeman" in the Persian Gulf, and the United States had given exten- sive amounts of arms to the Shah's armed forces. At the same time, Iran was supplying Israel with more than half of its oil, and it served as a moderating in- fluence in the Arab-Israeli conflict. Consequently, when domestic upheaval began to increase sharply in Iran in the fall of 1978, and the government of the Shah was gravely weakened, the United States, Israel, and Egypt, all of whom had close ties to Iran, became increasingly concerned. This concern mounted in mid-January 1979 when the Shah was forced to leave Iran and go into exile. The interim government of Shapur Bakhtiar then proved unable to cope with pressure from Islamic fundamentalist forces led by Ayatollah Khomeini, who returned from exile in early February and then almost immediately took control of the country.[102]

Khomeini's victory had a number of immediate effects on the Arab-Israeli conflict. Not only were Iranian sales of oil to Israel ended and diplomatic relations broken (the PLO was given the building that had housed the Israeli delegation in Tehran), but Khomeini also pledged support for the PLO in its conflict with Israel. Nonetheless, given the serious internal disorders in Iran, it appeared likely that it would be some time before the Khomeini regime would be able to supply the "rejectionists" with any substantive aid.

If the cause of the Arab "rejectionists" was strengthened by the events in Iran, the Soviet Union also benefited considerably from Khomeini's rise to power. As Iran moved out of the U.S. orbit, the United States lost not only its "policeman of the Persian Gulf," but also the sophisticated radar stations it had maintained in northern Iran for tracking Soviet missiles. As U.S. influence rapidly ebbed in Iran, Moscow may have hoped ultimately to replace U.S. influence with Soviet influence, although given the Islamic fundamentalist position of the Khomeini regime, this soon proved to be a difficult task.[103] In any case, the elimination of Iran from the U.S. Middle East alliance system was a major gain for the Soviet Union. As Soviet Middle East commentator Dmitry Volsky stated, "Whatever course the events in Iran may take, one thing is clear: never again will the West be able to rely on that country in its global strategy."[104]

Interestingly enough, as the Soviet Union's position in the Middle East began to improve following the Baghdad Conference and the upheaval in Iran, Moscow also made another of its periodic gestures toward Israel. Thus, a group of Israeli parliamentarians representing a number of Israeli parties, including Labor, Mapam, the National Religious Party, and the Israeli Communist party, were invited to Moscow at the invitation of the Soviet Peace Committee.[105] Reminiscent in many ways of the dispatch of Soviet representatives to Israel at the time of the United States' Middle East policy "reappraisal" in 1975 and Gromyko's private talk with Abba Eban in 1973, it seemed to be a Soviet effort, at a turning point in Middle East affairs, to try to gain Israeli support for the Soviet Middle East peace plan.

Meanwhile, after the failure of the Vance mission in December, the United States once again set out to try to bring about an Egyptian-Israeli settlement. Thus, special United States Ambassador Alfred Atherton visited the two countries in January; United States Defense Secretary Harold Brown visited them in February (along with Saudi Arabia) in yet another show of United States support for its Middle East allies following the fall of the Shah; and Cyrus Vance met with Israeli Foreign Minister Dayan and Egyptian Prime Minister Khalil in Camp David in late February.[106] The diplomatic momentum was then increased with a Begin-Carter meeting in Washington and Carter's final—and successful—visit to Egypt and Israel in mid-March.[107] The end result was a peace treaty signed by Begin and Sadat, and witnessed by Carter, in Washington on March 26, 1979.

The Egyptian-Israeli peace treaty, which was approved by the Israeli parliament by a vote of 95–18 with five absentions, was similar to its Camp David prototype in many ways (see Appendix C). Israel agreed to give up the entire Sinai Peninsula, including the airfields and the settlements, in stages over a three year period, and Egypt agreed to limit the forces it would station in the Sinai. As a gesture to Egypt, Israel also agreed to a limited forces zone on its side of the border. A United Nations force was to be installed along the border between Israel and Egypt, one that could be removed only with the unanimous approval of the permanent members of the United Nations Security Council. A second main principle of Camp David also became part of the treaty: the establishment of diplomatic, economic, and cultural relations, along with the passage of Israeli ships through the Suez Canal, and freedom of travel through the Straits of Tiran and the Gulf of Aqaba. Wording about linkage between the Egyptian-Israeli treaty and a more comprehensive peace settlement was included both in the treaty preamble and in a joint letter from Begin and Sadat to President Carter accompanying the treaty. The two Middle Eastern leaders also pledged to begin negotiations within a month of their treaty's ratification to implement the provisions of the Camp David agreement pertaining to the West Bank and Gaza. Sadat and Begin specifically stated that the purpose of their negotiations, in which the United States would "participate fully," and in which Jordan would be invited to participate, "shall be to agree, prior to the elections, on the modalities for establishing the elected self-government authority and defining its powers and responsibilities." Israel and Egypt set a one year "goal" to complete the negotiations, although no specific deadline was set. Following the talks, which Egypt and Israel pledged to negotiate in "good faith," the inhabitants of the West Bank and Gaza were to obtain full "autonomy," the Israeli military government and its civilian administration would be withdrawn, and the Israeli forces would be deployed into specified "security locations." As in Camp David, the issue of the ultimate disposition of the West Bank and Gaza, the nature of "autonomy," and the future role of Israel in the areas were left open.

In addition to agreeing to participate in the negotiations on West Bank autonomy, the United States also pledged increased economic and military aid to both Israel and Egypt, and in a special letter to Sadat and Begin, President Carter pledged that (subject to United States constitutional processes) the United States would intervene in case of an actual or threatened violation of the treaty and would move to establish a substitute multinational force between Israel and Egypt if the United Nations Security Council failed to create one. Israel, still concerned that the Sadat regime or a future Egyptian government might renege on the treaty, received additional U.S. assurances to compensate it for giving up the Sinai in a separate memorandum of agreement with the United States. In it the United States pledged to provide Israel with support in case of a demonstrated violation of the peace treaty, such as a blockade of Israel's use of international waterways, a violation of the treaty provisions concerning Egypt's force limitations in the Sinai Peninsula, or an armed attack against Israel. Additionally, the United States extended to 15 years the pledge to help provide Israel with oil that was first made at the time of the Sinai II agreement of September 1, 1975.[108]

As in the case of the Camp David agreements, President Carter quickly dispatched one of his top aides (Zbigniew Brzezinski) to the Middle East to help gain support for the Egyptian-Israeli treaty. Once again, however, the effort did not meet with success, as Jordan and Saudi Arabia, which Brzezinski had visited on his trip, voted along with the Arab "rejectionists" to impose sanctions against Egypt at the second Baghdad Conference, which met after the treaty signing. The sanctions included suspension of Egypt's membership in the Arab League, withdrawal of all Arab ambassadors from Cairo, the severing of all political and diplomatic relations with Egypt, and the cutting off of all economic aid to Egypt.[109] These provisions were voted unanimously (the Sudan and Oman, however, which continued to maintain ties to Egypt, did not attend the conference), and several Arab states also called for an oil embargo against the United States. Although no such embargo was adopted, the *Pravda* commentator who analyzed the second Baghdad Conference noted approvingly the "anti-imperialist" mood of the meeting.[110]

In assessing their position in the Middle East following the completion of the second Baghdad Conference, the Soviet leaders may well have been satisfied at the sharp improvement in their position—and the concommitant weakening of the U.S. position—since the low point of Soviet Middle East fortunes following the end of the civil war in Lebanon in October 1976. Their hopes of a unified "anti-imperialist" block of Arab states (albeit one without Egypt) seemed on the way to being realized, as even such one-time allies of the United States, as Saudi Arabia, Kuwait, and Jordan criticized the Egyptian-Israeli treaty and the U.S. role in achieving it. At the same time, the Saudi-Egyptian axis, once the dominant one in Arab politics, had broken apart. In addition, the once hostile Arab Ba'athist states, Syria and Iraq, were now cooperating, and this development, together with the ouster of the Shah of Iran, and the rise to power of pro-Soviet regimes in Ethiopia and Afghanistan seemed to tilt the Middle East balance of forces toward the Soviet Union.

It was thus from a very much improved Middle East position that Brezhnev met Carter at a summit conference in Vienna in June. At the summit itself, which was convened primarily for the signing of the SALT II agreement, there was little official mention of the Middle East.[111] According to Radio Moscow, however, Brezhnev openly criticized the Egyptian-Israeli treaty and reiterated the Soviet peace plan.[112] Brezhnev's position on the Middle East was repeated by Gromyko in his news conference following the summit, and the Soviet for-

eign minister further stated that the Soviet Union opposed the use of the United
Nations in policing the treaty, thus calling into question the future mandate of
the U.N. force stationed between Egypt and Israel in the Sinai that was due to
expire on July 24, 1979. (Indeed, the United States was to subsequently have to
provide a multinational force in the Sinai, as President Carter had promised
Sadat and Begin, because Moscow was to oppose the use of U.N. forces for this
purpose.) Gromyko went out of his way, however, to once again emphasize
the Soviet belief that Israel had the right to exist and, while again coming out for
an independent Palestinian state, he asserted that it could be a "small" one—yet
another means of reassurance to Israel (and to U.S. Jews whose support Moscow
may have seen necessary for the passage of the SALT agreement):

> The Soviet Union's principled position on Middle Eastern affairs was
> and remains the same as it was formulated many years ago. Namely:
> all the lands captured by Israel from the Arabs must be returned; the
> Palestine Arab people must be granted the opportunity to create its
> own, if only small, independent state ...
>
> All of the countries of that region, *including Israel, and nobody
> must have any doubt about it,* should have the possibility to exist and
> develop in the Middle East as independent sovereign states....[113] (em-
> phasis mine)

Following the Soviet-U.S. summit, the situation in the Middle East took
a sharp turn for the worse as far as Moscow was concerned as the "anti-Egyptian"
unity of the Arab world, so much in evidence at the second Baghdad Conference, rapidly dissipated and the internecine strife that had so long characterized
intra-Arab relations returned with a vengeance, with Iran playing a significant
role in the intra-Arab conflicts.

The first major problem for Moscow was to come with the renewal of the
Iraqi-Syrian feud at the end of July 1979. This was due, in part, to the fact that
Iraq's new president, Saddam Hussein, accused Syria of being involved in a plot
to overthrow him and, in part, to Syrian unwillingness to subordinate itself to
Iraq in the proposed union of the countries. It was not long before the old
animosity returned to the Syrian-Iraqi relationship, a development that was to
greatly weaken the "anti-imperialist" unity Moscow had wished for so long.[114]
Compounding this problem for Moscow was Iraq's severe crackdown on the Iraqi
Communist party, and a number of demonstratively anti-Communist and even
anti-Soviet statements by top Iraqi leaders, actions that seemed aimed at improving Iraq's ties to the strongly anti-Communist regime of Saudi Arabia.[115] Meanwhile, Moscow also had to be concerned about the Carter administration's efforts
to widen the Camp David process, although the Andrew Young fiasco seemed to
abort, at least temporarily, administration efforts to involve the PLO.[116] Yet

another problem for the Soviet Union came in regard to the new regime in Iran. The Khomeini regime soon came into conflict with its Arab neighbor Iraq, thus causing a further disruption in the Arab world, as Syria and Libya backed Iran, while Jordan, Saudi Arabia, and Kuwait, all of whom felt threatened by Khomeini's brand of Islamic fundamentalism, backed Iraq. Moscow was also worried about a possible move of Iran back toward the United States, as evidenced by Iranian Prime Minister Barzargan's decision in September 1979 to turn to the United States for spare parts for Iran's U.S.-supplied weapons.[117] Fortunately for Moscow, however, the hostage crisis erupted in November 1979, an event that led to Barzargan's resignation, and it was soon apparent that Iranian-U.S. relations had hit a new low.

Six weeks after the beginning of the hostage crisis, the Soviet Union invaded Afghanistan, an action that greatly angered most of the Arab and Islamic world.[118] The United States seized upon the invasion to try to rally the Muslim states of the Middle East, many of whom were suspicious of the United States because of its role in Camp David, against the Soviet Union, while at the same time stepping up its search for Middle Eastern bases and hastening the deployment of its military forces near the Persian Gulf, which Carter pledged to protect.[119] When the issue of Soviet intervention in Afghanistan came up for a vote in the United Nations in early January, only Ethiopia and South Yemen, among Moscow's Middle Eastern allies, voted against the resolution that condemned the Soviet Union, while Algeria and Syria abstained, with Libya taking a similar position by being absent from the vote.[120] Among the 104 countries voting against Moscow (only 18 states voted with the Soviet Union, while 30 abstained or were not present) was Iraq, whose president, Saddam Hussein, publicly condemned the invasion, thus further demonstrating Iraq's independence of Moscow.[121] Also voting against Moscow were Saudi Arabia, Jordan, and Kuwait all of whom Moscow had hoped to wean away from the West. Indeed, these three countries, along with the UAE, North Yemen, Morocco, and Tunisia now occupied a centrist position in Arab politics between Egypt and its allies (the Sudan and Oman), on the one side, and the Front of Steadfastness and Confrontation, on the other. As far as Iran was concerned, its Foreign Ministry issued a statement condemning the invasion, while its U.N. representative joined with the majority in voting for the anti-Soviet resolution.[122]

In an effort to overcome this Muslim backlash, which it feared the United States would be able to exploit, Moscow made several moves. In the first place, its most trusted Arab allies, who formed the Steadfastness and Confrontation Front, organized a meeting in Damascus in mid-January—two weeks before the Islamic Conference of Nations was scheduled to meet to discuss the invasion. The Steadfastness and Confrontation Front used its meeting as a platform to condemn the United States, while pledging friendship for the Soviet Union and solidarity with Iran. It also tried to divert the attention of the Arab world away from the Soviet invasion of Afghanistan by emphasizing U.S. support for

Camp David and calling for a postponement of the beginning of the Islamic Conference (which was to strongly condemn Moscow) until after January 26, 1980 because that was the date scheduled for the normalization of relations between Egypt and the "Zionist entity" (Israel).[123]

Indeed, the Steadfastness Front, or at least key components of it such as Syria, the PLO (primarily the Popular Front for the Liberation of Palestine and the Popular Democratic Front for the Liberation of Palestine), and the Peoples Democratic Republic of Yemen became almost adjuncts of Soviet policy during this period. Thus at the end of January, Gromyko visited Syria, and the joint communique issued at the end of his visit articulated the themes that Moscow and its Middle East allies were to use over the next few months to try to divert Muslim attention away from the invasion of Afghanistan and toward the activities of "American-supported" Israel in the West Bank and Gaza.

Moscow's invective against Israel reached a new high during Gromyko's visit, as the Soviet-Syrian communique attacked Israel not only for racial discrimination but also for the "desecration of objects of historical, religious and cultural value to the Arabs." The United States, however, received the brunt of the Soviet and Syrian criticism:

> Under the cover of an artifically fomented uproar over the events in Iran and Afghanistan, imperialist circles and their accomplices are striving to divert the Arab people's attention away from the struggle to liquidate the consequences of Israeli aggression, and are attempting to create a split in the ranks of the Arab and Moslem countries, drive a wedge between them and their friends—the USSR—and subvert the unity and principles of the non-aligned movement. [The USSR and Syria] condemn the continuing campaign by imperialist forces, led by the United States, which are displaying a false concern for Islam while simultaneously supporting Israel's seizure of the Holy places in Jerusalem [and] taking an openly hostile position toward the revolution in Iran.
>
> The facts indicate that imperialism has been and continues to be an enemy of all the Moslem countries as a whole and an enemy of Islam.[124]

Fortunately for Moscow, the expansion of Israeli settlements on the West Bank and the turnabout in the March 1, 1980 U.S. vote in the U.N. Security Council condemning Israeli policies were to prove most fortuitous for Soviet efforts to divert Arab and Muslim attention from Afghanistan to the Arab-Israeli conflict.

Several months later the ill-fated U.S. rescue mission in Iran seemed to provide a golden opportunity for Moscow to reinforce its ties with Iran while at the same time enabling the Soviet Union to demonstrate to the nations of the Middle East the dangers posed to them by the U.S. buildup in the Indian Ocean. It also aided Moscow in its efforts to divert Muslim attention from the Soviet invasion of Afghanistan, and Moscow lost little time in attacking the United States for the rescue attempt, comparing it to the raid by the Tel Aviv "cut-throats" at Entebbe,[125] and claiming that the raid was part of a larger plot to overthrow the government of Ayatollah Khomeini.[126] The Soviet Union also thrust itself forth again as the protector of Iran—and other Muslim countries. Intestingly enough, however, despite the Soviet attempt to act as Iran's champion at the Islamic Conference, which met several weeks after the abortive hostage rescue mission, it was to be Iran that was to lead the Islamic Conference in its denunciation of the Soviet Union's invasion and occupation of Afghanistan. Indeed, Iran went so far as to include, as official members of its own delegation, eight Afghan rebel leaders.[127] Foreign Minister Ghotbzadeh led the Iranian delegation and denounced the Soviet Union and the United States in equally harsh terms, condemning the Soviet Union's invasion of Afghanistan as "a flagrant violation of international law carried out in total disrespect for the sovereignty and territorial integrity of Afghanistan."[128] He also stated, in an obvious effort to prevent the conference from being diverted to the Arab-Israeli conflict, "For us, the liberation of Afghanistan is not less important than the liberation of Palestine." Ghotbzadeh was successful in his quest, as the Islamic Conference, despite the efforts of the Steadfastness Front, again called for the "immediate, total and unconditional withdrawal of all Soviet troops stationed on the territory of Afghanistan."[129]

Once again, as in the case following the Islamic Conference in January, Moscow and its Arab allies sought to deflect Muslim criticism by concentrating their attention on Israeli actions in the West Bank and Gaza Strip and purported U.S. support for them. Fortunately for Moscow, Israel was again to give the Soviet Union ammunition for its propaganda efforts. Thus, following a terrorist attack against Jews in the West Bank city of Hebron who were returning from Sabbath services, Israel expelled the mayor and religious leader of that city and the mayor of a nearby city who were accused of creating the atmosphere for the attack. A month later two West Bank Arab mayors were maimed by bombs, and at the same time, the Begin government decided to support a bill for the formal annexation of East Jerusalem that was introduced in the Israeli parliament. While Egypt suspended the autonomy talks in protest, Moscow seized on these events to claim that Egypt had capitulated to Israel and to demonstrate that by backing these actions, the United States (which had also condemned the annexation of East Jerusalem) was, in fact, an enemy of Islam. The Soviet Union also proclaimed its willingness to vote sanctions in the Security Council against Israel "by virtue of its solidarity with the Arab and other Islamic countries that considered it necessary for the Security Council to take some steps in connection with the Israeli occupier's defiant action."[130] Indeed, Moscow was to use the numerous condemnations of Israel by the U.N. in the spring and summer of 1980—condemnations that were spearheaded by its Arab allies—to try to divert attention from Afghanistan, where, despite a massive troop commitment, the Soviet Union was facing serious difficulties in suppressing the rebels.

By September, Moscow was to face an even more serious conflict—the outbreak of the Iran-Iraq war. Having no choice but to remain neutral,[131] Moscow could only stand by as Syria and Libya actively supported Iran, while Jordan and to a lesser degree Saudi Arabia and Kuwait backed Iraq. In addition, the United States was able to improve its position in the region as Iranian threats against Saudi Arabia and other Arab states of the Gulf both drove the Saudis to seek U.S. protection (the emplacement of the U.S. AWACS) and helped legitimize in the minds of many Gulf Arabs the U.S. military presence off their coasts.[132] In addition, prompted both by the war and the Soviet invasion of Afghanistan, the Gulf Cooperation Council was formed, an organization of six conservative monarchies, which Moscow feared would gravitate to the U.S. camp. Indeed, with the newly elected U.S. President Ronald Reagan calling for an anti-Soviet alliance of Middle Eastern states, the Soviet leadership may have feared that its position in the region was fast deteriorating.

In an effort to counter those negative trends, Brezhnev, in addition to calling for an end to the Iran-Iraq war "from which only the imperialists benefit," also called for the prohibition of both foreign military bases in the Persian Gulf and military alliances between the Persian Gulf states and nuclear powers— an obvious ploy to prevent the establishment of any formal military ties between the Gulf nations, directly threatened by Iran and indirectly by the Soviet Union, and the United States.[133] A second Soviet reaction to the war was the signing of a "Treaty of Friendship and Cooperation" with Syria, although negotiations concerning the treaty had been underway for a long period before the war erupted. It is interesting to note that while the treaty itself (at least as seen in its public clauses) was similar in many ways to other Soviet "Friendship and Cooperation" treaties with Third World states, it did have one unique aspect— its denunciation of "Zionism as a form of racism" both in the preamble and article 3.[134] Given Moscow's continued support of Israel's right to exist, its agreement to such a clause may be seen as a gesture to the hard-pressed Syrians. Indeed, one of the reasons why Syrian President Hafiz Asad signed the treaty with the Soviet Union was Syria's isolated regional position as well as its isolated position in the Arab world, except for its ties to the Steadfastness Front Arabs.

Asad, however, was to exploit Israel's shooting down of two Syrian helicopters in Lebanon in late April 1981 to try to move back into the Arab mainstream. He did this by moving Syrian SAM missiles into Lebanon, thereby breaking the tacit agreement he made with Israel in 1976 when Syrian troops first invaded Lebanon. In thus directly challenging Israel, which was only two months away from its national elections, Syria was obviously trying to rally Arab support to its side, and, as the crisis developed, Saudi Arabia and Kuwait did come out in support of Syria, although Iraq and Jordan, both now bitter enemies of Syria, hedged their support.[135] In any case, Moscow, while concerned both about the possible outbreak of a war and the mediation efforts of U.S. diplomatic troubleshooter Philip Habib, was pleased that its leading ally had at least partially moved out of its position of isolation in the Arab world. Moscow was also happy that the position of the United States was somewhat weakened as a result of the crisis. At this time, the Arab Foreign Ministers Conference, called on the initiative of Syria's Steadfastness Front allies Algeria and the PLO, in addition to pledging financial support for Syria, also warned the United States that continuation of its "unconditional support to Israel would lead to a serious confrontation between the Arab nation and the U.S."[136]

On June 9, 1981, however, the missile crisis seemed to pale in importance as another Middle Eastern crisis replaced it in the headlines.[137] On that date Israeli aircraft destroyed an Iraqi nuclear reactor that the vast majority of Israelis feared was being constructed to develop a nuclear weapon for use against Israel. The Israeli action inflamed the Arab world far more than did the Syrian-Israeli confrontation over the Syrian missiles in Lebanon, as many Arabs felt humiliated by the fact that the Israeli aircraft, which flew over Jordanian and Saudi airspace on the way to and from Iraq, were able to come and go unscathed while eliminating the most advanced nuclear installation of any Arab country. As might be expected, Moscow moved quickly to try to exploit this situation, not only condemning the Israeli raid but also pointing to the fact that the Israeli action was carried out with U.S.-supplied aircraft and that it took place despite—or indeed because of—the U.S. AWACS radar planes operating in Saudi Arabia.[138] Reagan's decision to postpone shipment of additional F-16 fighter-bombers to Israel because of the attack was deprecated by Moscow, which sought to exploit the Israeli action by utilizing it to focus Arab attention on the "Israeli threat" to the Arab world (rather than the "Soviet threat") and to underline the U.S. position in the region as Israel's chief supporter, while at the same time improving Soviet-Iraqi relations. In addition, Moscow evidently hoped that the Israeli attack would help to rebuild the "anti-imperialist" Arab unity, which had been so badly dissipated by the Iran-Iraq war. As a commentary by *Pravda* commentator Yuri Glukhov noted on June 16:

> [The Israeli raid] had again demonstrated the extent of the imperialist and Zionist threat hanging over the Arab countries forcing them to set aside their differences, *which have become more pronounced of late....*
>
> In order to carry out their schemes, the Israeli leaders and their patrons have also taken advantage of the situation that has come about in the Persian Gulf zone and the protracted and bloody conflict between Iraq and Iran. In recent months, Baghdad has virtually withdrawn from the Arabs' common front for the struggle to eliminate the consequences of Israeli aggression....
>
> The criminal actions of Tel Aviv and its sponsors have demonstrated once again that the only enemy of the Arab peoples is imperialism and its henchmen, and that no task is more important than closing ranks in the face of the danger threatening their vital interests.[139] (emphasis mine)

Moscow may have also seen the Israeli raid as undercutting Egyptian efforts to reenter the Arab mainstream, since it took place only four days after a Begin-Sadat summit. Indeed, Egypt had sold Iraq thousands of tons of Soviet ammunition and spare parts to aid it in its war with Iran[140] in a clear effort to rebuild Egyptian-Iraqi ties—something noted with displeasure in Moscow, which was concerned about Sadat's lessening isolation.[141] Fortunately for Moscow, the Israeli raid did serve to abort any Iraqi-Egyptian rapprochement, despite Sadat's denunciation of the Israeli action.

Moscow, however, was to be less successful in its goal of exploiting the Israeli raid to undermine the U.S. position in the Arab world, and in particular to improve Soviet ties with Iraq. While there had been calls in the Arab world to embargo oil to the United States because of the raid, the Reagan administration's decision to withhold a promised shipment of F-16 fighter-bombers to Israel and to join with Iraq in a U.N. Security Council vote condemning Israel seemed to deflate any such Arab pressures.[142] Indeed, the Iraqi-U.S. cooperation at the U.N. seemed to set the stage for improved Iraqi-U.S. relations: Iraqi President Saddam Hussein, on the ABC television program *Issues and Answers,* stated his interest in expanding diplomatic contacts with the United States and announced that he would treat the head of the U.S. interests section in the Belgian Embassy in Baghdad as the head of a diplomatic mission.[143]

In taking this posture, the Iraqi leader appeared to be trying to drive a wedge between the United States and Israel, which was very unhappy with the U.S. vote in the U.N. On the other hand, Moscow may have seen that the United States was seeking to drive a diplomatic wedge between the Soviet Union and Iraq. In any case, Soviet-Iraqi relations had been declining for a number of years, and they were not helped by Moscow's position of neutrality in the Iran-Iraq war. A further deterioration in Soviet-Iraqi relations had come in February 1981 at the Twenty-sixth CPSU Congress (which the Iraqi Ba'athists had not attended) when the head of the Iraqi Communist party (ICP), Aziz Mohammed, denounced the Iraqi government for its acts of repression against the ICP and the Iraqi Kurds. He also condemned the Iran-Iraq war and demanded the immediate withdrawal of Iraqi troops from Iran.[144] As Soviet-Iraqi relations were deteriorating, the United States moved to improve relations with the regime in Baghdad. Secretary of State Haig noted the possibility of improved Iraqi-U.S. relations in testimony to the Senate Foreign Relations Committee in mid-March (Iraq was seen as concerned by "the behavior of Soviet imperialism in the Middle Eastern area")[145] and followed this up by sending Deputy Assistant Secretary of State Morris Draper to Iraq in early April.[146] To improve the climate for the visit, the United States approved the sale to Iraq of five Boeing jetliners.[147] While nothing specific came out of Draper's talks, Washington continued to hope that because of Iraq's close ties with Jordan and Saudi Arabia, the regime in Baghdad might abandon its quasi-Steadfastness Front position and move toward a more centrist position in the Arab world on the issue of making peace with Israel. Indeed, Saddam Hussein himself, in his ABC interview, gave some hints about just such a move. In any case, despite the Israeli use of U.S.-made aircraft in the bombing of the reactor, it appeared as if the incident had led to an improvement rather than a deterioration in U.S.-Iraqi relations.

While the furor of the Israeli attack on the Iraqi reactor slowly died, Middle East tensions were kept alive by a number of other events during the summer, which Moscow sought to exploit. In the first place, following the reelection of Menachem Begin's Likud party, Israel launched a series of attacks against Palestinian positions in Lebanon in an effort to keep the PLO off balance and keep it from launching terrorist attacks against Israel. The fighting quickly escalated, with the PLO shelling towns in northern Israel and the Israelis bombing PLO headquarters in Beirut, causing a number of civilian casualities in the process. While the United States condemned the bombing of Beirut and again delayed the shipment of F-16s to Israel—while at the same time sending Habib back to the Middle East to work out a ceasefire (something he accomplished in late July)—Moscow seized the opportunity to once again link the Israeli actions to the United States and called for sanctions against Israel.[148] The bombing of Beirut also served to further inflame Arab tempers both against Israel and against the United States (there were once again calls for an oil boycott of the United States and heavy criticism of U.S. support of Israel not only from the Steadfastness Front but also from such centrist states as Jordan and Kuwait). All this activity, of course, served to further divert Arab attention from the continued Soviet occupation of Afghanistan while underlining the Soviet claim that it was U.S.-supported Israel, not the Soviet Union, that was the main threat to the Arab world.

No sooner had the furor over the bombing of Beirut quieted down than yet another Middle East crisis erupted as U.S. aircraft, operating from a naval task force in the Mediterranean, shot down two Libyan aircraft over the Gulf of Sidra.[149] Moscow lost little time in trying to exploit this incident to show the Arabs how dangerous it was for them to have a U.S. fleet operating off their shores; the Soviet Union obviously hoped to weaken the diplomatic legitimacy that U.S. forces near the Persian Gulf had obtained as a result of the Iran-Iraq war through their protective umbrella over the Arab Gulf states.[150]

If Moscow sought to exploit the Gulf of Sidra incident to encourage anti-U.S. feelings in the Arab world, it was also to move to exploit the Israeli-U.S. agreement "in principle" on strategic cooperation reached during Israeli Prime Minister Begin's visit to Washington in early September. Moscow had already deplored the reelection of Begin and the appointment of the "superhawk" Arik Sharon as Israel's defense minister and sought also to exploit Reagan's decision in mid-August to finally allow the F-16s to go to Israel. Indeed, several Soviet commentators actually linked the release of the F-16s to the U.S.-Libyan air clash that took place several days later.[151]

It was the strategic cooperation agreement (later to be signed when Sharon visited the United States at the end of November, albeit "suspended" when Israel formally annexed the Golan two weeks later), however, that came in for the most criticism. Moscow, which tends to have a military view of world events, may well have felt that the combination of the Israeli air force and army with the U.S. Sixth Fleet would militarily dominate the Middle East, while the potential U.S. use of Israeli air bases in the Negev and the stockpiling of equipment in Israel for the U.S. Rapid Deployment Force would greatly enhance the ability of the United States to deploy its ground forces in the Middle East.[152]

While Moscow sought to show that the Israeli-U.S. agreement, coming after the Israeli bombings of Beirut, the Iraqi reactor, and the Libyan-U.S. clash over the Gulf of Sidra was a policy aimed at threatening the entire Arab world, the Soviet leaders themselves may have felt some need to make a gesture toward Israel. Thus, during Gromyko's visit to the United Nations in late September, he agreed to meet Israeli Foreign Minister Yitzhak Shamir.[153] It appears as if Moscow's willingness to meet with the Israeli foreign minister, the first such official meeting in six years, was yet another Soviet effort, as in the past, at a time of flux in Middle Eastern politics to both maintain some contact with the Israelis and to seek Israeli support for Moscow's idea of an international conference on the Arab-Israeli conflict.[154]

The meeting between Shamir and Gromyko, which took place less than two weeks before the assassination of Anwar Sadat, provides a useful point of departure for evaluating Soviet policy toward Israel during the first phase of the Begin era.

CONCLUSIONS

In looking at the thrust of Soviet policy toward Israel during the Begin era, and Moscow's efforts to exploit the U.S.-Israeli relationship to improve its own position in the Middle East while weakening that of the United States, several major conclusions can be drawn. In the first place, the basic Soviet policy toward Israel did not undergo any major change from the pre-Begin period. Thus, despite the lack of diplomatic relations between the countries, the Soviet Union remained publicly committed to Israel's existence, as it had been before 1977, and the existence of Israel remained one of the three central points in the Soviet Middle East peace plan (the other two being the establishment of a Palestinian state and the total withdrawal of all Israeli forces from the lands captured in the 1967 war). Indeed, Soviet leaders from Communist party General Secretary Leonid Brezhnev to Foreign Minister Andrei Gromyko were to publicly espouse this position frequently during the 1977–81 period. It should be pointed out, however, that the Soviet view of an Arab-Israeli peace settlement differed sharply from the concept pursued by the United States during this period. While President Jimmy Carter called for a peace complete with diplomatic relations, economic ties, and cultural contacts—in other words a full normalization of relations between Israel and its Arab neighbors—Moscow seemed intent on achieving a far more limited settlement, one on the pattern of the North Korea-South Korea armistice, where, while the danger of a major war erupting would recede, sufficient hostility would remain so as to keep alive the possibility of war. Such a situation, for Moscow, would have several advantages. In the first place, given the very serious conflicts among many of the Arab states in the region, and the general suspicion in which the Communist parties of the Arab world are held, a common hostility to Israel is viewed by Moscow as the only basis for the "anti-imperialist" (anti-Western) Arab unity that the Soviet Union is trying to build, which would unite the feuding Arab states and the Arab Communist parties in a common front against what Moscow terms is the "linchpin" of Western imperialism—Israel. It is clear that Moscow hopes that the creation of such an "anti-imperialist" Arab unity (as in 1973) would weaken the Western (and especially the U.S.) position in the Middle East.

The second advantage for Moscow if it could achieve such a peace settlement is that by preserving a modicum of tension in the Arab-Israeli relationship—and the possibility of war—the Arabs would need Soviet military assistance. Given the fact that Soviet military aid is the major form of Soviet influence in the Arab world, this is a very important consideration.

A third advantage to Moscow of working toward such a settlement, rather than aiding the Arabs in destroying Israel, is that the United States would not be alienated. While the Soviet Union is working to undermine the U.S. position in the Middle East, the Soviet leadership still thinks it can obtain benefits from the United States and that the United States will not "link" Soviet activities in the Middle East (or elsewhere in the Third World) to bilateral U.S.-Soviet issues, except for instances where there is a large U.S. constituency supportive of a Third World state, as in the case of Israel. Thus, given the very close ties between the United States and Israel, and Moscow's continued desire for SALT and trade agreements with the United States (and its fear of a Sino-U.S. alignment), it would be counterproductive to Moscow's larger world interests to work for Israel's destruction. Indeed, the periodic meetings between Soviet and Israeli officials both at the U.N. and elsewhere, and the periodic Israeli delegations invited to Moscow, together with the frequent statements by Soviet officials that Israel has a right to exist, seem aimed at least in part at further reassuring the United States (as well as the U.S. Jewish community, whose influence Moscow sees as disproportionately large) that the Soviet Union is not working for Israel's destruction. It should, of course, be added that a second goal of such meetings and pronouncements, which were part of Soviet policy before as well as during the Begin era, may have been to demonstrate to the world that it was not just the United States that could talk to both sides of the Arab-Israeli conflict, but that Moscow could do so as well.

If there was little difference between the pre-Begin and Begin eras in the overall thrust of Soviet policy toward the Middle East, there were clearly differences of nuance, which centered on the Soviet reaction to U.S. efforts to achieve an Egyptian-Israeli agreement, and on Soviet efforts to play up the Arab-Israeli conflict so as to divert Arab attention from its invasion of Afghanistan.

When Begin took power in May 1977, Moscow immediately sought to exploit the new Israeli leader's statements about the West Bank to rebuild its relationship with Egypt. Moscow's efforts were to little avail, as Sadat proved unwilling to meet the Soviet price for improved relations. The Soviets were more successful with the United States, as the Carter administration, unable to bring about by itself the comprehensive peace it sought, turned to the Soviet Union for assistance. The joint Soviet-U.S. statement that followed, however, was only a temporary triumph for Soviet diplomacy: Sadat's visit to Jerusalem less than two months later reversed the thrust of U.S. policy in the region, as Washington, albeit only temporarily, returned to a quasi-Kissingerian step-by-step approach. For their part, the Soviet leaders sought to capitalize on Egypt's increasing estrangement from the rest of the Arab world by seeking to exploit the anti-Sadat alignment of Arab states that had arisen as a reaction to his visit to Jerusalem and to the prospect of an Egyptian-Israeli peace agreement. At the same time, Moscow also sought to deprecate the frequent conflicts between the United States and Israel over the proper strategy for achieving peace. Soviet diplomacy appeared to score a major victory following the Camp David agreements when virtually the entire Arab world denounced Sadat, and rapprochements took place between Syria and Iraq and between Jordan and the PLO, thus giving to the anti-Sadat forces a degree of internal unity they had not possessed before. The Soviet Union also profited from the fact that the rather heavy-handed efforts of the United States to pressure Israel into concessions, such as the Saunders and Vance missions in the fall of 1978, proved counterproductive because they stimulated the Begin government to take a harder line than before. Unfortunately for Moscow, however, the reeruption of the Syrian-Iraqi quarrel and the Soviet invasion of Muslim Afghanistan soon led to a dissipation of the "anti-imperialist" unity the Soviet Union had hoped was created by the anti-Egyptian Baghdad Conferences. Indeed, by 1980, the Arab world had fragmented into three blocs, with the centrists and the Egyptian bloc, along with Iraq, condemning the Soviet Union for invading Afghanistan, while only the Front of Steadfastness and Confrontation supported Moscow's policy. Indeed, Moscow was initially hard put to divert Arab attention from its actions in Afghanistan, but, fortunately for the Soviet Union, Israeli Prime Minister Begin was soon to give (unwitting) assistance to Moscow.

Thus, by promoting increased settlement on the West Bank, including in the city of Hebron, by agreeing to support a bill for the annexation of East Jerusalem, and by deporting a number of Arab officials from Hebron and its environs after a terrorist attack, Begin provided a great deal of grist for the Soviet propaganda mill. Not only was Moscow able, at least in part, to divert attention from Afghanistan (the frequent U.N. debates on the Arab-Israeli conflict in the period from March to August 1980 clearly helped Moscow's efforts), it was also able to weaken the position of the United States, which incurred Arab hostility because of its overall support for Israel. Whatever the domestic motivations behind Begin's moves on Hebron, the West Bank, and Jerusalem, their consequences in the international arena included a strengthening of the Soviet position, the weakening of the U.S. position, and the straining of U.S.-Israeli ties.

Yet, Moscow was not able to long savor the success of Begin's actions in enhancing the Soviet Union's Middle East position. In September 1980 a war broke out between Iran and Iraq, which served not only to further dissipate the "anti-imperialist" Arab unity that Moscow had hoped had been achieved because of Camp David, but that also considerably strengthened the U.S. Middle East position when Washington provided AWACS aircraft for the defense of Saudi Arabia and the basically pro-Western Gulf Cooperation Council came into being. Once again Moscow sought to reverse these unfavorable trends by capitalizing on Israeli actions, and once again Prime Minister Begin seemed to play into Soviet hands. Thus, the missile crisis with Syria in Lebanon, the Israeli strike against the Iraqi nuclear reactor, and the Israeli-PLO war in south Lebanon all provided Moscow with the opportunity to call for a rebuilding of the Arab's "anti-imperialist" unity. Unfortunately for Moscow, however, divisions in the Arab world ran too deep even for such Israeli actions to move them toward unity, although U.S.-Israeli ties were strained as President Reagan twice postponed promised shipments of F-16 fighter-bombers to Israel. Interestingly enough, Moscow had also evidently hoped to use the Israeli strike against the Iraqi nuclear reactor as a vehicle for improving Soviet-Iraqi relations, which had become increasingly strained in the 1977–81 period. Such was not to be the case, however, as perhaps ironically it was to be the United States rather than the Soviet Union that was to improve relations with Iraq as a result of the destruction of the reactor, despite the fact that Israel had utilized U.S.-supplied aircraft in its attack.

In sum, during the Begin era, Soviet-Israeli relations remained primarily a function of Soviet efforts to build an "anti-imperialist" unity among the Arab states of the region. While Moscow remained committed to Israel's continued existence, it sought to exploit Israeli actions on the West Bank and elsewhere in the Middle East in order to undermine the U.S. position in the Middle East while strengthening its own.

NOTES

1.   For studies of Soviet policy in the Middle East, see Robert O. Freedman, *Soviet Policy Toward the Middle East Since 1970*, 2nd ed. (New York:

Praeger, 1978); John D. Glassman, *Arms for the Arabs: The Soviet Union and War in the Middle East* (Baltimore: The Johns Hopkins University Press, 1975); and Yaacov Ro'i, *From Encroachment to Involvement: A Documentary Study of Soviet Policy in the Middle East* (Jerusalem: Israel Universities Press, 1974).

For a general study of possible Soviet objectives in the Middle East, see A. S. Becker and A. L. Horelick, *Soviet Policy in the Middle East* (Santa Monica, Calif.: Rand Publication R-504-FF, 1970). For a study of Soviet-Israeli relations, see Avigdor Dagan, *Moscow and Jerusalem* (New York: Abelard-Schuman, 1970).

2. For a study of U.S. policy in the 1947–49 period, see Herbert Feis, *The Birth of Israel* (New York: W. W. Norton, 1969).

3. Cf. Zionist Archives (Jerusalem), particularly documents S/25/9299 (31 July 1947); S/25/9299 (11 September 1947); S/25/486 (9 September 1947) and S/25/9299 (10 Ocotber 1947). See also document S/25/6600 (5 April 1947).

4. For an analysis of possible Soviet goals in aiding Israel in the 1947–49 period, see Yaacov Ro'i, *Soviet Decision-making in Practice: The USSR and Israel 1947-1954* (London: Transaction Press, 1980); Arnold Krammer, *The Forgotten Friendship: Israel and the Soviet Bloc 1947-1953* (Chicago: University of Illinois Press, 1974); and the Archival documents cited in note number 3 above.

5. For an excellent study of the Khrushchev-Nasser relationship, see Oles M. Smolansky, *The Soviet Union and the Arab East Under Khrushchev* (Lewisburg, Pa.: Bucknell University Press, 1974), chapters 1–5.

6. Ibid., chapters 6–8.

7. For a general analysis of the changes in Soviet policy toward the Arab-Israeli conflict in the period following the fall of Khruschchev, see Freedman, pp. 26–46.

8. Cf. Robert O. Freedman, "Moscow and the Communist Parties of the Middle East: An Uncertain Relationship," in *Soviet Economic and Political Relations with the Developing World*, ed. Roger Kanet and Donna Bahry (New York: Praeger, 1975), pp. 100–34.

9. For an analysis of the Soviet attitude toward U.S. Jewry, see Robert O. Freedman, "Soviet Jewry and Soviet-American Relations," in *The Decisive Decade: Soviet Jewry 1971-1980*, ed. Robert O. Freedman (forthcoming).

10. For a study of this incident and the subsequent Six-Day War, see Walter Laqueur, *The Road to Jerusalem* (New York: Macmillan, 1968).

11. For analyses of the diplomatic and military aspects of the War of Attrition, see Lawrence L. Whetten, *The Canal War* (Cambridge: MIT Press, 1974) and Alvin Z. Rubinstein, *Red Star on the Nile: The Soviet-Egyptian Influence Relationship Since the June War* (Princeton, N.J.: Princeton University Press, 1977).

12. For an analysis of the ceasefire violation, see Robert O. Freedman, "Detente and Soviet-American Relations in the Middle East During the Nixon Years," in *Dimensions of Detente*, ed. Della Sheldon (New York: Praeger, 1978), pp. 89–92. See also Mohammed Heikal, *The Road to Ramadan* (New York: Ballantine Books, 1975), pp. 89–94.

13. Freedman, "Detente and Soviet-American Relations" pp. 92–101.

14. For an analysis of the Soviet exodus from Egypt, see Galia Golan, *Yom Kippur and After: The Soviet Union and the Middle East Crisis,* (London: Cambridge University Press, 1977), pp. 23–26.

15. Ibid., chapter 3.

16. Cf. Freedman, "Detente and Soviet-American Relations," pp. 101–9.

17. For accounts of Kissinger's efforts, see William B. Quandt, *Decade of Decisions: American Policy Toward the Arab-Israeli Conflict 1967–1976* (Los Angeles: University of California Press, 1977), chapter 7; Matti Golan, *The Secret Conversations of Henry Kissinger* (New York: Bantam Books, 1976); and Edward R. F. Sheehan, *The Arabs, Israelis and Kissinger* (New York: Reader's Digest Press, 1976).

18. Cf. Golan, *Secret Conversations,* pp. 137–42.

19. For an account of Soviet aid to Syria during this period, see Freedman, *Soviet Policy,* pp. 163–67.

20. Ibid., pp. 198–203. For a discussion of many such Soviet signals to Israel, see Yaacov Ro'i, "The Soviet Attitude to the Existence of Israel," *The Limits to Power,* ed. Yaacov Ro'i (London: Croom Helm, 1979), pp. 232–53.

21. For an analysis of Soviet policy toward the PLO, see Galia Golan, *The Soviet Union and the Palestine Liberation Organization* (New York: Praeger, 1980).

22. For an analysis of the evolution of Soviet peace efforts, see Robert O. Freedman, "The Soviet Conception of a Middle East Peace Settlement," in Ro'i, ed., *The Limits to Power,* pp. 282–327.

23. For a discussion of Soviet policy during the civil war in Lebanon, see Freedman, *Soviet Policy,* chapter 7.

24. Ibid., pp. 271–73.

25. For the text of Carter's comments, see *Near East Report* 21(March 16, 1977): 42. Subsequent U.S. statements referred only to "minor modifications" of the 1967 borders.

26. For the text of Carter's comments, see *Near East Report* 21(March 23, 1977): 47.

27. For the early Israeli reaction to Carter's moves, see Yitzhak Rabin, *The Rabin Memoirs* (Boston: Little, Brown, 1979), pp. 292–300.

28. For a detailed analysis of the conflict in the Horn of Africa, see David Albright, "The Horn of Africa and the Arab-Israeli Conflict," in *World Politics and the Arab-Israeli Conflict* ed., Robert O. Freedman (New York: Pergamon, 1979), pp. 147–91.

29. Cf. *Tass,* International Service, May 23, 1977.

30. Cairo Radio Domestic Service, July 16, 1977.

31. Cf. *Pravda,* July 31, 1977 (International Week column).

32. Cited in the report by Don Oberdorfer in the July 30, 1977 issue of the *Washington Post.*

33. Cf. Moscow Radio Arabic language broadcasts to the Arab world, August 1 and 4, 1977.

34. *Time,* August 8, 1977, pp. 24–25 and report by Daniel Southerland in the August 9, 1977 issue of the *Christian Science Monitor.*

35. The text of the rejection was broadcast over Cairo Radio, Voice of Palestine, August 26, 1977.

36. Cf. *Pravda,* September 1, 1977 and Arafat's interview on Moscow Radio on August 30, 1977.

37. Cited in AP report from Beirut, *Baltimore Evening Sun,* September 14, 1977.

38. *New Times* no. 36, 1977, p. 1.

39. Carter interview with newspapermen, cited in *Near East Report* 21(November 2, 1977): 189.

40. Cited in report by Bernard Gwertzman, *New York Times,* October 8, 1977.

41. Author's interview with Marshall D. Shulman, Special Adviser to Secretary of State Cyrus Vance on Soviet Affairs, Washington, D.C., December 7, 1977. For other authoritative views of United States policy vis-á-vis the Soviet Union in the Middle East at this time, see the testimony of Shulman before the Subcommittee on Europe and the Middle East of the House Committee on International Relations (Department of State: Bureau of Public Affairs, October 16, 1977); and the interview of Secretary of State Vance with the editors of *U.S. News and World Report* (Department of State: Bureau of Public Affairs, October 31, 1977). For an analysis of the joint Soviet-American statement and its background, see the report by Robert G. Kaiser, *Washington Post,* October 7, 1977. National Security Advisor Zbigniew Brzezinski also took a positive view of Soviet willingness to aid in a peace settlement in an interview with the Canadian Television Network, in which he also stated that the United States had a "legitimate right to exercise its own leverage" to obtain a settlement (cited in report by Dusko Doder, *Washington Post,* October 3, 1977).

The United States was also working at this time to achieve a cooperative arrangement with the Soviet Union in the Indian Ocean, and this may have had an effect on the Carter administration's desire to sign the joint statement with the Soviet Union on the Middle East. Some commentators also have suggested that the joint statement was linked with a U.S. desire to get Soviet agreement in other areas of Soviet-U.S. relations such as the SALT talks, but this was denied by Vance in his interview with the editors of *U.S. News and World Report.* For the general thrust of Soviet-U.S. relations at this time, see Robert O. Freedman, "The Soviet Image of the Carter Administration's Policy Toward the USSR," *Korea and World Affairs* 4 (Summer 1980): 229–67.

42. Radio Moscow, in Arabic, October 3, 1977.

43. Radio Moscow, in Arabic, October 3, 1977.

44. *Tass,* in English, October 28, 1977.

45. *Pravda,* October 29, 1977.

46. Dmitry Volsky, "Middle East: Key to the Puzzle," *New Times* no. 47, 1977, pp. 21–22.

47. See the report in the *New York Times,* October 3, 1977.

48. For the text of Carter's U.N. address, see the *New York Times,* October 5, 1977.

49. For Dayan's view of Carter and the diplomacy leading to the working paper, see Moshe Dayan, *Breakthrough: A Personal Account of the Egyptian-*

Israeli Peace Negotiations (New York: Alfred A. Knopf, 1981), pp. 55–71.

50. Cf. *Izvestia,* October 19, 1977, and *Pravda,* October 29, 1977.

51 For Israeli reactions to the Sadat visit, see Dayan, *Breakthrough,* chapter 6 and Ezer Weizmann, *The Battle for Peace* (New York: Bantam Books, 1981), pp. 56–72.

52. For an analysis of this event, see Albright, "The Horn of Africa."

53. Gandhi, however, was to return to power in early 1980. For a good study of the geopolitics of the Indian Ocean, see A. J. Cottrell and R. M. Burrell, "Soviet-U.S. Naval Competition in the Indian Ocean," *Orbis* 18 (Winter 1975): 1109–128.

54. Both Algeria and South Yemen could, however, perhaps be counted on to give lip service to the rejectionist cause for domestic political purposes or to gain more Soviet aid; and Algeria might trade off its help to the hardline rejectionists like Libya and Iraq for support in its confrontation with Morocco over the former Spanish Sahara, which Morocco and Mauratania had annexed. Indeed, the Morocco-Algeria confrontation had heated up considerably at the time of the Sadat visit, following the capture of French citizens by Algerian-backed Polisario guerrillas and French military moves to try to obtain their release. (See the report by Paul Lewis, *New York Times,* November 3, 1977). In addition, King Hussan of Morocco warned on November 6, 1977 that his troops would exercise the right of pursuit of Polisario guerrillas into Algeria—a warning that was rejected by Algeria. Interestingly enough, the United States, while an ally and military supplier of Morocco, was in the process of negotiating major natural gas import deals with Algeria and by 1976 had become the main trading partner of Algeria (see the report by Jonathan C. Randal, *Washington Post,* November 4, 1977).

55. Cf. *Pravda,* November 20 and 22, 1977; *New Times* no. 49, 1977, pp. 8–9 ("President Sadat's Canossa"); and Radio Moscow, in Arabic, November 23, 1977 (commentary by Vladimir Bilyakov).

56. Cited in *New York Times,* December 12, 1977.

57. Radio Moscow, Domestic Service, December 18, 1977.

58. Cf. report by John Cooley in the January 11, 1978 issue of the *Christian Science Monitor;* AP report in the *New York Times* on January 12 citing U.S. State Department spokesman Hodding Carter III; and the report by Drew Middleton in the March 27, 1978 issue of the *New York Times.*

59. Baghdad INA, in Arabic, December 5, 1977.

60. The text of the Tripoli Declaration was broadcast by Tripoli Radio in Arabic, December 5, 1977.

61. Cf. *Tass* report, in English, December 5, 1977. See also A. Usvatov, "The Middle East," *New Times* no. 50, 1977, pp. 12–13, and Radio Moscow, "Window on the Arab World," December 5, 1977.

62. For a discussion of this incident, see *Middle East Intelligence Survey* 5 (February 1–15, 1978): 167.

63. Cf. Weizmann, *The Battle for Peace,* pp. 272–81 for the Israeli diplomatic and military response to the attack.

64. *Pravda,* March 21, 1978.

65. *Pravda,* March 26, 1978. See Dayan, *Breakthrough,* p. 122 on the negative diplomatic consequences for Israel of its limited invasion of Lebanon.

66. Cited in the report by Christopher Wren in the March 30, 1978 issue of the *New York Times.*

67. *Izvestia,* June 10, 1978.

68. See Weizmann, *The Battle for Peace,* pp. 119-20 for an analysis of the autonomy plan.

69. *Pravda,* January 8, 1978.

70. See Dayan, *Breakthrough,* pp. 111-14 on the events leading to the recall of the delegation.

71. *Pravda,* January 22, 1978.

72. *Izvestia,* February 16, 1978. The Israelis, however, saw Sadat's visit as a great diplomatic success for Egypt (Cf. Weizmann, *The Battle for Peace,* p. 251).

73. *Pravda,* February 26, 1978.

74. Cf. Dayan, *Breakthrough,* pp. 122-29.

75. *Pravda,* March 11, 1978.

76. Y. Katin, "Useful Talks," *New Times* no. 18, 1978, p. 10. See also *Pravda,* April 23, 1978.

77. *New York Times,* May 2, 1978.

78. For a description of the meeting in England that took place in Leeds Castle, see Dayan, *Breakthrough,* pp. 138-47.

79. For Israeli descriptions of the often very difficult negotiations at Camp David, see Dayan, *Breakthrough,* pp. 153-159 and Weizmann, *The Battle for Peace,* pp. 342-77.

80. For the military and political implications of these concessions, see Weizmann, *The Battle for Peace,* pp. 90-92, 132, 175-76, 184, 208, 231.

81. For the texts of the Camp David agreements and the accompanying letters, see *The Camp David Summit* (Washington: United States Department of State Publication No. 8954, September 1978).

82. *Pravda,* September 24, 1978.

83. For an Israeli critique of U.S. handling of King Hussein, see Dayan, *Breakthrough,* p. 201.

84. Leonid Medvenko, "Middle East: Fictions and Realities," *New Times* no. 40, 1978, p. 6.

85. A. Stepanov, "Hour of Trial for the Palestinians," *New Times* no. 41, 1978, p. 7.

86. *Pravda,* October 7, 1978.

87. Radio Moscow, Domestic Service, October 28, 1978 (International Diary Program).

88. *Pravda,* November 2, 1978.

89. For a discussion of Egyptian tactics, see Dayan, *Breakthrough,* pp. 206-21.

90. For an examiniation of the domestic opposition facing Begin, see the "News Analysis" by William Clairborne, *Washington Post,* October 3, 1978, and the chapters by Pollock and Torgovnik in this volume.

91. Dayan, *Breakthrough,* p. 194.

92. For an analysis of the reaction to Saunders, see the report by John M. Goshko, *Washington Post,* October 27, 1978.

93. Cited in Reuters report, *Baltimore Sun,* October 26, 1978.

94.   *Pravda,* November 1, 1978.

95.   *Izvestia,* November 2, 1978.

96.   For a report on the results of the Baghdad Conference, see Baghdad INA, November 5, 1978, in *Foreign Broadcast Information Service Daily Report: Middle East and North Africa,* November 6, 1978, pp. A-13—A-15. See also Amman Ar-Ra'y, in Arabic, November 6, 1978, in the same source, pp. A-19-20.

97.   Radio Moscow (in Arabic to the Arab world), November 6, 1978.

98.   "Wanted! Not a Bogus Settlement," *New Times* no. 50, 1978, p. 1.

99.   For an analysis of these negotiations, see Dayan, *Breakthrough,* pp. 199-249.

100.   Ibid., pp. 250-51.

101.   Cf. report by Paul Hoffman, *New York Times,* December 15, 1978.

102.   For an analysis of the events in Iran, see Barry Rubin, *Paved with Good Intentions: The American Experience in Iran* (New York: Oxford, 1970).

103.   For an analysis of Soviet difficulties with Khomeini's Iran, see Robert O. Freedman, "Soviet Policy Toward the Middle East Since the Invasion of Afghanistan," *Columbia Journal of International Affairs* 34 (Fall/Winter 1980-81): 290-321.

104.   Dmitry Volsky, "Vicious Circle," *New Times* no. 5, 1979, p. 8.

105.   For a Soviet description of the visit, see L. Lebedev and Y. Tyunkov, "Useful Exchange of Views," *New Times* no. 51, 1978, p. 15.

106.   Cf. Dayan, *Breakthrough,* pp. 260-64 for his rather pessimistic view of this meeting.

107.   Ibid., p. 282.

108.   See Appendix C for a list of the additional promises.

109.   For a list of the actions taken against Egypt and the dynamics of the second Baghdad Conference, see *The Middle East* no. 55 (May 1979): 12, 37-39.

110.   *Pravda,* March 27, 1979.

111.   A discussion of the summit is found in Freedman, "The Soviet Image," pp. 259-60.

112.   *Tass,* in English, June 17, 1979 (*Foreign Broadcast Information Service: Daily Report USSR,* June 18, 1979, p. AA-11).

113.   Radio Moscow, Domestic Service, June 25, 1979. For a Soviet view of the general Middle Eastern situation at this time, see the interview of Yevgeny Primakov in the Beirut publication *Monday Morning* (*Foreign Broadcast Information Service: Daily Report USSR,* July 6, 1979, pp. H-1 to H-11).

114.   For an analysis of the resumption of the Iraq-Syria quarrel, see Graham Benten, "After the Coup Attempt," *The Middle East* no. 59 (September 1979): 13-14.

115.   For an analysis of the Iraqi-Soviet relationship at this time, see Robert O. Freedman, "Soviet Policy Toward Ba'athist Iraq," in *The Soviet Union in the Third World,* ed., Robert H. Donaldson, (Boulder, Colo.: Westview Press, 1981), pp. 161-191.

116.   O. Volgin, "Palestinians Stand Firm," *New Times* no. 35, 1979, p. 14. The U.S. Ambassador to the U.N., Andrew Young, had been forced to resign after an "unauthorized" meeting with the PLO U.N. representative in New York.

117. For a Soviet reaction to Barzargan's decision, see Alexander Usvatov, "Iran's Troubled August," *New Times* no. 36, 1979, pp. 10–11.

118. For the background to the Soviet decision to invade Afghanistan, see Robert O. Freedman, *Soviet Policy Toward the Middle East Since 1970,* 3rd ed., (New York: Praeger, 1982), chapter 10.

119. For the Soviet reaction to Carter's moves, see *Pravda,* January 7, 1980.

120. Cf. *Baltimore Sun,* January 16, 1980 for a list of the states supporting Moscow or abstaining in the U.N. vote.

121. Cited in report by Douglas Watson in the *Baltimore Sun,* January 21, 1980.

122. Cited in report by Michael Weisskopf, *Washington Post,* January 2, 1980. Afghanis and Iranians stormed the Soviet Embassy in Teheran but were driven off by Iranian police. One year later, however, the Iranian authorities were much slower to come to the defense of the embassy.

123. For the text of the Steadfastness Front declaration, see Radio Damascus, Domestic Service, January 16, 1980 (translated in *Foreign Broadcast Information Service: Middle East,* January 17, 1980, pp. A–2–6.)

124. *Pravda,* January 30, 1980 (translated in *Current Digest of the Soviet Press* vol. 32 no. 4, pp. 19–20).

125. *Pravda,* April 26, 1980.

126. *Pravda,* May 1, 1980.

127. Cited in report by Marvine Howe, *New York Times,* May 19, 1980.

128. Cited in report by Marvine Howe, *New York Times,* May 20, 1980.

129. The text of the resolution is found in the *New York Times,* May 23, 1980.

130. *Pravda,* August 22, 1980 (translated in *Current Digest of the Soviet Press* vol. 32 no. 34, p. 13).

131. For an analysis of the Soviet decision to declare neutrality, see Freedman, "Soviet Policy Since the Invasion of Afghanistan," pp. 299–301.

132. For an analysis of the new diplomatic situation caused by the war, see "U.S. Defense Umbrella, Shelter or Storm," *The Middle East,* (December 1980): 10–13.

133. Brezhnev initially made his call for the neutralization of the Persian Gulf during a trip to India in mid-December 1980, and repeated it during his speech to the Twenty-sixth Party Congress in February 1981. (For the text of his proposal, see Freedman, "Soviet Policy Since the Invasion of Afghanistan," pp. 304–5.)

134. For the text of the treaty, see *Pravda,* October 9, 1980. For a discussion of Soviet-Syrian relations, see Galia Golan, "Syria and the Soviet Union since the Yom Kippur War," *Orbis* 21 (Winter 1978): 777–801. See also Robert O. Freedman, "Soviet Policy Toward Syria Since Camp David," *Middle East Review* 14, (Fall-Winter 1981–82): 31–42.

135. The missile crisis is discussed in detail in Freedman, "Soviet Policy Since Camp David."

136. Cited in *Jerusalem Post,* May 24, 1981.

137. Moscow, however, had not forgotten the missile crisis and in early July carried out a joint military exercise with Syria including, for the first time,

naval landings. For a report on the exercise, which could be seen as a Soviet show of support for Syria after Begin's reelection, see the UPI report in the *New York Times,* July 10, 1981.

138. Cf. *Pravda,* June 10, 11, and 16, 1981.

139. Translated in *Current Digest of the Soviet Press* vol. 33 no. 24, p. 17.

140. Cf. report by Nathaniel Harrison, *Christian Science Monitor,* April 1, 1981.

141. Cf. Andrei Stepanov, "Taking Up a Point" (Soviet Neutrality in the Iran-Iraq War), *New Times* no. 17, 1981, p. 31.

142. Cf. report by Michael J. Berlin, *Washington Post,* June 19, 1981.

143. Cited in report by Edward Cody, *Washington Post,* June 29, 1981.

144. Aziz Mohammed's speech was also printed in *Pravda,* March 3, 1981.

145. Cited in report by Bernard Gwertzman, *New York Times,* March 20, 1981.

146. Cf. report by Don Oberdorfer, *Washington Post,* April 11, 1981.

147. Ibid. Permission for the sale of the planes had been previously refused.

148. Cf. *Tass* statement in *Pravda,* July 22, 1981.

149. For an analysis of the background to this incident, see the report by Bernard Gwertzman, *New York Times,* August 21, 1981. For an examination of Kaddafi's attempt to improve his diplomatic position, see Claudia Wright, "Libya Comes in From the Cold," *The Middle East* (August 1981): 18–25.

150. Cf. *Tass,* International Service, in Russian, August 20, 1981 (translated in *Foreign Broadcast Information Service: USSR,* August 20, 1981, p. H–2).

151. Cf. *Pravda,* August 23, 1981 and Radio Moscow, in English, August 29, 1981. Criticism of the U.S. action came from such centrist Arab states as Jordan, Kuwait, Bahrein, and the United Arab Emirates, and from the Secretary of the Gulf Cooperation Council, and the Organizaton of African Unity (Cf. *Foreign Broadcast Information Service: Middle East and Africa,* August 20 and 21, 1981).

152. Cf. *Pravda,* September 8, 12, 14, 25, 1981. The actual agreement, signed in December, was far more modest, but Moscow sought to extract the maximum in propaganda value from it both when Begin came to the United States in September to negotiate the general principles of the agreement and when Sharon came in November to sign the detailed agreement.

153. The meeting was at Shamir's initiative.

154. Cf. *Tass,* International Service, in Russian, September 25, 1981 (*Foreign Broadcast Information Service: USSR,* September 25, 1981, p. CC–3) and Radio Moscow, in English, to North America, October 5, 1981 (*Foreign Broadcast Information Service: USSR,* October 6, 1981, p. H–4) and report by William Clayborn, *Washington Post,* September 26, 1981.

8   Autonomy, the Palestinians, and International Law: The Begin Legacy

Robert A. Friedlander

The *Los Angeles Times'* revelation on July 5, 1981 that four successive presidential administrations have conducted secret talks with PLO representatives served once more to remind the U.S. public that the United States, no matter who occupies the White House, is both concerned with and committed to a resolution of the Palestinian problem.[1] And the negative response of Prime Minister Menachem Begin that very day to queries on the PLO connection by two ABC television news correspondents[2] also demonstrates that, as in the past, the Begin regime (or for that matter any Israeli government) will continue advocating the exclusion of the PLO from every proposed territorial settlement as essential to its own political survival. Thus, the impasse continues, for neither side has been willing to divorce the Palestinian issue from that of the role of the Palestine Liberation Organization.[3]

Former Undersecretary of State George Ball, a persistent pro-Arabist since leaving the diplomatic ranks, has summed up the charges levied against Israeli territorial policies in general and the Begin settlements record in particular:

For 14 years Israel has imposed an increasingly repressive military occupation of 1.3 million Palestinians in the West Bank and Gaza Strip, while, through its settlements policy, engineering a progressive land grab in the West Bank. It now controls one-third of both land and water resources and the process of absorption continues relentlessly.[4]

The other side of the coin is the fact that after nearly three and a half decades of existence, Israel is still a nation under seige, "faced with implacable Arab resistance, reviled as an alien wedge in the Arab heartland, and threatened with terrorism and invasion to which it could only respond with armed vigilance."[5] The Palestinian question not only continues to isolate Israel from its Arab neighbors, but has become a divisive force within the Israeli body politic.[6]

In the eyes of its Arab adversaries, along with their friends and sympathizers, Israel has been a continual transgressor of international law since its creation more than 30 years ago.[7] Concomitant with this view is the inference by the so-called moderate Arab states, never explicitly pronounced, that if Israel would cease its violations, it would receive some form of legal recognition.[8] Even the PLO at various times, for its own purposes, has hinted moderation in private contacts with Western diplomats and government representatives.[9] Its public stance, however, has never changed—being that of implacable hostility to the so-called "Zionist entity," an Arab "rejectionist" euphemism for the sovereign state of Israel.[10]

A distinguished Palestinian scholar has recently observed that "[t]he Arab world is a baffling political universe."[11] How else can one account for the continued and contumacious refusal of the Arab bloc (Egypt excepted) to recognize Israel's existence, despite the fact that it has been a member state of the United Nations for nearly a generation?[12] It may very well be that the continued Arab refusal to accept Israel's legitimacy goes a long way in explaining the Israeli refusal to recognize Palestinian national claims. At the very heart of the Arab-Israeli confrontation are seemingly incompatible nationalistic aspirations and ideologies. What is at issue in the emergence of Palestinian nationalism is not a question of right and wrong, but rather two conflicting sets of rights.[13] These claims are not necessarily mutually exclusive, but due to the combined pressures of religion and politics, neither side will concede "the right of the other to lead a sovereign political existence in that strip of territory both consider their homeland."[14]

Unhappily, the United Nations, originally a symbol of the triumphant Allies' commitment to international law and the maintenance of world peace, has exacerbated the Middle Eastern dilemma. The modern state of Israel was, in effect, a U.N. creation, but the precipitate British withdrawal from their Palestinian Mandate on May 15, 1947, helped change the course of history. When the guerrilla Arab Liberation Army, the Jordanian Arab Legion, and the armies of the Arab League invaded Israel upon the proclamation of its independence, the United Nations Partition Plan adopted by the General Assembly on November 29, 1947, became void *ab initio*. With its termination the projected Palestinian state, which was to have included Judea and Samaria (the West Bank), but not Jerusalem, also fell victim to the Arab League invasion.

The armistice concluding the first Arab-Israeli war,[15] sometimes called the Israeli War of Independence, left Israel in physical possession of approximately 30 percent more territory than had been granted to it under the original United Nations Partition plan. Of even greater significance, the Arab League invaders not only were in possession of 129 square miles of territory assigned to Israel by the Partition instrument, but also Egypt and Jordan had unilaterally absorbed the very territories from which the United Nations had intended to create an

Arab Palestine. The end result was that Jordan controlled over 82 percent of the former Mandate, whereas the new state of Israel was in possession of barely more than 17 percent. At the conclusion of a military conflict, under customary international law, the victor is entitled to annex territory belonging to the vanquished, and where neither side prevails, de facto possession can lead to permanent acquisition. This is exactly what took place.[16]

In retrospect, perhaps the most enduring and unfortunate legacy of that first Arab-Israeli war was the failure to create the Palestinian state envisaged by the United Nations Partition agreement. In flagrant disregard of the Arab League, King Abdullah of Transjordan on December 1, 1948 annexed the Palestinian territory acquired in that war but also offered Jordanian citizenship to the 400,000 Palestinian refugees. Despite this annexation, which lead to the proclamation on April 26, 1949 of the new Hashemite Kingdom of Jordan,[17] Abdullah continued secret negotiations with the Israeli government.[18] This was one of the reasons why he was assassinated on July 20, 1951, while praying at the Omar Mosque in East Jerusalem (obtained through conquest by the Arab Legion). The location of that untoward event was especially significant, since Jerusalem—intended under the 1947 U.N. plan to be an international city—represents the second major obstacle to any Arab-Israeli accommodation.

"I am an old man. I would like to pray at Beyt al/Maqdis (in Jerusalem) before my death."[19] These words spoken by the late Arabian King Feisal, following the 1973 October or Yom Kippur War, are a pointed reminder that the Palestinian issue is far from being the only major controversy between Jews and Arabs. The Jewish capture of East Jerusalem during the Six-Day War, or third Arab-Israeli conflict, has created an additional territorial bone of contention, severely traumatized by the July 1980 vote of the Israeli Knesset to make Jerusalem the de jure capital of Israel,[20] though it had already been the de facto capital since 1967. Prime Minister Menachem Begin's decision to move his office to East Jerusalem further aggravated an already volatile situation,[21] but the Israeli prime minister rejected all protests, maintaining in a letter to Egyptian President Anwar Sadat, "Jerusalem is and will be one, under Israel's sovereignty, its indivisible capital."[22]

Small wonder that one knowledgeable academic commentator has called Jerusalem "the thorniest issue in the Arab-Israeli conflict...."[23] According to Saudi Arabian Crown Prince Fahd bin Abdul Aziz, in an official government statement, until the Jerusalem conundrum is resolved to Arab satisfaction, any talk of accommodation is "pure imagination and dreams."[24] Yet Moshe Dayan, foreign minister at the time of the Camp David agreements and a declared moderate on the Palestinian issue, denounces the U.N. for attempting to make East Jerusalem sacrosanct and protected by international law, while West Jerusalem becomes fair game for any Arab territorial depredation. "What was there holy about the military conquest by the Jordanian Army in 1948 and profane about our victory in the 1967 war—a war that also started with Jordan's attack on Israel?"[25] * The sad truth is that the Palestinian and Jerusalem issues have been inextricably intertwined, with the United Nations creating a political Gordian knot of almost limitless dimensions.

The role of the United Nations has been curious to say the least. Following the first Arab-Israeli conflict, the United Nations Relief and Works Agency (UNRWA) was established to aid in the shelter, food, clothing, education, and medical care of the Palestinian refugees. (The United States was the largest contributor to UNRWA funds.) The results were less than satisfactory, and the refugee camps earned their place in modern history. Of considerable significance is the fact that only the Kingdom of Jordan accepted Palestinian refugees in large numbers within its boundaries and extended to them Jordanian citizenship. A few Arab states, primarily Lebanon, allowed Palestinians to enter and to work but refused to grant them permanent status. Egypt created the Gaza Strip settlement camps, utilizing the misery of the Palestinian refugees for propaganda and political purposes. Israeli occupation of these areas after the 1967 war led to a definite improvement in living standards and economic opportunities, but the overall result was comparable to a U.S. urban minority group moving up from ghetto to slum. And the refugees, when subjected to Israeli political controls, responded with a heightened national consciousness.[26]

Since mid-December 1948, the United Nations General Assembly has repeatedly insisted upon the Palestinian refugees' right of return and compensation for their material losses.[27] During the last decade, simultaneous with the growth of the Arab oil weapon, U.N. pronouncements have sharpened to the point where, in the essence of Assembly declarations, "displaced Palestinians have not only an absolute right to return to the Israeli state but also have the right to do so for the purpose of pursuing their separate nationalist identity." To Israelis this is in effect another way of implementing the avowed PLO goal of Israel's destruction.[28]

The third Arab-Israeli conflict, popularly termed the Six-Day War, dramatically transformed the nature of the Israeli state with the conquest and occupation of the Sinai, Gaza, West Bank, and Golan territories, along with East Jerusalem. An additional 2,986 square miles of territory came under Israeli rule, not counting 23,622 square miles in the Sinai Peninsula, which has now reverted to Egypt under the terms of the Egyptian-Israeli peace treaty.[29] Of even greater consequence, Israel acquired an Arab Palestinian population of approximately one million.[30] Pro-Arab commentators have condemned the 1967 conflict as an

---

*Technically, the 1967 war began with an Israeli attack on Egypt following Egypt's decisions to order the U.N. buffer force out of the Sinai, close the Straits of Tiran to Israeli shipping, and mass Egyptian forces on Israel's border. Israel asked Jordan to stay out of the war, but King Hussein refused.—ED.

Israeli war of aggression, but a majority of legal and political analysts view the Six-Day War as basically a defensive action on the part of Israel.[31] After cessation of hostilities, however, the mildly antagonistic mood of the United Nations membership radically worsened.[32]

U.N. Security Council Resolution 242, passed by unanimous vote on November 22, 1967 called upon Israel to withdraw from Arab territories occupied during the Six-Day War and declared as inadmissible "the acquisition of territory by war...."[33] This is not only *contra* to customary international law, *pre* and *post* Charter, but also

> ... if acquisition by war is inadmissible, one might question what right the Kingdom of Jordan had in the West Bank, and, in addition, what right Egypt had in the Gaza Strip. It would appear that territory which can be gained by the sword can also be lost by the sword.[34]

Admittedly, Resolution 242 sought "acknowledgement of the sovereignty, territorial integrity and political independence of every state in the area and their right to live in peace within secure and recognized boundaries free from force or threats of force...."[35] But despite this oblique affirmation of Israel's right to exist, the main thrust of the Security Council's declaration was that Israel had committed aggressive conquest.[36]

It is also significant that the Security Council, during the Yom Kippur War, avoided any condemnation of the Arab attack in the cease-fire Resolution 338 of October 22, 1973[37] and merely contented itself with the creation of an international peace-keeping force. When the tide of battle finally turned in favor of Israel, pressure by the U.N. majority and the two superpowers brought the October conflict to a halt, but the restrictive principles of Resolutions 242 and 338 continued to be applied to Israel alone.[38] The end result has been a political and diplomatic impasse broken only by the high drama of Sadat's journey to Jerusalem, the Camp David summit, and the Israeli-Egyptian treaty of peace.

For more than three decades United Nations impartiality and its self-proclaimed role of moral suasion have become, at least for the Israelis, inherently suspect.

> [F]ollowing each Arab-Israeli major war, the same "settlement"... was imposed by the Powers in concert with the United Nations: restoration to the Arabs for their losses in return for some ambiguous semantic exercise.... And between the wars, the Arabs were allowed to wage war on Israel to the best of their ability (marauding, harassment, boycotts, fedayeen actions, artillery barrages, etc.).[39]

Yet, despite a hostile international climate,[40] Israel has refused to negotiate the modalities of its own demise, relying upon the ancient legal maxim—*jus ex injuria non oritur*—rights do not arise from wrongs.

Three United Nations events during the years immediately following the Yom Kippur War indicate without question that the non-Western and Soviet bloc majority in the United Nations is acting on the premise that Israel has no legal foundation in international law and therefore has no right to exist as a nation-state. On November 13, 1974, Yasir Arafat, chairman of the Palestinian Liberation Organization, was accorded the status of a head of state and by formal invitation addressed the U.N. General Assembly, waving a gun and an olive branch. In his colorful speech, denouncing "racist Zionism" and Jewish aggression, there was no mention whatsoever of either an Arab or a Palestinian recognition of the state of Israel.[41] Less than two weeks later, on November 22, 1974, the U.N. General Assembly voted overwhelmingly for two resolutions that officially endorsed the creation of a Palestinian state and granted to the PLO, a private group of nonstate actors engaged in global terrorist activities, permanent observer status at the U.N.[42] Then, on November 10, 1975, in its most controversial action to date, the General Assembly by a vote of 70 to 29, with 27 abstentions, condemned Zionism "as a form of racism and racial discrimination."[43] Considering the role that Zionism had played in the establishment of Israel as a nation-state, the implication was obvious.

Even more significant than the wording of these resolutions themselves, was the repeated failure of the General Assembly either to take cognizance of Security Council Resolution 242, which had called for recognition of the political sovereignty and territorial integrity of *all* belligerents involved in the 1967 war, or to indicate in any way whatsoever the authentic existence of Israel and its rightful place as a U.N. member state. In the words of U.S. Ambassador Daniel Patrick Moynihan, "the U.N. was chipping away at the legitimacy of the State of Israel, all but declaring it an illegal entity...."[44] Petroleum politics, petrodollar diplomacy, and Third World hostility have combined in attempting to deny to Israel her lawful position in the world community of nations and to strip away her historic and legal foundations.[45]

What is, exactly, the meaning of General Assembly declarations and Security Council resolutions? Is there such a thing as U.N. law, and what is its relationship to the operation of the international state system? Although these questions are and have been the subjects of intense and inexorable scholarly debate, certain basic assumptions are clear enough. The General Assembly's voting function is merely recommendatory, while the resolutions of the Security Council (subject to great power veto) have some enforcement mechanisms attached when they implement a decision of the International Court of Justice (ICJ) or when they deal with matters of international peace and security. Whereas the four Arab-Israeli wars fall under that category, the Palestinian question does not. Moreover, "peremptory language in a resolution cannot convert a mere recommendation which Member States may or may not accept, into a decision legally binding on them."[46]

At best, General Assembly resolutions may be considered authoritative interpretations of the Charter,[47] but that in turn raises the issue of what is the nature of the Charter itself with respect to the function of international law? The best view is that "the Charter is an international compact creating rights and obligations for states,"[48] but those rights and obligations pertain merely to the members of the organization who upon entering the United Nations have pledged themselves to be bound. Obviously, given the history of the past 35 years, those pledges have not been honored with much fidelity.[49]

Thus, the U.N. approach to the Palestinian question for more than a generation has been political rather than legal, and this continues to obscure the juridical aspects of the problem. As with all self-determination claims, both people and territory are inextricably intertwined.[50] But without territory, there can be no assertion of injury,[51] and therein lies the rub. For Arab protestations and the United Nations' majority notwithstanding, "the West Bank and the Gaza Strip are not 'Arab' territories in the legal sense, but territories of the Mandate which have never been recognized as belonging to either Israel or Jordan."[52] One U.S. law professor and former Justice Department official, carrying that proposition to its logical extension, argues that Israel is a trustee-occupant of the West Bank territory.[53] Another U.S. legal academic, and current director of the U.S. Arms Control and Disarmament Agency, claims that the status of the West Bank territory survived the British Mandate,

> ...and will continue until Jordan and Israel settle what is essentially a territorial dispute between them, make peace, and divide the land in accordance with the provisions of Security Council Resolution 242, which is based on the Mandate.[54]

Customary international law recognizes several different ways for the acquisition of territory, among them occupation, prescription, and subjugation. Occupation refers to the establishment of a physical presence in an area over which no other state has exercised authority and control (which may or may not pertain to portions of the Mandate following British withdrawal). Prescription is the international counterpart to the common law domestic concept of adverse possession, the elements of which include: (1) the exercise of sovereignty authority, (2) peaceful and uninterrupted possession, (3) open and notorious possession, (4) continuous possession. A minority view holds that prescriptive title becomes valid by means of time held and effective control. Subjugation is the acquisition of territory by forcible annexation, generally confirmed by treaties and conventions.[55] Until that time, the occupying power remains in lawful possession.[56] Under this analysis the West Bank settlements policy of the Begin government is legally permissible, although politically controversial.

What of the Palestinians themselves? Have they a valid claim to national legitimacy, and are there any other claims deserving of an international remedy? According to the United Nations Charter and literally dozens of General Assembly resolutions, all peoples have the right to determine their freedom of action without external interference, and every state is obliged to refrain from any forcible activity that would deprive said people of that inherent right. Official publications and influential committees of the United Nations have designated self-determination as a "human right," although that proclaimed right must obviously be exercised on a collective rather than an individual basis.[57] But peoplehood is not necessarily statehood, and if the link between people and territory becomes severed, the prior claim of right is rendered inoperative.[58]

Despite the fact that for 18 years the Palestinians residing in Gaza and the West Bank did not seek to establish their own national identity, and despite the fact that the quest for an independent Palestinian state began in earnest only after the 1967 war,[59] past history has given way to current realities. The Begin regime has yet to face up to the new international climate and change of Western attitudes, regarding the Palestinian Arabs of the West Bank and Gaza territories, on the Palestinian right to express themselves politically, which favor the establishment of a Palestinian political entity.[60] Whether a Palestinian state made up of the West Bank and the Gaza territories would constitute a viable economic entity (an important requisite for internal stability) is no longer a relevant question, given the current dynamics of the world community.

A serious complicating factor is that most members of the U.N. and some Western states recognize the PLO as the representative of the Palestinian people. The PLO position on Israel has not changed, notwithstanding the diplomatic support of the past decade, as exemplified by Chairman Yasir Arafat's pleas to the Arab rulers in July 1981: "I want your swords, not your blessings."[61] As Israeli dove Yehoshafat Harkabi sadly observes, "[t]he PLO position represents the absolutist-totalistic nature of the Arab position in the most blatant terms."[62] The Reagan White House (as opposed to its predecessor) has periodically condemned the PLO as a terrorist organization,[63] but mixed signals have been sent to the Israelis.[64] The same could be said at best, or at worst, for U.N. General Assembly Resolution 3089D, voted in the wake of the Yom Kippur War,[65] for by its deliberately vague wording, the implication is that the content of the resolution embraces "all or part of the existing Israeli state...."[66]

Under this kind of unremitting pressure, Israeli governments have slowly, but perceptibly, yielded previously asserted uncompromising stands.[67] The most dramatic and potentially far-reaching shift in the official Israeli attitude is associated with the concept of autonomy for the West Bank, first proposed in 1967 by Yigal Allon and offered in one form or another (on several occasions to King Hussein) by succeeding Israeli government officials down to the Camp David accords ten years later.[68] Autonomy, however, whatever else it stands for, is not self-determination.[69] One might even maintain that it exists only in the eye of the beholder.

Autonomy throughout modern history in both theory and practice has been largely a suspect phenomenon. With the singular exception of the South Tyrol New Autonomy Statute of 1972, (the jury is still out as to whether or not it has succeeded),[70] autonomy when it was attempted has either worked very badly or not at all.[71] Its role as a legal norm is inherently suspect, for it is first and foremost a political remedy, and a transitory one at that. Autonomous relationships in the current century were mainly designed as placebos to frustrate nationalist movements and to vitiate secessionist pressures.[72] In almost every instance where some degree of autonomy has been granted to dissident populations, the donation was made with reluctance, and the reception took place without gratitude. As a political device, autonomy is transitory at best and designed to be of a stopgap nature.

From the perspective of international law, autonomy has been of minor legal consequence. It may be generally defined as self-regulation (sometimes mistakenly called home rule), wherein the grantee remains tied to a superior sovereignty. Even when such political instrumentality was accepted by all interested parties, that tenuous relationship ultimately dissolved into either separation or severance. At best, it is a stopgap measure leading to independence. At worst, it "is a vague and obscure term subject to doubt and debate."[73] Whatever its intended function, autonomy does not and cannot represent a permanent resolution to the nationalist quarrels between a secessionist-minded population and a dominant political order.[74]

Despite the high drama of Anwar Sadat's journey to Jerusalem in November 1977, his historic quest for peace, although unrealized at the time, predated the 1973 October war.[75] Whether the first autonomy proposals offered by Prime Minister Menachem Begin to President Jimmy Carter during Begin's visit to Washington in December 1977, and then presented to the Knesset upon his return,[76] were a political reflex action or the product of long-term thinking is a moot historical question, for the Camp David accords diverged sharply from the December plan.[77] Begin's original proposals contained 26 points , which provided for Palestinian self-regulation (mistakenly referred to as self-rule) by means of "administrative autonomy" to be exercised by an administrative council in matters of religion, culture, education, social problems, and economic concerns, but Israel would still hold sovereign authority and therefore continue to maintain powers of internal and external security. Arab inhabitants of the West Bank would be permitted to retain, or to opt for, Jordanian citizenship if they so desired.[78] This meant that the Palestinians "could determine the placing of sewer pipes in Hebron, but could not build an army, hoist a flag, compose a new anthem or print money."[79] As might have been expected, Sadat uniformly rejected these suggestions.

One major difficulty from the very start in undertaking a viable autonomy program was the deeply-held, rather unusual convictions of the Israeli prime minister. Not only had Begin committed himself to the Biblical version of *Eretz Israel*, the composition of which included Judea and Samaria (the West Bank territories),[80] but he also espoused the concept of personal autonomy as opposed to territorial autonomy. Juridically, this meant he was advocating that a collective theory be extended to individuals, and in any case, the legal feasibility of such an approach is strongly suspect.[81] However, several U.S. scholars have incorporated personal or individual autonomy into their own construct of democratic constitutionalism.[82]

The September 17, 1978 Camp David accords seemed to represent a major step forward in the autonomy process.[83] Though the term "administrative council" appears only once in the "Framework for Peace," the term "self-governing authority" received four different references. According to the Camp David "Framework," the previous Begin formula of permanent autonomous status was transformed into a five year "transitional period," after which negotiations between all parties involved—Israel, Egypt, Jordan, and the inhabitants of the West Bank and Gaza—are to decide upon a permanent solution based upon the principles of U.N. Security Council Resolution 242. Moreover, the language of the document explicitly pledged that Israel would withdraw its armed forces and redeploy its security modalities so that a local police force could be operated by the self-governing authority. However, a vague and indeterminate reference was also made to the need for all necessary measures that would insure the security of Israel, as well as its neighbors, during the autonomy transitional period.

It soon developed that the Israeli-Egyptian signatories had differing interpretations regarding the nature of the self-governing authority, the extent of autonomous powers, and the control of security in the occupied territories. The Egyptian model stressed "full autonomy," in which elected representatives of a self-governing authority (SGA) "will be able to take their decisions and formulate their own policies." When coupled with an insistence upon the "unqualified withdrawal" of the Israeli military government and redeployment of the Israeli armed forces "into specified security locations," the overall import is one of independence in everything but name.[84]

The Israeli model, on the other hand, sought to include state lands, international communications, currency regulation, natural resources, radio and television stations, plus internal security as part of the "residual powers" that would continue to be exercised by Israel.[85] Reportedly, 19 points of agreement had been reached in the Egyptian-Israeli autonomy talks during January-February 1980,[86] but the major substantive points at issue were not resolved. The Jerusalem conundrum, wholly avoided by the Camp David "Framework," was raised in letters written by the three signatory heads of government on September 17 and September 22, 1978, and then faded into the background.[87] In effect, the parties agreed to disagree.

Notwithstanding the Jordanian refusal to enter into any discussions regarding the proposed autonomy,[88] notwithstanding the failure of any Palestinian groups or representative figures to participate in the negotiations,[89] and notwithstanding the Begin regime's settlements policy (a source of continued friction), a precedent-shattering treaty of peace between Israel and Egypt was signed on March 26, 1979,[90] and diplomatic normalization has now occurred between the two countries, including periodic meetings between President Sadat and Prime Minister Begin. But there the matter rests, and, if anything, the June 1981

Israeli election has complicated rather than ameliorated tensions between the Israelis and their Palestinian population.

Since the U.S. presidential election of 1980 and the start of the Reagan administration, there has been much talk of new diplomatic initiatives, and considerable debate as to whether the Camp David agreement has any further relevance to the current dormant Middle East peace process. In retrospect, Camp David was a spectacular *coup de theatre* for Jimmy Carter, though it could not salvage his presidency. A successful outcome, in one form or another, was probably inevitable and, from the standpoint of both Begin and Sadat, certainly desirable.

There is a good deal also to be said for one critic's sardonic comment that the Maryland summit was merely "a clumsily improvised search for a comprehensive Middle East settlement."[91] Many well-informed observers consider Camp David a closed chapter, at best victim of a natural death when there was no more to be gained from it.[92] Viewed from the Palestinian perspective, it was a "non-starter" to begin with, viable only insofar as it was a logical step toward the Israeli-Egyptian treaty of peace.[93] Nevertheless, no matter what the present verdict, Camp David proved that there is an alternative to confrontation politics.[94]

A major obstacle still to be surmounted is Menachem Begin's legalistic interpretation of the obligations that Israel has undertaken and his frequent reinterpretation of prior agreed-upon understandings. When the legal advisor to the Ministry of Foreign Affairs can write of the Camp David "Framework" that it "does not necessarily convey the idea of a binding international agreement," though admitting that its intention was to conclude such an obligation,[95] what can Israel's friends and allies, let alone her new treaty partner, actually believe? Narrow legalistic formularizing often leads to suspicion and mistrust. It is not surprising, therefore, that Begin's critics on the autonomy issue and the peace process have become so savage and unrelenting.[96]

The bitterly fought and sharply fragmented June 1981 Israeli parliamentary elections "revealed a country passionately divided by ideology, class, age, attitudes toward Orthodox faith and law—and crucially, ethnic origin."[97] Added to this was the fierce personal vendetta between Begin and Shimon Peres, leader of the Labor party, which climaxed in a series of angry insults exchanged during and after their televised debate on June 25, 1981, the second such confrontation in Israeli political history.[98] Autonomy was barely mentioned, which should not have been surprising since Peres, a former proponent of the "Jordanian option," seemed at times to outposture Begin as a proponent of West Bank settlement.[99] For his part, the Israeli prime minister sought to transform the campaign into a referendum on his leadership and on his increasingly tough stance toward the autonomy issue. Seven weeks following the Likud's narrow victory, the autonomy talks between Egypt and Israel resumed in Cairo after a 16 month hiatus, but they appeared to have no direction and no momentum.[100]

The truth is that Israeli public opinion, no matter what its political orientation, had come to view the prospect of an independent Palestinian state "as a Trojan horse for terrorism...."[101] None of the four Arab-Israeli wars has resulted in an improvement of the Palestinian position. The Egyptian-Israeli rapprochement has meant peace only for those two countries, the recovery of most of the Sinai for Egypt, a stronger military position for Israeli vis-á-vis her Arab antagonists, but no discernible progress in self-regulation, let alone self-determination, for either Gaza or the West Bank. The United Nations, if anything, has grown more strident and more hostile in its attitude toward Begin's Israel, and the new Reagan administration does not seem any more sympathetic to the Israeli hardline position than did the prior government of Jimmy Carter. Begin has managed to isolate Israel with respect to world public opinion, and his current policies appear, in the eyes of many, to vitiate the promise of Camp David. Whatever the actuality, the present Begin image remains that of the former Irgun street fighter.

History will be kinder to Menachem Begin than his contemporaries have demonstrated to date, for the Egyptian-Israeli peace treaty, and all that it implies, is from any historical viewpoint, a stunning personal achievement. But as with other historical monuments, time appears to have passed the Israeli prime minister by. And the real meaning of his endeavors is obscured by an increasing inflexibility and aggressiveness. Begin has turned Israel's war with the PLO into a personal vendetta, in much the same way that Jimmy Carter personalized the Iranian hostage seizure into a quarrel with the Ayatollah Khomeini. In each case the result has been a zero-sum game.

Camp David and the Egyptian peace were Begin's triumphs. Palestinian nationalism is his tragedy. What the Israelis and the Palestinians now require "is not a war of liberation but a peace of liberation."[102] The Begin syndrome can only provide endless recrimination. One must not forget that the rule of law is also the rule of reason. Yet these are sadly undervalued commodities in contemporary Middle Eastern politics.

NOTES

1. See the *Miami Herald,* July 6, 1981; *Chicago Tribune,* July 6, 1981.

2. ABC-TV *Issues and Answers* interview with Menachem Begin, Jerusalem, July 5, 1981.

3. An unwillingness to compromise by the reputedly flexible Moshe Dayan, then foreign minister and the allegedly moderate King Hussein, during their last secret meeting, is illustrative of the PLO's corrosive influence. See Moshe Dayan, "Encounters," *The Atlantic,* June 1981, pp. 73–75.

4. George W. Ball, "No More Blank Checks," *Washington Post,* June 15, 1981, p. A 11, col. 1. Ball strongly implies that Israel is on the verge of apartheid policy toward the Palestinians.

5. Robert Alter, "Deformations of the Holocaust," *Commentary,* February 1981, p. 52.

6. See, particularly, Bernard Avishai, "Begin vs. Begin," *The New York Review of Books,* May 31, 1979, pp. 35–41.

7. See, generally, Jordan J. Paust and Albert P. Blaustein, eds., *The Arab Oil Weapon* (Dobbs Ferry, N.Y.: Oceana Publications, 1977); John Norton Moore, ed., *The Arab-Israeli Conflict: Readings and Documents* (Princeton, N.J.: Princeton University Press, 1977); and Arab rhetoric in *UN Chronicle,* February 1981, pp. 7–19.

8. Security Council Resolution 242, 22 U.N. SCOR (1967), sought to develop a framework for mutual recognition, but it has not only been rejected by all of Israel's Arab adversaries, but also has been essentially discarded by the European Economic Community (EEC), mainly on a French initiative. See Sally Baumann Reynolds, "France vs. Israel," *Commentary,* April 1981, pp. 55–56, 59. On the origins and background of Resolution 242, see Institute for the Study of Diplomacy, *U.N. Security Council Resolution 242: A Case Study in Diplomatic Ambiguity* (Washington, D.C.: Georgetown University School of Foreign Service, 1981).

9. A typical example of friendly Western politicians is Paul Findley, "Israel's Rationale is Unacceptable," *Miami Herald,* June 14, 1981.

10. PLO attacks were sharpened considerably in December 1980. Menahem Milson, "How to Make Peace with the Palestinians," *Commentary,* May 1981, p. 28. Cf. also Robert A. Friedlander, "The PLO and the Rule of Law: A Reply to Dr. Anis Kassim," *Denver Journal of International Law and Policy* 10 (Winter 1981): 221–35.

11. Walid Khalidi, "Regiopolitics: Toward a U.S. Policy on the Palestinian Problem," *Foreign Affairs* 59 (Summer 1981): 1052.

12. Israel's independence was proclaimed on May 14, 1948. Admission to the United Nations occurred on May 11, 1949.

13. Yoram Dinstein, "Self-Determination in the Middle East Conflict," in *Self-Determination: National, Regional, and Global Dimensions,* eds. Yonah Alexander and Robert A. Friedlander (Boulder, Colo.: Westview Press 1980), pp. 252 and 255, argues persuasively that both sides "are entitled to self-determination" and that they both have "incontrovertible" rights. Cf. also the statement of former French President Valerie Giscard d'Estaing, *New York Times,* March 13, 1980 and the French Socialist-Communist Cabinet agreement in *Time,* July 6, 1981, p. 28.

14. Nissim Rejawn, quoted by Harry N. Howard, "Nationalism in the Middle East," *Orbis* 10 (Winter 1967): 1211.

15. Iraq refused to sign and is still technically in a state of war with Israel. Representatives of the other belligerents in the first Arab-Israeli conflict never actually met, since the negotiations were conducted by the U.N. Conciliation Commission.

16. Aside from Arab intransigence over whether Israel has a right to exist, Israeli territory acquired in the War of Independence was never questioned, since its Arab antagonists had similarly increased their holdings. Besides, Israel had become (over Arab opposition) a member of the United Nations. For an anti-Arab critique, claiming that "Egypt's seizure of the Gaza Strip, and Jordan's seizure

and subsequent annexation of the West Bank and the old city of Jerusalem, were unlawful," see Stephen M. Schwebel, "What Weight to Conquest?", in Moore, *Arab-Israeli Conflict*, p. 359.

17. George Lenczowski, *The Middle East in World Affairs,* 4th ed. (Ithaca, N.Y.: Cornell University Press, 1980), p. 475.

18. Guido Valabrega, *La Revolucion Arabe* (Barcelona: Editorial Bruguera, 1971), pp. 102-3; Israel Pocket Library, *History from 1880* (Jerusalem: Keter Books, 1973), p. 160. King Hussein continued over the years to make contact with Israeli leaders. See Eitan Haber, Zeev Schiff, and Ehud Yaari, *The Year of the Dove* (New York: Bantam Books, 1979), pp. 81-82; Dayan, "Encounters," pp. 73-75.

19. David Ignatius, "Arabs, Israelis Stand Pat on Jerusalem, Leaving the Emotional Issue Festering," *Wall Street Journal,* January 27, 1981.

20. *New York Times,* July 31, 1980. The U.N. Security Council voted 14 to zero, deploring the Israeli action, with the U.S. in abstention. Israel became a target for repeated U.N. denunciations in the months that followed. See, for example, *UN Chronicle* (August 1980): 20-30 and (September–October 1980): 13-18.

21. *Newsweek,* July 14, 1980, p. 40; *New York Times,* August 14, 1980. Still, as of April 30, 1982, Begin had not moved his office.

22. *Time,* August 25, 1980, p. 33. There is also no "moderate" PLO position on Jerusalem. See Arafat statement, *Blade* (Toledo), July 26, 1981, p. 1.

23. Amos Perlmutter, "A Palestinian Entity?", *International Security* 5 (Spring 1981): 115. On the legal issues involved, see Mark Gruhin, "Note—Jerusalem: Legal & Political Dimensions in a Search for Peace," *Case-Western Reserve Journal of International Law* 12 (Winter 1980): 169-213.

24. Quoted by Ignatius, "Arabs," p. 26.

25. Dayan, "Encounters," p. 82. West German publisher Axel Springer maintains "that undivided Jerusalem is the symbol and manifestation of Israel's right to self-determination and its *raison d'etre." Die Welt,* September 6, 1980.

26. Marie Syrkin, "The Palestinian Refugees: Resettlement, Repatriation, or Restoration?", in *Israel, the Arabs, and the Middle East,* eds. Irving Howe and Carl Gershman (New York: Bantam Books, 1972), pp. 157-72, 179-85.

27. Cf. Kurt Rene Radley, "The Palestinian Refugees: The Right to Return in International Law," *American Journal of International Law* 72 (July 1978): 599-608.

28. Ibid., p. 607.

29. Statistics provided by the Israeli Government Tourist Office, New York City. Cf. Israel Pocket Library, *History,* p. 203.

30. Lenczowski, *The Middle East,* p. 452. The total population of Israel by 1981 was 3,900,000.

31. Cf. for example, Ibrahim F.I. Shihata, "Destination Embargo of Arab Oil: Its Legality under International Law," in Paust and Blaustein, *Arab Oil Weapon,* pp. 105-7; Eugene M. Fisher and M. Cherif Bassiouni, *Storm over the Arab World: A People in Revolution* (Chicago: Follett, 1972), pp. 250-57; William B. Quandt, *Decade of Decisions: American Policy Toward the Arab-Israeli Conflict, 1967-1976* (Berkeley, Los Angeles, and London: University of California Press, 1977), pp. 39-59; Lenczowski, *The Middle East,* pp. 448-50;

Yoram Dinstein, "The Legal Issues of 'Para-War' and Peace in the Middle East," *St. John's Law Review* 44 (January 1970): 468–70; Rosalyn Higgins, "The June War: The United Nations and Legal Background," in Moore, *Arab-Israeli Conflict,* pp. 539–51; Schwebel, "Conquest," p. 359; Amos Shapira, "The Six Day War and the Right to Self-Defense," *Israel Law Review* 6 (October 1971): 65–80; Julius Stone, *Conflict Through Consensus: United Nations Approaches to Aggression* (Baltimore and London: The Johns Hopkins University Press, 1977), p. 58; and Michael Walzer, *Just and Unjust Wars: A Moral Argument with Historical Illustrations* (New York: Basic Books, 1977), pp. 82–85, who terms "[t]he Israeli first strike . . . a clear case of legitimate anticipation." Stanley Hoffman, *Duties Beyond Borders: On the Limits and Possibilities of Ethical International Politics* (Syracuse, N.Y.: Syracuse University Press, 1981), p. 60, admits, "I have mixed feelings on the matter." Former U.N. Ambassador Charles W. Yost, "The Arab-Israeli War: How it Began," in Moore, *Arab-Israeli Conflict,* p. 293, claims both sides "blundered into it."

32. Radley, "Palestinian Refugees," p. 604.

33. Security Council Resolution 242, 22 U.N. SCOR (1967), reprinted in Moore, *Arab-Israeli Conflict,* p. 1084. The resolution did not explicitly call for a total Israeli withdrawal, however, hence the wording "occupied territories" instead of "the occupied territories."

34. Dinstein, "'Para-War,'" p. 481. See also Schwebel, "Conquest," p. 359.

35. A summary of the Security Council debate can be found in Report of the Security Council 16 July 1967–15 July 1968, 23 U.N. GAOR (Supp. No. 2), U.N. Doc. A/7202 (1968).

36. Differences between the French and English versions of Resolution 242 led to still further controversy. See Toribio de Valdes, "The Authoritativeness of the English and French Texts of Security Council Resolution 242 (1967) on the Situation in the Middle East," *American Journal of International Law* 71 (April 1977): 311–16.

37. Security Council Resolution 338, U.N. Doc. S/RES/338 (1973), reprinted in Moore, *Arab-Israeli Conflict,* p. 1189. See the trenchant analysis of Eugene V. Rostow, "The Illegality of the Arab Attack on Israel of October 6, 1973," in the same source, pp. 462–472, 474–475.

38. All things are possible in the international arena, even if not always predictable. Anwar Sadat, writing in the fiftieth anniversary issue of *Foreign Affairs,* complained of the wars imposed on Egypt "by Israeli expansionism. . . ." Anwar Sadat, "Where Egypt Stands," *Foreign Affairs* 51 (October 1972): 123. The journey from Cairo to Jerusalem lit the lamp of hope in an era of despair, and the light still flickers.

39. Gil Carl AlRoy, "The Middle East Conflict and International Politics," in Howe and Gershman, *Middle East,* p. 382.

40. Dinstein, "'Para-War,'" p. 478, sardonically refers to the "many previous dinosaur-like pronouncements of the United Nations: interesting, impressive, and irrelevant." See also the piquant comments of former U.N. Ambassador, Daniel Patrick Moynihan, *A Dangerous Place* (New York: Berkeley Books, 1980), pp. 172–73, 191–92.

41. *UN Monthly Chronicle* (December 1974): 80–82.

42.   Question of Palestine, General Assembly Resolution 3236 (XXIX), 29 U.N. GAOR, U.N. Doc. A/RES/3236 (1976), reprinted in Moore, *Arab-Israeli Conflict*, pp. 1204–205 and *UN Monthly Chronicle* (December 1974): 36–37; Observer Status for Palestine Liberation Organization, General Assembly Resolution 3237 (XXIX), 29 U.N. GAOR, U.N. Doc. A/RES/3237 (1974), reprinted in *ibid.*, pp. 37–38.

43.   Zionism as a Form of Racism, General Assembly Resolution 3379 (XXX), 30 U.N. GAOR, U.N. Doc. A/RES/3379 (1975), reprinted in Moore, *Arab-Israeli Conflict*, pp. 1236–37. On the true meaning of this resolution and the reaction of the U.S. delegation, see Moynihan, *A Dangerous Place*, pp. 194–206. The U.S. Ambassador emotionally embraced the Israeli Ambassador after the votes were tallied.

44.   Ibid., p. 295.

45.   See, for example, the brief comments of Eugene V. Rostow, "Palestinian Self-Determination: Possible Futures for the Unallocated Territories of the Palestinian Mandate," *Yale Studies in World Public Order* 5 (Spring 1979): 169.

46.   Julius Stone, "No Peace—No War in the Middle East," in Moore, *Arab-Israeli Conflict*, p. 321.

47.   See Separate Opinion of Judge Percy Spender, Certain Expenses of the United Nations (1962), I.C.J., pp. 184–197.

48.   Richard J. Tyner, "Wars of National Liberation in Africa and Palestine: Self-Determination for Peoples or Territories?", *Yale Studies in World Public Order* 5 (Spring 1979): 259.

49.   For a short synopsis of the international legal system, see Robert A. Friedlander, "International Law is What the Lawyers Say It Is," *Student Lawyer* (December 1975): 10–13, *et seq.*

50.   See, generally, Alexander and Friedlander, *Self-Determination.*

51.   Harold S. Johnson and Baljit Singh, "Self-Determination and World Order," in Alexander and Friedlander, *Self-Determination,* 350–351, 354–357.

52.   Rostow, "Palestinian Self-Determination," p. 153. See also Schwebel, "Conquest," p. 359: "Egypt's seizure of the Gaza Strip and Jordan's seizure and subsequent annexation of the West Bank and the old city of Jerusalem were unlawful." Rosalyn Higgins, "The June War," in Moore, *Arab-Israeli Conflict*, p. 553: "Israel is in legal terms entitled to remain in the territories she now holds."

53.   Allan Gerson, "Trustee-Occupant" The Legal Status of Israel's Presence in the West Bank," *Harvard International Law Journal* 14 (Winter 1973): 1–49.

54.   Rostow, "Palestinian Self-Determination," p. 161. Ya'akov Meron, "Waste Land (Mewat) in Judea and Samaria," *Boston College International and Comparative Law Review* 4 (Spring 1981): 2, contends "that there is no basis under any national legal system or principle of international law for the assertion that Judea and Samaria are wholly state-owned lands."

55.   This was the primary purpose of the Helsinki Final Act of 1975. See Douglas G. Scrivner, "Comment—The Conference on Security and Cooperation in Europe: Implications for Soviet-American Detente," *Denver Journal of International Law and Policy* 6 (Spring 1976): 122–28.

56.   Gerson, "Legal-Status," pp. 6-7. Cf. also Doris Graber, *The Development of the Law of Belligerent Occupation, 1863-1914* (New York: Columbia University Press, 1949), especially pp. 37-69, 110-116, for the traditional view, and Brice M. Clagett and O. Thomas Johnson, Jr., "May Israel as a Belligerent Occupant Lawfully Exploit Previously Unexploited Oil Resources of the Gulf of Suez?", *American Journal of International Law* 72 (July 1978): 559-60. Neither Israel nor Egypt ever ratified the Hague Convention No. IV (1907).

57.   Cf. the discussions of Robert A. Friedlander, "Self-Determination: A Legal-Political Inquiry," in Alexander and Friedlander, *Self-Determination,* pp. 309-16; Dinstein, "Self-Determination," same source, pp. 243-51.

58.   Dinstein, "Self-Determination," p. 253.

59.   Ibid., pp. 254-55; Lenczowski, *The Middle East,* pp. 453-54. *Nations and States: An Enquiry into the Origins of Nations and the Politics of Nationalism* (Boulder, Colo.: Westview Press, 1977), pp. 269-270; and Stone, "Self-Determination," p. 216, both date the origin of a national consciousness from the first Palestinian National Congress of May 1964. Syrkin, "The Palestinian Refugees," in Moore, *Arab-Israeli Conflict,* p. 171, a decade ago, saw the Palestinian national movement as a possible "synthetic creation ... in the anti-Israeli arsenal." On the other hand, one pro-Palestinian scholar, Ann Mosely Lesch, *Arab Politics in Palestine, 1917-1939: The Frustration of a National Movement* (Ithaca, N.Y.: Cornell University Press, 1980) asserts that the seeds of Palestinian nationalism, sown in the interwar period, were ultimately frustrated by clannish and organizational rivalries. The late Israeli scholar, Gershom Scholem, believed the Israelis "educated the Arabs about nationalism. It was our very existence that created Arab national consciousness." Interview in *The New York Review of Books,* August 14, 1980, p. 22.

60.   See, for example, the final declaration of the Venice Economic Summit in the *New York Times,* June 14, 1980, p. 4. President Jimmy Carter, during the first week of August 1979, compared the Palestinian cause to the Civil Rights Movement in the United States. "Concern Covers Palestinians," *Spokesman-Review* (Spokane), August 12, 1979; Eleanor Randolph, "Carter's Mideast Remark Resented," *Los Angeles Times,* August 2, 1979.

61.   *Blade* (Toledo), July 17, 1981. The PLO has continued to reject any settlement based on Security Council Resolution 242. See "PLO Takes Hard Line in U.N.," *Spokesman-Review* (Spokane), August 13, 1979.

62.   Yehoshafat Harkabi, *Arab Strategies and Israel's Response* (New York: The Free Press, 1977), pp. 34-35.

63.   Doyle McManus, "Intentions of Unruly PLO are Difficult to Pin Down," *Blade* (Toledo), July 5, 1981.

64.   See, for example, "What Israel's Election Means to Mideast, U.S.," *U.S. News & World Report,* July 13, 1981, p. 30; *Blade* (Toledo), July 19, 1981.

65.   General Assembly Resolution 3089 D (XXVIII), 28 U.N. GAOR (Supp. No. 30), U.N. Doc. A/9030 (1973).

66.   Radley, "The Palestinian Refugees," p. 605. See the puzzled comments of the Barbados representative to the General Assembly reported on p. 608.

67.   Much of the initial credit, for the wrong reasons, should go to former

Secretary of State Henry Kissinger. See Matti Golan, *The Secret Conversations of Henry Kissinger: Step by Step Diplomacy in the Middle East,* trans. by Ruth Geyra Stern and Sol Stern (New York: Quadrangle/The New York Times, 1976).

68.   See statement by Professor Bernard Reich, in "The Middle East, 1974: New Hopes, New Challenges," U.S. Congress, House, Committee on Foreign Affairs, *Hearings before the Subcommittee on the Near East and South Asia,* 93rd Cong., 2d Sess., 1974, p. 124; Haber, Schiff, and Yaari, *Year of the Dove,* pp. 81–82; and Mark Heller, "Begin's False Autonomy," *Foreign Policy* 37 (Winter 1979–80): 115–16, which claims current autonomy proposals originated during 1973 as a means of masking Israel's intention to remain on the West Bank.

69.   Sanford R. Silverburg, "In Perpetuation of Myth: National Self-Determination *de lege ferenda,*" *Glendale Law Review* 2 (1978): 288, holds that separation, federation, and regionalism are all forms of the self-determination process. For a recent legal analysis of the relationship between self-determination theory and historical practice as it relates to the Palestinians, see John A. Collins, "Note—Self-Determination in International Law: The Palestinians," *Case Western Reserve Journal of International Law* 12 (Winter 1980): 137–67.

70.   Christoph Schruer, "Autonomy in South Tyrol," paper presented at Conference on Models of Autonomy, Tel-Aviv University Faculty of Law, January 30, 1980.

71.   It is not working in the Basque Country despite the liberal Basque Autonomy Statute. Raymond Carr and Juan Pablo Fusi, *Spain: Dictatorship to Democracy,* 2nd ed. (London: George Allen & Unwin, 1981), pp. 248–52.

72.   This is precisely the argument, not always well-balanced, of Heller, "Begin's False Autonomy," pp. 111–25.

73.   Yoram Dinstein, "Final Summary," Conference on Models of Autonomy, Tel Aviv, January 31, 1980.

74.   For a *contra* view, see Louis B. Sohn, "The Concept of Autonomy in International Law and the Practice of the United Nations," *Israel Law Review* 15 (April 1980): 180–90.

75.   See Sadat, "Where Egypt Stands," p. 122.

76.   Milson, "Peace," p. 25.

77.   *Ibid.* Haber, Schiff, and Yaari, *Year of the Dove,* p. 106, note that Begin first "raised the idea of self-rule in 1975," as leader of the opposition. Heller, "Begin's False Autonomy," p. 116, claims that "until 1977 it was Begin who . . . objected most strenuously to the slightest hint of autonomy, home rule, or self-government."

78.   Haber, Schiff, and Yaari, *Year of the Dove,* p. 107. The full text of the autonomy proposal can be found in the *New York Times,* December 29, 1977.

79.   Haber, Schiff, and Yaari, *Year of the Dove,* p. 108.

80.   Heller, "Begin's False Autonomy," pp. 119–20, 124–25, argues that this biblical commitment will prevent any Begin government from offering terms acceptable to the Palestinians.

81.   Dinstein, "Final Summary," Conference on Models of Autonomy; Meir Gabai, "Legal Aspects of the Autonomy Proposal for Judea, Samaria, and the Gaza District," paper presented at the same conference, Tel Aviv, January 30, 1980.

82.   Myres S. McDougal, Harold D. Lasswell, and Lung-Chu Chen, *Human Rights and World Public Order: The Basic Policies of an International Law of Human Dignity* (New Haven, Conn.: Yale University Press, 1980), p. 472.

83.   For the full text of the agreement and other related documents, see Marilou M. Righini, ed., *International Legal Materials* no. 17 (November 1978): pp. 1463-74; *Israel Law Review* no. 15 (April 1980): 284-90, 293-301.

84.   See David Landau, "Egyptian View of Autonomy," *Jerusalem Post,* February 6, 1980, p. 5. Still, by permitting Israel to withdraw to "specified security locations," Israel's security could be protected, since these "security locations" would control access to the West Bank (and Israel) from the Jordan Valley.

85.   David Landau, "Some Progress Seen in Autonomy Talks," *Jerusalem Post,* February 1, 1980. On March 20, 1979, Begin told the Israeli Knesset: "We agreed to give autonomy to the Arab residents in Judea, Samaria, and Gaza. We never agreed that full autonomy would be given to the areas which are Judea, Samaria and Gaza...." Quoted by Meron, "Waste Land," p. 37.

86.   David Landau, "Some Accord on Autonomy's Powers," *Jerusalem Post,* February 3, 1980.

87.   *International Legal Materials,* p. 1473; *Israel Law Review,* pp. 297-99.

88.   Moshe Sharon, "Peace Without Penalties," *Jerusalem Post,* September 26, 1980, asserts that King Hussein very much prefers his de facto accommodations with Israel to a more risky de jure settlement.

89.   Milson, "Peace," pp. 25-26, reports that at first there were Israeli-Palestinian contacts, but PLO pressure ended this prospect. For the increasingly bitter attitude of the West Bank Palestinian population, see the sharply critical article by Amnon Kapeliouk, "La determination des palestinians de l'interieur," *Le Monde Diplomatique,* June 1980.

90.   *International Legal Materials* 18 (March 1979): 362-96; *Israeli Law Review* 15 (April 1980): 302-28. For excellent short analyses of the treaty and related issues, see John F. Murphy, "To Bring an End the State of War," *Vanderbilt Journal of Transnational Law* 12 (Fall 1979): 912-24; Richard W. Nelson, "Comment—Peacekeeping Aspects of the Egyptian-Israeli Peace Treaty and Consequences for United Nations Peacekeeping," *Denver Journal of International Law and Policy* 10 (Fall 1980): 113-53.

91.   Stanley Hoffman, "Foreign Policy: What's to be Done?", *The New York Review of Books,* April 30, 1981, p. 33.

92.   Ron Ben-Yishai, "Israel's Move," *Foreign Policy* 42 (Spring 1981): 43; M. Cherif Bassiouni, "An Analysis of Egyptian Peace Policy toward Israel: From Resolution 242 (1967) to the 1979 Peace Treaty," *Case Western Reserve Journal of International Law* 12 (Winter 1980): 26.

93.   Mohammed Sid-Ahmed, "Shifting Sands of Peace in the Middle East," *International Security* 5 (Summer 1980): 78-79.

94.   Perlmutter, "A Palestinian Entity?", p. 112, believes that Begin "unwittingly" opened the door for an eventual Palestinian autonomous polity. The analysis of Bernard Reich, Sanford R. Silverburg, and Donald S. Stein, "The Middle East Peace Process: Sisyphus Reexamined," *Suffolk Transnational Law Journal* 4 (1980): 44-46, is a very optimistic one but provides a useful historical account of the overall peace process.

95.   Ruth Lapidoth, "The Relation between the Camp David Framework and the Treaty of Peace—Another Dimension," *Israel Law Review* 15 (April 1980): 192. The consequences of this type of rationalization were easily predictable. See Christopher S. Wren, "Distrust Mars Egyptian-Israeli Ties More Than a Year after Peace Pact," the *New York Times*, August 18, 1980, who warned: "Less than a year and a half after Egypt and Israel signed a celebrated peace treaty, their new relationship has become mired in mistrust and recriminations." As with the French Bourbon monarchy, in the Middle East, *plus ca change, plus ca la meme chose.*

96.   Cf. Heller, "Begin's False Autonomy," pp. 111–23; Avishai, "Begin vs. Begin," pp. 35–41. The passion of Begin's critics can lead to irrational distortion, such as the claim that Begin desires "a Jewish state on both sides of the Jordan River," by Arthur H. Samuelson, "Israeli Expansionism," *Harper's*, February 1980, p. 28.

97.   Bernard Avishai, "The Victory of the New Israel," *The New York Review of Books*, August 13, 1981, p. 45. Marie Syrkin, "How Begin Threatens Israel," *The New Republic*, September 16, 1981, p. 23, overstates her case when she refers to the Israeli election campaign as "fratricidal."

98.   *Miami Herald,* June 26, 1981.

99.   Avishai, "The Victory," p. 48.

100.   *Plain Dealer* (Cleveland), September 24, 1981.

101.   Avishai, "The Victory," p. 49.

102.   Dinstein, "Self-Determination," p. 255.

Appendix A: Soviet-U.S. Joint Statement of October 1, 1977

Having exchanged views regarding the unsafe situation that remains in the Middle East, A.A. Gromyko, member of the Politburo of the CPSU Central Committee and USSR Minister of Foreign Affairs, and U.S. Secretary of State C. Vance have the following statement to make on behalf of their countries, which are co-chairmen of the Geneva Peace Conference on the Middle East:

1. Both sides are convinced that the vital interests of the peoples of this area, as well as the interests of strengthening peace and international security in general, urgently dictate the necessity of achieving as soon as possible a just and lasting settlement of the Arab-Israeli conflict. This settlement should be comprehensive, incorporating all the parties concerned and all questions.

The Soviet and American sides believe that, within the framework of a comprehensive settlement of the Middle East problem, all specific questions of the settlement should be resolved, including such key issues as withdrawal of Israeli armed forces from territories occupied in the 1967 conflict; the resolution of the Palestinian questions, including ensuring the legitimate rights of the Palestinian people; termination of the state of war and establishment of normal peaceful relations on the basis of mutual recognition of the principles of sovereignty, territorial integrity and political independence. Both sides believe that, in addition to such measures for ensuring the security of the borders between Israel and the neighboring Arab states as the establishment of demilitarized zones and the agreed stationing in them of U.N. troops or observers, international guarantees of such borders, as well as of the observance of the terms of the settlement, can also be established, should the contracting parties so desire. The Soviet Union and the United States of America are ready to participate in these guarantees, subject to their constitutional processes.

2. The Soviet and American sides believe that the only right and effective way for achieving a fundamental solution to all aspects of the Middle East problem in its entirety is negotiations within the framework of the Geneva peace conference specially convened for these purposes, with participation in its work of the representatives of all the parties involved in the conflict, including those of the Palestinian people, and legal and contractual formulization of the decisions reached at the conference.

In their capacity as cochairmen of the Geneva conference, the USSR and the U.S. affirm their intention through joint efforts and in their contacts with the parties concerned to facilitate in every way the resumption of the work on the conference no later than December 1977. The cochairmen note that there still exist several questions of a procedural and organizational nature that remain to be agreed upon by the participants in the Geneva Conference.

3. Guided by the goal of achieving a just political settlement in the Middle East and of eliminating the explosive situation in this area of the world, the USSR and the U.S. appeal to all the parties in the conflict to understand the necessity for careful consideration of each other's legitimate rights and interests and to demonstrate mutual readiness to act accordingly.

Source: *Pravda*, October 2, 1977 (translated in *Current Digest of the Soviet Press* 29 (1977): 8-9).

Appendix B: Camp David Agreements

Text of Agreements signed September 17, 1978

I. A FRAMEWORK FOR PEACE IN THE MIDDLE EAST AGREED AT CAMP DAVID

Muhammad Anwar al-Sadat, President of the Arab Republic of Egypt, and Menachem Begin, Prime Minister of Israel, met with Jimmy Carter, President of the United States of America, at Camp David from September 5 to September 17, 1978, and have agreed on the following framework for peace in the Middle East. They invite other parties to the Arab-Israeli conflict to adhere to it.

PREAMBLE

The search for peace in the Middle East must be guided by the following:

—The agreed basis for a peaceful settlement of the conflict between Israel and its neighbors is United Nations Security Council Resolution 242, in all its parts.

—After four wars during thirty years, despite intensive human efforts, the Middle East, which is the cradle of civilization and the birthplace of three great religions, does not yet enjoy the blessings of peace. The people of the Middle East yearn for peace so that the vast human and natural resources of the region can be turned to the pursuits of peace and so that this area can become a model for coexistence and cooperation among nations.

—The historic initiative of President Sadat in visiting Jerusalem and the reception accorded to him by the Parliament, government and people of Israel, and the reciprocal visit of Prime Minister Begin to Ismailia, the peace proposals made by both leaders, as well as the warm reception of these missions by the peoples of both countries, have created an unprecedented opportunity for peace which must not be lost if this generation and future generations are to be spared the tragedies of war.

—The provisions of the Charter of the United Nations and the other accepted norms of international law and legitimacy now provide accepted standards for the conduct of relations among all states.

—To achieve a relationship of peace, in the spirit of Article 2 of the United Nations Charter, future negotiations between Israel and any neighbor prepared to negotiate peace and security with it, are necessary for the purpose of carrying out all the provisions and principles of Resolutions 242 and 338.

—Peace requires respect for the sovereignty, territorial integrity and political independence of every state in the area and their right to live in peace within secure and recognized boundaries free from threats or acts of force. Progress toward that goal can accelerate movement toward a new era of reconciliation in the Middle East marked by cooperation in promoting economic development, in maintaining stability, and in assuring security.

—Security is enhanced by a relationship of peace and by cooperation between nations which enjoy normal relations. In addition, under the terms of peace treaties, the parties can, on the basis of reciprocity, agree to special security arrangements such as demilitarized zones, limited armaments areas, early warning stations, the presence of international forces, liaison, agreed measures for monitoring, and other arrangements that they agree are useful.

FRAMEWORK

Taking these factors into account, the parties are determined to reach a just, comprehensive, and durable settlement of the Middle East conflict through the conclusion of peace treaties based on Security Council Resolutions 242 and 338 in all their parts. Their purpose is to achieve peace and good neighborly relations. They recognize that, for peace to endure, it must involve all those who have been most deeply affected by the conflict. They therefore agree that this framework as appropriate is intended by them to constitute a basis for peace not only between Egypt and Israel, but also between Israel and each of its other neighbors which is prepared to negotiate peace with Israel on this basis. With that objective in mind, they have agreed to proceed as follows:

A.   West Bank and Gaza

1.   Egypt, Israel, Jordan and the representatives of the Palestinian people should participate in negotiations on the resolution of the Palestinian problem in all its aspects. To achieve that objective, negotiations relating to the West Bank and Gaza should proceed in three stages:

(a)   Egypt and Israel agree that, in order to ensure a peaceful and orderly transfer of authority, and taking into account the security concerns of all the parties, there should be transitional arrangements for the West Bank and Gaza for a period not exceeding five years. In order to provide full autonomy to the inhabitants, under these arrangements the Israeli military government and its civilian administration will be withdrawn as soon as a self-governing authority has been freely elected by the inhabitants of these areas to replace the existing military government. To negotiate the details of a transitional arrangement, the Government of Jordan will be invited to join the negotiations on the basis of this framework. These new arrangements should give due consideration both to the principle of self-government by the inhabitants of these territories and to the legitimate security concerns of the parties involved.

(b)   Egypt, Israel, and Jordan will agree on the modalities for establishing the elected self-governing authority in the West Bank and Gaza. The delegations of Egypt and Jordan may include Palestinians from the West Bank and Gaza or other Palestinians as mutually agreed. The parties will negotiate an agreement which will define the powers and responsibilities of the self-governing authority to be exercised in the West Bank and Gaza. A withdrawal of Israeli armed forces will take place and there will be a redeployment of the remaining Israeli forces into specified security locations. The agreement will also include arrangements for assuring internal and external security and public order. A strong local police force will be established, which may include Jordanian citizens. In addition, Israeli and Jordanian forces will participate in joint patrols and in the manning of control posts to assure the security of the borders.

(c)   When the self-governing authority (administrative council) in the West Bank and Gaza is established and inaugurated, the transitional period of five years will begin. As soon as possible, but not later than the third year after the beginning of the transitional period, negotiations will take place to determine the final status of the West Bank and Gaza and its relationship with its neighbors, and to conclude a peace treaty between Israel and Jordan by the end of the transitional period. These negotiations will be conducted among Egypt, Israel, Jordan, and the elected representatives of the inhabitants of the West Bank and Gaza. Two separate but related committees will be convened, one committee, consisting of representatives of the four parties which will negotiate and agree on the final status of the West Bank and Gaza, and its relationship with its neighbors, and the second committee, consisting of representatives of Israel and representatives of Jordan to be joined by the elected representatives of the inhabitants of the West Bank and Gaza, to negotiate the peace treaty between Israel and Jordan, taking into account the agreement reached on the final status of the West

Bank and Gaza. The negotiations shall be based on all the provisions and principles of UN Security Council Resolution 242. The negotiations will resolve, among other matters, the location of the boundaries and the nature of the security arrangements. The solution from the negotiations must also recognize the legitimate rights of the Palestinian people and their just requirements. In this way, the Palestinians will participate in the determination of their own future through:

1) The negotiations among Egypt, Israel, Jordan and the representatives of the inhabitants of the West Bank and Gaza to agree on the final status of the West Bank and Gaza and other outstanding issues by the end of the transitional period.

2) Submitting their agreement to a vote by the elected representatives of the inhabitants of the West Bank and Gaza.

3) Providing for the elected representatives of the inhabitants of the West Bank and Gaza to decide how they shall govern themselves consistent with the provisions of their agreement.

4) Participating as stated above in the work of the committee negotiating the peace treaty between Israel and Jordan.

2.   All necessary measures will be taken and provisions made to assure the security of Israel and its neighbors during the transitional period and beyond. To assist in providing such security, a strong local police force will be constituted by the self-governing authority. It will be composed of inhabitants of the West Bank and Gaza. The police will maintain continuing liaison on internal security matters with the designated Israeli, Jordanian, and Egyptian officers.

3.   During the transitional period, representatives of Egypt, Israel, Jordan, and the self-governing authority will constitute a continuing committee to decide by agreement on the modalities of admission of persons displaced from the West Bank and Gaza in 1967, together with necessary measures to prevent disruption and disorder. Other matters of common concern may also be dealt with by this committee.

4.   Egypt and Israel will work with each other and with other interested parties to establish agreed procedures for a prompt, just and permanent implementation of the resolution of the refugee problem.

B.   Egypt-Israel

1.   Egypt and Israel undertake not to resort to the threat or the use of force to settle disputes. Any disputes shall be settled by peaceful means in accordance with the provisions of Article 33 of the Charter of the United Nations.

2.   In order to achieve peace between them, the parties agree to negotiate in good faith with a goal of concluding within three months from the signing of this Framework a peace treaty between them, while inviting the other parties to the conflict to proceed simultaneously to

negotiate and conclude similar peace treaties with a view to achieving a comprehensive peace in the area. The Framework for the Conclusion of a Peace Treaty between Egypt and Israel will govern the peace negotiations between them. The parties will agree on the modalities and the timetable for the implementation of their obligations under the treaty.

C. Associated Principles

1. Egypt and Israel state that the principles and provisions described below should apply to peace treaties between Israel and each of its neighbors—Egypt, Jordan, Syria and Lebanon.

2. Signatories shall establish among themselves relationships normal to states at peace with one another. To this end, they should undertake to abide by all the provisions of the Charter of the United Nations. Steps to be taken in this respect include:

 (a) full recognition;

 (b) abolishing economic boycotts;

 (c) guaranteeing that under their jurisdiction the citizens of the other parties shall enjoy the protection of the due process of law.

3. Signatories should explore possibilities for economic development in the context of final peace treaties, with the objective of contributing to the atmosphere of peace, cooperation and friendship which is their common goal.

4. Claims Commissions may be established for the mutual settlement of all financial claims.

5. The United States shall be invited to participate in the talks on matters related to the modalities of the implementation of the agreements and working out the timetable for the carrying out of the obligations of the parties.

6. The United Nations Security Council shall be requested to endorse the peace treaties and ensure that their provisions shall not be violated. The permanent members of the Security Council shall be requested to underwrite the peace treaties and ensure respect for their provisions. They shall also be requested to conform their policies and actions with the undertakings contained in this Framework.

For the Government of the Arab
Republic of Egypt:

For the Government of
Israel:

A. SADAT

M. BEGIN

Witnessed by: JIMMY CARTER
            Jimmy Carter, President of the
            United States of America

II. FRAMEWORK FOR THE CONCLUSION OF A PEACE TREATY
     BETWEEN EGYPT AND ISRAEL

In order to achieve peace between them, Israel and Egypt agree to negotiate in good faith with a goal of concluding within three months of the
signing of this framework a peace treaty between them.

It is agreed that:

The site of the negotiations will be under a United Nations flag at a
location or locations to be mutually agreed.

All of the principles of U.N. Resolution 242 will apply in this resolution of the dispute between Israel and Egypt.

Unless otherwise mutually agreed, terms of the peace treaty will be
implemented between two and three years after the peace treaty is signed.

The following matters are agreed between the parties:

(a) the full exercise of Egyptian sovereignty up to the internationally
recognized border between Egypt and mandated Palestine;

(b) the withdrawal of Israeli armed forces from the Sinai;

(c) the use of airfields left by the Israelis near El Arish, Rafah, Ras en
Naqb, and Sharm el Sheikh for civilian purposes only, including possible commercial use by all nations;

(d) the right of free passage by ships of Israel through the Gulf of Suez
and the Suez Canal on the basis of the Constantinople Convention of
1888 applying to all nations; the Strait of Tiran and the Gulf of Aquaba
are international waterways to be open to all nations for unimpeded
and nonsuspendable freedom of navigation and overflight;

(e) the construction of a highway between the Sinai and Jordan near
Elat with guaranteed free and peaceful passage by Egypt and Jordan;
and

(f) the stationing of military forces listed below.

Stationing of Forces

A. No more than one division (mechanized or infantry) of Egyptian
armed forces will be stationed within an area lying approximately 50 kilo-
meters (km) east of the Gulf of Suez and the Suez Canal.

B. Only United Nations forces and civil police equipped with light weapons to perform normal police functions will be stationed within an area
lying west of the international border and the Gulf of Aqaba, varying in
width from 20 km to 40 km.

C. In the area within 3 km east of the international border there will be
Israeli limited military forces not to exceed four infantry battalions, and
United Nations observers.

D. Border patrol units, not to exceed three battalions, will supplement
the civil police in maintaining order in the area not included above.

The exact demarcation of the above areas will be as decided during the
peace negotiations.

Early warning stations may exist to insure compliance with the terms of the agreement.

United Nations forces will be stationed: (a) in part of the area in the Sinai lying within about 20 km of the Mediterranean Sea and adjacent to the international border, and (b) in the Sharm el Sheikh area to ensure freedom of passage through the Strait of Tiran; and these forces will not be removed unless such removal is approved by the Security Council of the United Nations with a unanimous vote of the five permanent members.

After a peace treaty is signed, and after the interim withdrawal is complete, normal relations will be established between Egypt and Israel, including diplomatic, economic and cultural relations; termination of economic boycotts and barriers to the free movement of goods and people; and mutual protection of citizens by the due process of law.

Interim Withdrawal

Between three months and nine months after the signing of the peace treaty, all Israeli forces will withdraw east of a line extending from a point east of El Arish to Ras Muhammad, the exact location of this line to be determined by mutual agreement.

For the government of the Arab Republic of Egypt:

For the Government of Israel:

A. SADAT

M. BEGIN

Witnessed by:

JIMMY CARTER
Jimmy Carter, President
of the United States of America

Source: "The Camp David Summit," U.S. Department of State publication no. 8954, 1978, pp. 6–11.

Appendix C: The Israeli-Egyptian Peace Treaty

Treaty of Peace between the Arab
Republic of Egypt and the State of Israel

The Government of the Arab Republic of Egypt and the Government of the State of Israel;

Preamble

Convinced of the urgent necessity of the establishment of a just, comprehensive and lasting peace in the Middle East in accordance with Security Council Resolutions 242 and 338;

Reaffirming their adherence to the "Framework for Peace in the Middle East Agreed at Camp David," dated September 17, 1978;

Noting that the aforementioned Framework as appropriate is intended to constitute a basis for peace not only between Egypt and Israel but also between Israel and each of its other Arab neighbors which is prepared to negotiate peace with it on this basis;

Desiring to bring to an end the state of war between them and to establish a peace in which every state in the area can live in security;

Convinced that the conclusion of a Treaty of Peace between Egypt and Israel is an important step in the search for comprehensive peace in the area and for the attainment of the settlement of the Arab-Israeli conflict in all its aspects;

Inviting the other Arab parties to this dispute to join the peace process with Israel guided by and based on the principles of the aforementioned Framework;

Desiring as well to develop friendly relations and cooperation between themselves in accordance with the United Nations Charter and the principles of international law governing international relations in times of peace;

Agree to the following provisions in the free exercise of their sovereignty, in order to implement the "Framework for the Conclusion of a Peace Treaty Between Egypt and Israel";

Article I

1. The state of war between the Parties will be terminated and peace will be established between them upon the exchange of instruments of ratification of this Treaty.

2. Israel will withdraw all its armed forces and civilians from the Sinai behind the international boundary between Egypt and mandated Palestine, as provided in the annexed protocol (Annex I), and Egypt will resume the exercise of its full sovereignty over the Sinai.

3. Upon completion of the interim withdrawal provided for in Annex I, the Parties will establish normal and friendly relations, in accordance with Article III (3).

Article II

The permanent boundary between Egypt and Israel is the recognized international boundary between Egypt and the former mandated territory of Palestine, as shown on the map at Annex II, without prejudice to the issue of the status of the Gaza Strip. The Parties recognize this boundary as inviolable. Each will respect the territorial integrity of the other, including their territorial waters and airspace.

Article III

1. The Parties will apply between them the provisions of the Charter of the United Nations and the principles of international law governing relations among states in times of peace. In particular:

    a. They recognize and will respect each other's sovereignty, territorial integrity and political independence;

    b. They recognize and will respect each other's right to live in peace within their secure and recognized boundaries;

    c. They will refrain from the threat or use of force, directly or indirectly, against each other and will settle all disputes between them by peaceful means.

2. Each Party undertakes to ensure that acts or threats of belligerency, hostility, or violence do not originate from and are not committed from within its territory, or by any forces subject to its control or by any other forces stationed on its territory, against the population, citizens or property of the other Party. Each Party also undertakes to refrain from organizing, instigating, inciting, assisting or participating in acts or threats of belligerency, hostility, subversion or violence against the other Party, anywhere, and undertakes to ensure that perpetrators of such acts are brought to justice.

3. The Parties agree that the normal relationship established between them will include full recognition, diplomatic, economic and cultural relations, termination of economic boycotts and discriminatory barriers to the free movement of people and goods, and will guarantee the mutual enjoyment by citizens of the due process of law. The process by which they undertake to achieve such

a relationship parallel to the implementation of other provisions of this Treaty is set out in the annexed protocol (Annex III).

Article IV

1.   In order to provide maximum security for both Parties on the basis of reciprocity, agreed security arrangements will be established including limited force zones in Egyptian and Israeli territory, and United Nations forces and observers, described in detail as to nature and timing in Annex I, and other security arrangements the Parties may agree upon.

2.   The Parties agree to the stationing of United Nations personnel in areas described in Annex I. The Parties agree not to request withdrawal of the United Nations personnel and that these personnel will not be removed unless such removal is approved by the Security Council of the United Nations, with the affirmative vote of the five Permanent Members, unless the Parties otherwise agree.

3.   A Joint Commission will be established to facilitate the implementation of the Treaty, as provided for in Annex I.

4.   The security arrangements provided for in paragraphs 1 and 2 of this Article may at the request of either party be reviewed and amended by mutual agreement of the Parties.

Article V

1.   Ships of Israel, and cargoes destined for or coming from Israel, shall enjoy the right of free passage through the Suez Canal and its approaches through the Gulf of Suez and the Mediterranean Sea on the basis of the Constantinople Convention of 1888, applying to all nations. Israeli nationals, vessels and cargoes, as well as persons, vessels and cargoes destined for or coming from Israel, shall be accorded non-discriminatory treatment in all matters connected with usage of the canal.

2.   The Parties consider the Strait of Tiran and the Gulf of Aqaba to be international waterways open to all nations for unimpeded and non-suspendable freedom of navigation and overflight. The Parties will respect each other's right to navigation and overflight for access to either country through the Strait of Tiran and the Gulf of Aqaba.

Article VI

1.   This Treaty does not affect and shall not be interpreted as affecting in any way the rights and obligations of the Parties under the Charter of the United Nations.

2.   The Parties undertake to fulfill in good faith their obligations under this Treaty, without regard to action or inaction of any other party and independently of any instrument external to this Treaty.

3.   They further undertake to take all the necessary measures for the application in their relations of the provisions of the multilateral conventions

to which they are parties, including the submission of appropriate notification to the Secretary General of the United Nations and other depositaries of such conventions.

4. The Parties undertake not to enter into any obligation in conflict with this Treaty.

5. Subject to Article 103 of the United Nations Charter, in the event of a conflict between the obligations of the Parties under the present Treaty and any of their other obligations, the obligations under this Treaty will be binding and implemented.

Article VII

1. Disputes arising out of the application or interpretation of this Treaty shall be resolved by negotiations.

2. Any such disputes which cannot be settled by negotiations shall be resolved by conciliation or submitted to arbitration.

Article VIII

The Parties agree to establish a claims commission for the mutual settlement of all financial claims.

Article IX

1. This Treaty shall enter into force upon exchange of instruments of ratification.

2. This Treaty supersedes the Agreement between Egypt and Israel of September, 1975.

3. All protocols, annexes, and maps attached to this Treaty shall be regarded as an integral part hereof.

4. The Treaty shall be communicated to the Secretary General of the United Nations for registration in accordance with the provisions of Article 102 of the Charter of the United Nations.

ANNEX I

Protocol Concerning Israeli Withdrawal
and Security Agreements

Article I–Concept of Withdrawal

    1.   Israel will complete withdrawal of all its armed forces and civilians from the Sinai not later than three years from the date of exchange of instruments of ratification of this Treaty.

    2.   To ensure the mutual security of the Parties, the implementation of phased withdrawal will be accompanied by the military measures and establishment of zones set out in this Annex and in Map 1, hereinafter referred to as "the Zones."

    3.   The withdrawal from the Sinai will be accomplished in two phases:

        a.   The interim withdrawal behind the line from east of El Arish to Ras Mohammed as delineated on Map 2 within nine months from the date of exchange of instruments of ratification of this Treaty.

        b.   The final withdrawal from the Sinai behind the international boundary not later than three years from the date of exchange of instruments of ratification of this Treaty.

    4.   A Joint Commission will be formed immediately after the exchange of instruments of ratification of this Treaty in order to supervise and coordinate movements and schedules during the withdrawal, and to adjust plans and timetables as necessary within the limits established by paragraph 3, above. Details relating to the Joint Commission are set out in Article IV of the attached Appendix. The Joint Commission will be dissolved upon completion of final Israeli withdrawal from the Sinai.

Article II–Determination of Final Lines and Zones

    1.   In order to provide maximum security for both Parties after the final withdrawal, the lines and the Zones delineated on Map 1 are to be established and organized as follows:

        a.   Zone A

           (1)   Zone A is bounded on the east by line A (red line) and on the west, by the Suez Canal and the east coast of the Gulf of Suez, as shown on Map 1.

           (2)   An Egyptian armed force of one mechanized infantry division and its military installations, and field fortifications, will be in this Zone.

           (3)   The main elements of that Division will consist of:

               (a)   Three mechanized infantry brigades.

               (b)   One armored brigade.

               (c)   Seven field artillery battalions including up to 126 artillery pieces.

(d)   Seven anti-aircraft artillery battalions including individual surface-to-air missiles and up to 126 anti-aircraft guns of 37 mm and above.

(e)   Up to 230 tanks.

(f)   Up to 480 armored personnel vehicles of all types.

(g)   Up to a total of twenty-two thousand personnel.

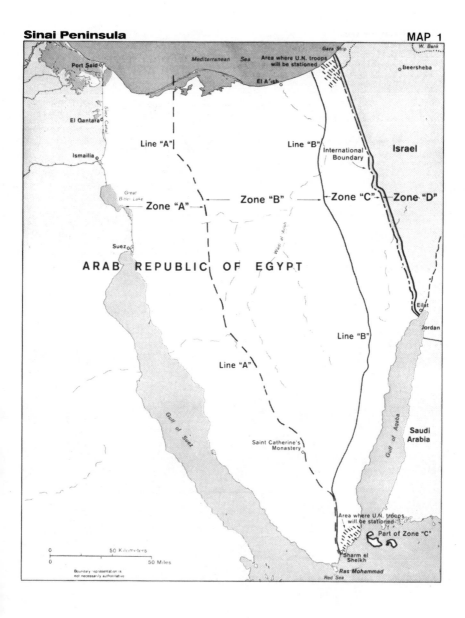

Sinai Peninsula   MAP 1

b. Zone B

(1)   Zone B is bounded by line B (green line) on the east and by
line A (red line) on the west, as shown on Map 1.

(2)   Egyptian border units of four battalions equipped with light
weapons and wheeled vehicles will provide security and supplement
the civil police in maintaining order in Zone B. The main elements

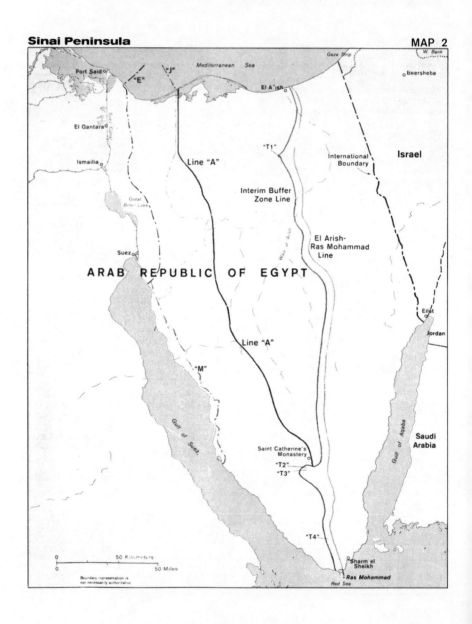

of the four Border Battalions will consist of up to a total of four thousand personnel.

(3)　Land based, short range, low power, coastal warning points of the border patrol units may be established on the coast of this Zone.

(4)　There will be in Zone B field fortifications and military installations for the four border battalions.

c.　Zone C

(1)　Zone C is bounded by line B (green line) on the west and the International Boundary and the Gulf of Aqaba on the east, as shown on Map 1.

(2)　Only United Nations forces and Egyptian civil police will be stationed in Zone C.

(3)　The Egyptian civil police armed with light weapons will perform normal police functions within this Zone.

(4)　The United Nations Force will be deployed within Zone C and perform its functions as defined in Article VI of this Annex.

(5)　The United Nations Force will be stationed mainly in camps located within the following stationing areas shown on Map 1, and will establish its precise locations after consultations with Egypt:

　　(a)　In that part of the area in the Sinai lying within about 20 Km. of the Mediterranean Sea and adjacent to the International Boundary.

　　(b)　In the Sharm el Sheikh area.

d.　Zone D

(1)　Zone D is bounded by line D (blue line) on the east and the international boundary on the west, as shown on Map 1.

(2)　In this Zone there will be an Israeli limited force of four infantry battalions, their military installations, and field fortifications, and United Nations observers.

(3)　The Israeli forces in Zone D will not include tanks, artillery and anti-aircraft missiles except individual surface-to-air missiles.

(4)　The main elements of the four Israeli infantry battalions will consist of up to 180 armored personnel vehicles of all types and up to a total of four thousand personnel.

2.　Access across the international boundary shall only be permitted through entry check points designated by each Party and under its control. Such access shall be in accordance with laws and regulations of each country.

3.　Only those field fortifications, military installations, forces, and weapons specifically permitted by this Annex shall be in the Zones.

Article III—Aerial Military Regime

1.　Flights of combat aircraft and reconnaissance flights of Egypt and Israel shall take place only over Zones A and D, respectively.

2.   Only unarmed, non-combat aircraft of Egypt and Israel will be stationed in Zones A and D, respectively.

3.   Only Egyptian unarmed transport aircraft will take off and land in Zone B and up to eight such aircraft may be maintained in Zone B. The Egyptian border units may be equipped with unarmed helicopters to perform their functions in Zone B.

4.   The Egyptian civil police may be equipped with unarmed police helicopters to perform normal police functions in Zone C.

5.   Only civilian airfields may be built in the Zones.

6.   Without prejudice to the provisions of this Treaty, only those military aerial activities specifically permitted by this Annex shall be allowed in the Zones and the airspace above their territorial waters.

Article IV—Naval Regime

1.   Egypt and Israel may base and operate naval vessels along the coasts of Zones A and D, respectively.

2.   Egyptian coast guard boats, lightly armed, may be stationed and operate in the territorial waters of Zone B to assist the border units in performing their functions in this Zone.

3.   Egyptian civil police equipped with light boats, lightly armed, shall perform normal police functions within the territorial waters of Zone C.

4.   Nothing in this Annex shall be considered as derogating from the right of innocent passage of the naval vessels of either party.

5.   Only civilian maritime ports and installations may be built in the Zones.

6.   Without prejudice to the provisions of this Treaty, only those naval activities specifically permitted by this Annex shall be allowed in the Zones and in their territorial waters.

Article V—Early Warning Systems

Egypt and Israel may establish and operate early warning systems only in Zones A and D respectively.

Article VI—United Nations Operations

1.   The Parties will request the United Nations to provide forces and observers to supervise the implementation of this Annex and employ their best efforts to prevent any violation of its terms.

2.   With respect to these United Nations forces and observers, as appropriate, the Parties agree to request the following arrangements:

   a.   Operation of check points, reconnaissance patrols, and observation posts along the international boundary and line B, and within Zone C.

   b.   Periodic verification of the implementation of the provisions of this Annex will be carried out not less than twice a month unless otherwise agreed by the Parties.

c. Additional verifications within 48 hours after the receipt of a request from either Party.

d. Ensuring the freedom of navigation through the Strait of Tiran in accordance with Article V of the Treaty of Peace.

3. The arrangements described in this article for each zone will be implemented in Zones A, B, and C by the United Nations Force and in Zone D by the United Nations Observers.

4. United Nations verification teams shall be accompanied by liaison officers of the respective Party.

5. The United Nations Force and observers will report their findings to both Parties.

6. The United Nations Force and Observers operating in the Zones will enjoy freedom of movement and other facilities necessary for the performance of their tasks.

7. The United Nations Force and Observers are not empowered to authorize the crossing of the international boundary.

8. The Parties shall agree on the nations from which the United Nations Force and Observers will be drawn. They will be drawn from nations other than those which are permanent members of the United Nations Security Council.

9. The Parties agree that the United Nations should make those command arrangements that will best assure the effective implementation of its responsibilities.

Article VII—Liaison System

1. Upon dissolution of the Joint Commission, a liaison system between the Parties will be established. This liaison system is intended to provide an effective method to assess progress in the implementation of obligations under the present Annex and to resolve any problem that may arise in the course of implementation, and refer other unresolved matters to the higher military authorities of the two countries respectively for consideration. It is also intended to prevent situations resulting from errors or misinterpretation on the part of either Party.

2. An Egyptian liaison office will be established in the city of El-Arish and an Israeli liaison office will be established in the city of Beer-Sheba. Each office will be headed by an officer of the respective country, and assisted by a number of officers.

3. A direct telephone link between the two offices will be set up and also direct telephone lines with the United Nations command will be maintained by both offices.

Article VIII—Respect for War Memorials

Each Party undertakes to preserve in good condition the War Memorials erected in the memory of soldiers of the other Party, namely those erected by

Israel in the Sinai and those to be erected by Egypt in Israel, and shall permit access to such monuments.

Article IX—Interim Arrangements

The withdrawal of Israeli armed forces and civilians behind the interim withdrawal line, and the conduct of the forces of the Parties and the United Nations prior to the final withdrawal, will be governed by the attached Appendix and Map 2.

APPENDIX TO ANNEX I

Organization of Movements in the Sinai

Article I—Principles of Withdrawal

1. The withdrawal of Israeli armed forces and civilians from the Sinai will be accomplished in two phases as described in Article I of Annex I. The description and timing of the withdrawal are included in this Appendix. The Joint Commission will develop and present to the Chief Coordinator of the United Nations forces in the Middle East the details of these phases not later than one month before the initiation of each phase of withdrawal.

2. Both Parties agree on the following principles for the sequence of military movements.

   a. Notwithstanding the provisions of Article IX, paragraph 2, of this Treaty, until Israeli armed forces complete withdrawal from the current J and M Lines established by the Egyptian-Israeli Agreement of September 1975, hereinafter referred to as the 1975 Agreement, up to the interim withdrawal line, all military arrangements existing under that Agreement will remain in effect, except those military arrangements otherwise provided for in this Appendix.

   b. As Israeli armed forces withdraw, United Nations forces will immediately enter the evacuated areas to establish interim and temporary buffer zones as shown on Maps 2 and 3, respectively, for the purpose of maintaining a separation of forces. United Nations forces' deployment will precede the movement of any other personnel into these areas.

   c. Within a period of seven days after Israeli armed forces have evacuated any area located in Zone A, units of Egyptian armed forces shall deploy in accordance with the provisions of Article II of this Appendix.

   d. Within a period of seven days after Israeli armed forces have evacuated any area located in Zones A or B, Egyptian border units shall deploy in accordance with the provisions of Article II of this

Appendix, and will function in accordance with the provisions of Article II of Annex I.

e. Egyptian civil police will enter evacuated areas immediately after the United Nations forces to perform normal police functions.

Sinai Peninsula MAP 3

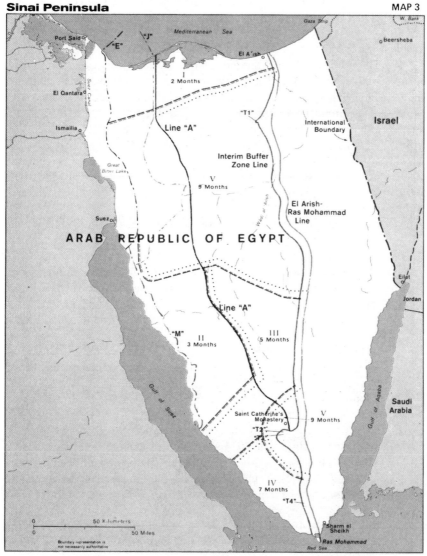

..... Israeli Sub-Phase Line
——— Egyptian Sub-Phase Line
▬▬ U.N. Sub-Phase Buffer Zone

Representation of original map included in treaty.

f.   Egyptian naval units shall deploy in the Gulf of Suez in accordance with the provisions of Article II of this Appendix.

g.   Except those movements mentioned above, deployments of Egyptian armed forces and the activities covered in Annex I will be effected in the evacuated areas when Israeli armed forces have completed their withdrawal behind the interim withdrawal line.

Article II—Subphases of the Withdrawal to the Interim Withdrawal Line

1.   The withdrawal to the interim withdrawal line will be accomplished in subphases as described in this Article and as shown on Map 3. Each subphase will be completed within the indicated number of months from the date of the exchange of instruments of ratification of this Treaty.

a.   First subphase: within two months, Israeli armed forces will withdraw from the area of El Arish, including the town of El Arish and its airfield, shown as Area I on Map 3.

b.   Second subphase: within three months, Israeli armed forces will withdraw from the area between line M of the 1975 Agreement and line A, shown as Area II on Map 3.

c.   Third subphase: within five months, Israeli armed forces will withdraw from the area east and south of Area II, shown as Area III on Map 3.

d.   Fourth subphase: within seven months, Israeli armed forces will withdraw from the area of El Tor-Ras El Kenisa, shown as Area IV on Map 3.

e.   Fifth subphase: Within nine months, Israeli armed forces will withdraw from the remaining areas west of the interim withdrawal line, including the areas of Santa Katrina and the areas east of the Giddi and Mitla passes, shown as Area V on Map 3, thereby completing Israeli withdrawal behind the interim withdrawal line.

2.   Egyptian forces will deploy in the areas evacuated by Israeli armed forces as follows:

a.   Up to one-third of the Egyptian armed forces in the Sinai in accordance with the 1975 Agreement will deploy in the portions of Zone A lying within Area I, until the completion of interim withdrawal. Thereafter, Egyptian armed forces as described in Article II of Annex I will be deployed in Zone A up to the limits of the interim buffer zone.

b.   The Egyptian naval activity in accordance with Article IV of Annex I will commence along the coasts of Areas I, III, and IV, upon completion of the second, third, and fourth subphases, respectively.

c.   Of the Egyptian border units described in Article II of Annex I, upon completion of the first subphase one battalion will be deployed in Area I. A second battalion will be deployed in Area II upon completion of the second subphase. A third battalion will be deployed in Area III upon completion of the third subphase. The second and third battalions mentioned above may also be deployed in any of the subsequently evacuated areas of the southern Sinai.

3.   United Nations forces in Buffer Zone I of the 1975 Agreement will redeploy to enable the deployment of Egyptian forces described above upon the completion of the first subphase, but will otherwise continue to function in accordance with the provisions of that Agreement in the remainder of that zone until the completion of interim withdrawal, as indicated in Article I of this Appendix.

4.   Israeli convoys may use the roads south and east of the main road junction east of El Arish to evacuate Israeli forces and equipment up to the completion of interim withdrawal. These convoys will proceed in daylight upon four hours notice to the Egyptian liaison group and United Nations forces, will be escorted by United Nations forces, and will be in accordance with schedules coordinated by the Joint Commission. An Egyptian liaison officer will accompany convoys to assure uninterrupted movement. The Joint Commission may approve other arrangements for convoys.

Article III—United Nations Forces

1.   The Parties shall request that United Nations forces be deployed as necessary to perform the functions described in this Appendix up to the time of completion of final Israeli withdrawal. For that purpose, the Parties agree to the redeployment of the United Nations Emergency Force.

2.   United Nations forces will supervise the implementation of this Appendix and will employ their best efforts to prevent any violation of its terms.

3.   When United Nations forces deploy in accordance with the provisions of Articles I and II of this Appendix, they will perform the functions of verification in limited force zones in accordance with Article VI of Annex I, and will establish check points, reconnaissance patrols, and observation posts in the temporary buffer zones described in Article II above. Other functions of the United Nations forces which concern the interim buffer zone are described in Article V of this Appendix.

Article IV—Joint Commission and Liaison

1.   The Joint Commission referred to in Article IV of this Treaty will function from the date of exchange of instruments of ratification of this Treaty up to the date of completion of final Israeli withdrawal from the Sinai.

2.   The Joint Commission will be composed of representatives of each Party headed by senior officers. This Commission shall invite a representative of the United Nations when discussing subjects concerning the United Nations, or when either Party requests United Nations presence. Decisions of the Joint Commission will be reached by agreement of Egypt and Israel.

3.   The Joint Commission will supervise the implementation of the arrangements described in Annex I and this Appendix. To this end, and by agreement of both Parties, it will:

a.   coordinate military movements described in this Appendix and supervise their implementation;

b.   address and seek to resolve any problem arising out of the implementation of Annex I and this Appendix, and discuss any violations reported by the United Nations Force and Observers and refer to the Governments of Egypt and Israel any unresolved problems;

c.   assist the United Nations Force and Observers in the execution of their mandates, and deal with the timetables of the periodic verifications when referred to it by the Parties as provided for in Annex I and in this Appendix;

d.   organize the demarcation of the international boundary and all lines and zones described in Annex I and this Appendix;

e.   supervise the handing over of the main installations in the Sinai from Israel to Egypt;

f.   agree on necessary arrangements for finding and returning missing bodies of Egyptian and Israeli soldiers;

g.   organize the setting up and operation of entry check points along the El Arish-Ras Mohammed line in accordance with the provisions of Article 4 of Annex III;

h.   conduct its operations through the use of joint liaison teams consisting of one Israeli representative and one Egyptian representative, provided from a standing Liaison Group, which will conduct activities as directed by the Joint Commission;

i.   provide liaison and coordination to the United Nations command implementing provisions of the Treaty, and, through the joint liaison teams, maintain local coordination and cooperation with the United Nations Force stationed in specific areas or United Nations Observers monitoring specific areas for any assistance as needed;

j.   discuss any other matters which the Parties by agreement may place before it.

4.   Meetings of the Joint Commission shall be held at least once a month. In the event that either Party or the Command of the United Nations Force requests a special meeting, it will be convened within 24 hours.

5.   The Joint Committee will meet in the buffer zone until the completion of the interim withdrawal and in El Arish and Beer-Sheba alternately afterwards. The first meeting will be held not later than two weeks after the entry into force of this Treaty.

Article V—Definition of the Interim Buffer Zone and Its Activities

1.   An interim buffer zone, by which the United Nations Force will effect a separation of Egyptian and Israeli elements, will be established west of and

adjacent to the interim withdrawal line as shown on Map 2 after implementation of Israeli withdrawal and deployment behind the interim withdrawal line. Egyptian civil police equipped with light weapons will perform normal police functions within this zone.

2. The United Nations Force will operate check points, reconnaissance patrols, and observation posts within the interim buffer zone in order to ensure compliance with the terms of this Article.

3. In accordance with arrangements agreed upon by both Parties and to be coordinated by the Joint Commission, Israeli personnel will operate military technical installations at four specific locations shown on Map 2 and designated as T1 (map central coordinate 57163940), T2 (map central coordinate 59351541), T3 (map central coordinate 5933-1527), and T4 (map central coordinate 611-30979) under the following principles:

    a. The technical installations shall be manned by technical and administrative personnel equipped with small arms required for their protection (revolvers, rifles, sub-machine guns, light machine guns, hand grenades, and ammunition), as follows:

    T1—up to 150 personnel

    T2 and T3—up to 350 personnel

    T4—up to 200 personnel.

    b. Israeli personnel will not carry weapons outside the sites, except officers who may carry personal weapons.

    c. Only a third party agreed to by Egypt and Israel will enter and conduct inspections within the perimeters of technical installations in the buffer zone. The third party will conduct inspections in a random manner at least once a month. The inspections will verify the nature of the operation of the installations and the weapons and personnel therein. The third party will immediately report to the Parties any divergence from an installation's visual and electronic surveillance or communications role.

    d. Supply of the installations, visits for technical and administrative purposes, and replacement of personnel and equipment situated in the sites, may occur uninterruptedly from the United Nations check points to the perimeter of the technical installations, after checking and being escorted by only the United Nations forces.

    e. Israel will be permitted to introduce into its technical installations items required for the proper functioning of the installations and personnel.

    f. As determined by the Joint Commission, Israel will be permitted to:

    (1) Maintain in its installations fire-fighting and general maintenance equipment as well as wheeled administrative vehicles and mobile engineering equipment necessary for the maintenance of the sites. All vehicles shall be unarmed.

    (2) Within the sites and in the buffer zone, maintain roads,

water lines, and communications cables which serve the sites. At each of the three installation locations (T1, T2 and T3, and T4), this maintenance may be performed with up to two unarmed wheeled vehicles and by up to twelve unarmed personnel with only necessary equipment, including heavy engineering equipment if needed. This maintenance may be performed three times a week, except for special problems, and only after giving the United Nations four hours notice. The teams will be escorted by the United Nations.

g.   Movement to and from the technical installations will take place only during daylight hours. Access to, and exit from, the technical installations shall be as follows:

(1)   T1: through a United Nations check point, and via the road between Abu Aweigila and the intersection of the Abu Aweigila road and the Gebel Libni road (at Km. 161), as shown on Map 2.

(2)   T2 and T3: through a United Nations checkpoint and via the road constructed across the buffer zone to Gebel Katrina, as shown on Map 2.

(3)   T2, T3, and T4: via helicopters flying within a corridor at the times, and according to a flight profile, agreed to by the Joint Commission. The helicopters will be checked by the United Nations Force at landing sites outside the perimeter of the installations.

h.   Israel will inform the United Nations Force at least one hour in advance of each intended movement to and from the installations.

i.   Israel shall be entitled to evacuate sick and wounded and summon medical experts and medical teams at any time after giving immediate notice to the United Nations Force.

4.   The details of the above principles and all other matters in this Article requiring coordination by the Parties will be handled by the Joint Commission.

5.   These technical installations will be withdrawn when Israeli forces withdraw from the interim withdrawal line, or at a time agreed by the parties.

Article VI–Disposition of Installations and Military Barriers

Disposition of installations and military barriers will be determined by the Parties in accordance with the following guidelines:

1.   Up to three weeks before Israeli withdrawal from any area, the Joint Commission will arrange for Israeli and Egyptian liaison and technical teams to conduct a joint inspection of all appropriate installations to agree upon condition of structures and articles which will be transferred to Egyptian control and to arrange for such transfer. Israel will declare, at that time, its plans for disposition of installations and articles within the installations.

2.   Israel undertakes to transfer to Egypt all agreed infrastructures, utilities, and installations intact, inter alia, airfields, roads, pumping stations, and ports.

Israel will present to Egypt the information necessary for the maintenance and operation of these facilities. Egyptian technical teams will be permitted to observe and familiarize themselves with the operation of these facilities for a period of up to two weeks prior to transfer.

3. When Israel relinquishes Israeli military water points near El Arish and El Tor, Egyptian technical teams will assume control of those installations and ancillary equipment in accordance with an orderly transfer process arranged beforehand by the Joint Commission. Egypt undertakes to continue to make available at all water supply points the normal quantity of currently available water up to the time Israel withdraws behind the international boundary, unless otherwise agreed in the Joint Commission.

4. Israel will make its best effort to remove or destroy all military barriers, including obstacles and minefields, in the areas and adjacent waters from which it withdraws, according to the following concept:

a. Military barriers will be cleared first from areas near populations, roads, and major installations and utilities.

b. For those obstacles and minefields which cannot be removed or destroyed prior to Israeli withdrawal, Israel will provide detailed maps to Egypt and the United Nations through the Joint Commission not later than 15 days before entry of United Nations forces into the affected areas.

c. Egyptian engineers will enter those areas after United Nations forces enter to conduct barrier clearance operations in accordance with Egyptian plans to be submitted prior to implementation.

Article VII—Surveillance Activities

1. Aerial surveillance activities during the withdrawal will be carried out as follows:

a. Both Parties request the United States to continue airborne surveillance flights in accordance with previous agreements until the completion of final Israeli withdrawal.

b. Flight profiles will cover the Limited Forces Zones to monitor the limitations on forces and armaments, and to determine that Israeli armed forces have withdrawn from the areas described in Article II of Annex I, Article II of this Appendix, and Maps 2 and 3, and that these forces thereafter remain behind their lines. Special inspection flights may be flown at the request of either Party or of the United Nations.

c. Only the main elements in the military organizations of each Party, as described in Annex I and in this Appendix, will be reported.

2. Both Parties request the United States operated Sinai Field Mission to continue its operations in accordance with previous agreements until completion of the Israeli withdrawal from the area east of the Giddi and Mitla Passes. Thereafter, the Mission will be terminated.

Article VIII–Exercise of Egyptian Sovereignty
     Egypt will resume the exercise of its full sovereignty over evacuated parts of
the Sinai upon Israeli withdrawal as provided for in Article I of this Treaty.

ANNEX II

Map of the Sinai Peninsula

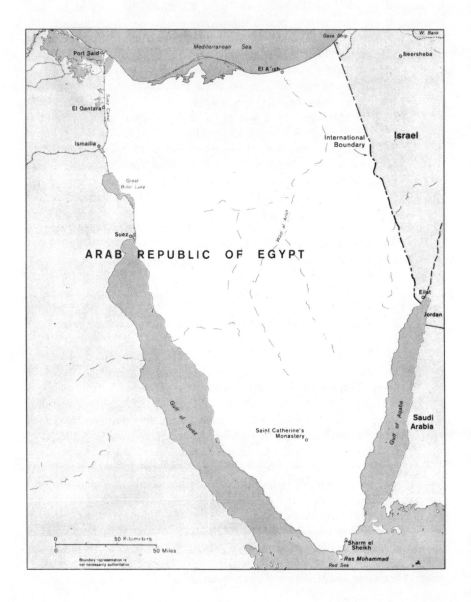

ANNEX III

Protocol Concerning Relations of the Parties

Article 1–Diplomatic and Consular Relations
The Parties agree to establish diplomatic and consular relations and to exchange ambassadors upon completion of the interim withdrawal.

Article 2–Economic and Trade Relations
1. The Parties agree to remove all discriminatory barriers to normal economic relations and to terminate economic boycotts of each other upon completion of the interim withdrawal.
2. As soon as possible, and not later than six months after the completion of the interim withdrawal, the Parties will enter negotiations with a view to concluding an agreement on trade and commerce for the purpose of promoting beneficial economic relations.

Article 3–Cultural Relations
1. The Parties agree to establish normal cultural relations following completion of the interim withdrawal.
2. They agree on the desirability of cultural exchanges in all fields, and shall, as soon as possible and not later than six months after completion of the interim withdrawal, enter into negotiations with a view to concluding a cultural agreement for this purpose.

Article 4–Freedom of Movement
1. Upon completion of the interim withdrawal, each Party will permit the free movement of the nationals and vehicles of the other into and within its territory according to the general rules applicable to nationals and vehicles of other states. Neither Party will impose discriminatory restrictions on the free movement of persons and vehicles from its territory to the territory of the other.
2. Mutual unimpeded access to places of religious and historical significance will be provided on a nondiscriminatory basis.

Article 5–Cooperation for Development and Good Neighborly Relations
1. The Parties recognize a mutuality of interest in good neighborly relations and agree to consider means to promote such relations.
2. The Parties will cooperate in promoting peace, stability and development in their region. Each agrees to consider proposals the other may wish to make to this end.
3. The Parties shall seek to foster mutual understanding and tolerance and will, accordingly, abstain from hostile propaganda against each other.

Article 6—Transportation and Telecommunications

1.   The Parties recognize as applicable to each other the rights, privileges and obligations provided for by the aviation agreements to which they are both party, particularly by the Convention on International Civil Aviation, 1944 ("The Chicago Convention") and the International Air Services Transit Agreement, 1944.

2.   Upon completion of the interim withdrawal any declaration of national emergency by a party under Article 89 of the Chicago Convention will not be applied to the other party on a discriminatory basis.

3.   Egypt agrees that the use of airfields left by Israel near El Arish, Rafah, Ras El Nagb and Sharm El Sheikh shall be for civilian purposes only, including possible commercial use by all nations.

4.   As soon as possible and not later than six months after the completion of the interim withdrawal, the Parties shall enter into negotiations for the purpose of concluding a civil aviation agreement.

5.   The Parties will reopen and maintain roads and railways between their countries and will consider further road and rail links. The Parties further agree that a highway will be constructed and maintained between Egypt, Israel and Jordan near Eilat with guaranteed free and peaceful passage of persons, vehicles and goods between Egypt and Jordan, without prejudice to their sovereignty over that part of the highway which falls within their respective territory.

6.   Upon completion of the interim withdrawal, normal postal, telephone, telex, data facsimile, wireless and cable communications and television relay services by cable, radio and satellite shall be established between the two Parties in accordance with all relevant international conventions and regulations.

7.   Upon completion of the interim withdrawal, each Party shall grant normal access to its ports for vessels and cargoes of the other, as well as vessels and cargoes destined for or coming from the other. Such access shall be granted on the same conditions generally applicable to vessels and cargoes of other nations. Article 5 of the Treaty of Peace will be implemented upon the exchange of instruments of ratification of the aforementioned treaty.

Article 7—Enjoyment of Human Rights

The Parties affirm their commitment to respect and observe human rights and fundamental freedoms for all, and they will promote these rights and freedoms in accordance with the United Nations Charter.

Article 8—Territorial Seas

Without prejudice to the provisions of Article 5 of the Treaty of Peace each Party recognizes the right of the vessels of the other Party to innocent passage through its territorial sea in accordance with the rules of international law.

AGREED MINUTES

Article I

Egypt's resumption of the exercise of full sovereignty over the Sinai provided for in paragraph 2 of Article I shall occur with regard to each area upon Israel's withdrawal from that area.

Article IV

It is agreed between the parties that the review provided for in Article IV (4) will be undertaken when requested by either party, commencing within three months of such a request, but that any amendment can be made only with the mutual agreement of both parties.

Article V

The second sentence of paragraph 2 of Article V shall not be construed as limiting the first sentence of that paragraph. The foregoing is not to be construed as contravening the second sentence of paragraph 2 of Article V, which reads as follows:

> "The Parties will respect each other's right to navigation and overflight for access to either country through the Strait of Tiran and the Gulf of Aqaba."

Article VI (2)

The provisions of Article VI shall not be construed in contradiction to the provisions of the framework for peace in the Middle East agreed at Camp David. The foregoing is not to be construed as contravening the provisions of Article VI (2) of the Treaty, which reads as follows:

> "The Parties undertake to fulfill in good faith their obligations under this Treaty, without regard to action or inaction of any other Party and independently of any instrument external to this Treaty."

Article VI (5)

It is agreed by the Parties that there is no assertion that this Treaty prevails over other Treaties or agreements or that other Treaties or agreements prevail over this Treaty. The foregoing is not to be construed as contravening the provisions of Article VI (5) of the Treaty, which reads as follows:

> "Subject to Article 103 of the United Nations Charter, in the event of a conflict between the obligations of the Parties under the present Treaty and any of their other obligations, the obligations under this Treaty will be binding and implemented."

Annex I

Article VI, Paragraph 8, of Annex I provides as follows:

"The Parties shall agree on the nations from which the United Nations forces and observers will be drawn. They will be drawn from nations other than those which are permanent members of the United Nations Security Council."

The Parties have agreed as follows:

"With respect to the provisions of paragraph 8, Article VI, of Annex I, if no agreement is reached between the Parties, they will accept or support a U.S. proposal concerning the composition of the United Nations force and observers."

Annex III

The Treaty of Peace and Annex III thereto provide for establishing normal economic relations between the Parties. In accordance therewith, it is agreed that such relations will include normal commercial sales of oil by Egypt to Israel, and that Israel shall be fully entitled to make bids for Egyptian-origin oil not needed for Egyptian domestic oil consumption, and Egypt and its oil concessionaries will entertain bids made by Israel, on the same basis and terms as apply to other bidders for such oil.

For the Government of the   For the Government
    Arab Republic of Egypt: of Israel:

Witnessed by:

Jimmy Carter, *President*
of the United States of America

JOINT LETTER FROM PRESIDENT SADAT AND PRIME MINISTER BEGIN TO PRESIDENT CARTER

The President   March 26, 1979
The White House

Dear Mr. President:

This letter confirms that Israel and Egypt have agreed as follows:

The Governments of Israel and Egypt recall that they concluded at Camp David and signed at the White House on September 17, 1978, the annexed documents entitled "A Framework for Peace in the Middle East Agreed at Camp David" and "Framework for the conclusion of a Peace Treaty between Israel and Egypt."

For the purpose of achieving a comprehensive peace settlement in accordance with the above-mentioned Frameworks, Israel and Egypt will proceed with the implementation of those provisions relating to the West Bank and the Gaza Strip. They have agreed to start negotiations within a month after the exchange of the instruments of ratification of the Peace Treaty. In accordance with the "Framework for Peace in the Middle East," the Hashemite Kingdom of Jordan is invited to join the negotiations. The Delegations of Egypt and Jordan may include Palestinians as mutually agreed. The purpose of the negotiation shall be to agree, prior to the elections, on the modalities for establishing the elected self-governing authority (administrative council), define its powers and responsibilities, and agree upon other related issues. In the event Jordan decides not to take part in the negotiations, the negotiations will be held by Israel and Egypt.

The two Governments agree to negotiate continuously and in good faith to conclude these negotiations at the earliest possible date. They also agree that the objective of the negotiations is the establishment of the self-governing authority in the West Bank and Gaza in order to provide full autonomy to the inhabitants.

Israel and Egypt set for themselves the goal of completing the negotiations within one year so that elections will be held as expeditiously as possible after agreement has been reached between the parties. The self-governing authority referred to in the "Framework for Peace in the Middle East" will be established and inaugurated within one month after it has been elected, at which time the transitional period of five years will begin. The Israeli military government and its civilian administration will be withdrawn, to be replaced by the self-governing authority, as specified in the "Framework for Peace in the Middle East." A withdrawal of Israeli armed forces will then take place and there will be a redeployment of the remaining Israeli forces into specified security locations.

This letter also confirms our understanding that the United States Government will participate fully in all stages of negotiations.

Sincerely yours,

For the Government of Israel:

Menachem Begin

For the Government of the Arab Republic of Egypt:

Mohamed Anwar El-Sadat

LETTER FROM PRESIDENT CARTER TO PRIME MINISTER BEGIN ABOUT THE DEPLOYMENT OF A UN OR AN ALTERNATE MULTINATIONAL FORCE

His Excellency
   Menachem Begin,
     Prime Minister of the
       State of Israel.

March 26, 1979

Dear Mr. Prime Minister:

I wish to confirm to you that subject to United States Constitutional processes:

In the event of an actual or threatened violation of the Treaty of Peace between Israel and Egypt, the United States will, on request of one or both of the Parties, consult with the Parties with respect thereto and will take such other action as it may deem appropriate and helpful to achieve compliance with the Treaty.

The United States will conduct aerial monitoring as requested by the Parties pursuant to Annex I of the Treaty.

The United States believes the Treaty provision for permanent stationing of United Nations personnel in the designated limited force zone can and should be implemented by the United Nations Security Council. The United States will exert its utmost efforts to obtain the requisite action by the Security Council. If the Security Council fails to establish and maintain the arrangements called for in the Treaty, the President will be prepared to take those steps necessary to ensure the establishment and maintenance of an acceptable alternative multi-national force.

Sincerely,

Jimmy Carter

**EXCHANGE OF LETTERS BETWEEN PRESIDENT CARTER
AND PRIME MINISTER BEGIN REGARDING THE
EXCHANGE OF AMBASSADORS BETWEEN EGYPT AND ISRAEL**

His Excellency   March 26, 1979
  Menachem Begin,
    Prime Minister of the
      State of Israel

Dear Mr. Prime Minister:

I have received a letter from President Sadat that, within one month after Israel completes its withdrawal to the interim line in Sinai, as provided for in the Treaty of Peace between Egypt and Israel, Egypt will send a resident ambassador to Israel and will receive in Egypt a resident Israeli ambassador.

I would be grateful if you will confirm that this procedure will be agreeable to the Government of Israel.

Sincerely,

Jimmy Carter

The President, March 26, 1979
The White House

Dear Mr. President:

I am pleased to be able to confirm that the Government of Israel is agreeable to the procedure set out in your letter of March 26, 1979 in which you
state:

"I have received a letter from President Sadat that, within one month
after Israel completes its withdrawal to the interim line in Sinai, as provided
for in the Treaty of Peace between Egypt and Israel, Egypt will send a
resident ambassador to Israel and will receive in Egypt a resident Israeli
ambassador."

Sincerely,

Menachem Begin

III MEMORANDA OF AGREEMENT

Memorandum of Agreement between the Governments of the United States of America and the State of Israel

March 26, 1979

Recognizing the significance of the conclusion of the Treaty of Peace
between Israel and Egypt and considering the importance of full implementation of the Treaty of Peace to Israel's security interests and the contribution
of the conclusion of the Treaty of Peace to the security and development of
Israel as well as its significance to peace and stability in the region and to the
maintenance of international peace and security; and

Recognizing that the withdrawal from Sinai imposes additional heavy
security, military and economic burdens on Israel;

The Governments of the United States of America and of the State of
Israel, subject to their constitutional processes and applicable law, confirm as
follows:

1. In the light of the role of the United States in achieving the Treaty of
Peace and the parties' desire that the United States continue its supportive
efforts, the United States will take appropriate measures to promote full observance of the Treaty of Peace.

2. Should it be demonstrated to the satisfaction of the United States
that there has been a violation or threat of violation of the Treaty of Peace,
the United States will consult with the parties with regard to measures to halt
or prevent the violation, ensure observance of the Treaty of Peace, enhance

friendly and peaceful relations between the parties and promote peace in the region, and will take such remedial measures as it deems appropriate, which may include diplomatic, economic and military measures as described below.

3.   The United States will provide support it deems appropriate for proper actions taken by Israel in response to such demonstrated violations of the Treaty of Peace. In particular, if a violation of the Treaty of Peace is deemed to threaten the security of Israel, including, inter alia, a blockade of Israel's use of international waterways, a violation of the provisions of the Treaty of Peace concerning limitation of forces or an armed attack against Israel, the United States will be prepared to consider, on an urgent basis, such measures as the strengthening of the United States presence in the area, the providing of emergency supplies to Israel, and the exercise of maritime rights in order to put an end to the violation.

4.   The United States will support the parties' rights to navigation and overflight for access to either country through and over the Strait of Tiran and the Gulf of Aqaba pursuant to the Treaty of Peace.

5.   The United States will oppose and, if necessary, vote against any action or resolution in the United Nations which in its judgment adversely affects the Treaty of Peace.

6.   Subject to Congressional authorization and appropriation, the United States will endeavor to take into account and will endeavor to be responsive to military and economic assistance requirements of Israel.

7.   The United States will continue to impose restrictions on weapons supplied by it to any country which prohibit their unauthorized transfer to any third party. The United States will not supply or authorize transfer of such weapons for use in an armed attack against Israel, and will take steps to prevent such unauthorized transfer.

8.   Existing agreements and assurances between the United States and Israel are not terminated or altered by the conclusion of the Treaty of Peace, except for those contained in Articles 5, 6, 7, 8, 11, 12, 15 and 16 of Memorandum of Agreement between the Government of Israel and the Government of the United States (United States-Israeli Assurances) of September 1, 1975.

9.   This Memorandum of Agreement sets forth the full understandings of the United States and Israel with regard to the subject matters covered between them hereby, and shall be implemented in accordance with its terms.

Memorandum of Agreement between the Governments
of the United States and Israel—Oil

March 26, 1979

The oil supply arrangement of September 1, 1975, between the Governments of the United States and Israel, annexed hereto, remains in effect. A memorandum of agreement shall be agreed upon and concluded to provide an oil supply arrangement for a total of 15 years, including the 5 years provided in the September 1, 1975 arrangement.

The memorandum of agreement, including the commencement of this arrangement and pricing provisions, will be mutually agreed upon by the parties within sixty days following the entry into force of the Treaty of Peace between Egypt and Israel.

It is the intention of the parties that prices paid by Israel for oil provided by the United States hereunder shall be comparable to world market prices current at the time of transfer, and that in any event the United States will be reimbursed by Israel for the costs incurred by the United States in providing oil to Israel hereunder.

Experts provided for in the September 1, 1975, arrangement will meet on request to discuss matters arising under this relationship.

The United States administration undertakes to seek promptly additional statutory authorization that may be necessary for full implementation of this arrangement.

M. Dayan   Cyrus R. Vance
For the Government   For the Government
of Israel   of the United States

Annex to the Memorandum of Agreement concerning Oil

Annex

Israel will make its own independent arrangements for oil supply to meet its requirements through normal procedures. In the event Israel is unable to secure its needs in this way, the United States Government, upon notification of this fact by the Government of Israel, will act as follows for five years, at the end of which period either side can terminate this arrangement on one-year's notice.

(a) If the oil Israel needs to meet all its normal requirements for domestic consumption is unavailable for purchase in circumstances where no quantitative restrictions exist on the ability of the United States to procure oil to meet its normal requirements, the United States Government will promptly make oil available for purchase by Israel to meet all of the aforementioned normal requirements of Israel. If Israel is unable to secure the necessary means to transport such oil to Israel, the United States Government will make every effort to help Israel secure the necessary means of transport.

(b) If the oil Israel needs to meet all of its normal requirements for domestic consumption is unavailable for purchase in circumstances where quantitative restrictions through embargo or otherwise also prevent the United States from procuring oil to meet its normal requirements, the United States Government will promptly make oil available for purchase by Israel in accordance with the International Energy Agency conservation and allocation formula, as applied by the United States Government, in order to meet Israel's essential requirements. If Israel is unable to secure the necessary means to transport such oil to Israel, the United States Government will make every effort to help Israel secure the necessary means of transport.

Israeli and United States experts will meet annually or more frequently at the request of either party, to review Israel's continuing oil requirement.

IV ADDRESSES DELIVERED AT THE PEACE SIGNING CEREMONY ON THE WHITE HOUSE LAWN– 26 MARCH 1979

PRESIDENT CARTER

During the past 30 years, Israel and Egypt have waged war. But for the past 16 months, these same two great nations have waged peace.

Today we celebrate a victory, not of a bloody military campaign, but of an inspiring peace campaign. Two leaders who loom large in the history of nations, President Anwar Sadat and Prime Minister Menachem Begin, have conducted this campaign with all the courage, tenacity, brilliance and inspiration of any generals who have ever led men and machines onto the field of battle.

At the end of this campaign, the soil of the two lands is not drenched with young blood. The countrysides of both lands are free from the litter and the carnage of a wasteful war.

Mothers in Egypt and Israel are not weeping today for their children fallen in senseless battle. The dedication and determination of these two world statesmen have borne fruit. Peace has come to Israel and to Egypt.

I honor these two leaders and their Government officials who have hammered out this peace treaty which we have just signed. But most of all, I honor the people of these two lands whose yearning for peace kept alive the negotiations which today culminate in this glorious event.

We have won, at last, the first step of peace. A first step on a long and difficult road. We must not minimize the obstacles which still lie ahead. Differences still separate the signatories to this treaty from one another. And also from some of their neighbors who fear what they have just done.

To overcome these differences, to dispel these fears, we must rededicate ourselves to the goal of a broader peace with justice for all who have lived in a state of conflict in the Middle East.

We have no illusions. We have hopes, dreams and prayers, yes. But no illusions. There now remains the rest of the Arab world whose support and whose cooperation in the peace process is needed and honestly sought.

I am convinced that other Arab people need and want peace. But some of their leaders are not yet willing to honor these needs and desires for peace. We must now demonstrate the advantages of peace and expand its benefits to encompass all those who have suffered so much in the Middle East.

Obviously, time and understanding will be necessary for people, hitherto enemies, to become neighbors in the best sense of the word. Just because a paper is signed, all the problems will not automatically go away. Future days will require the best from us to give reality to these lofty aspirations.

Let those who would shatter peace, who would callously spill more blood, be aware that we three and all others who may join us will vigorously wage peace. So let history record that deep and ancient antagonisms can be settled without bloodshed and without staggering waste of precious lives, without rapacious destruction of the land.

It has been said, and I quote:

"Peace has one thing in common with its enemy, with the fiend it battles, with war: Peace is active, not passive; peace is doing, not waiting; peace is aggressive, attacking; peace plans its strategy and encircles the enemy; peace marshals its forces and storms the gates; peace gathers its weapons and pierces the defense. Peace, like war, is waged."

It is true that we cannot enforce trust and cooperation between nations, but we can use all our strength to see that nations do not again go to war. Our religious doctrines—all our religious doctrines gives us hope.

In the Koran, we read: "But if the enemy inclines towards peace, do thou also incline towards peace. And trust in God, for He is the One that heareth and knoweth all things."

And the Prophet Isaiah said: "Nations shall beat their swords into plowshares, and their spears into pruning hooks. Nation shall not lift up sword against nation. Neither shall they learn war any more."

So let us now lay aside war; let us now reward all the children of Abraham who hunger for a comprehensive peace in the Middle East. Let us now enjoy the adventure of becoming fully human, fully neighbors, even brothers and sisters.

We pray God, we pray God together, that these dreams will come true. I believe they will. Thank you very much.

PRESIDENT SADAT

President Carter, dear friends. This is certainly one of the happiest moments in my life. It is a historic turning point of great significance for all peaceloving nations. Those among us who are endowed with vision cannot fail to comprehend the dimension of our sacred mission. The Egyptian people with their heritage and unique awareness of history have realized from the very beginning the meaning and value of this endeavor. In all the steps I took I was not performing a personal mission. I was merely expressing the will of a nation. I am proud of my people and of belonging to them.

Today a new dawn is emerging out of the darkness of the past. A new chapter is being opened in the history of co-existence among nations, one that's worthy of our spiritual values and civilization. Never before have men encountered such a complex dispute which is highly charged with emotions. Never before did men need that much courage and imagination to confront a single challenge. Never before had any cause generated that much interest in all four corners of the globe.

Men and women of good will have labored day and night to bring about this happy moment. Egyptians and Israelis alike pursued their sacred goal undeterred by difficulties and complications. Hundreds of dedicated individuals on both sides have given generously of their thought and effort to translate the cherished dream into a living reality. But the man who performed the miracle was President Carter. Without any exaggeration, what he did constitutes one of the greatest achievements of our time. He devoted his skill, hard work and above all his firm belief in the ultimate triumph of good against evil to insure the success of our mission. To me he has been the best companion and partner along the road to peace.

With his deep sense of justice and genuine commitment to human rights we were able to surmount the most difficult obstacles. There came certain moments when hope was eroding and retreating in the face of pride. However, President Carter remained unshaken in his confidence and determination. He is a man of faith and compassion. Before anything else, the signing of the peace treaty and the exchange of letters is a tribute to the spirit and ability of Jimmy Carter.

Happily he was armed with the blessing of God and the support of his people. For that, we are grateful to each and every American who contributed in his own way to the success of our endeavor. We are also heartened by the understanding of hundreds of thousands of Israelis who remained unwavering in their commitment to peace. The continuation of this spirit is vital to the coronation of our efforts.

We realize that difficult times lay ahead. The signing of these documents marks only the beginning of peace. But it is an indispensible start. Other steps remain to be taken without delay or procrastination. Much will depend upon the success of these steps. We are all committed to pursue our efforts until the fruits of the comprehensive settlement we agreed upon are shared by all parties to the conflict.

President Carter once said that the United States is committed without reservation to seeing the peace process through until all parties to the Arab-Israeli conflict are at peace. We value such a pledge from a leader who raised the banner of morality and ethics as a substitute for power politics and opportunism. The steps we took in the recent past will serve Arab vital interests. The liberation of Arab land and the reinstitution of Arab authority in the West Bank and Gaza would certainly enhance our common strategic interests. While we take the initiative to protect these interests, we remain faithful to our Arab commitment. To us, this is a matter of destiny. Pursuing peace is the only avenue which is compatible with our culture and creed.

Let there be no more war or bloodshed between Arabs and the Israelis. Let there be no more suffering or denial of rights. Let there be no more despair or loss of faith. Let no mother lament the loss of her child. Let no young man waste his life on a conflict from which no one benefits. Let us work together until the day comes when they beat their swords into plowshares and their spears into pruning hooks; and God does call to the abode of peace; He does guide whom He pleases to His way. Thank You.

PRIME MINISTER BEGIN

"Mr. President of the United States of America, Mr. President of the Arab Republic of Egypt, Mr. Vice-President, Mr. Speaker of the House of Representatives, Mr. Speaker of the Knesset, Members of the Cabinet of the United States, of Egypt, of Israel, Members of the Congress, and the Knesset, Your Excellencies, Chairman of the Board of Governors of the Jewish Agency, Chairman of the Executive of the Zionist Organization, distinguished guests, ladies and gentlemen."

"I have come from the land of Israel, the land of Zion and Jerusalem, and here I stand, in humility and with pride, as a son of the Jewish people, as one of the generation of the holocaust and redemption. The ancient Jewish people gave the world the vision of eternal peace, of universal disarmament, of abolishing the teaching and learning of war. Two prophets, Yeshayahu Ben Amotz and Micha Hamorashti, having foreseen the spiritual unity of man under God—with His word coming forth from Jerusalem—gave the nations of the world the following vision expressed in identical terms:

"And they shall beat their swords into ploughshares and their spears into pruning hooks. Nation shall not lift up sword against nation; neither shall they know war anymore."

Despite the tragedies and disappointments of the past we must never forsake that vision, that human dream, that unshakeable faith. Peace is the beauty of life. It is sunshine. It is the smile of a child, the love of a mother, the joy of a father, the togetherness of a family. It is the advancement of man, the victory of a just cause, the triumph of truth. Peace is all of these and more, and more."

These are words I uttered in Oslo on December tenth 1978 while receiving the second half of the Nobel Peace Prize—the first half went, and rightly so, to President Sadat—and I took the liberty to repeat them here, on this momentous, historic occasion.

It is a great day in the annals of two ancient nations, Egypt and Israel, whose sons met in our generation five times on the battlefield, fighting and falling. Let us turn our hearts to our heroes and pay tribute to their eternal memory; it is thanks to them that we could have reached this day.

However, let us not forget that in ancient times our two nations met also in alliance. Now we make peace, the cornerstone of cooperation and friendship.

It is a great day in your life, Mr. President of the United States. You have worked so hard, so insistently, so consistently, for this goal; and your labors and your devotion bore God-blessed fruit. Our friend, President Sadat, said that you are the "unknown soldier" of the peace-making effort. I agree, but, as usual, with an amendment. A soldier in the service of peace you are; you are, Mr. President, even, horrible dictu, an *intransigent fighter* for peace. But Jimmy Carter, the President of the United States, is not completely unknown. And so is his effort, which will be remembered for generations to come.

It is, of course, a great day in your life, Mr. President of the Arab Republic of Egypt. In the face of adversity and hostility you have demonstrated the human value that can change history: civil courage. A great field commander once said: civil courage is sometimes more difficult to show than military courage. You showed both. But now is the time, for all of us, to show *civil courage* in order to proclaim to our peoples, and to others: no more war, no more bloodshed, no more bereavement—peace unto you, Shalom, Salaam— forever.

And it is, ladies and gentlemen, the third greatest day in my life. The first was May the Fourteenth 1948 when our flag was hoisted, our independence in our ancestors' land was proclaimed after one thousand eight hundred and seventy-eight years of dispersion, persecution, and physical destruction. We fought for our liberation—alone—and won the day. That was spring; such a spring we can never have again.

The second day was when Jerusalem became one city, and our brave, perhaps most hardened soldiers, the parachutists, embraced with tears and kissed the ancient stones of the remnants of the western wall destined to protect the chosen place of God's glory. Our hearts wept with them—in remembrance.

"Omdot hoyu ragleinu b'sha'arayich yerushalayim, yerushalayim habnuya k'ir sh-chubrah la yachdav." (Psalm 122)

This is the third day in my life. I have signed a treaty of peace with our neighbor, with Egypt. The heart is full and overflowing. God gave me the strength to survive the horrors of Nazism and of a Stalinite concentration camp, to persevere, to endure, not to waiver in, or flinch from, my duty, to accept abuse from foreigners and, what is more painful, from my own people, and from my close friends. This effort too bore some fruit.

Therefore it is the proper place, and appropriate time to bring back to memory the song and prayer of Thanksgiving I learned as a child in the home of father and mother, that doesn't exist any more, because they were among the six million people, men, women and children, who sanctified the Lord's name with their sacred blood, which reddened the rivers of Europe from the Rhine to the Danube, from the Bug to the Volga—because, *only because* they were born Jews, and because they didn't have a country of their own, neither a valiant

Jewish army to defend them, and because, nobody, nobody came to their rescue, although they cried out: save us, save us, de profundis, from the depths of the pit and agony; that is the song of degrees written two millennia and five hundred years ago when our forefathers returned from their first exile to Jerusalem, to Zion.

"Shir hamama'alot b'shuv adonai, et shivat zion hayinu k'cholmim. As yimalei t'zechok pinu ulshoneinu rinah. As yomru vagoyim higdil adonai la'asot im eileh, higdil adonai la'asot imanu hayinu s'meichim. Shuva adonai et sh'viteinu ka'afikim banegev. Ha' azorim b'dimah b'rinah yikzoru. Haloch yeilech uvacho nosei meshech—hazarah bo-yavo b'rinah nosei alumotav." (Psalm 126)

I will not translate. Every man, whether Jew or Christian or Moslem can read it in his own language. It is Psalm 126.

Source: *Documents Pertaining to the Conclusion of Peace* (Washington: Embassy of Israel, 1979).

Appendix D: Preelection Polls and Knesset Results, 1981 Israeli Elections[a]

	1977[b] vote	Jan. 1981	Feb. 1981	March 1981	April 1981	Early May 1981	Late May 1981	Early June 1981	Mid June 1981	Late June 1981	Election Results June 30, 1981
Likud	(43)	20	20	33	35	41	45	46	49	42	48
Labor	(32)	58	45	45	46	41	42	40	37	42	47
National Religious Party	(12)	11	10	9	10	9	7	8	9	8	6
Aguda	(5)	5	6	5	5	6	5	5	5	6	4
TAMI (Abuhatzeira)	-	-	-	-	-	-	-	3	1	2	3

	36%	26%	23%	21%	25%	22%	14%	22%	12.5%
Telem (Dayan)		19	9	4	4	4	3	3	2
Citizens Rights & Peace	(1)		2	3	2	2	2	3	1
Shinui	b 2	1	2	1	1	1	1	1	2
Tehiya	4	3	3	4	3	3	3	4	3
Democratic Front for Peace & Equality (Communists)	(5)								4
Undecided	36%	26%	23%	21%	25%	22%	14%	22%	12.5%

aNumber of seats projected or won (except for "Undecided").

bIn 1977 the Democratic Movement for Change, led by Yigal Yadin won 15 seats. The party had dissolved by early 1981 with only one faction, Shinui, running a party list.

Sources: Jerusalem Post, February 3, March 13, 31, April 14, May 6, 12, June 2, 12, 21—all 1981. *Haknesset V'Hamemshalah* (results of the elections to the Tenth Knesset, 1981).

Bibliography

BOOKS

Abramov, S.Z. *Perpetual Dilemma.* New York: Associated University Presses, 1976.

Arian, Asher. *The Elections in Israel 1977.* Jerusalem: Jerusalem Academic Press, 1980.

Aronoff, Myron J. *Power and Ritual in the Israel Labor Party: A Study in Political Anthropology.* Amsterdam and Assen: Van Gorcum, 1977.

Crossman, Richard. *The Diaries of a Cabinet Minister.* New York: Holt, Rinehart and Winston, 1975–1976.

Curtis, Michael, ed. *Religion and Politics in the Middle East.* Boulder, Colo.: Westview Press, 1981.

Dagan, Avigdor. *Moscow and Jerusalem.* New York: Abelard-Schuman, 1970.

Dayan, Moshe. *Breakthrough: A Personal Account of the Egyptian-Israeli Peace Negotiations.* New York: Alfred A. Knopf, 1981.

Duverger, Maurice. *Political Parties.* London: Methuen, 1959.

Eban, Abba. *Abba Eban: An Autobiography.* New York: Random House, 1977.

Freedman, Robert O. *Soviet Policy Toward the Middle East Since 1970.* 3rd ed. New York: Praeger, 1982.

————, ed. *World Politics and the Arab-Israeli Conflict.* New York: Pergamon, 1979.

Golan, Galia. *The Soviet Union and the Palestine Liberation Organization.* New York: Praeger, 1980.

————. *Yom Kippur and After: The Soviet Union and the Middle East Crisis.* London: Cambridge University Press, 1977.

Golan, Matti. *The Secret Conversations of Henry Kissinger: Step by Step Diplomacy in the Middle East,* translated by Ruth Geyra Stern and Sol Stern. New York: Quadrangle/The New York Times, 1976.

Gorni, Yosef. *Achdut Ha'avoda 1919–1930: Hayesodot Haraayonim Ve-ha-Shita* (Achdut Ha'avoda 1919–1930: The Ideological Principles and the

267

Political System). Ramat Gan: Hakibbutz Hameuchad Publishing House, 1973.

Graber, Doris. *The Development of the Law of Belligerent Occupation, 1863-1914.* New York: Columbia University Press, 1949.

Haber, Eitan, Zeev Schiff, and Ehud Yaari. *The Year of the Dove.* New York: Bantam Books, 1979.

Harari, Yechiel. *Arabs of Israel in 1978* (Hebrew) No. 30. Givat Haviva, Israel: Institute for Arab Studies, 1980.

———. *The Elections in the Arab Sector–1977* (Hebrew), no. 6. Givat Haviva, Israel: Institute for Arab Studies, 1978.

———. *The Municipal Elections in the Arab Sector–1978* (Hebrew). Givat Haviva, Israel: Institute for Arab Studies, n.d.

Harkabi, Yehoshafat. *Arab Strategies and Israel's Response.* New York: The Free Press, 1977.

Hoffman, Stanley. *Duties Beyond Borders: On the Limits and Possibilities of Ethical International Politics.* Syracuse, N.Y.: Syracuse University Press, 1981.

Institute for the Study of Diplomacy. *U.N. Security Council Resolution 242: A Case Study in Diplomatic Ambiguity.* Washington, D.C.: Georgetown University School of Foreign Service, 1981.

Isaac, Rael Jean. *Israel Divided: Ideological Politics in the Jewish State.* (Baltimore: The Johns Hopkins University Press, 1976.

———. *Party and Politics in Israel: Three Visions of a Jewish State.* New York: Longman, 1981.

Krammer, Arnold. *The Forgotten Friendship: Israel and the Soviet Bloc 1947-1953.* Chicago: University of Illinois Press, 1974.

Laqueur, Walter. *The Road to Jerusalem.* New York: Macmillan, 1968.

Lenczowski, George. *The Middle East in World Affairs.* 4th. ed. Ithaca, N.Y.: Cornell University Press, 1980.

Lesch, Ann Mosely. *Arab Politics in Palestine, 1917-1939: The Frustration of a National Movement.* Ithaca, N.Y.: Cornell University Press, 1980.

Lustick, Ian. *Arabs in the Jewish State: Israel's Control of a National Minority.* Austin: University of Texas Press, 1980.

McDougal, Myres, Harold D. Lasswell, and Lung-Chu Chen. *Human Rights and World Public Order: The Basic Policies of an International Law of Human Dignity.* New Haven, Conn.: Yale University Press, 1980.

Medding, Peter Y. *Mapai in Israel: Political Organization and Government in a New Society.* Cambridge: Cambridge University Press, 1972.

Moore, John Norton, ed. *The Arab-Israeli Conflict: Readings and Documents.* Princeton, N.J.: Princeton University Press, 1977.

Moynihan, Daniel Patrick. *A Dangerous Place.* New York: Berkeley Books, 1980.

Paust, Jordan J. and Albert P. Blaustein, eds. *The Arab Oil Weapon.* Dobbs Ferry, N.Y.: Oceana Publications, 1977.

Penniman, Howard R., ed. *Israel at the Polls: The Knesset Elections of 1977.* Washington, D.C.: American Enterprise Institute, 1979.

Quandt, William. *Decade of Decisions.* Berkeley: University of California Press, 1977.

Rabin, Yitzhak. *The Rabin Memoirs.* Boston: Little, Brown, 1979.

Ro'i, Yaacov. *From Encroachment to Involvement: A Documentary Study of Soviet Policy in the Middle East.* Jerusalem: Israel Universities Press, 1974.

————. *Soviet Decision-making in Practice: The USSR and Israel 1947–1954.* London: Transaction Press, 1980.

———— ed. *The Limits to Power: Soviet Policy in the Middle East.* London: Croom Helm, 1979.

Rubin, Barry. *Paved with Good Intentions: The American Experience in Iran.* New York: Oxford, 1970.

Shapiro, Yonatan. *The Formative Years of the Israeli Labour Party: The Organization of Power.* London and Beverly Hills: Sage, 1976.

Sharkansky, Ira. *Whither the State.* Chatam, N.J.: Chatam House, 1979.

Sheehan, Edward R.F. *The Arabs, Israelis and Kissinger.* New York: Reader's Digest Press, 1976.

Smolansky, Oles M. *The Soviet Union and the Arab East Under Khrushchev.* Lewisburg, Pa.: Bucknell University Press, 1974.

Smooha, Sammy. *Israel: Pluralism and Conflict.* Berkeley and Los Angeles: University of California Press, 1978.

————. *The Orientation and Politicization of the Arab Minority in Israel.* Occasional Papers on the Middle East, No. 2. Haifa, Israel: Institute for Middle East Studies, 1980.

State of Israel, Ministry of Treasury. *Government Corporation Report.* no. 18. Jerusalem, March 1980.

Stendel, Uri. *Minorities in Israel* (Hebrew). Jerusalem: Information Center and the Office of the Adviser to the Prime Minster on Arab Affairs, 1971.

Stone, Julius. *Conflict Through Consensus: United Nations Approaches to Aggression.* Baltimore and London: The Johns Hopkins University Press, 1977.

Weizmann, Ezer. *The Battle for Peace.* New York: Bantam Books, 1981.

Whetten, Lawrence L. *The Canal War.* Cambridge, Mass.: MIT Press, 1974.

Wildavsky, Aaron. *The Politics of the Budgetary Process.* 2nd ed. Boston: Little, Brown 1974.

————. *Speaking Truth to Power.* Boston: Little, Brown, 1979.

Zuckerman, Alan. *The Politics of Faction.* New Haven, Conn.: Yale University Press, 1979.

ARTICLES

Albright, David. "The Horn of Africa and the Arab-Israeli Conflict." In *World Politics and the Arab-Israeli Conflict,* edited by Robert O. Freedman, pp. 147–91. New York: Pergamon, 1979.

Alter, Robert. "Deformations of the Holocaust." *Commentary,* February 1981, pp. 48–54.

Aronoff, Myron J. "The Decline of the Israeli Labor Party: Causes and Significance." In *Israel at the Polls: The Knesset Elections of 1977,* edited by

Howard R. Penniman, pp. 115–45. Washington, D.C.: The American Enterprise Institute Studies in Political and Social Processes, 1979.

Avishai, Bernard. "Begin vs. Begin." *The New York Review of Books,* May 31, 1979, pp. 35–41.

Bassiouni, M. Cherif. "An Analysis of Egyptian Peace Policy Toward Israel: From Resolution 242 (1967) to the 1979 Peace Treaty." *Case Western Reserve Journal of International Law* 12 (Winter 1980).

Cottrell, A.J. and R.M. Burrell. "Soviet-U.S. Naval Competition in the Indian Ocean." *Orbis* 18 (Winter 1975): 1109–28.

Dinstein, Yoram. "The Legal Issues of 'Para-War' and Peace in the Middle East." *St. John's Law Review* 44 (January 1970).

————. "Self-Determination in the Middle East Conflict." In *Self-Determination: National, Regional and Global Dimensions,* edited by Yonah Alexander and Robert A. Friedlander, pp. 243–57. Boulder, Colo.: Westview Press, 1980.

Don-Yehiya, Eliezer. "Secularization, Negation and Integration: Concepts of Traditional Judaism in Zionist Socialism" (Hebrew). *Kivunim* 8 (Summer 1980): 29–46.

Elazar, Daniel J. "The New Sadducees." *Midstream* 24 (August/September, 1978): 20–25.

————. "Toward a Renewed Zionist Vision." *Forum* 26 (1977): 52–69.

Freedman, Robert O. "Detente and Soviet-American Relations in the Middle East During the Nixon Years", in *Dimensions of Detente* (ed. Della Sheldon) (New York: Praeger, 1978), pp. 84–121.

————. "Moscow and the Communist Parties of the Middle East: An Uncertain Relationship," in *Soviet Economic and Political Relations with the Developing World* (eds. Roger Kanet and Donna Bahry) (New York: Praeger 1975) pp. 100–134.

————. "The Soviet Conception of a Middle East Peace Settlement," in Yaakov Ro'i (ed.), *The Limits to Power: Soviet Policy in the Middle East* (London: Croom Helm, 1979), pp. 282–327.

————. "Soviet Policy Toward the Middle East Since the Invasion of Afghanistan", *Columbia Journal of International Affairs,* Vol. 34 no. 2 (Fall/Winter 1980–81), pp. 290–321.

————. "Soviet Policy Toward Syria Since Camp David." *Middle East Review* 14, (Fall/Winter 1981-82): 31–42.

Friedlander, Robert A. "International Law is What the Lawyers Say It Is." *Student Lawyer* (December 1975): 10–13, *et seq.*

————. "The PLO and the Rule of Law: A Reply to Dr. Anis Kassim." *Denver Journal of International Law and Policy* 10 (Winter 1981).

Golan, Galia. "Syria and the Soviet Union since the Yom Kippur War." *Orbis* 21 (Winter 1978): 777–801.

Gerson, Allan. "Trustee-Occupant: The Legal Status of Israel's Presence in the West Bank." *Harvard International Law Journal* 14 (Winter 1973).

Katin, Y. "Useful Talks." *New Times* (Moscow) no. 18, 1978, p. 10.

Khalidi, Walid. "Regiopolitics: Toward a U.S. Policy on the Palestinian Problem." *Foreign Affairs* 59 (Summer 1981): 1050–63.

Lebedev, L. and Y. Tyunkov. "Useful Exchange of Views." *New Times* (Moscow) no. 51, 1978, p. 15.

Liebman, Charles S. and Eliezer Don-Yehiya. "Symbol System of Zionist Socialism: An Aspect of Israeli Civil Religion." *Modern Judaism* 1 (September 1981): 121-48.

————. "Zionist Ultranationalism and its Attitude Toward Religion." *Journal of Church and State* 23 (Spring 1981): 259-64.

Lipset, S.M. "Bureaucracy and Social Reform." In *Complex Organizations: A Sociological Reader,* edited by A. Etzioni, pp. 260-67. New York: Rinehart and Winston, 1961.

Margalit, Dan. "Let's Begin All Over Again?" (Hebrew). *Ha'aretz* Magazine, October 19, 1979.

Milson, Menahem. "How to Make Peace with the Palestinians." *Commentary,* May 1981, pp. 25-35.

Nakhleh, Khalil. "Reassessing the Struggle Inside." *Arab Perspectives* 2 (April 1981): 4-9.

Nelson, Richard W. "Comment—Peacekeeping Aspects of the Egyptian-Israeli Peace Treaty and Consequences for United Nations Peacekeeping." *Denver Journal of International Law and Policy* 10 (Fall 1980).

Neumann, Sigmund. "Toward a Comparative Study of Political Parties." In *Modern Political Parties,* edited by Sigmund Neumann. Chicago: University of Chicago Press, 1965.

Paine, Robert. "When Saying is Doing." In *Politically Speaking: Cross-Cultural Studies of Rhetoric,* edited by Robert Paine, pp. 9-23. Philadelphia: Institute for the Study of Human Issues, 1981.

Perlmutter, Amos. "A Palestinian Entity?" *International Security* 5 (Spring 1981): 103-16.

Radley, Kurt Rene. "The Palestinian Refugees: The Right to Return in International Law." *American Journal of International Law* 72 (July 1978).

Ro'i, Yaacov. "Soviet Attitudes Toward the Existence of Israel." In *The Limits to Power,* edited by Yaacov Ro'i, pp. 232-53. London: Croom Helm, 1979.

Rostow, Eugene V. "Palestinian Self-Determination: Possible Futures for the Unallocated Territories of the Palestinian Mandate." *Yale Studies in World Public Order* 5 (Spring 1979).

Sandler, Shmuel. "The National Religious Party: Israel's Third Party." *Jerusalem Letter* 24 (October 28, 1979).

Shapira, Amos. "The Six Day War and the Right to Self-Defense." *Israel Law Review* 6 (October 1971).

Silverburg, Sanford R. "In Perpetuation of Myth: National Self-Determination *de lege ferenda.*" *Glendale Law Review* 2 (1978).

Stepanov, A. "Hour of Trial for the Palestinians." *New Times* (Moscow) no. 41, 1978, p. 7.

Syrkin, Marie. "The Palestinian Refugees: Resettlement, Repatriation, or Restoration?" In *Israel, the Arabs, and the Middle East* edited by Irving Howe and Carl Gershman, pp. 157-85. New York: Bantam Books, 1972.

Torgovnik, Efraim. "Accepting Camp David: the Role of Party Factions in Israel

Policy Making." *Middle East Review* 11 (Winter 1978–79): 18-25.

————. "A Movement for Change in a Stable System." In *Israel at the Polls*, edited by H. Penniman, pp. 147–72. Washington, D.C.: American Enterprise Institute for Public Policy Research, 1979.

————. "Party Factions and Election Issues." In *The Elections in Israel 1969*, edited by Asher Arian, pp. 21–40. Jerusalem: Jerusalem Academic Press, 1972.

Tuma, Emil. "Reply to Nakhleh's 'Liberation Mentality'." *New Outlook*, June 1981, pp. 30-33.

Twersky, David, "Labor Prepares for Battle." *Jewish Frontier* (March 1981): 4-7.

Wright, Claudia. "Libya Comes in from the Cold." *The Middle East*, August 1981, pp. 18–25.

Yaron, Zvi. "Religion in Israel." *American Jewish Year Book*. New York: American Jewish Committee and Philadelphia: Jewish Publication Society of America, 1975, pp. 174-223.

Index

273

About the Authors

DR. MYRON ARONOFF, Professor of Political Science, Department of Political Science, Rutgers University. He is author of *Power and Ritual in the Israeli Labor Party* (Amsterdam and Assen: Van Gorcum, 1977) and editor of *Political Anthropology* (New Brunswick: Transaction Press, 1980).

DR. DANIEL ELAZAR, Senator Norman H. Patterson Professor of Intergovernmental Relations, Bar Ilan University, Israel and Director for the Center for the Study of Federalism, Temple University. Among his publications are *Community and Polity: The Organizational Dynamics of American Jewry* (Philadelphia: The Jewish Publication Society of America, 1976) and "Toward a Renewed Zionist Vision," *Forum* 26 (1977).

DR. ROBERT O. FREEDMAN, Dean of the Graduate School and Professor of Political Science of the Baltimore Hebrew College. He is the author of *Economic Warfare in the Communist Bloc: A Study of Soviet Economic Pressure Against Yugoslavia, Albania, and Communist China* (New York: Praeger, 1970) and *Soviet Policy Toward the Middle East Since 1970* (New York: Praeger, 1982) and editor of *World Politics and the Arab-Israeli Conflict* (New York: Pergamon, 1979).

DR. ROBERT FRIEDLANDER, Professor of Law, Pettit College of Law, Ohio Northern University. He is the author of *Terrorism: Documents of International and Local Control* (Dobbs Ferry, N.Y.: Oceana Publications, 1979/81) (3 volumes) and coeditor of *Self-Determination: National, Regional and Global Dimensions* (Boulder, Colo.: Westview Press, 1980).

DR. IAN LUSTICK, Associate Professor of Government, Dartmouth College. He is the author of *Arabs in the Jewish State: Israel's Control of a National Minori-*

ty (Austin: University of Texas Press, 1980) and *Israel and Jordan: The Implications of an Adversarial Partnership* (Berkeley: University of California, Institute of International Studies, 1978).

DR. DAVID POLLOCK, Assistant Professor, George Washington University and Consultant on the Middle East. He is the author of *The Politics of Pressure: American Arms and Israeli Policy Since the Six-Day War* (Westport, Conn.: Greenwood Press, 1982) and coauthor of *The Iranian Revolution: Implications for the Middle East* (Washington: U.S. Government Printing Office, 1980).

ALEX RADIAN is an Instructor in the Department of Political Science at the Hebrew University.

DR. IRA SHARKANSKY, Professor of Political Science at Hebrew University, Jerusalem. Among his publications are *The United States: A Study of a Developing Country* (New York: David McKay, 1975) and *The Routines of Politics* (New York: Van Nostrand Reinhold New Perspectives in Political Science, 1970).

DR. EFRAIM TORGOVNIK, Professor of Political Science, Department of Political Science of Tel Aviv University. Among his publications are *Determinants in Managerial Selections* (International Management, Washington, D.C., 1969) and "Accepting Camp David: The Role of Party Factions in Israel Policy Making," *Middle East Review* II (Winter 1978–79).